WOMEN, CRIME, AND FORGIVENESS IN EARLY MODERN PORTUGAL

Women, Crime, and Forgiveness in Early Modern Portugal

DARLENE ABREU-FERREIRA
University of Winnipeg, Canada

Routledge
Taylor & Francis Group
LONDON AND NEW YORK

First published in paperback 2024

First published 2015 by Ashgate Publishing

Published 2016 by Routledge
4 Park Square, Milton Park, Abingdon, Oxon OX14 4RN

and by Routledge
605 Third Avenue, New York, NY 10158

Routledge is an imprint of the Taylor & Francis Group, an informa business

Publisher's Note
The publisher has gone to great lengths to ensure the quality of this reprint but points out that some imperfections in the original copies may be apparent.

British Library Cataloguing in Publication Data
A catalogue record for this book is available from the British Library

The Library of Congress has cataloged the printed edition as follows:
Abreu-Ferreira, Darlene.
Women, crime, and forgiveness in early modern Portugal / by Darlene Abreu-Ferreira.
pages cm
Includes bibliographical references and index.
ISBN 978-1-4724-4231-4 (hardcover : alk. paper)

1. Women—Portugal—Social conditions—16th century. 2. Women—Portugal—Social conditions—17th century. 3. Crime—Portual—History. 4. Women—Crimes against—Portugal—History. 5. Female offenders—Portugal—History. 6. Pardon—Portugal—History. 7. Portugal—History—16th century. 8. Portugal—History—17th century. I. Title.
HQ1697.A27 2015
305.409469—dc23

2014031159

ISBN 13: 978-1-47-244231-4 (hbk)
ISBN 13: 978-1-03-292522-6 (pbk)
ISBN 13: 978-1-31-554664-3 (ebk)

DOI: 10.4324/9781315546643

Contents

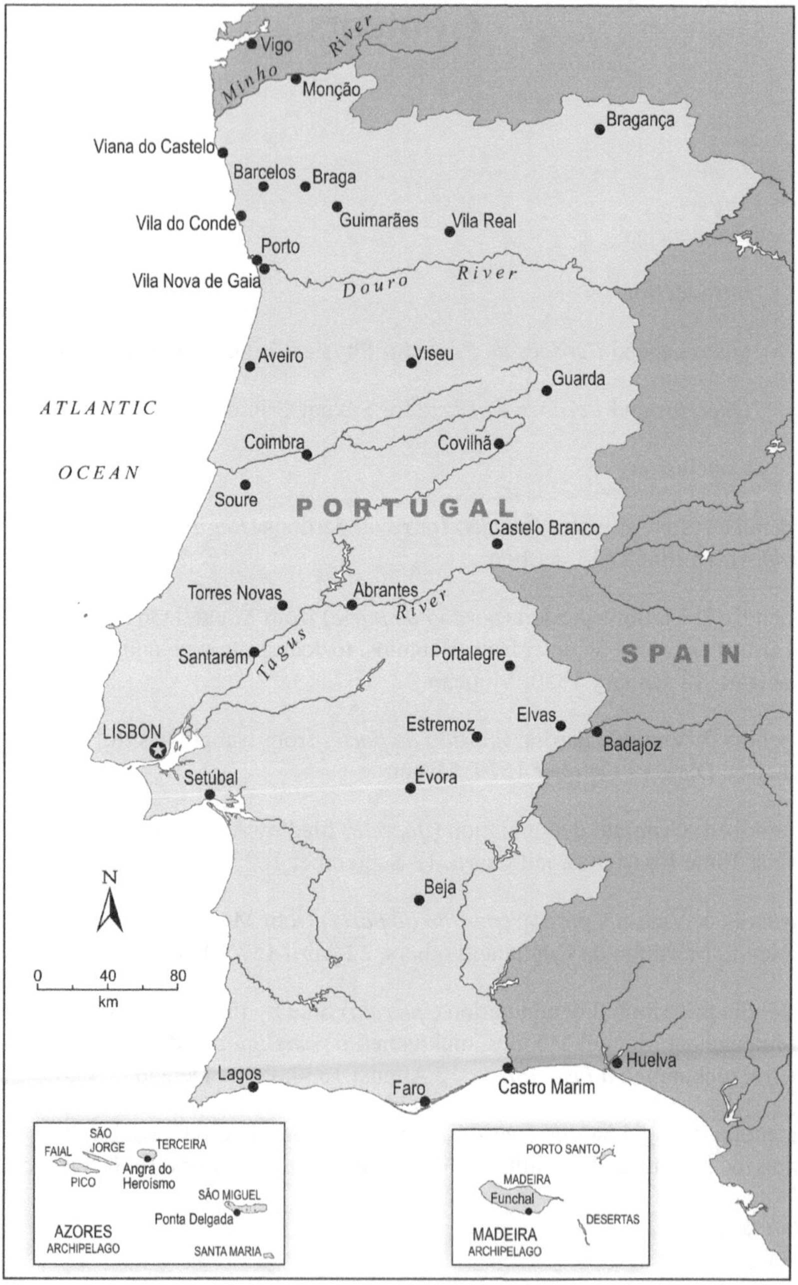

Map Portugal and the Atlantic Archipelagos of Madeira and the Azores, courtesy of Weldon Hiebert, Department of Geology, University of Winnipeg.

List of Tables

Abbreviations

ADAH	Arquivo Distrital de Angra do Heroísmo
ADE	Arquivo Distrital de Evora
ADF	Arquivo Distrital de Faro
ADP	Arquivo Distrital do Porto
ADVC	Arquivo Distrital de Viana do Castelo
AHMP	Arquivo Histórico Municipal do Porto
AMVC	Arquivo Municipal de Viana do Castelo
BPARPD	Biblioteca Pública e Arquivo Regional de Ponta Delgada
IAN/TT	Instituto de Aquivos Nacionais/Torre do Tombo (Lisbon)

Acknowledgements

The present study would not have been possible without the much-appreciated research grants from the Social Sciences and Humanities Research Council of Canada (SSHRC), and additional assistance from the Research Office at the University of Winnipeg. Travel to and from the archives, and the gathering of archival materials, is a laborious and expensive exercise, and I am exceedingly grateful for the financial support I have received. Jennifer Cleary, at the University of Winnipeg's Research Office, is a grant application goddess.

Once in the archives, the task of locating the precious documents that I sought, written in a language that was quite foreign to me at the start of this journey, would have been impossible without the assistance of some generous individuals inside and outside those archives. I met Amélia Polónia and Silvestre Lacerda during my early stumbles in Porto, and they have remained constants in my subsequent trips to Portugal. I am also thankful to the archivists in other locations who have facilitated my research, in particular António Maranhão Peixoto in the Arquivo Municipal de Viana do Castelo, Maria Olinda Alves Pereira in the Arquivo Distrital de Viana do Castelo, Isabel Cid in the Arquivo Distrital de Evora, Miguel Vargas in the Arquivo Distrital de Faro, and Jorge Mello Manoel in the Arquivo Distrital de Ponta Delgada.

A big thank you is also owed to Isabel Maria de Barros Dias, who kindly lent me her apartment in Lisbon, and to Fernanda Olival and Isabel dos Guimarães Sá, who have patiently helped me with numerous queries. A big hug to the sisters Lucy and Fátima Gonçalves Pereira, whose warmth and gregarious spirit made my visits to Lisbon and Abrantes much more pleasant and productive. While I was working on my PhD in the 1990s, I had the good fortune to meet Fátima Sequeira Dias in Ponta Delgada, São Miguel, and she became an instant friend. Always a fountain of information, always generous with her time and home, Fátima's untimely death has left a big void for many of us, professionally and personally. Thank you to the staff at a number of research libraries, especially those at the Biblioteca Nacional (Lisbon), Biblioteca Municipal (Porto), Thomas Fisher Rare Book Library and Robarts Library (University of Toronto), and the Newberry Library (Chicago). I am indebted to many historians and other scholars, on both sides of the Atlantic, whose published works have been crucial to my own study, and to the anonymous readers of this manuscript who nudged me to reconsider some presuppositions. Thank you, Jan McTavish, for the encouragement and constructive comments on an earlier version of the manuscript. Thank you also to the editorial team at Ashgate Publishing, particularly the proof-reader extraordinaire.

I have depended on the no-nonsense advice of Daniel Vickers long after we both left Memorial University of Newfoundland, and the encouragement of Valerie Burton, still causing trouble at Memorial. After agreeing to look over one early draft of the present study, Danny told me, 'You can do better.' I trust that I have. Thank you also to Merry Wiesner-Hanks for her support over the years, and for telling me, 'You have got to stop before you finish because you will never be finished.' A big thank you to my academic family at the Association for Spanish and Portuguese Historical Studies, most notably David Higgs, Carla Rahn Phillips, Ivana Elbl, and Frank Dutra, all of whom embraced me into the fold. As the adviser for my post-doctoral fellowship at the University of Toronto, David Higgs was fond of saying that he liked my work because it was based on archival evidence, not on 'hot air from New York.' Safe journeys, Prof. Higgs.

I am grateful for the support from my colleagues at the University of Winnipeg, particularly Jennifer Brown and Robert Young, who generously read and edited a number of research grant proposals; Don Bailey, 'pour les soirées du bon vivant'; Angela Joy Schippers, for managing the front office of the Department of History with remarkable skill and diplomacy; the helpful staff at the university library, particularly those hard-working women in inter-library loan services, Lynne Schultz and Heather Mathieson, and Kim Nguyen at the reserve desk; and my dedicated research assistants, especially Myriame Orloff and Erica Kolomic who organized the pardon database, Marieke Gruwel who tackled sixteenth-century Portuguese parish records with astonishing good cheer and uncanny ability, and William Temple who handled his teaching assistantship positions with professional integrity. Thank you as well to my non-academic friends who have been kind enough not to ask me, 'Aren't you done, yet?' The late Renate Eigenbrod, friend and neighbour, was someone who would have genuinely celebrated this humble accomplishment of mine, and she is greatly missed.

I also thank my siblings, Joe, Ted, Theresa, and Susy, who contributed to my research efforts by generously driving me to and from airports on countless occasions, and my sister-in-law, Grace, who helped me unravel some Portuguese terms. I dedicate this book to my mother, Balbina, *a cevadinha das fontes*, who never had the chance to go to school beyond grade three, but whose love of learning I have inherited. May that love flow into the next generation: Jodie Lynn, Michael (and their brother, Jacob), Sarah, Dylan, Angie, Jordyn, Riley, Jaden, and Ryder. Finally, I thank my wife for looking after all my travel plans and accommodations overseas, accompanying me during the most arduous research trips, looking after our home during my many absences, preparing countless delicious meals, yet finding the time to proofread the endless drafts of this manuscript, and squeezing in a foot massage when most needed. Alright, so I didn't have one, but it would have been nice.

Chapter 1
Introduction

Catarina da Ascenção was a child, perhaps only an infant, when she lost her mother, Catarina Tavares. The date of birth for the former, or date of death for the latter, is not known, but the two names were recorded in a *querela* launched on 6 October 1632 in Ponta Delgada, São Miguel (Azores). The *querela* was the official accusation of a crime committed against an individual, and once a *querela* was registered by the plaintiff with the local authorities, the investigation of the alleged crime began. In this case, the text informed us that a crime had been committed against Catarina da Ascenção's interests, but because she was a minor, her widowed father, André de Castro, filed the complaint on her behalf.

In his denunciation, André stated that he was the executor of the will of the late Catarina Tavares, his wife, and as legal administrator of his daughter Catarina da Ascenção, he filed a complaint against Domingos Gonçalves, *trabalhador* or labourer. André explained further that his daughter was entitled to inherit all the estate of her late mother, and that estate included a cart and two bulls, one named Virtugo and the other Fidalgo. One day in September past, after the end of the threshing, the defendant took the cart and the bulls from the barn, and had been using the animals without permission. From one brief accusation we learn that a wife could and did leave all her worldly goods to her daughter, not her husband; that sometimes agricultural animals were given names that poked fun at the elite (a *fidalgo* was a member of the nobility); and that helping others with their harvest was one thing, helping oneself was another. Domingos was accused of theft.[1]

On the surface, this case appeared to deal with a relatively benign incident, but the way in which André de Castro framed his complaint says a great deal about the place of women in seventeenth-century Portugal, particularly vis-à-vis property ownership and inheritance rights. Before she died, Catarina Tavares, wife, was legally entitled to half of the family estate; before she died, Catarina Tavares, mother, looked after her young daughter's future with the best means at her disposal. Although Tavares appointed her husband as executor of her will, she declared her daughter her universal heir. Everything that belonged to the first Catarina belonged to the second, her mother's namesake. For extra protection, baby Catarina was also named 'of the Ascension', perhaps in the hope that someday the daughter's soul would ascend to heaven and join her mother's.

---

1 Biblioteca Pública e Arquivo Regional de Ponta Delgada (BPARPD), Fundo Judicial, *Livro de Autos de Querellas [sic] dos Tabeliães Francisco Serrão, António Pereira, Jorge da Costa, Francisco Pavão, Pedro Ferreira Serrão, Gregório Sanches, Francisco de Carvalho[?], Lourenço Preto da Costa, Pedro Correia Chaves, Simão da Cunha, João de la Paz, Jerónimo Rebelo, Francisco Cardoso Machado*, NOT.601 (1606–1654), f.79v–80v (henceforth, *Livro de Autos de Querelas*).

Catarina Tavares' will has not been found, so that all we know of her intentions are the fragments from her widowed husband's statements in his *querela*, the resolution of which impinged on the property that belonged to Catarina's heir. In early modern Portugal, that type of impingement was at the root of many, if not most, criminal cases. This premise was entrenched in early modern Portuguese law that allowed for the victim of a crime to pardon the wrongdoer. Thus, André de Castro could have allowed his *querela* to take its course, and hope for a guilty verdict against Domingos Gonçalves, in which case André would get back the cart and the two bulls, plus damages. Alternatively, André could have agreed to pardon Domingos for his indiscretion, and ostensibly forgo any further claim. Such a pardon could have been granted either before or after sentencing, and would have been useful to Domingos who was embroiled in a judicial procedure that could have proven tenuous and costly. Portuguese law recognized and indeed encouraged such pardons, but the law also aimed to minimize the impact these types of settlements could have had on the rights of inheritance. The present study examines that potential impact, particularly as it applied to women caught in the system of granting legal pardons to individuals accused of committing crimes.

The Road to Forgiveness

A system was in place in many parts of early modern Europe (c.1500–1700) through which a convicted criminal could appeal for clemency or a full pardon from the Crown, and this phenomenon has been studied by a number of historians, particularly in Spain[2] and in France.[3] In Portugal, too, the Crown reserved for itself

---

2 For Spain, see Ángel Alloza Aparicio, *La Vara Quebrada de la Justicia: un estúdio sobre la delincuencia madrileña entre los siglos XVI y XVIII* (Madrid: Catarata, 2000); Ricardo Córdoba de la Llave, *El instinto diabólico: Agresiones Sexuales en la Castilla Medieval* (Córdoba: Universidad de Córdoba, 1994); Rafael Narbona Vizcaíno, *Pueblo, Poder y Sexo. Valencia Medieval (1306–1420)* (Valencia: Diputació de València, 1992); Julián Viejo Yharrassarry, 'La segunda dote', Cuadernos de Sección. *Historia y Geografia* 8 (1986): 33–46; Ma Immaculada Rodriguez Flores, *El Perdon Real en Castilla (Siglos XIII–XVIII)* (Salamanca: Universidad de Salamanca, 1971); Francisco Tomás y Valiente, *El derecho penal de la monarquía absoluta* (Madrid: Tecnos, 1969).

3 For France, see Jean-Pascal Gay, 'Acheter la Grâce en France du XVe au XVIIe Siècle', in Benoît Garnot, ed., *Justice et Argent: Les crimes et les peines pécuniaires du XIIIe au XXIe siècle* (Dijon: Editions Universitaires de Dijon, 2005), 237–57; Marie-Sylvie Dupont-Bouchat, 'Le crime pardonné: La justice réparatrice sous l'Ancien Régime (XVIe–XVIIIe siècles)', *Criminologie* 32, no. 1 (1999): 31–56; Claude Gauvard, *'De Grace Especial': Crime, Etat et Société en France à la Fin du Moyen Age*, 2 vols (Paris: Publications de La Sorbonne, 1991); Robert Muchembled, *Le Temps des Supplices: De l'Obéissance sous les Rois Absolus, XVe–XVIIIe Siècle* (Paris: Armand Colin Editeur, 1992), and *La Violence au Village: Sociabilité et comportements populaires en Artois du XVe au XVIIe siècle* (Turnhout: Editions Brepols I.G.P., 1989); Natalie Zemon Davis, *Fiction in the Archives: Pardon Tales and Their Tellers in Sixteenth-Century France* (Stanford: Stanford

the prerogative of granting royal pardons to convicted criminals, an appeal process that promoted the Crown's image as the benevolent arbitrator, and generated fees that supported religious and other institutions. Portuguese historians have published a number of studies based on pardon documents that focussed on mainland Portugal in the late Middle Ages or early modern periods,[4] or on the Atlantic islands and African posts.[5] For the most part, these studies were based on a quantitative analysis of royal pardons granted under the reign of a particular monarch. Generally their findings indicated that the Crown acquiesced most often to appeals related to crimes against the state, particularly breaking out of prison, followed by crimes against the person including homicide and other types of physical assault.

In early modern Portugal, the mechanism for obtaining a royal pardon included a unique component: the culprit first had to obtain a written and notarized pardon from

University Press, 1987); Pierre Ribière, 'Délits sexuels dans les lettres de rémission du comte Jean IV d'Armagnac', in *La Faute, la Répression et le Pardon. Actes du 107e Congrès National des Sociétés Savantes, Brest, 1982*, 2 vols, (Paris: Comité des Travaux Historiques et Scientifiques, 1984), I: 369–81.

4 Luís Miguel Duarte, *Justiça e Criminalidade no Portugal Medievo (1459–1481)* (Lisbon: Fundação Calouste Gulbenkian, 1999); Isabel Maria de Moura Ribeiro de Queirós, 'Theudas e Mantheudas: A criminalidade feminina no reinado de D. João II através das cartas de perdão (1481–1485)' (master's thesis, Universidade do Porto, 1999); Paulo Drumond Braga, 'Perdões Concedidos a Moradores em Evora no Reinado de D. João IV', in *Actas do Congresso de História no IV Centenário do Seminário de Evora*, 529–38 (Evora: s.n., 1994); Isabel M.R. Mendes Drumond Braga, 'A criminalidade em Portalegre no reinado de D. João III: delitos e perdões', *A Cidade: Revista Cultural de Portalegre*, no. 8, Nova Série (1993): 65–81; Luís Miguel Duarte and Maria da Conceição Falcão Ferreira, 'Dependentes das Elites Vimarenses Face à Justiça no Reinado de D. Afonso V', *Revista da Faculdade de Letras* 6 (Porto, 1989): 175–221.

5 Paulo Drumond Braga, *Do Crime ao Perdão Régio (Açores, Séculos XVI–XVIII)* (Ponta Delgada: Instituto Cultural de Ponta Delgada, 2003); Isabel M.R. Mendes Drumond Braga and Paulo Drumond Braga, 'A Criminalidade nos Açores no Reinado de D. Sebastião: delitos e perdões', 523–43, and Fernando Calapez Corrêa, 'Aspectos da Criminalidade nos Açores: as Cartas de Perdão e de Legitimação Concedidas no Período das Guerras da Restauração', in *O Faial e a Periferia Açoriana nos Sécs. XV a XIX. Actas do Colóquio realizado nas ilhas do Faial e Pico de 10 a 13 de Maio de 1993* (Horta: Núcleo Cultural da Horta, 1995), 545–57; João dos Santos Ramalho Cosme and Maria de Deus Beites Manso, 'Cartas de perdão e legitimação concedidas aos moradores do arquipélago da Madeira (1531–1557)', in *Actas do II Colóquio Internacional de História da Madeira* (Funchal: Centro de Estudos de História do Atlântico, 1989), 155–70; Aires dos Passos Vieira, 'Subsídios para a história da criminalidade da Madeira nas épocas de Filipe II e III', in *Actas III Colóquio Internacional de História da Madeira* (Funchal: Centro de Estudos do Atlântico, 1993), 473–92; João dos Santos Ramalho Cosme, 'Cartas de perdão e legitimação concedidas a açorianos (1642–1748)', *Boletim do Instituto Histórico da Ilha Terceira* 48 (1990): 317–48; Vítor Luís Pinto Gaspar da Conceição Rodrigues, 'A Guiné nas cartas de perdão (1463–1500)', in *Sociedade, Cultura e Mentalidades na Época do 'Cancioneiro Geral'*, in *Actas do Congresso Internacional 'Bartolomeu Dias e a sua Época'*, 4 vols (Lisbon: Instituto de Investigação Científica Tropical, 1989), IV: 397–412.

the victim(s) – a *perdão de parte* – and women featured greatly in that process, as the instigator or more notably as the victim in its many manifestations. The *perdão de parte* has not been examined very much in Portuguese historiography, possibly because it is a more difficult document to find, in comparison to the royal pardons which were registered in the royal chancelleries in a series appropriately entitled *Perdões e Legitimações* (Pardons and Legitimizations), and are easily accessible at the national archives in Lisbon. For their part, the victims' pardons are randomly scattered in notarial collections, the vast majority of which are not indexed, and stored in the national archives, in district archives across the country, and in the Atlantic Islands.[6] How many *perdões de parte*[7] reached the Crown and led to successful remissions is impossible to determine, but one study of victims' pardons in Porto from the second half of the eighteenth century found that only approximately 16 per cent of prisoners in the local jail could expect to receive a pardon.[8]

The victim's pardon was attached to the culprit's appeal to the Crown, and the royal pardon was the Crown's response to that appeal.[9] As the historian António Manuel Hespanha has pointed out, in theory, the king could not pardon a crime for which there was a victim without first the accused obtaining the victim's pardon, for it was understood that the offended party received, with the sentence, the right to render a punishment, and the right to a portion of the compensation that was inflicted on the perpetrator. In reality, these limits on the Crown were not insurmountable.[10] A list of prices for royal pardons was compiled in 1517, called the *Regimento dos Perdões*, and the document included an addendum at the bottom of the list which is especially pertinent for the present study.

> And in all the cases and pardons that are declared in this *Regimento* always in order for a pardon to be granted in each case the said our Chief Justices [*Desembargadores*] must see the *perdões de parte* from the victims when there are victims. And without which no pardons shall be granted. And if the harm is

[6] For other studies of the *perdão de parte*, see Hugo Ribeiro da Silva and Susana Cardoso, 'Escrituras de perdão num notário do Porto (1650–1700)', *Revista da Faculdade de Letras, HISTORIA* 5 (Porto, 2004): 167–92; Dina Catarina Duarte Alves, 'Violência e perdão em Óbidos (1595–1680)' (master's thesis, Faculdade de Letras, Universidade de Coimbra, 2003); Isilda Braga da Costa Monteiro, 'A Litigiosidade e o "perdão" em Vila Nova de Gaia (séculos XVII e XVIII)', *Revista de Ciências Históricas* 11 (Universidade Portucalense, 1996): 101–12.

[7] The plural for *perdão de parte* is *perdões de parte*.

[8] Ana Sofia Vieira Ribeiro, 'Convívios difíceis: viver, sentir e pensar a violência no Porto de setecentos (1750–1772)' (master's thesis, Faculdade de Letras, Universidade do Porto, 2008), 33. I am grateful to Amélia Polónia of the Faculdade de Letras, Universidade do Porto, for providing me with access to this study.

[9] The legal requirement for a notarized *perdão de parte* can be traced to at least as far back as the fifteenth century, though few notary collections have survived from that era. For a *perdão de parte* from 1473, see Duarte, *Justiça e Criminalidade* (Document no. 67), 618.

[10] António Manuel Hespanha, *As Vésperas do Leviathan: Instituições e Poder Poltítico, Portugal – Séc. XVII* (Coimbra: Livraria Almedina, 1994), 481–2.

> caused only to Justice and there are no victims the said pardons shall be granted without [the] *perdão de parte* for such is how we have always done and we have it that it be done thus.[11]

The national ordinances also instructed the *Desembargadores* how to proceed with appeals, and stressed that the *perdão de parte* was an essential part of the process,[12] but recognition of the rights of the victim was open to some negotiation, as exemplified in the listed costs outlined in the above-mentioned *Regimento* that applied to a culprit who sought a reprieve from the penalty of exile. In such a case the Crown allowed that a royal pardon was possible even without a *perdão de parte*, as long as a third of the sentence had already been served (see Appendix 1). In fact, under certain circumstances, a royal pardon could be granted outright without a victim's pardon. For instance, the law permitted that any renegade criminal who helped justice officials apprehend her or his accomplices could receive a royal pardon for the crime the accused had committed.[13] Some royal pardons registered in the chancelleries did not make any reference to a *perdão de parte*, either because the scribe failed to note it, or because it was not part of the deliberations. Nevertheless, the victim's pardon was ostensibly an indispensable part of royal pardons, in Portugal and in the rest of Iberia. In his study of pardons and patronage in early modern Spain, Salustiano de Dios found an example of a petition for a pardon from two brothers whose petition was contested. The victim of their aggression petitioned the Crown as well, and asked the Crown not to grant them a pardon because they had caused him grave injuries and he had not pardoned them.[14]

It is not known whose petition was successful in that particular case, but if the Crown was recruiting soldiers, the two brothers would have been awarded certain concessions. As Dios pointed out, the reasons for granting a royal pardon in Spain were numerous, but most notably to supply troops for wars, with Portugal, Granada, North Africa, and the Indies.[15] The capricious and arbitrary nature of the system of royal pardons has been documented in Portugal as well, particularly in relation to the practice of granting general pardons to criminals who joined

---

11 Instituto de Arquivos Nacionais/Torre do Tombo (IAN/TT), *Maço 2 de Leis*, no. 49, f.1–8, in Duarte, *Justiça e Criminalidade* (Document no.118), 726–32 (see Appendix 1). For a record that shows the Crown ordering its officials to grant a royal pardon without the *perdão de parte*, see Duarte, *Justiça e Criminalidade* (Document no.75), 624–5.

12 *Ordenações Afonsinas*, Livro 1, Título 4, no. 5; *Ordenações Manuelinas*, Livro 1, Título 3, no. 3; *Ordenações Filipinas*, Livro 1, Título 3, no. 9. The three collections of national laws from the early modern period were published in the 1980s by the Gulbenkian Foundation, and the three sets are also available on-line.

13 *Ordenações Filipinas*, Livro 5, Título 116; see also Título 36, No.7. For a look at the strategies used by an informer during a criminal trial in Rome, see Thomas V. Cohen, 'Three Forms of Jeopardy: Honor, Pain, and Truth-Telling in a Sixteenth-Century Italian Courtroom', *Sixteenth Century Journal* 29, no. 4 (Winter 1998): 975–98.

14 Salustiano de Dios, *Gracia, Merced y Patronato Real: La Camara de Castilla Entre 1474–1530* (Madrid: Centro de Estudios Constitucionales, 1993), 331, note 258.

15 Dios, *Gracia, Merced*, 329.

military and colonizing campaigns.[16] Such pardons would generally apply to men only, but women, too, were affected by those policies, most notably as pawns in the colonizing project. For instance, in 1569, Diogo Martines, living in exile in Rio de Janeiro, received a royal pardon for his unspecified crime after having married the recently arrived orphan, Maria Brás. It is doubtful she had much choice in the matter, or the victim(s) of Diogo's initial crime.[17] Yet contemporaries were aware that fairness was essential for the integrity of the pardon system. A text from the sixteenth century, believed to have been written by Rui Gonçalves, affirmed that it was proper for a prince to show clemency and pardon malefactors, but that the prince needed to be temperate with his generosity.[18]

The studies conducted by Portuguese historians of the royal pardons confirmed that, statistically speaking, early modern Portugal was not very different from the rest of Western Europe: among the known convicted criminals, men outnumbered women by a wide margin. In a quantitative analysis of nearly 7,500 royal pardons in late medieval France, Claude Gauvard found that only 4 per cent of petitioners who received pardons were women, though he cautioned that the sources dealt primarily with serious crimes, such as homicide.[19] Similar findings were recorded for early modern Portugal, regardless of the reigning monarch or the geographical region under study. For instance, during the reign of King D. João III (r.1521–1557), 130 royal pardons were awarded to residents of Portalegre, 120 for men and 10 for women. Between 1593 and 1641, residents in Madeira received 113 royal pardons, 107 granted to men, 6 to women. King D. João IV (r.1640–1656) granted 33 pardons to individuals in Evora, of which only 2 were granted to women. Finally, of the 660 residents of the Azores Archipelago who received a royal pardon between the sixteenth and eighteenth centuries, only 46, or 7 per cent, were women.[20]

---

16 Américo A. Taipa de Carvalho, 'Condicionalidade sócio-cultural do Direito Penal', *Boletim da Faculdade de Direito, Universidade de Coimbra* 58 (1982): 1075 [1039–45]; Hirondino da Paixão Fernandes, *Bibliografia do Distrito de Bragança: Documentos (textos) Publicados, 569–1870* (Bragança: Câmara Municipal de Bragança, 1996), 90–91; Eduardo Correia, 'A evolução histórica das penas', *Boletim da Faculdade de Direito* 53 (1977): 104–5 [51–310].

17 Geraldo Pieroni, 'Fui desterro para os culpados: A Inquisição portuguesa e os banidos no Brazil colonial', *Portuguese Studies Review* 15, no. 1/2 (2007): 276–7 [267–80].

18 Rui Gonçalves, *Memorial au rei D. João III sobre os perdões* (Lisbon: João Barreira, 15??), f.12v–13v.

19 Gauvard, *'De Grace Especial'*, I:300–307. See also Zoë A. Schneider, 'Women before the Bench: Female Litigants in Early Modern Normandy', *French Historical Studies* 23, no. 1 (Winter 2000): 16 [1–32]; Malcolm M. Feeley and Deborah L. Little, 'The Vanishing Female: The Decline of Women in the Criminal Process, 1687–1912', *Law & Society Review* 25, no. 4 (1991): 720 [719–58]; Muchembled, *La Violence au Village*, 19; Malcolm Greenshields, 'Women, Violence, and Criminal Justice Records in Early Modern Haute Auvergne (1587–1664)', *Canadian Journal of History/Annales Canadiennes d'Histoire* 12 (August 1987): 182 [175–94].

20 Braga, 'A criminalidade em Portalegre', 72; Vieira, 'Subsídios para a História', 474; Braga, 'Perdões concedidos', 534; Braga, *Do Crime ao Perdão*, 21–5.

Addressing this question of sex ratios in criminal activity in pre-modern France, Natalie Zemon Davis contended that part of the discrepancy was explained by the fact that crimes conventionally associated with women, particularly witchcraft and infanticide, were not pardonable.[21] This argument cannot be sustained, at least not for Portugal, because the pardons registered in the royal chancelleries represent an incomplete set of pardons that were granted, not of the applications that were denied, and nothing is known about the latter. In principle, not every crime was pardonable. Those accused of crimes of treason, sodomy, false witness, counterfeit money, theft, witchcraft, pandering, heresy, resisting arrest, or violent abduction were excluded from royal pardons.[22] In reality, political and military imperatives, particularly in relation to the overseas colonizing project, were motivating factors in the ways in which clemency was awarded, and, as already mentioned, those political and military imperatives favoured convicted men.[23] Furthermore, the systemic wage gap that existed between women and men made the cost of a royal pardon more prohibitive for women. Overall, though, the evidence suggests that women received fewer royal pardons because women committed fewer crimes. So why conduct a study of women and crime?

While some studies of the Portuguese royal pardons provided a broad framework with which to evaluate the preponderance of certain crimes over time, the emphasis of those studies was on the recipients of the royal pardons only, resulting in a very male-centred image of the past – yet again. Partly this was due to the nature of the document, which by necessity addressed the concerns of the applicant – the culprit – first and foremost. Consequently, the focus of most of the existing studies has been on a quantitative discussion of the crimes committed by the supplicant, with very little analysis of the possible consequences of the harm committed by all of those overwhelmingly male supplicants. The aftermath of the conflict that necessitated a royal pardon can never be fully measured, but the ramifications of those acts of violence that made the record books are worthy of some serious consideration.

Those possible ramifications, and the ways individuals attempted to deal with them, are at the heart of the present study. The victim's pardon is one of the few available sources that provide some glimpses into the wider consequences of criminal behaviour, and the steps available to some of those victims to resolve the problems they faced. As this study will show, while most crimes were committed by men, many of those crimes had a great impact on women's lives. Women were members of families whose menfolk were embroiled in criminality, and, consequently, women were confronted with the effects of criminal acts.

It must be stressed outright that despite its title, the present investigation is not a study of criminality per se. Such a study would require bona fide criminal records – court transcripts, depositions, testimonials, prison rolls – all of which

21 Davis, *Fiction in the Archives*, chapter 3.

22 *Ordenações Filipinas*, Livro 5, Título 138, no. 2.

23 Carvalho, 'Condicionalidade sócio-cultural', 1077.

generally have not survived for early modern Portugal.[24] Studies of other European regions showed an increase in litigation in the early modern period, but, without proper documentation, such an assertion cannot be made for Portugal.[25] According to one Spanish commentator from the seventeenth century, the Portuguese needed the severe hand of the Crown to keep them in line for they had a tendency to turn minor arguments into major disputes and fights, with outrageous consequences to families and communities. Writing more than 100 years later, a Portuguese observer disagreed with this sentiment and in fact claimed that the Portuguese character was essentially peaceful and tranquil, even in the face of the most serious affronts, at least among the *Minhotos*.[26]

Although the victim's pardon dealt with some element of a criminal act, it is, in itself, insufficient for the study of crime. The *perdão de parte* aimed first and foremost to minimize the conflict that erupted at some point, because its objective was to stress the *goodwill* between the parties, in order to assure the Crown that the accusation initially made against the perpetrator merited reconsideration. Some of the victims' pardons were rich in detail about the confrontation that led to an accusation, but most left out crucial information with which the historian could reconstruct a possible landscape of criminal activity.

Notwithstanding these limitations, the victim's pardon reflects something about a conflict and the place of women in it. It provides a framework through which the lives of women can be explored. In effect, the *perdão de parte* allows us to examine early modern Portuguese women in a unique perspective because it gave women a voice in a legal process that was otherwise dominated by men. The formulaic nature of the notarial record represents a transmission of legal practice coupled with editorial insertions from the notary; nevertheless the document

[24] Ribeiro, 'Convívios difíceis', 19; José Damião Rodrigues, 'Criminalidade e Violência em Ponta Delgada no Final do Antigo Regime (1706–1817): Para uma outra leitura das relações sociais', in *Colóquio Comemorativo dos 450 Anos da Cidade de Ponta Delgada. Actas* (Ponta Delgada: Universidade dos Açores, 1999), 153–78; António Manuel Hespanha, 'Da "Iustitia" à "Disciplina": textos, poder e política penal no antigo regime', in António Hespanha, ed., *Justiça e Litigiosidade: História e Prospectiva* (Lisbon: Fundação Calouste Gulbenkian, 1993), 287–379. The trials conducted by the Portuguese Holy Office of the Inquisition (1538–1821) are outside the purview of the present study.

[25] Christopher W. Brooks, *Lawyers, Litigants and English Society Since 1450* (London: The Hambledon Press, 1998); Laura Gowing, 'Language, Power and the Law: Women's Slander Litigation in Early Modern London', in Jennifer Kermode and Garthine Walker, eds, *Women, Crime and the Courts in Early Modern England* (Chapel Hill and London: University of North Carolina Press, 1994), 26–47.

[26] D. Agustín Manuel y Vasconcelos, *Vida y Acciones del Rey Don Juan el Segundo, Decimotercio de Portugal* (Madrid: En la Imprensa de Maria de Quiñones, 1639), 277–8; Pe Agostinho Rebelo da Costa, *Descrição Topográfica e Histórica da Cidade do Pôrto*, Second Edition (Porto: Na Officina de António Alvarez Ribeiro, r.1945 [1789]), 18. The *Minhotos* are the people who live in northern Portugal in the areas between the rivers Douro and Minho.

contains important clues to an individual's sense of priorities, and to her or his self-fashioning.[27] One can acknowledge the 'palpable dishonesty of many of these documents', as James Farr found in his own work, yet still make useful observations about the world in which those documents were created.[28] As Laurie Nussdorfer has pointed out, notary documents 'abound with representations of the spoken word', while Malcolm Greenshields found that legal documents 'provide one of the few opportunities we have to witness the speeches of the illiterate'.[29]

Since the law was constructed and administered predominantly by men, and most criminal acts were perpetrated by men against men, the official record under-represented, indeed, it misrepresented women's historical agency in the world of crime and its aftermath. Most women were not just bystanders, passive individuals who had to contend with things that happened to them – no more than most men. Women were not relegated to the background while men acted out their aggression. The *perdão de parte* shows that women were directly implicated in that aggression, sometimes as the aggressors themselves or accomplices, sometimes as the victims of the aggression, but most often, and most importantly, women were directly involved in the deliberations, negotiations, conciliations, and compromises that were crucial to the resolution of those conflicts that caused havoc in their lives and their families. In fact, the *perdão de parte* illustrates women's active participation in a legal, economic, social, and cultural phenomenon.

Crime and Property Matters

On the surface, most early modern European women were subjected to patriarchal systems that attempted to limit and control their lives; further down, on the ground – maybe even underground – where the root of the matter was found, the interdependency between women and men was the rule, not the exception. In Portugal, evidence of that interdependency was readily found in a myriad of notarized documents, including the *perdão de parte*. Portuguese law stipulated that a convicted person who sought a royal pardon had to obtain a pardon from the victim, whether that victim was a woman or man, young or old, rich or poor.

27 For a look at some new questions around women's voices and women's agency as depicted in legal records from pre-modern England, see Bronach Kane and Fiona Williamson, eds, *Women, Agency and the Law, 1300–1700* (London: Pickering & Chatto, 2013).

28 James R. Farr, *A Tale of Two Murders: Passion and Power in Seventeenth-Century France* (Durham and London: Duke University Press, 2005), 3.

29 Laurie Nussdorfer, 'Writing and the Power of Speech: Notaries and Artisans in Baroque Rome', in Barbara B. Diefendorf and Carla Hesse, eds, *Culture and Identity in Early Modern Europe (1500–1800): Essays in Honor of Natalie Zemon Davis* (Ann Arbor: University of Michigan Press, 1993), 108 [103–8]; Malcolm Greenshields, *An Economy of Violence in Early Modern France: Crime and Justice in the Haute Auvergne, 1587–1664* (University Park: Pennsylvania State University Press, 1994), 62.

The reasons for this were linked to the laws of inheritance in the land. In Portugal, crime, like property, was a family affair.[30]

The act of granting a pardon to a perpetrator had economic ramifications for the pardoner and her or his heirs because the pardon was above all a renunciation of all potential claims for damages. This is essentially why we find women involved in such a legal process. Portuguese laws of inheritance stated that spouses shared equally in family property, and all legitimate children were entitled to an equal portion of their parents' estate. Upon the death of one spouse, the portion of the family estate that belonged to the deceased was divided between the surviving spouse and the children of that matrimony.[31] For this reason, early modern Portugal had, or was supposed to have, a *Juíz dos Orfãos* or orphan judge in each judicial district, a Crown agent who was responsible for looking after the interests of minor children who had lost one or both parents.[32]

The legislation pertaining to the orphan judge assumed a patriarchal stance, but also wavered at times in order to safeguard the rights of children. Thus, the law held that upon the death of the mother, the father of minor children was the legitimate administrator of their estate, whereas the law made no such declaration about the widowed mother. Widowed women could be trustees and guardians of their children, but that practice was not considered self-evident to the lawmakers, who felt the need to impose certain conditions on female guardians. For instance, in order to maintain her position as administrator of her children's portion of the family estate, a widow was expected to remain chaste and unmarried.[33] Doubtless those constraints were in place to allow authorities to meddle when the stakes were worth meddling into, but the exigencies of everyday life meant that, for most people, the practical solution was to by-step ideology. In his work on orphans in the Portuguese empire, Timothy Coates found that occasionally observers raised concerns about the misappropriation of monies that belonged to orphans, particularly by stepfathers, to which problem the Crown responded that 'mothers should be placed in charge of these estates.'[34]

---

[30] For similar arguments about early modern Spain, see Scott Taylor, *Honor and Violence in Golden Age Spain* (New Haven and London: Yale University Press, 2008), 200–201.

[31] *Ordenações Filipinas*, Livro 4, Título 46, 94, 95, 96, 97.

[32] The legislation stipulated that an orphan judge would be appointed to each settlement with 400 residents or more. See *Ordenações Filipinas*, Livro 1, Título 88. For a review of the insufficient presence of royal judicial agents across most of Portugal in the early modern period, see Anabela Ramos, *Violência e Justiça em Terras do Montemuro, 1708–1820* (Viseu: Palimage Editores, 1998), 78–81; António Manuel Hespanha, 'Sábios e Rústicos: a violência doce da razão jurídica', *Revista Crítica de Ciências Sociais*, no. 25/26 (December 1988): 47–8 [31–60]; António Manuel Hespanha, 'Centro e periferia nas estruturas administrativas do Antigo Regime', *Ler História*, no. 8 (1986): 43, 57–8 [35–60].

[33] For the legislation on women trustees and guardians, see *Ordenações Filipinas*, Livro 4, Título 102, no. 3 and 4. For a discussion of the situation in Spain, see Grace E. Coolidge, '"Neither dumb, deaf, nor destitute of understanding": Women as Guardians in Early Modern Spain', *Sixteenth Century Journal* 36, no. 3 (Fall 2005): 673–93.

[34] Timothy J. Coates, *Convicts and Orphans: Forced and State-Sponsored Colonizers in the Portuguese Empire, 1550–1775* (Stanford: Stanford University Press, 2001), 125.

While widowers were not expected to adhere to the same moral code that applied to widows, the law recognized that, fathers, too, could lapse in more concrete terms, to the detriment of the children's best interests. For this reason, the orphan judge was instructed to intervene regardless of the sex of the deceased parent, order an inventory of the estate of the deceased, and determine the appropriate allotment of the assets to which the minor children were entitled. Regardless of who administered those assets – father, mother, or trustee – the children's portions had to be handed over to them once they reached maturity, and according to the official inventory. Those inventoried portions could not be altered, at least not legally, without the consent from the authorities.[35]

In the case discussed at the beginning of this chapter, for instance, any settlement made between the widower André de Castro and the accused Domingos Gonçalves would have necessitated the approval of the local orphan judge who would represent the minor child, Catarina da Ascenção. In the absence of children, the birth family of the deceased was entitled to a share of the patrimony.[36] Thus, when an individual was injured, maimed, or killed, a number of people could make a legal claim against the potential loss of revenue or other material gain that might have been accrued had the victim lived a long and healthy life. This potential was at the crux of the victim's pardon.

Time after time the formula used in the *perdão de parte* underscored the fact that the pardoner relinquished all future claims on behalf of her or himself, and on behalf of all other present and future heirs, regardless of the ultimate outcome of the criminal act. By requiring the victim's pardon in the judicial appeal process, state legislation highlighted the obligation of the criminal to the victim's family in very tangible terms. In the absence of a state-sponsored social net, the family had to ensure it looked after its own, and the law promoted the private arrangements which were implicit in the *perdão de parte* negotiated at the local level.

It is not clear why so many of the *perdões de parte* made no reference to the legal requirement that the surviving spouse was informed and agreed to the terms of the obligations implicit in the pardon, while other pardons included this crucial clause. For instance, on 22 August 1552, João Anes and Bastião Afonso, both inmates in the Porto prison, granted each other a pardon for the injuries each caused the other, an agreement that was approved by their wives, Isabel Gonçalves and Catarina Rodrigues, respectively. Furthermore, the document specified that the broad renunciation made by those four included the rights of their children, as well as the brothers and sisters of the two men, as each side released each other's family from any future claim.[37] Unusual for its precision, this victim's pardon,

---

35 *Ordenações Filipinas*, Livro 1, Título 88, nos 4–9.

36 *Ordenações Filipinas*, Livro 4, Título 96. For an example of a step-mother losing inheritance to an entailment to the blood relatives of the deceased, see Maria de Lurdes de Rosa, *O Morgadio em Portugal, sécs. XIV–XV: modelos e práticas de comportamento linhagístico* (Lisbon: Editorial Estampa, 1995), 176–7.

37 Arquivo Distrital do Porto (ADP), Fundo Notarial, Po.1, 3a Se, no. 4–7, Livro 7 (1552), f.23–25.

this one addressed the possible claims of all those who, according to Portugal's inheritance laws, had their inheritance potentially jeopardized.

The victim's pardon, therefore, is an excellent tool for the study of early modern Portuguese women, and in fact this type of document can be used to emphasize the experiences of women confronted with difficult decisions. The law that governed pardons required and enabled women as well as men to forego some of which they were entitled to, but because women's earning opportunities were generally more limited than those of their male counterparts, it could be argued that the proportion of what women relinquished was potentially of greater significance to women than was the case for men. Because early modern Portuguese women could and did actively participate in the granting of pardons, the process highlights the uniqueness of the legal position of Portuguese women vis-à-vis their female counterparts elsewhere in Europe. In fact, Portuguese women had more in common with other women in the Iberian Peninsula than with women in the rest of the continent because Portugal and Spain inherited and developed similar legal codes. Not surprisingly, recent scholarship shows that in contrast to the conventional view about the oppression and discrimination of women in Spain, the reality is that they enjoyed greater legal protection than women elsewhere in Western Europe.[38] The same held true for Portuguese women.

The basis for that unique position is difficult to trace because the Portuguese laws in effect in the sixteenth and seventeenth centuries were developed over time in the Middle Ages, and few of those laws provided a justification for their existence. While there were some relatively mild modifications over time, the laws pertaining to inheritance rights, and all related laws such as those that applied to pardons, remained fundamentally the same throughout this period. Early modern Portuguese women did not see the diminishing of their traditional rights to family property to the extent that has been documented for other parts of Europe.[39] From a legal perspective, it appears that Portuguese women enjoyed more autonomy than women elsewhere, but this position needs some cautious qualification. The difference between the law and practice cannot be overstated, and some studies have shown that the more was at stake, the more pressure on the family to concentrate its wealth on a male heir.[40] Undoubtedly not every family adhered to the principles

---

[38] See, for example, Lisa Vollendorf, *The Lives of Women: A New History of Inquisitional Spain* (Nashville: Vanderbilt University Press, 2005), and Allyson M. Poska, *Women and Authority in Early Modern Spain: The Peasants of Galicia* (Oxford: Oxford University Press, 2005).

[39] See, for example, Merry E. Wiesner, *Women and Gender in Early Modern Europe*, 3rd ed. (Cambridge: Cambridge University Press, 2008); Ulinka Rublack, *The Crimes of Women in Early Modern Germany* (Oxford: Clarendon Press, 1999); Judith M. Bennett and Amy M. Froide, eds, *Singlewomen in the European Past, 1250–1800* (Philadelphia: University of Pennsylvania Press, 1999); Amy Louise Erickson, *Women and Property in Early Modern England* (London and New York: Routledge, 1993).

[40] James L. Boone III, 'Parental Investment and Elite Family Structure in Preindustrial States: A Case Study of Late Medieval-Early Modern Portuguese Genealogies', *American Anthropologist* 88, no. 4 (December 1986): 859–78.

of Portugal's laws on partible inheritance, but sometimes the custom was to favour daughters over sons, if it could benefit the family overall.[41] In fact, the family came first, to the detriment of the individual son or daughter, a practice that continued to the modern era. As Brian Juan O'Neill found for the nineteenth and twentieth centuries, 'case after case indicates that despite the existence of a formal rule of equality between heirs, on a practical level there is a distinct inequality between one favoured heir and many secondary, tacitly excluded heirs'.[42]

It is evident from the surviving records that some of the basic principles required by law were not followed, or so much pertinent detail was left out of the narrative that it is difficult to determine whether or not the rules were followed. In theory, an incomplete pardon could have been challenged by any number of potential heirs, but how often did that happen? Who would have had the know-how, the courage, and the financial means to engage in such a lengthy and expensive procedure? If possession is nine-tenths of the law, then clearly those who possessed the most feared the law the least. First, the experiences of women and men of the elite were fundamentally different from those below them. Second, law or no law, early modern Portuguese women lived under a patriarchal system that placed the male head of the household well above his wife and dependents.

As already mentioned, on its own, the victim's pardon is inadequate for the study of crime, but it is also a limited source for the study of women, and society more generally. In addition to the problems inherent in its truncated formula, the pardon document also offers problems of quantification. We do not know how many victims' pardons have survived for any particular district, but given that the notary collections are burgeoning with other types of documents, and only rarely contain a *perdão de parte*, we can surmise that the vast majority of early modern Portuguese people did not visit a notary's office to regulate their conflicts. Most disputes were resolved informally, or remained unresolved, and left little trace for curious researchers. For these reasons the present study uses a combination of legal sources to mine for information about women's strategies in the face of legal troubles.

The Sources

The present study relies heavily on national laws that were in effect in the sixteenth and seventeenth centuries, and on manuscript sources held in a number of Portuguese

41 Mafalda Soares da Cunha and Nuno Gonçalo Monteiro, 'Aristocracia, Poder e Família em Portugal, Séculos XV–XVIII', in Mafalda Soares da Cunha and Juan Hernández Franco, eds, *Sociedade, Família e Poder na Peninsula Ibérica: Elementos para uma História Comparativa* (Lisbon and Murcia: Edições Colibri/CIDHUS/Universidade de Evora/ Universidad de Murcia, 2010), 47–75. For examples of this practice in colonial Brazil, see Muriel Nazzari, 'Parents and Daughters: Change in the Practice of Dowry in São Paulo (1600–1770)', *Hispanic American Historical Review* 70, no. 4 (November 1990): 639–65; Alida C. Metcalf, 'Fathers and Sons: The Politics of Inheritance in a Colonial Brazilian Township', *Hispanic American Historical Review* 66, no. 3 (August 1986): 455–84.

42 Brian Juan O'Neill, *Social Inequality in a Portuguese Hamlet: Land, Late Marriage, and Bastardy, 1870–1978* (Cambridge: Cambridge University Press, 1987), 176.

municipal and district archives, as well as in Portugal's national archives in Lisbon. Early modern Portuguese legislation was organized in three major compilations that were codified in three different periods. The *Ordenações Afonsinas*, completed around 1446, bear the name of King D. Afonso V (r.1438–1481), though the work began in the reign of King D. João I (r.1384–1433); the *Ordenações Manuelinas* were completed in 1521, under the reign of King D. Manuel I (r.1495–1521); and the *Ordenações Filipinas* were published in 1603 during the reign of King D. Filipe II (r.1598–1621), though the compilation was completed in 1595, under the reign of King D. Filipe I (r.1580–1598).[43] Each set of ordinances consists of five volumes of national laws, and, as would be expected, there is much overlap between the three compilations, though there were substantive modifications and alterations since the initial set of 1446. Yet some Portuguese historians claim that the laws of Portugal from the fifteenth century differed very little from those of the eighteenth, and that, in fact, the latter version of the ordinances, the *Ordenações Filipinas*, was not repealed entirely until the second half of the nineteenth century with the publication of the modern penal codes.[44]

This corpus of legislation provides a legal framework in which the archival findings can be contextualized, and the archival sources used for this study consist primarily of samples of victims' pardons and denunciations. The victim's pardon, or *perdão de parte,* was found in notary collections in the district archives of Viana do Castelo, Porto, Evora, and Faro, in addition to the national archives in Lisbon (the Torre do Tombo), as well as the district archives in Ponta Delgada, São Miguel, and Angra do Heroísmo, Terceira (Azores). What precipitated the need for a victim's pardon was an infraction for which an official complaint had been launched – the *querela* – but few of these have survived for the sixteenth and seventeenth centuries.[45] Fortunately one volume entitled *Livro de Autos de Querelas* (1606–1654) was found in the district archives of Ponta Delgada, a registry of the initial denunciations launched by individuals to authorities about wrongdoings that merited an investigation.[46]

Early modern Portuguese law allowed for ordinary people to come forward and initiate a judicial procedure against anyone who had caused them harm.[47] In theory, that was the law; in practice, it is difficult to determine to what extent early modern people felt comfortable with, had access to, and made use of the legal system as a means to resolve their disputes. All we have are remnants, bits and

---

43 From 1580 to 1640, Portugal was under the Spanish Crown, with three consecutive Spanish rulers, Filipe II (r.1580–1598), Filipe III (r.1598–1621), and Filipe IV (r.1621–1640), though in Portugal they were known as Filipe I, Filipe II, and Filipe III, respectively.

44 Carvalho, 'Condicionalidade sócio-cultural', 1059, 1071.

45 In one other study of a later series of *querelas* from Ponta Delgada, the author found that the surviving evidence was minimal for the first two decades of the eighteenth century, and sporadic thereafter. Rodrigues, 'Criminalidade e Violênica'.

46 See note 1.

47 For the law on the *querelas* and the judicial procedure around them, see *Ordenações Filipinas*, Livro 5, Título 117 and 124.

pieces of parts of the process, with which we aim to examine what often were complex problems, the context for which is often missing. As will be discussed later, the vast majority of victims' pardons made specific reference to a complaint having been launched at some undetermined time, but there is no way to know how many of the initial denunciations led to victims' pardons.

The Querela

According to the law, the *querela* or official accusation had to be presented by the offended individual to the judge within a year and a day of the crime. Most victims launched their complaints to the ordinary judge (*Juíz Ordinário*), an official who was elected by the local municipal council, or to the outside judge (*Juíz de Fora*), someone from outside the area he served, an official appointed by the Crown ostensibly to assure impartiality in the local judicial system. When neither of those two officials was available, the senior member of the municipal council (*Vereador*) was the acting judge. Portuguese law also dictated that a corregidor (*Corregedor*), the Crown overseer in each district or *comarca*, visit his constituencies regularly to ensure that justice was being served, and to hold a travelling court to hear *querelas* where no other judge existed. Criminal cases were thus first dealt with at the local level, and then could be appealed to the corregidor, or to a higher court, the *Relação da Casa do Porto* in Porto, that covered northern Portugal, or the *Casa da Suplicação* in Lisbon, that covered the rest of Portugal and the Atlantic islands. That had been the model promulgated by lawmakers, but studies have shown that the system was seriously weakened by a general lack of proper oversight by the corregidors, and the absence of the outside judge from most localities.[48]

The majority of the *querelas* found for this study were heard at the home of the outside judge in Ponta Delgada, with the rest registered with the local judge, or with the Crown magistrate (*Ouvidor Geral*), or even at the palace of the Count of Vila Franca, São Miguel (Azores).[49] The count was especially visible in 1641, when he heard four of the five *querelas* registered that year, and in 1646 when he heard five of the ten. The count's seigneurial powers included the administration of justice on the island, and in fact he was the *Major Alcaide* of the region, but no reason was supplied for why he dealt with those specific cases. Wherever

48 For an overview of the judicial system in early modern Portugal, see, for example, Alves, 'Violência e Perdão'; Ramos, *Violência e Justiça*; Hespanha, 'Sábios e Rústicos'; Fortunato de Almeida, 'Organização político-administrativa portuguesa dos sécs. XVII e XVIII', in António Manuel Hespanha, ed., *Poder e Instituições na Europa do Antigo Regime: Colectânia de Textos* (Lisbon: Fundação Calouste Gulbenkian, 1988), 323–94. For a more recent reassessment of this question, see António Manuel Hespanha, 'A monarquia: a legislação e os agentes', in José Mattoso, ed., *História da Vida Privada em Portugal: A Idade Moderna*, 4 vols (Lisbon: Círculo de Leitores e Temas e Debates, 2011), II: 12–31.

49 In fact, the count had an impressive title: Excellentissimo Senhor Dom Rodrigo da Câmara, Count of Vila Franca, Major Alcaide, General Captain and Governor of His Majesty's Council.

the venue, however, the scribe followed a formula as outlined in the national ordinances. In the cases of physical injury, for instance, the complainant had to show 'open and bloody injuries, or swollen and black marks and bruises, whether [the injuries happened] on purpose or in an argument, and failing to show this, it [the complaint] will not be accepted'.[50] The judicial scribe was also instructed to write down the statements made by the accusers in their own voice, word per word, and not to make any alterations to the details reported by the victims.[51] There is no way to verify the extent to which this directive was followed, but in all likelihood some of the victims' expressions filtered through the recorded narrative.

The *querelas* in the collection under discussion were registered by 13 different scribes, from 1606 to 1654, and they dealt with complaints from a small region in an outlying island in the middle of the Atlantic, namely the small city of Ponta Delgada in São Miguel, Azores – an island approximately 1,500 kilometres west of Portugal.[52] They cannot be said to represent the range of criminal activity in early modern Portugal, but they serve to highlight the ways in which some ordinary people used the judicial system to deal with conflict and personal trauma. These sources are inadequate for any meaningful quantifiable analysis, but they offer fascinating insights into the daily activities and mindset of a few individuals who otherwise would not have made the official record. While the plaintiffs' narratives must be viewed with great caution, enough can be garnered from them to better situate our imaginings of those few troubled moments in their lives. The objective was not to assess the validity of their claims, but rather to examine what the claimants believed to be valid and valued. A lot of creativity went into fashioning each individual *querela*, and likewise we can be creative in discerning between possibility and probability. Undoubtedly each denunciation was the result of some harmful incident, but the partiality of those narratives cannot be ignored.[53]

---

[50] 'feridas abertas e sangoentas, ou pisaduras e nodoas inchadas e negras, quer diga que foi de preposito, quer em rixa; e não as mostrando, não lhe será recebida'. *Ordenações Filipinas*, Livro 5, Título 117, no. 1. See also Alves, 'Violência e perdão', 95–6, and Ramos, *Violência e Justiça*, 31–3.

[51] *Ordenações Filipinas*, Livro 5, Título 117, no. 11. See also Marcello Caetano, *História do Direito Português (sécs. xii–xvi)* (Lisbon: Editorial Verbo, 2000), 383–4.

[52] For a discussion of the judicial infrastructure in São Miguel, see Ma Margarida de Sá Nogueira Lalanda, 'Os municípios micaelenses nos séculos XVI e XVII', in Alberto Vieira, ed., *O Município no Mundo Português: Seminário Internacional, Funchal, 26 a 30 Outubro de 1998* (Funchal: Região Autónoma da Madeira/Centro de Estudos de História do Atlântico, 1998), 235–68.

[53] Due to the deterioration of the collection, duplication of the manuscript was limited to certain sections only, and thus the present discussion deals with a sample of *querelas* from 1629 to 1652. Furthermore, no *querela* was deciphered for the years 1637 and 1638 because those pages were damaged.

Table 1.1 Criminal accusations (*querelas*) in Ponta Delgada, São Miguel, Azores, 1629–1652

	Female plaintiff	**Male plaintiff**	**Female defendant**	**Male defendant**
assault (65)	22	57	40	104
concubinage (3)		3	3	3
false testimony (1)		1		3
homicide (3)	1	3	3	9
illegal trading (2)		2		3
rape/deflower (9)	12	3	1	9
theft (14)	1	16	8	24
witchcraft (1)	1		4	
TOTAL (98)	37	85	59	155

Source: Biblioteca Pública e Arquivo Regional de Ponta Delgada (São Miguel, Azores), Fundo Judicial, *Livro de Autos de Querelas*, NOT.601 (1606–1654)

Ninety-four *querelas* were transcribed and translated for this study, and as Table 1.1 indicates, the majority of complaints filed between 1629 and 1652 dealt with physical assault and injury, while the second most common accusation was for theft.[54] Men outnumbered women in all categories of crimes, as plaintiffs and as defendants, except in the category of rape/deflower, where women appeared more often as the plaintiff. Although these numbers provide a useful breakdown of the sex ratio of the accusers and the accused, they do not represent all the individuals involved in each particular case because sometimes the scribe used vague terminology to refer to certain people also implicated in a case. The same was true with the scribe's references to the listed witnesses, of which 489 were named in total, 159 women and 330 men, with the occasional imprecise remark about the sisters or the neighbours of so-and-so. Nevertheless, albeit a small sample, the *querelas* reveal that men were at the forefront of criminal acts reported to judicial officials.

The numbers shown in Table 1.1 confirm what has been found in studies of crime for other parts of Europe, with a few notable exceptions registered in Ponta Delgada. It is noteworthy, for instance, that there was an equal number of men and women who were accused of concubinage, in all three cases the accusation stemming from a male judicial official. This topic is discussed further in Chapter 3, but suffice to state here that the cases involved single women and married men. Although a small number, the three examples point to the possibility that officials in Ponta Delgada did not necessarily disregard the sexual transgressions of married men. Equally intriguing was the female defendant in the category of rape/deflower, an unusual circumstance that is examined more closely in Chapter 3, as well. As will be shown, the female defendant in question was not accused of

[54] Because some of the complaints dealt with more than one crime, the number of crimes is slightly higher than the number of *querelas* registered.

raping or deflowering anyone; rather, she was allegedly involved in facilitating the sexual exploitation of a young woman by a married man. This latter example, combined with the number of female defendants in the columns for injury and homicide, demonstrated that while women were a minority in reported cases of aggression, they could and did occasionally commit serious crimes, or were said to have committed those crimes. It needs to be stressed that *querelas* were accusations against certain individuals, not confirmation of their guilt.

The *querelas* were registered in a fairly consistent formula, starting with the date and place where the complaint was written down, usually at the lodgings and in the presence of the judge or another judicial official, before whom the plaintiff appeared and related her or his accusation, the details of which included the name of the accused and the place where the alleged incident occurred, and occasionally the time and date of the incident. The monthly and yearly breakdown of the *querelas* shown in Table 1.2 shows that a slightly higher number of complaints were registered in the spring and summer months. Possibly the numbers reflect a greater opportunity for people to interact and enter into disputes during the longer days of the year, when more time was spent outdoors, in the fields. Nearly all accusations indicated the location for the reported infraction, and 48 of these made reference to the outdoors, though 32 of the 48 merely inferred that the incident took place outside, with no further specifics. Although 29 *querelas* referred to agriculture, either in connection to the conflict or as the occupation of the individuals named in the registry, including witnesses, another 25 plaintiffs claimed that the conflict erupted in their own home. Five infractions took place in the defendants' home, while yet another five occurred in someone else's residence, including the quarrel that escalated at around 2 o'clock, after dinner, on Monday, 1 June 1651, at the home of Ursula Ferreira, when Cecilia de Sousa and her mother attacked Catarina de Almeida.[55] Other conflicts broke out at a ball game, along the shoreline or harbour, on the street, at the slaughterhouse or at the mill, and in prison.

One of the most important omissions in the *querelas* is the viewpoint of the defendant, hence the narrative invariably presented the accuser as an innocent bystander, someone who was minding her or his own business, going about in peace and tranquillity ('em paz e pacífica'). In the cases of physical assault, for instance, we are told that without any confrontation and seemingly from nowhere, the accused attacked or harmed the plaintiff, with fists, teeth, and nails, or stones, sticks, knives, spears, swords, and guns, or a combination thereof. These attacks often resulted in black and bloody bruises and blemishes, scratches and swollen body parts, twisted or broken limbs, or worse. The complainant displayed the injuries to the judge, and the scribe vouched for the veracity and severity of those injuries. Not surprisingly, the scribe's description of the injuries was recorded in non-medical terms; rather, the scribe aimed to pinpoint the exact location of the visible wound(s), and estimated the size of the bruise(s) or cut(s) in relation to recognizable objects, such as a coin, an egg, or the palm of his hand.

---

55 BPARPD, *Livro de Autos de Querelas*, f.171–172.

Table 1.2 Yearly and monthly distribution of criminal accusations (*querelas*) in Ponta Delgada, São Miguel, Azores, 1629–1652

	J	F	M	A	M	J	J	A	S	O	N	D	T
1629		2	2						1				5
1630		1					1	1					3
1631			1										1
1632					2	1			3	1	1	1	9
1633				1	2	1		1			1		6
1634	1			1					1				3
1635							1	2					3
1636						1		1					2
1637													-
1638													-
1639						1			2			1	4
1640		1			1								2
1641		1	1			2				1			5
1642													0
1643					1				1				2
1644		1		1	1	1	2						6
1645	3		1										4
1646					3	4		2	1				10
1647						1	1						2
1648								2	1	1			4
1649		1	1			1	1			2		1	7
1650	2	1			1		1	2	1				8
1651						2			2				4
1652	1					3							4
TOTAL	7	8	6	3	11	18	7	11	13	5	2	3	94

Source: Biblioteca Pública e Arquivo Regional de Ponta Delgada (São Miguel, Azores), Fundo Judicial, *Livro de Autos de Querelas*, NOT.601 (1606–1654)

The judge accepted to proceed with the accusation once the plaintiff swore on the holy scriptures, and named the witnesses, which, in this sample, varied in number from one to 23; regardless of the number of witnesses listed, the accuser always reserved the right to name some more at a later date, if necessary. The accuser, judge, and scribe signed the document, unless the accuser was a woman, in which case the need for her signature was either ignored, or someone signed on her behalf. Only rarely did women sign their own querela, a testimony to women's low literacy rate, although the inability to sign one's name was not necessarily a sign that the individual could not read, for writing and reading were taught separately in the early modern period.[56] Furthermore, other notarized records reveal that while mothers could not sign the documents, their daughters could, an indication that female literacy rates increased with the younger generations.[57]

Nevertheless, women's poor access to formal education was a topic of heated debate in Portugal, particularly in the eighteenth-century pamphlet literature,[58] but there is some evidence that not all women readily embraced book learning. For instance, in her last testament dated 31 July 1461, Beatriz Galvoa outlined how the female community in Evora was to continue to operate, a community that she had founded years earlier along with her sister Inês Galvoa, and their associate, Beatriz de Elvas. One of the cardinal rules that Beatriz Galvoa highlighted was that no woman who entered the community was to be taught to read, and if a woman entered who already knew how to read, she was not to use a book for prayer but rather to pray with the beads along with the other sisters. Moreover, to avoid dangers and other ills, no man, cleric or secular, was to read to the sisters.[59] The representativeness of these sentiments is difficult to determine, but the archival findings point to a general state of illiteracy, particularly among women. Yet, several notarized records referred to women counting money, suggesting that those women were at least numerate.[60] It is also worth noting that in early modern Portugal, women had the legal right to sign their own documents, and those who could, did so. The vast majority of notarized documents ended with a declaration that the woman had someone sign on her behalf because she did not know how to write, not because she was prohibited by law or custom from doing it herself.

Although formulaic, the *querela* registries revealed some important details about relationships between a few individuals who made up an early modern community. To avoid repetition, this study focusses on a sample of *querelas* that highlight the intrinsic (mis)understandings within and between families, neighbours, and acquaintances, some of whom may have been forgiven along the way, in some form or another. Although we do not know how many, or if

---

56 Lisa Vollendorf, 'Navigating the Atlantic Divide: Women, Education, and Literacy in Iberia and the Americas', in Sarah E. Owens and Jane E. Mangan, eds, *Women of the Iberian Atlantic* (Baton Rouge: Louisiana University Press, 2012), 18–36; Yolanda Gamboa-Tusquets, 'María de Zayas, or Memory Chains and the Education of a Learned Woman', in Anne J. Cruz and Rosilie Hernández, eds, *Women's Literacy in Early Modern Spain and the New World* (Burlington: Ashgate, 2011), 209–24; Sara T. Nalle, 'Literacy and Culture in Early Modern Castile', *Past and Present*, no. 125 (November 1989): 65–96.

57 See, for example, ADP, Fundo Notarial, Po.4, 1a Se, no. 39 (1648–1649), f.57v–59, and f.91v–93.

58 Pedro Miguel Reboredo Marques, '"Não são femeas, ou machos as almas com distinção": Estratégias de valorização da mulher em papéis volantes setecentistas', *Portuguese Studies Review* 13, no. 1/2 (Fall–Winter 2005/2007): 305–29.

59 João Luís Inglês Fontes, 'A Pobre Vida no Feminino: O Caso das Galvoas de Evora', in Ana Isabel Buelcu, João Silva de Sousa, and Maria Adelaide Miranda, eds, *O Corpo e o Gesto na Civilização Medieval* (Lisbon: Edições Colibri/Universidade Nova de Lisboa, 2006), 157–78.

60 I am grateful to Jan McTavish for bringing this point to my attention.

any, of these *querelas* were resolved informally, through some form of mediation, reconciliation, and concessions, the gap between the time of the infraction and the formal accusation could be a hint that some attempts were made to negotiate a settlement. Only 50 of the registered sample of *querelas* under study had a clear indication of the time or date for the reported crime, and of those, only 12 were reported on the same day that the incident occurred. Another 17 were registered one day later, 6 registered two days later, 3 registered three days later, and 12 accusations were made several days after the incident took place.

There were a number of possible reasons for the delay between the alleged criminal act and the visit to the judge's quarters, not least of which was the distance the plaintiff had to travel to reach the authorities. Although the majority of the complaints filed in Ponta Delgada were launched by local residents, some complainants came from other parts of São Miguel, and one even came from another island. On 4 June 1652, Francisco Vaz Falcão, from the island of Santa Maria, filed a complaint against four members of an elite household who had beaten up his daughter, Maria Velha, a 24-year-old *moça donzela*, or young maiden. Francisco explained that the incident had happened in early May, but he had to travel to Ponta Delgada because no one in Santa Maria would accept his complaint due to the influence of the accused.[61] In another *querela* the plaintiff alerted authorities more than two months after he had been assaulted, but he explained that he had been bedridden for 39 days due to the injuries he incurred from the assault, and he had a medical certificate to prove it.[62] Still, it is worth noting that nearly half of the *querelas* examined for this study did not stipulate when the reported crime took place, suggesting that some time had lapsed, during which time informal discussions were held but eventually broke down. It is possible that, in some cases, those discussions resumed at some point during the judicial process, leading to informal agreements, or to a visit to the notary to initiate a victim's pardon.

The Perdão de Parte

A total of 224 *perdões de parte* was examined for this study, from the sixteenth to the eighteenth centuries, found in a number of Portuguese archives.[63] As was the case with the *querelas*, most victims' pardons were more directly connected to male supplicants and male defendants, and most crimes dealt with physical

61 BPARPD, *Livro de Autos de Querelas*, f.175–175v.

62 BPARPD, *Livro de Autos de Querelas*, f.143–143v.

63 The total number of victims' pardons collected for this study is largely a reflection of the accessibility and availability of sources, as well as the duplication services provided in each archive. After an initial gathering of a number of samples, I returned to the three major centres in Portugal – Evora, Lisbon, and Porto – to conduct a more thorough search in each respective archive. Many more notarized pardons were found in the national archives in Lisbon, and in the district archives in Porto, but, two years later, the orders for the duplication from those two sites still had not been fulfilled.

injuries (see Table 1.3).[64] The statistical challenges with this type of document are particularly remarkable in the rape/deflower category. Without additional information, we can but accept the unreliability of these figures, given that of the 17 pardons from Viana do Castelo, three dealt with cases of rape/deflower, and of the 44 from Porto, six were connected to rape/deflower, whereas of the 99 pardons in Evora, only two related to rape/deflower, and none of Faro's 38 pardons mentioned sexual assault of any sort. There is no reason to believe that men in northern Portugal were more inclined to sexually assault women, or that women in the northern regions were more prone to report or pardon those types of crimes. Only further investigation, and a much larger corpus of documentation, could reveal the possible reasons for the discrepancies of this nature. At the present, the available evidence is not significant enough to allow for detection of regional differences.

Table 1.3 Pardons from victims of crime (*perdões de parte*) to their perpetrators, Portugal, 1544–1754

	1	**2**	**3**	**4**	**5**	**6**	**7**	**8**	**9**
Azores (11)	5	5		1					
Evora (99)	66	22	2	3	1	2			3
Faro (38)	28	3		1	3		2		1
Lisbon (15)	9	1		2		1		2	
Porto (44)	21	6	6	1	3	1	2	1	3
Viana do Castelo (17)	8	2	3	2					2
TOTAL (224)	137	39	11	10	7	4	4	3	9

Source: Notarial Collections (see footnotes for specifics)

Legend:

1 = injury
2 = homicide
3 = rape/deflower
4 = adultery
5 = theft
6 = concubinage
7 = slander
8 = escape from prison
9 = other (resisting authority, abduction, vandalism, unlawful weapons and unknown)

Notwithstanding the challenges with the documentation, the few scattered victims' pardons gathered for this study indicated that women were not necessarily dependent on a male figure to validate their decision to grant a pardon to their aggressors. For example, of the 11 *perdões de parte* related to sexual assault (or loss of virginity, deflowering, and sexual dishonour), women granted five on their own; two women were accompanied by their fathers, and one by her mother; another had her uncle involved in the accusation and pardon process; a wife and husband pardoned the culprit on behalf of their daughter; and a wife and husband pardoned the man who they had accused of physical assault and attempted rape of the wife. The questions of distinctions between rape and deflowering are addressed

64 See endnotes for specific references to individual cases.

in greater detail in Chapter 3, but it should be noted that the 11 cases listed in Table 1.3 contained a number of ways to refer to different forms of sexual assault or exploitation. The most common euphemism used was in reference to the woman having been deflowered, or to her loss of virginity and honour, found in 9 of the 11 *perdões de parte* in this category. The other two examples used less equivocal language, relying instead on the verb 'to force' to indicate the sexual assault.

The victims' pardons related to sexual crimes highlighted women's unique vulnerability as women, but as Table 1.4 illustrates, women were also implicated in the pardoning process for other forms of reported violence. As already noted, most pardons were granted by men to other men for cases of physical injuries amongst themselves, but as discussed in Chapter 2, the records showed that women had much at stake in those aggressions and the subsequent pardons. Women's involvement in the settlements between (male) victims and (male) perpetrators was particularly acute in cases of homicide, the only category of crime (with the exception of sexual assault) where women outnumbered men as pardoners. Admittedly, part of the reason for this high number of women in pardons for homicide was connected to one particular case that involved a large family, with many female members, who pardoned two young men for killing their kinswoman. Nevertheless, the archival records showed that more men were killed by other men, which, consequently, left the burden on women to deal with those untimely deaths. Significantly, only one pardon was found for a woman accused of homicide, compared to 56 male defendants in that category of crime. Some if not most of those pardoned men would have had families whose lives were altered as well, but as was the case with the *querelas*, the victim's pardon reflected the incident predominantly from the victim's point of view, albeit under the influence of some undisclosed forces.

Table 1.4 Female/male ratio in pardons from victims of crimes (*perdões de parte*) for cases of physical injury and homicide, Portugal, 1544–1754

	Pardoner (female)	**Pardoner (male)**	**Pardoned (female)**	**Pardoned (male)**
injury	32	139	10	178
homicide	45	25	1	56
TOTAL	77	164	11	234

Source: Notarial Collections (see footnotes for specifics)

The victim's pardon, too, followed a general formula that included the date of its creation and the place where it was created, usually at the notary's office or at the home of the pardoner. A pardon was granted for a variety of reasons, but many of the same reasons came up in the documents. In cases of assault, for instance, the most often-cited justifications for granting a pardon were that the plaintiff was mistaken about the identity of the culprit, had been misinformed, could not see well because it was night time, it was accidental, it was the plaintiff's fault, or the injuries were minor, were all healed, and left no mark or deformity. Above all, the pardoner invariably stressed that the incident was insignificant and had not been due to any old feud, otherwise there would be suspicions of possible premeditation.

Other formulaic clauses included the insistence that the pardoner was acting of her or his own volition, without any constraint from anybody, but for the love of God who also pardoned one's sins, and to clear one's conscience. Because the pardon was supposedly granted for free, the plaintiff wanted nothing from the defendant, and the pardoner pledged never to renege on any of the terms of the pardon. This pledge was given on behalf of the pardoner and on behalf of any present or future heirs, an important clause because, as already mentioned, by law the victim of a crime was entitled to some form of compensation and satisfaction from the perpetrator of the crime, which translated to a portion of the amount of the penalty. The pardon also included a clause with which the plaintiff pledged her or his properties as a guarantee that the terms of the pardon would be honoured forever, otherwise the defendant reserved the right to seek damages from the plaintiff for any expenses incurred due to the reneging of the agreement, sometimes for double the amount of those expenses.[65] While the pardon was ostensibly granted for free, a common condition inserted in the text was that the defendant had to pay for her or his own legal costs in obtaining a release from the justice system.

Although the pardon was granted to the individual(s) who had been charged with a crime, the text was addressed to the Crown, for it would be used by the defendant in her or his appeal to the king for clemency.[66] The pardoner thus made a plea to His Majesty's justices to show mercy and not to proceed against the accused, for the plaintiff was willing to let matters drop, and they, plaintiff and defendant, had always been and still were good friends. In essence the victim's pardon was part of the process in a conflict between private and public (state) interests. With the victim's pardon, the victim renounced and extinguished all penal and civil laws that applied in cases of injuries to the individual person; what remained was the 'public offense' of the crime, which was the portion that was dealt with a royal pardon.[67] For this reason, most victims' pardons included a declaration that the victims had

---

[65] For examples of such agreements, see ADP, Fundo Notarial, Po.4, 1a Se, no. 47 (1656), f.96–96v; Arquivo Distrital de Evora (ADE), Fundo Notarial, Francisco Jorge (notary), Estremoz, Séries 28 (1677), f.128–131.

[66] Portugal had a number of queens regent, especially in the Middle Ages, though their regency did not go uncontested. See, for example, Judite A. Gonçalves de Freitas, 'D. Leonor de Aragão: imagens de contestação e poder', in Ana María da Costa Toscano and Shelley Godsland, eds, *Mulheres Más: Percepção da Mulher Transgressora no Mundo Luso-Hispânico*, 2 vols (Porto: Universidade Fernando Pessoa, 2004), I: 73–86, and Isabel de Barros Dias, 'Uso pragmático do *topos* má na segunda redacção da *Crónica de 1344*', in the same volume, 123–40. In the early modern period, D. Catarina de Austria, wife of D. João III, was regent (1557–1562) for her grandson, D. Sebastião, and D. Luíza de Gusmão, wife of D. João IV, was regent (1656–1662) for her son, D. Afonso VI. The only two reigning queens in Portugal were D. Maria I (r.1777–1799) and D. Maria II (r.1834–1853).

[67] Francisco Tomás y Valiente, 'El perdon de la parte ofendida en el derecho penal castellano', *Anuario de Historia del Derecho Español* 31, no. 1, Serie 1a (Madrid, 1961): 89–93 [55–114].

'forgiven' their part, and they asked His Majesty's justices to forgive theirs, as well. To further arouse the sympathy of judicial authorities, pardoners often stressed the poverty or youthfulness of the culprit, and the unintentional nature of the incident. If the plaintiff had filed a *querela*, it had been done on impulse, in a fit of anger and passion. In essence, the gravity of the crime was downplayed, the consequences were dismissed, and the need for retribution was nullified.

Finally, the pardon document typically ended with the notary stating that he had read the script back to the pardoner and had explained the laws that pertained to pardons, including those that dealt with renunciations, and invariably the pardoner agreed to a sweeping renunciation of all laws, rights and privileges, ordinances and liberties, and anything else that could in any way affect the validity of the pardon contract. The notary often accepted the pardon on behalf of the defendant, who usually was absent from this final stage of the deliberations, and on behalf of anyone else who might have been implicated by the ramifications of the pardon. The notary also acknowledged that he recognized the pardoners, or the witnesses vouched for their identity. Everyone signed the document, in one form or another, or had someone sign it on their behalf.

Given the required formula, the legal clauses of the pardon document sometimes took up more space than the stated reasons for the pardon, and often the stated reasons lacked conviction to the modern reader. Undoubtedly negotiations took place that led to the visit to or from the notary, and the ultimate acquiescence of the victim of a crime to forgo entitlements to justice and restitution. It is doubtful that altruism was as rampant in early modern Portugal as these documents suggest. Rather, because the accused was not allowed to buy her or his way out of the crime committed, and the victim was not supposed to have alerted justice officials for frivolous reasons, the pardon document had to be worded in such a way that stressed the need for compassion over compensation.

Whatever was discussed and agreed to behind the scenes, whatever pressures, threats, and manipulations, whatever promises, compulsions, and compromises, all of that was left out of the legal document called *perdão de parte*, the victim's pardon. As was the case with the *querelas*, the notarized pardon reflected the official presentation of the plaintiff's point of view only; again, we have no record of the defendant's response and counterarguments. In essence, the *perdão de parte* was a retraction of the *querela*, and similar points were raised in both types of documents, except in reverse. Whereas in the *querela* the plaintiff emphasized the severity of the injury, the evil intentions of the enemy who harboured ill feelings due to an old festering feud, and the helplessness and utter innocence of the victim, the pardon addressed the same issues but presented them from the other side of the spectrum.[68] In both cases the details often appeared convoluted, exaggerated, and even absurd, but they reflected the ultimate intent of each document: one was to ensure a conviction, the other to prevent it.

---

68 The legislation differentiated between old and new feuds, and allotted penalties accordingly. *Ordenações Filipinas*, Livro 5, Título 122.

The *querelas* showed that women were sometimes involved in criminal activity for which reason they, too, could have granted or sought a pardon. Overall, though, the *querelas* and the *perdões de parte* indicated that most crime was committed by men against other men. That is one point of view, but the present study looked at those records from another angle. The following chapters examine not only the crimes that affected women more directly, but also those crimes between men that had a clear impact on women and their families more broadly. In fact, the crimes themselves are not examined in any great length – we lack the documentary tools for such an exercise – but rather the focus is on what those recorded crimes tell us about the options open to women whose lives were affected by crime.

Documents cannot represent a reality but rather a process, a complex process that involved a fabrication of events to show the protagonist in a favourable light. What would the narrative look like if one had access to other versions of the events recorded in the documents under discussion? The available sources revealed very little about any particular case. We do not know the final outcome of the *querelas* discussed here, or of the *perdões de parte*. No *querela* was found with its corresponding pardon, or vice versa. In fact, we do not know whether any of the *querelas* from Ponta Delgada generated any pardons, though most pardon documents referred to *querelas*. Sometimes the victim's pardon indicated that the culprit had been sentenced already, but we cannot know whether or not those sentences were carried out.

Another potentially complementary set of records was found in Ponta Delgada, the *Livro para o Rol dos Culpados* (1644–1734), a docket of criminal accusations and the final sentence for each *querela*, the entries registered in alphabetical order according to the culprit's first name. Because of the deterioration of many of the folios, only a limited sample of this list was consulted, approximately 20 folios that contained 215 entries, covering the names from Agueda to Miguel.[69] Unfortunately, the entries were truncated and sorely incomplete, with the actual crime indicated for only 50 per cent of the cases, while the final penalty was seldom mentioned. Nevertheless, the *Rol dos Culpados* served to confirm what was also found in the collection of *querelas*, namely that crime was primarily a male domain, both as plaintiffs and as defendants. Of the 215 entries of *culpados* examined, 30 were for female defendants and 188 male, with 143 male and 52 female plaintiffs named, one of whom was Ursula Rodrigues, daughter of Francisco Rodrigues, who filed a *querela* against Francisco Esteves for 'desfloramento' or deflowering. The case was registered on 15 October 1686, but the outcome was not recorded.[70]

---

[69] BPARPD, Fundo Judicial, *Livro para o Rol dos Culpados* (1644–1734), NOT. 554 (henceforth, *Rol dos Culpados*). It was an imperfect system, to say the least. It appears that the scribe kept a separate folio for each letter of the alphabet, but a registry for a Pedro was inserted on f.17v, left on its own, whereas f.17 ended with António and f.18 began with Fausino. Due to damaged folios, my own sample consists of two separate sections, f.15–23 and f.30–38.

[70] BPARPD, *Rol dos Culpados*, f.19.

Many of the entries in the *Rol dos Culpados* had marginal notes as well, sometimes up to three marginal scribbles, in different handwriting, indicating that a number of scribes were involved in maintaining these records. For instance, Isabel Rodrigues, wife of Agostinho de Oliveira, filed a *querela* against Domingas Colassa, wife of Manuel Rodrigues Salazar, on or around 24 March 1683. On the right margin of this entry, in faded ink, a scribe noted that the accused was 'presa e corre livramento', while on the left margin another scribe wrote that she was free per sentence by the outside judge on 25 January 1693. For a crime that was not identified in this registry, Domingas was imprisoned, released to deal with her case, and finally discharged, a process that appeared to have lasted nearly 10 years.[71]

Although potentially rich in details for statistical analysis, the docket list from Ponta Delgada was of limited use for this study because none of the names found in the *Rol dos Culpados* matched the names in the *Livro de Autos de Querelas*. Admittedly, part of the problem is that, due to the deterioration of both sets of documents, the present examination dealt with a sample from each collection only, and not their entirety, and possibly a more thorough comparison of the two texts would reveal some overlap. In fact, most of the entries in the *Rol dos Culpados* dated from the late seventeenth and early eighteenth centuries, whereas the *Livro de Autos de Querelas* ended in the mid-1650s. Nevertheless, it is curious to note that no *querela* was found for Isabel Luís, wife of Pedro Lopes, even though her *querela* was listed in the *Rol dos Culpados* on 26 April 1644, a *querela* that she had initiated against Manuel, brother of the wife of Filipe Cordeiro of Ponta Delgada. The case was noted as 'tem sumario q obriga' – that is, there was enough evidence to proceed. On the right margin of the docket entry a scribe wrote the word 'morto' or dead, presumably in connection to the accused.[72]

The circumstances of Manuel's death were not recorded, but it is doubtful that he was executed for whatever crime Isabel reported to authorities. Studies of the early modern Portuguese judicial system indicated that the Crown rarely applied the harsh penalties outlined in the law books, some of which included torture, mutilation, and death by fire.[73] The death sentence, in particular, was seldom carried out prior to the eighteenth century, and was often replaced with exile.[74] Depending on the severity of the crime, a convicted person could be banished or exiled internally or externally. In the former case, the individual was forced to live

[71] BPARPD, *Rol dos Culpados*, f.15.

[72] BPARPD, *Rol dos Culpados*, f.32.

[73] In the books, the death sentence applied to a number of crimes. See *Ordenações Filipinas*, Livro 5, Título 3, 6, 12, 13, 17, 18, 25, 35, 39, 41, 51–4, 58, and 60.

[74] This argument was promoted in particular by Hespanha, 'Da "Iustitia" à "Disciplina"'; for some reinterpretations of this theme, see Ana Cristina Araújo, 'Cerimónias de execução pública no Antigo Regime – escatologia e justiça', *Revista de História da Sociedade e da Cultura* 1 (2001): 169–211; Ramos, *Violência e Justiça*; Maria Teresa Costa Ferreira Cardoso, 'Os presos da Relação do Porto. Entre a cadeia e a Misericórdia (1735 a 1740)' (master's thesis, Universidade do Minho, Braga, 2005). I am indebted to an anonymous reader for bringing this last study to my attention.

outside the district where the crime was committed, or move to a depopulated town, called a *couto de homiziados*, generally located along the territorial borders where frontiers had to be defended.[75] In the sample of documents analysed for this study, the *couto* that showed up most often was Castro Marim, in southeastern Portugal, near the Spanish border. For more serious crimes, culprits were more likely to be exiled overseas, a punishment that met the needs of the country's imperial ambitions. As Isabel dos Guimarães Sá has shown, this practice was already well established in the fifteenth century when Garcia de Resende, the Portuguese royal chronicler, reported that King D. João II (r.1481–1495) cautioned the judges of the supreme court to spare the lives of convicted criminals because Portugal 'had many islands to populate'.[76]

Undoubtedly the sentence of exile caused hardships to the recipients of those sentences, and to their families left behind, and this reality must have led to some negotiations for the much-coveted *perdão de parte*. As already noted, however, we do not know the conviction rate of those named in the *querelas* from Ponta Delgada, and whether or not any of those accusers were compelled to withdraw, or minimize, their accusations at the notary's office. This study is based on samples of two distinctly different yet complimentary types of sources, each of which is part of a different scenario. These sources, combined, point to some possibilities, and very few certainties.

What is certain is that some women could and did take steps to deal with difficult situations, with or without their menfolk. Women registered *querelas*, and sometimes had *querelas* registered against them. Women also sought or granted pardons, by themselves or other family members. Women were engaged in these matters due to one crucial factor: they could and did own property. As property owners, or as individuals who had the legal right to own or inherit property, women had the power and authority to demand for redress for wrongs committed against themselves or members of their families. They also had the power and authority to renounce their claims for any redress, and they did that through a notarized victim's pardon. Thus, the *perdão the parte* provides some hints about what was negotiable, and what was not. Notwithstanding the possible intervention

[75] For example, in 1454, the crown granted a privilege to the town of Bragança, with which to increase its population base. The privilege stipulated that 200 native Portuguese could move there to live without being persecuted for any crime they had committed. Fernandes, *Bibliografia do Distrito de Bragança*, 89.

[76] Isabel dos Guimarães Sá, 'Os Espaços de reclusão e a vida nas margens', in José Mattoso, ed., *História da Vida Privada em Portugal: A Idade Moderna*, 4 vols (Lisbon: Círculo de Leitores e Temas e Debates, 2011), II: 293 [276–99]. See also Timothy J. Coates, 'Crime and Punishment in the Fifteenth-Century Portuguese World: The Transition from Internal to Imperial Exile', in Donald J. Kagay and L.J. Andrew Villalon, eds, *The Final Argument: The Imprint of Violence on Society in Medieval and Early Modern Europe* (Woodbridge: Boydell Press, 1998), 119–39. For a discussion of the criminal settlements in Spain, published in the same volume, see Theresa M. Vann, 'Criminal Settlement in Medieval Castilian Towns', 83–94.

and manipulation of the notary who turned the pardoners' words into a written text, the notarized pardon allows for an analysis of some social mores.[77]

The objective of this study is to look at the possible motivations in and ultimate consequences of the seemingly benign practice of pardoning someone who had caused an injury or damage. Rather than turning these women into heroes, this study examines their options, their arguments, their tactics, and their means of survival in a challenging environment. While the number of women fully identified in the pardon document was significantly smaller than the number of men, the acts initiated or publicly ritualized by men had an impact on many unnamed women (and men). Even if the record keepers only recorded one man forgiving the assault of another man, chances are that one or both of those men were married, and had children. An injured male was an injured family; a murdered man was a widow struggling to eke out a living in an arduous and labour-intensive world of agriculture in the rural areas, or making ends meet with the egregiously low wages for female service in urban centres. An injured or murdered woman could also be a calamity for a household, but the records show that, overall, men were more prone than women to harm one another, and thus women more than men were left to pick up and deal with the broken pieces.

As already mentioned, it is difficult to gauge the extent to which early modern Portuguese people availed themselves of the victim's pardon to resolve conflicts, but one long-term study of a series of notary collections pointed to some significant changes over time. In her examination of the *perdões de parte* from 1601 to 1800 related to residents of Vila Nova de Gaia, a town located across from Porto at the mouth of the Douro River (see map), Isilda Monteiro found that there was a substantial increase in the number of notarized victims' pardons between the seventeenth and eighteenth centuries. In one particular series, she found 97 pardons for the seventeenth century, compared to 911 for the eighteenth, and of those a total of 587, or 62 per cent, were written up after 1771. Gaia had approximately 7,000 inhabitants in 1623 and 18,000 by 1785, but this demographic increase did not suffice to explain the seemingly major shift in conflict resolution in the area. Instead, Monteiro contented that the change may be linked to a specialization among the notaries, the successful promotion of their services, and a general recognition that victims' pardons had to be formalized in writing whereas they used to be done orally.

77 For a discussion of the notarial record, and the challenges therein, see, for example, Laurie Nussdorfer, *Brokers of Public Trust: Notaries in Early Modern Rome* (Baltimore: Johns Hopkins University Press, 2009), and Nussdorfer, 'Writing and the Power of Speech'; José Mariz, *Tabeliães e Notários: Estudos e documentos técnicos* (Lisbon: Instituto Português de Arquivos, 1989); Rosa María Capel Martinez, 'Los Protocolos Notariales en la Historia de la Mujer en la España del Antiguo Régimen', in *Ordenamiento jurídico y realidad social de las mujeres, siglos XVI a XX: Actas de las IV Jornadas de Investigación Interdisciplinaria* (Madrid: Universidad Autónoma de Madrid, 1986), 169–79; Barbara Roth-Lochner, 'L'Evolution de l'activité notariale à Genève aux XVIIe et XVIIIe siècles', *Revue d'histoire moderne et contemporaine* Tome 32 (January–March 1986): 97–113; Fernando Bandeira Ferreira, António Maria Pereira, and Augusto M. Veloso Ferreira, 'Le notariat portugais', *Archivum: Revue Internationale des Archives* 12 (1962): 21–30; I. de Sousa Duarte, *Legislação do Notariado Portuguez até ao Anno de 1882* (Lisbon: Livraria Ferreira, 1884).

The evidence for the verbal agreement is by its very nature difficult to locate, but another possible explanation that Monteiro proposed was that in the second half of the eighteenth century there was a more interventionist judicial system in place which led to an increase in the initial *querelas*. Some of the pardons that she looked at stipulated that the pardoner had felt obliged to file an accusation against the perpetrator. Local judges, having been informed of the infraction, often by the surgeon who had treated injuries which had resulted from arguments, 'encouraged' plaintiffs to pursue the case.[78]

We may never understand the underlying reasons behind a decision to grant a pardon, or the wider implications of such a decision, but the probabilities are worth exploring. While thoughts of reconciliation, compensation, accommodation, and co-operation arouse sympathetic feelings, coercion can manifest itself in many guises. The existing documents said very little about the conversations and negotiations that took place before a notary was paid a fee to write up an agreement with long-term reverberations and repercussions. The procedure cost money, so the ends must have justified the means, for at least some of the parties involved in the transaction. Undoubtedly some women and men, especially those of limited financial resources, were compelled to acquiesce to an arrangement not necessarily to their benefit. Conversely, others must have attained a sense of empowerment, however fleetingly, and may have profited enormously, financially or otherwise. Ultimately, though, the *perdão de parte* was not necessarily a means through which a victim forgave the perpetrator of a crime, despite the rhetoric to that effect. As will be shown, the victim's pardon was a way to forgo any claim for the potential loss – in earnings, in property value, in honour – as a result of criminal activity. In early modern Portugal, pardon and forgiveness were not synonymous.

If we know little about what went on before the pardon document was written up, we know even less about what happened afterward. The survival of evidence for the sixteenth and seventeenth centuries is piecemeal, at best, and not just in Portugal. In his study of early modern France, Stuart Carrol found that often there is no beginning or end, and 'the task of reconstruction will require imagination and some educated guesswork'.[79] With the *perdão de parte*, we have a piece of the narrative that came about somewhere along the way, but its precise location on the trajectory must always elude us. It would be useful to know, for instance, whether or not the victim's pardon was part of a successful petition for clemency from the culprit to the Crown. An attempt was made to match the notarized *perdão de parte* with the royal pardons recorded in the chancelleries, but that objective soon proved too futile to pursue. Time has not been kind to the Portuguese archives of the early modern period, particularly in relation to those related to the judicial process. The initial plan had been to gather enough examples from each district archive with which to address possible differences between regions and time periods – north and south, rural and urban, coastal and interior, mainland and Atlantic islands – but

[78] Monteiro, 'A litigiosidade', 104–6.

[79] Stuart Carroll, *Blood and Violence in Early Modern France* (Oxford: Oxford University Press, 2006), 22.

that objective had to be abandoned, as well. A proper examination of the victims' pardons scattered in Portuguese notarial archives would require an inordinate amount of time onsite, and a well-organized team of researchers. It is not a job for one lone historian living in Winnipeg.

Women in the Archives

While the loss of or inaccessibility to documentation from early modern Portugal is significant, Portuguese archives store vast holdings of records that have not been tapped into, especially by historians outside of Portugal. The notarial collections, in particular, are a rich source of information for any number of historical inquiries about women and their families, with great numbers of records that pertain to dowries, testaments, and disputes close to home, to long-distance trade and property transactions further afield. Seldom indexed and often difficult to decipher, the notary record presents enormous challenges for the historian, but equally enormous rewards. The present study is a humble attempt to reveal a fraction of its potential.

The potential of the notarial record for the study of women's history has been recognized elsewhere in Europe, and those studies showed that there was some discernible regional difference in the way women could use the notary to conduct business. In France, for example, only men and widows could deal with notaries on their own; married women needed the consent of their husbands, and single women that of their legal guardians.[80] Yet many women initiated their own notarized documents despite the legal restrictions. One notable example found in Montpellier by Valérie Lafage shows that on 11 November 1622 a woman walked into a notary's office with her husband to write up her testament, with which document she left the bulk of her estate to her husband, but also made some provisions for her sisters and brothers. Her husband disapproved of the division of her assets and therefore he refused to authorize her testament. Later that same day, the woman returned to the notary's office on her own, asked the notary to annul her first testament, and had a new one written up, at which point she left everything to her siblings and nothing to her husband. In fact, she accused her husband of taking some of her jewellery and asked authorities to go after him for those items.[81]

Early modern Portuguese women faced no legal restrictions in the use of the notary to conduct a transaction of whatever sort, as long as they were of legal age and dealt with their own property only. The same rules applied to women and to men, though legislators assumed that husbands conducted most legal proceedings, for the laws that dealt with joint property always addressed the man, and placed restrictions on his autonomy. Thus, the law stipulated that in any legal procedures that involved common property, the scribe and judge were not to proceed with any

[80] Julie Hardwick, 'Women "Working" the Law: Gender, Authority, and Legal Process in Early Modern France', *Journal of Women's History* 9, no. 3 (Autumn 1997): 32 [28–49].

[81] Valérie Lafage, '*Punir, récompenser*: l'enseignement des testaments montpelliérains (1554–1622)', *Seizième Siècle* no. 3 (2007): 238 [225–48].

complaints or appeals unless the supplicant, if married, provided the appropriate power of attorney from his wife. Judicial sentences that pertained to common property were invalidated if the power of attorney from the wife and the interests of minor children were not included in the deliberations.[82]

Those were the rules; those were not necessarily the practices. The notarial collections contain countless contracts initiated by women, but the same collections contain countless more done by men without any reference to their women. There were not more men than women in early modern Portugal. On the contrary, as the demographic studies noted below indicate, in some areas of Portugal there was a veritable absence of men, especially younger men. There is no getting around it. The custom generally speaking must have been that if 'the man of the house' was about the house, he would look after the affairs pertaining to that house, with or without the consent of his wife, depending on his disposition and the complacency of the local scribe. Perhaps those notarized contracts that identified men only did not deal with common property, but the sheer volume of such transactions points to possible divergences between women's legal entitlements and women's ability to lay claim to those entitlements. Not every husband obeyed the law; not every wife could disobey her husband. Nevertheless, if the husband was absent or otherwise engaged, or if there was no husband at all, women went about their business as well as they could, and the records showed that many of them did well enough. Some male contemporaries raised a hue and cry about the number of women left on their own due to the incidence of male work in overseas trade and migration to overseas posts. Significantly, the concern was not based on the difficulties that women faced having to raise their families on their own, but rather on the autonomy that these women enjoyed.[83]

In her study of Vila do Conde in the sixteenth century, the historian Amélia Polónia confirmed that women were heavily engaged in the local economy due to the significant and lengthy absences of local men. In fact, she found that 'besides educating, endowing and marrying off their children, women took charge of family transactions and they managed them skilfully and aggressively, as reflected in the frequency of notary records registering women's involvement in public actions'.[84] The most common transactions that Polónia highlighted for women in

82 *Ordenações Filipinas*, Livro 1, Título 74, no. 22, and Livro 3, Título 63, no. 1–4; see also Livro 3, Título 47, and Título 70, no. 4.

83 Maria Margarida Caeiro, 'Estereotipos femininos quinhentistas: O testemunho de António Ribeiro Chiado', in *O Rosto Feminino da Expansão Portuguesa, Actas I, Congresso Internacional (Lisboa, 21–25 de Novembro de 1994)* (Lisbon: Comissão para a Igualdade e para os Direitos das Mulheres, 1995), 141 [137–43]; see also Isabel Carita, 'A mulher que fica – dois exemplos vicentinos', in the same volume, 131–5.

84 Amélia Polónia, 'Women's Contribution to Family, Economy and Social Range of Maritime Communities in Sixteenth-Century Portugal', *Portuguese Studies Review* 13, no. 1/2 (Fall–Winter 2005/2007): 277 [269–85]. For similar findings in the city of Porto, see Amândio Jorge Morais Barros, 'Mulheres e comércio. Linhas de intervenção da mulher portuense no negócio durante o século XVI', in the same volume, 229–68.

Vila do Conde were connected to 'money collections and quittances' (36 per cent), 'negotiation of assets' (28 per cent), and 'judicial interventions' (15 per cent).[85] The present study looks at some of those 'judicial interventions', namely the *perdão de parte*, and argues that these transactions were intricately linked to those others that dealt with finances and property, and to broader questions of inheritance. As seen with the example of Catarina da Ascenção noted earlier, the crime that her father reported was not an isolated case of theft, but rather was related to property that the young Catarina had inherited from her late mother. At a fundamental level, nearly every crime was a property crime in early modern Portugal, a reality that was understood in the granting of the victim's pardon. For this reason, women had a vested interest in things criminal in their midst.

The Land and Its People

This study looks at some women and men who were enmeshed in criminal procedures in a region in south-western Europe that is little understood outside its borders.[86] Early modern Portugal was the little country that could, and did, for a while. Its exploits overseas in the fifteenth and sixteenth centuries reached epic proportions, at least in some Portuguese historiographical circles, though some contemporaries were aware of the problems those ambitions occasioned. In his poem entitled 'Corre sem vela e sem leme' ('Going about without a sail and rudder'), the Portuguese Renaissance poet Luís de Camões (1525?–1579?) sketched a dubious picture of the world around him.

> Rudderless and without sail proceeds
> this chaotic age
> as a great gale rages,
> and the danger no one heeds
> is not expressed on any page[87]

There was much cause for concern with the state of Portugal's fortunes in the sixteenth century, especially in the second half when the Crown's overseas empire project started to show signs of serious trouble, and not enough resources were allocated to deal with the troubles closer to home. 'Camões' lifespan', Douglas Wheeler has pointed out, 'marked both the high tide and ebbing of Portuguese imperial power'. As an agent for the Portuguese Crown, Camões spent time

---

85 Polónia, 'Women's Contribution', 278.

86 The people who show up in the records under examination in the present study do not represent the diversity that existed in early modern Portugal. For instance, the vast majority of cases did not refer to an individual's skin colour or other ethnic/racial markers, but distinctions along colour lines were certainly observed at the time. An examination of other types of sources that speak to those colour lines is currently underway.

87 Landeg White, trans., *The Collected Lyric Poems of Luís de Camões* (Princeton and Oxford: Princeton University Press, 2008), 289–90.

in several overseas posts, and was witness to much of what was laudable and reprehensible in Portugal's overseas aspirations. Despite his long career as a public servant, and writing his country's greatest epic poem, *Os Lusíadas* (The Lusiads), Camões is believed to have lived his last years in abject poverty.[88]

Portugal's home front is more pertinent to the present study and the evidence indicates that the country experienced some significant demographic shifts between the sixteenth and seventeenth centuries. Portugal's first national census was conducted from 1527 to 1532, from which records the country's population for that time has been estimated at 1.25 to 1.5 million. Lisbon, Portugal's capital city, had 65,000 people in 1527, 100,000 in 1550, and 165,000 in 1620. As one Portuguese historian concluded, it was a monstrous city, a head too big for such a small nation. The other major centres, Porto, Coimbra, Evora, and Elvas, for instance, ranged in population between 16,000 and 20,000 in the first half of the seventeenth century. In 1641, Portugal had six provinces, in which there were 27 districts called *comarcas*, 18 cities, 408 towns, and 200 counties. Aside from Lisbon, Portugal's population was most dense in the northern region between the Minho and Douro rivers. Already in the Middle Ages, the area between the rivers Lima (Viana do Castelo) and Ave (Vila do Conde) had 576 parishes, while the region between Guimarães and Montelongo had only 90.[89] As David Birmingham has stated, Portugal was topographically and demographically lopsided with its soil 'fertile but scarce in the north and plentiful but sterile in the south'.[90] The observation may be exaggerated, but in comparison to the soil in other regions, particularly those in northern Europe, Portugal's soil was poor for agriculture.

The first half of the sixteenth century has been dubbed Portugal's Golden Age, and Lisbon, especially, underwent phenomenal growth at that time. From the 1490s to the 1590s, 'the customs receipts at Lisbon grew a massive seventeen-fold', as the capital city boasted an international community of merchants and merchandise, and became the largest city of the Iberian Peninsula. Yet, A.R. Disney cautions that the perception of a Golden Age was largely based on the re-export of luxury items from Portugal's overseas posts, not from any comprehensive economic and commercial development in the country itself. Beyond the glitter from the capital, much of Portugal remained relatively isolated and inaccessible in the early modern period, renowned for its debilitating lack of transportation systems, though less so along the

---

88 Douglas L. Wheeler, *Historical Dictionary of Portugal* (Metuchen and London: Scarecrow Press, 1993), 52–3.

89 A.H. de Oliveira Marques, *História de Portugal*, 8th ed. (Lisbon: Palas Editores, 1978), 371–2, 399; Joaquim Veríssimo Serrão, *O Tempo Dos Filipes em Portugal e no Brasil (1580–1668)* (Lisbon: Edições Colibri, 2004), 165–6; Caetano, *História do Direito*, 177; Lívio da Costa Guedes, 'Aspectos do Reino de Portugal nos séculos XVI e XVII: A 'Descrição' de Alexandre Massaii (1621). II Tratado', *Boletim do Arquivo Histórico Militar* 58 (Lisbon, 1989): 84 [13–201]. For a partial transcript of the census conducted in 1527, see Braamcamp Freire, 'Povoação de Entre Doiro e Minho no XVI século', *Archivo Histórico Portuguez* 3 (Lisbon, 1905): 241–73.

90 David Birmingham, *A Concise History of Portugal*, 2nd ed. (Cambridge: Cambridge University Press, 2003), 25.

coast and major rivers.[91] With the Crown's focus on overseas exploration and trade, the economy in the metropolis was neglected to the point that Portugal became more and more reliant on imports of foodstuffs and manufactured goods, especially cereals and textiles, while its own production focussed more and more on market commodities such as salt, cork, wine, and olives. In the sixteenth and seventeenth centuries Portugal battled a trade deficit on an almost continuous basis.[92]

The focus on overseas trade and exploration also had significant demographic consequences. An examination of the 1527–1532 census shows that 21 per cent of the nation's households were headed by women, widowed (17 per cent) and single (4 per cent). Historians contend that that high number of female-headed households was a consequence of the Portuguese overseas expansion which gobbled up a significant number of the country's young men.[93] Indeed, by 1641 the country's population had decreased by nearly 20,000 from the figures registered more than a century earlier. Some studies show that by 1527, approximately 80,000 men had left Portugal for India, with only a fraction of them ever returning to their homeland.[94] Contemporaries observed and critiqued this phenomenon, such as Sá de Miranda who lamented in 1535 that with the scent of cinnamon, Lisbon depopulated the rest of the country as the capital attracted vast numbers of migrants who migrated further afield from its port. Already in the sixteenth century, the expression 'fumos da India' ('smoke from India') designated the illusion associated with the great wealth the Crown exhibited, which soon became apparent was more than the overseas empire could sustain.[95] In 1526, Lisbon contributed 35 per cent of the

---

91 Foreign travellers in particular noted problems in Portugal's transportation systems. See, for example, Basílio de Vasconcelos, *'Itinerário' do Dr. Jerónimo Münzer (excertos)* (Coimbra: Imprensa da Universidade, 1931); Frère Claude de Bronseval, *Peregrinatio Hispanica: Voyage de Dom Edme de Saulieu, Abbé de Clairvaux, en Espagne et au Portugal (1531–1533)* (Paris: Presses Universitaires de France/Fondation Calouste Gulbenkian, 1970); Jeroen Dewulf, 'As cartas do humanista Nicolau Clenardo sobre Portugal', in Luís Adão da Fonseca, Luís Carlos Amaral, and Maria Fernanda Ferreira Santos, eds, *Os Reinos Ibéricos na Idade Média: Livro de Homenagem ao Professor Doutor Humberto Carlos Baquero Moreno*, 2 vols (Porto: Faculdade de Letras da Universidade do Porto/Livraria Civilização Editora, 2003), II: 581–9; P. François de Tours, 'Voyage du P. François de Tours en Espagne et en Portugal (1698–1700)', *Revue Hispanique* 53 (1921): 469–549; A.H. de Oliveira Marques, *Portugal Quinhentista (Ensaios)* (Lisbon: Quetzal Editores, 1987).

92 Serrão, *O Tempo Dos Filipes*, 155; A.R. Disney, *A History of Portugal and the Portuguese Empire*, 2 vols (Cambridge: Cambridge University Press, 2009), I: 145–9. See also Carl A. Hanson, *Economy and Society in Baroque Portugal, 1668–1703* (Minneapolis: University of Minnesota Press, 1981), especially 126–40.

93 Polónia, 'Women's Contribution', 276.

94 Coates, *Convicts and Orphans*, 5; João José Alves Dias, 'Os Fogos Femininos nos Municípios do Séc. XVI', in *A Mulher na Sociedade Portuguesa: Visão Histórica e Perspectivas Actuais. Colóquio 1985, Actas*, 2 vols (Coimbra: Universidade de Coimbra, 1986), II: 224–5 [223–7].

95 José Hermano Saraiva, *História de Portugal*, 5th ed. (Mem Martins: Publicações Europa-América, 1998), 160, 170.

Crown's revenues, but from 1550–1700, Lisbon experienced 157 incidents of demographic crises, due to epidemics and food shortages.[96]

Writing in the seventeenth century, Manoel Severim de Faria (1583–1655) reflected on the depopulation problem in Portugal, for which he listed three reasons: the demands of Portugal's overseas projects, the lack of viable employment which prevented many from earning enough to get married and raise a family, and the lack of available land due to the concentration of seigneurial holdings.[97] Other commentators pointed to other causes for Portugal's troubles, including natural disasters beyond anyone's control. Francisco Dias, posted in Porto in 1548 as the Crown's procurator, had to flee the region in 1568 during an outbreak of the plague that killed an estimated 8,000 people.[98] Reports from the seventeenth century indicated that some coastal areas along Portugal's north coast were eroding, as sand bars invaded cultivated areas, while threats of corsair attack were a longstanding problem.[99] Portugal experienced significant increases in mortality rates during several periods of epidemics, six cases of the plague or influenza in the sixteenth century, and 29 cases of epidemics in the seventeenth, including typhoid fever, plague, flu, and variola or smallpox.[100] These crises were compounded by food shortages which were a common problem in early modern Portugal, reaching serious levels in 1556–1557, 1561–1562, 1582–1583, 1596–1597, 1621, 1627, 1632, 1655, 1659, and so forth.[101]

In his description of Portugal written in the early seventeenth century, Duarte Nunes de Leão noted the lack of grains in Portugal, for which he named two reasons: not enough was planted, and too much of what was planted was sent to overseas posts. He also felt that too many people did not want to work the

---

96 Teresa Rodrigues, *Crises de Mortalidade em Lisboa, Séculos XVI e XVII* (Lisbon: Livros Horizonte, 1990), 39, 98.

97 Manoel Severim de Faria, *Noticias de Portugal* (Lisbon: Na Offic. De Antonio Gomes, r.1791 [1655]), 14–20.

98 Francisco Dias, *Memorias Quinhentistas Dum Procurador Del-Rei No Pôrto* (Porto: Câmara Municipal do Porto, 1937 [158?]), 12–14, 22–4, 102, 124.

99 Alberto Antunes de Abreu, 'O Arquivo e as Origens da Santa Casa da Misericórdia de Fão', *Boletim Cultural de Esposende* no. 4 (December 1983): 115 [105–20]; Guedes, 'Aspectos do Reino', 84. See also Isabel Maria Ribeiro Mendes, 'A Defesa do Termo de Lisboa em 1594–1595: Documento do Arquivo de Simancas', *Revista da Faculdade de Letras* no. 12, 5a Se (December 1989): 97–116.

100 Maria João Guardado Moreira and Teresa Rodrigues Veiga, 'Modelos de mortalidade em Portugal', *Ler História* 49 (2005): 145–69. In fact, Portugal had to deal with the plague 27 times between 1410 and 1603. Isabel M.R. Mendes Drumond Braga, 'Para a história do medo no Portugal quinhentista: peste e religiosidade', *Revista de Ciências Históricas* (Universidade Portucalense) 8 (1993): 83 [83–96]. See also José Pereira da Costa, 'O Municipalismo no Arquipélago da Madeira, 1470–1550', in Alberto Vieira, ed., *O Município no Mundo Português: Seminário Internacional, Funchal, 26 a 30 Outubro de 1998* (Funchal: Região Autónoma da Madeira/Centro de Estudos de História do Atlântico, 1998), 196 [183–210].

101 Marques, *História de Portugal*, 373.

land, and instead preferred to go to school to pick up a profession or trade. Still, he highlighted the fact that while Portugal did not produce enough cereals for its own needs, it had an overabundance of other foodstuffs, such as chestnuts, vegetables, fruits, meats, wines, olive oil, and salt, with which Portugal traded for the cereals.[102] Although the author did not elaborate, women would have been engaged heavily in the production and distribution of those foodstuffs, for few of them would have had the opportunity to go to school to improve their work options. The *querela* and the *perdão de parte* corroborate with other evidence that shows that early modern women were seldom identified through their work labels, yet a closer reading of some of these records reveals something about women's means to earn a living. Examples from both sets of documents occasionally reveal women in a work-related activity when they were harmed: they were on the land, on their way to the vineyards, or sewing at home, sometimes on their own, often with other members of their families.

Demographic studies showed that family sizes in early modern Portugal were relatively small. One study of baptismal records from 1543 to 1610 for Póvoa de Varzim, a northern coastal village of approximately 107 households in 1517, revealed that about half of the households had only one child, and the other half the majority had two or three.[103] Nor was the situation necessarily different in larger centres such as Lisbon. A parish list of those who had been confessed in the Santiago district of Lisbon between 1630 and 1680 indicated that the average household consisted of four to five people, including very young children.[104] In another study of a broader corpus of parish records, the historian Maria Norberta Amorim determined that the number of births in early modern Portugal varied from 3 to 5 per household. Amorim stressed the regional variation in her demographic findings, a variation that was especially acute between northern and southern Portugal.[105] As she explained, the northern region has the most fertile land and better climate, and thus it experienced a lower death rate and was spared other demographic crises. By contrast, Amorim found that in the south death rates were higher than in the north, and that women married at an earlier age in the south. For

[102] Duarte Nunes de Leão, *Descripção do Reino de Portugal* (Lisbon: Na Of. de Simão Thaddeo Ferreira, 1785 [1610]), 148–51.

[103] Manuel Amorim, 'A Vila da Póvoa de Varzim no Século XVI', in *Colóquio 'Santos Graça' de Etnografia Marítima, Actas III: Povoamento, Administração, Aspectos sociais* (Póvoa de Varzim: Câmara Municipal da Póvoa de Varzim, 1985), 115–17 [97–201].

[104] Fernanda Olival, 'Os lugares e espaços do privado nos grupos populares e intermédios', in José Mattoso, ed., *História da Vida Privada em Portugal: A Idade Moderna*, 4 vols (Lisbon: Círculo de Leitores e Temas e Debates, 2011), II: 245 [244–75].

[105] For a discussion of the differences in housing styles between the north and south, see Maria Angela Beirante, 'Espaços de sociabilidade nas cidades medievais portuguesas', in Luís Adão da Fonseca, Luís Carlos Amaral, and Maria Fernanda Ferreira Santos, eds, *Os Reinos Ibéricos na Idade Média: Livro de Homenagem ao Professor Doutor Humberto Carlos Baquero Moreno*, 2 vols (Porto: Faculdade de Letras da Universidade do Porto/ Livraria Civilização Editora, 2003), II: 940 [939–45].

example, from 1680 to 1799, women in Couto do Mosteiro (in the central region) married on average at 28.2 years of age, whereas in the south, in Selmes, by the late eighteenth century women were marrying at an average of 22.1 years. As for men, their average age of marriage was slightly higher than that of women in all regions except in the parish of Ronfe (in Minho) where it was 27.6 for women and 27.8 for men, with frequent cases when the woman was older than the man.[106]

Amorim also found that the differences between the average age of marriage in Portugal and in Spain were quite remarkable, especially among women. Prior to 1700, the average age in marriage in Portugal for women was 25.6 to 27.1, and 26.0 to 26.7 for men; in Spain, the average for women was 20.7 to 24.8, and 22.3 to 27.2 for men, and Amorim concluded that the late marriage in Portugal was due to the absence of men who had migrated to overseas posts.[107] More comparative studies are needed to account for regional differences, though, because Spain, too, experienced great losses and depopulation due to famines and epidemics, as well as migration to the Indies, where hundreds of thousands migrated from the late sixteenth century onward.[108] Furthermore, there were significant regional differences within Spain itself, where in Galicia, for instance, women remained single well into their late twenties and thirties, and even later in the Basque country.[109] It should be noted as well that the above figures do not apply to women of the elite, who generally married at a very young age. One study of marriage rates among women of the upper nobility in the second half of the seventeenth century showed that on average the women were 17 years old when they first entered matrimony.[110]

Anecdotal evidence from the early modern period supported some of the above-mentioned differences between southern and northern Portugal, though it should be noted that the observations were generally made by northerners. In a text written c.1512 that describes the general district of Guimarães in northern Portugal, its author, 'Mestre António', observed that the region produced many healthy children and that women gave birth in their fifties, many of them having up to 20 children and raising them all without any difficulty, compared to other districts where the birth rate was much lower. He even offered an example of one woman of 97 years of age who lived outside of Braga but who could still walk to the city without any difficulties, and she had a combined total of 109

106 Maria Norberta Amorim, 'Comportamentos demográficos de Antigo Regime na Península Ibérica', *Ler História* 47 (2004): 164–5 [147–70]. See also Emília Salvado Borges, *Homens, Fazenda e Poder no Alentejo de Setecentos: O Caso de Cuba* (Lisbon: Edições Colibri, 2000), 79.

107 Amorim, 'Comportamentos demográficos', 158–9.

108 William D. Phillips, Jr. and Carla Rahn Phillips, *A Concise History of Spain* (Cambridge: Cambridge University Press, 2010), 165; Poska, *Women & Authority*, 42–3.

109 Poska, *Women & Authority*, especially chapter 2.

110 Nuno Gonçalo Monteiro, 'Casa, casamento e nome: fragmentos sobre relações familiares e indivíduos', in José Mattoso, ed., *História da Vida Privada em Portugal: A Idade Moderna*, 4 vols (Lisbon: Círculo de Leitores e Temas e Debates, 2011), II: 138 [130–58].

children, grandchildren, and great-grandchildren.[111] For his part, Duarte Nunes de Leão claimed that Portugal had such pure air and water that it produced healthy folk who lived long lives, and that no one got sick except for reasons of eating and drinking too much. In fact, he beamed, Portuguese women were so full of vitality that they had babies well into their fifties.[112] There is no way to gauge how many women saw that as a benefit.

Conventional histories of Portugal sometimes ignore the Atlantic islands, the archipelagos of Madeira and the Azores, but they show up in the records used in this study, particularly the latter. Both regions were instrumental in supplying mainland Portugal with essential foodstuffs, predominantly sugar from Madeira (subsequently supplanted by sugar production in Brazil), and wheat from the Azores. Writing in the mid-sixteenth century, João Brandão noted that the Atlantic islands provided a substantial source of revenue for the Crown.[113] While Madeira concentrated on sugar production, the Azores became 'Portugal's bread basket', but the nine islands of the Azorean Archipelago were demographically small. One study estimated that in 1587 the Azores had on average 3.5 people per household.[114] The island of São Miguel had 20,000 inhabitants, Terceira had 17,000, Faial had 3,500, and the remaining small islands averaged between 1,500 and 3,000 inhabitants, or even fewer.[115] The two major cities on the islands, Angra,

---

111 Luciano Ribeiro, 'Uma Descrição de Entre Douro e Minho', *Boletim Cultural da Câmara Municipal do Porto* (1959): 457 [441–60].

112 Leão, *Descripção do Reino*, 152. See also Manoel de Faria y Sousa (1590–1649), *Epitome de las Historias Portuguesas* (Lisbon: Na Officina de Francisco Villela, 1673), 294, 325, 378, and Gaspar Barreiros, *Chorographia de alguns lugares que stam em hum caminho que fez Gaspar Barreiros o anno de M.D.XXXXVI* (Coimbra: Universidade de Coimbra, 1968 [1561]), 53v, 103, 129v, 166, 207v, and 234, for example.

113 João Brandão (de Buarcos), *Grandeza e Abastança de Lisboa em 1552*, José da Felicidade Alves, org. (Lisbon: Livros Horizonte, 1990 [1552]), 43.

114 For a demographic study of a community in Flores island, see Luís Filipe Vieira, 'Leitura social e cultural da morte em Santa Cruz das Flores (1676–1725)', in *O Faial e a Periferia Açoriana nos Sécs. XV a XIX. Actas do III Colóquio. Nos 550 anos do Descobrimento das Flores e do Corvo* (Horta: Núcleo Cultural da Horta, 2002), 507–25.

115 The other islands are Corvo, Flores, Graciosa, São Jorge, Pico, and Santa Maria. For studies of the Azores Archipelago, see Avelino de Freitas Meneses and João Paulo Oliveira e Costa, eds, *O reino, as ilhas e o mar oceano: Estudos em homenagem a Artur Teodoro de Matos*, 2 vols (Lisbon and Ponta Delgada: Universidade dos Açores/Universidade de Lisboa, 2007), and *O Faial e a Periferia Açoriana nos Sécs. XV a XIX: Actas do Colóquio realizado nas ilhas do Faial e Pico de 10 a 13 de Maio de 1993* (Horta: Núcleo Cultural da Horta, 1995), and subsequent volumes from more recent colloquia. See also João Marinho dos Santos, *Os Açores nos Sécs. XV e XVI*, 2 vols (Angra do Heroísmo: Dir. Regional dos Assuntos Culturais, 1989); Avelino de Freitas de Meneses, *Os Açores e o Domínio Filipino (1580–1590)*, 2 vols (Angra do Heroísmo: Instituto Histórico da Ilha Terceira, 1987); António dos Santos Pereira, *A Ilha de S. Jorge (Séculos XV–XVII): Contribuição para o seu estudo* (Ponta Delgada: Universidade dos Açores/Departamento de História, 1987); João Marinho dos Santos, 'Ponta Delgada – Nascimento e Primeira Infância de uma Cidade', *Revista de História Económica e Social* 1 (January–June 1978): 33–53.

the capital of Terceira,[116] had between 8,000 and 9,000 people, followed by Ponta Delgada, the capital of São Miguel, with approximately 5,500. Horta, the capital of Faial, had 1,500 residents in the latter part of the sixteenth century.[117]

The archipelago's administrative apparatus and the bishopric were headquartered in Angra, Terceira, but for the purposes of this study São Miguel is of special interest because an important source of criminal accusations was found in Ponta Delgada.[118] By 1568 the island already boasted 24 churches, and experienced a steady rate of growth in the seventeenth century. Nevertheless, as was the case in many other regions of Portugal, a constant for all municipalities in São Miguel was the safeguarding of food supplies for their communities, with food patrols placed at key points in the district to ensure that basic necessities were not hoarded and shipped away for profit. Other protected items were leather, linen, woad, coal, lumber, and tree bark, all essential for the local economy.[119] The region also experienced some devastating natural disasters, particularly earthquakes. For instance, an earthquake in São Miguel during the night of 21–22 October 1522 resulted in more than 4,000 deaths.[120]

Overall, mainlanders and islanders alike had to contend with their fair share of natural disasters, poor harvests, seigneurial exactions, and royal impositions to

---

[116] In the early modern period, the capital of Terceira Island was Angra, but the city was renamed Angra do Heroísmo in the nineteenth century.

[117] Vasconcelos, 'Itinerário' do Dr. Jerónimo Münzer, 64–5; Iria Gonçalves, 'Um Problema a Resolver: A Vereação de Velas e os Consumos Essenciais', in *O Faial e a Periferia Açoriana nos Sécs. XV a XIX: Actas do Colóquio realizado nas ilhas do Faial e Pico de 10 a 13 Maio de 1993* (Horta: Núcleo Cultural da Horta, 1995), 175–88. Other studies concluded that the population in the Azores was slightly below these numbers. See, Meneses, *Os Açores*, I: 333.

[118] For a look at the role of the central government in the administration of justice in the Azores, see José Damião Rodrigues and Rui Cunha Martins, 'A Construção de um Espaço: os Açores e o Olhar do Poder Cental', in *O Faial e a Periferia Açoriana nos Sécs. XV a XIX. Actas do Colóquio realizado nas ilhas do Faial e Pico de 10 a 13 de Maio de 1993* (Horta: Núcleo Cultural da Horta, 1995), 75–83.

[119] Lalanda, 'Os Municípios Micaelenses', 266, Note 74. See also Nelson Veríssimo, 'Poder Municipal e Vida Quotidiana: Machico no Século XVII', in Alberto Vieira, ed., *O Município no Mundo Português: Seminário Internacional, Funchal, 26 a 30 Outubro de 1998* (Funchal: Região Autónoma da Madeira/Centro de Estudos de História do Atlântico, 1998), 292–3 [291–302].

[120] Francisco Ferreira Drumond, *Apontamentos Topográficos, Políticos, Civis e Ecclesiásticos para a História das nove Ilhas dos Açores servindo de suplemento aos Anais da Ilha Terceira* (Angra do Heroísmo: Instituto Histórico da Ilha Terceira, 1990), 52–70; Pe Manuel Luís Maldonado (1644–1711), *Fenix Angrence*, 3 vols, trans. Helder Fernando Parreira de Sousa Lima (Angra do Heroísmo: Instituto Histórico da Ilha Terceira, r.1990), II: 38, 124–33, 231, 305–10. Also see Ana Maria Pereira Ferreira, 'Alguns sismos e vulcões nas ilhas do Faial, Pico e S. Jorge nos séculos XVI e XVII', in *O Faial e a Periferia Açoriana nos Séculos XV a XX. Actas do Colóquio realizado nas ilhas do Faial e S. Jorge de 12 a 15 de Maio de 1997* (Horta: Núcleo Cultural da Horta, 1997), 103–111.

support the national projects overseas. With the discovery of gold mines in Brazil in the early eighteenth century, Portugal enjoyed some financial stability, but the majority of people would have hardly noticed the difference.[121] Most people were too busy making a living from their little plots of land, along the gentle coasts of the Azores, up the mountains in Madeira, in the fertile valleys in northern Portugal, and on the plains in the central regions and the Algarve. Most people got married and had children, some out of wedlock; most people got along most of the time, but some were the source of enough disorder to cause consternation at home and in their communities. A fraction of those troubles necessitated judicial intervention, producing a few fragments that substantiate this study.

Portuguese Now and Then

Whether the text was produced by a notary or by someone else, the written language found in archival documents from the sixteenth and seventeenth centuries raises serious questions about interpretation and presentation in a modern context, and a few liberties were taken to facilitate the discussion. For instance, some of the occupational titles and legal terms from early modern Portugal are difficult to translate into modern English. Attempts were made to come up with an approximate equivalent, but occasionally it was deemed easier to use the term found in the text, and provide an explanation in the text or in a footnote.[122] For example, many texts referred to young people as *manceba* or *mancebo*, to denote someone who was young and not married, but the age of that young person could vary widely. Sometimes the text implied that the term was used for a child, other times for someone already more than 25 years old, the age of majority at the time. In fact, the national census of 1527–1532 referred to *mancebos* of 18 to 30 years of age who lived with their parents.[123]

A few Portuguese terms have been used in the text because there is no clear equivalent in English, and a constant side note would become tedious. For example, *Fidalgo* and *Cavaleiro* were titles used to denote various levels of nobility and knighthood, used for men of that class. Members of the high nobility and aristocracy were titled *Dona* (D.) for women, and *Dom* (D.) for men.[124] A royal princess was the *Infanta* and a prince was the *Infante*. There were some regional

---

121 Almeida, 'Organização político-administrativa', 356–7; A.A. Marques de Almeida, *Aritmética como Descrição do Real (1519–1679)*, 2 vols (Lisbon: Imprensa Nacional/Casa da Moeda, 1994), I: 183.

122 All translations are mine, and all errors therein.

123 João José Alves Dias, *Gentes e Espaços: Edição crítica do 'Numeramento de 1527–1532' e Dicionário Corográfico do Portugal Quinhentista, Comarca de Entre Douro e Minho* (Cascais: Patrimonia Historica, 1999), 27.

124 For the rules on how to address members of the nobility and aristocracy, and on the proper use of honorific titles, see *Ordenações Filipinas*, Livro 5, Appendices: 'Alvará de 16 de Setembro de 1597', 'Alvará de 3 de Novembro de 1597', and 'Alvará de 3 de Dezembro de 1611', 1333–6.

idiosyncrasies, such as in the city of Porto, where an upstanding and honourable urban resident could be distinguished with the title of *cidadão*, or male citizen.[125] Similarly, the title *Licenciado* was used to designate a man with a certain amount of university training, a licentiate. Tellingly, there were no female equivalents of these titles, though in a play written by Gil Vicente (c.1465–c.1537), female shepherds were compared favourably with 'todas as cidadãs', or all the female citizens.[126] Further down the ladder still, the landed or tenant farmer was called a *lavrador*, an occupational label generally used by the record keeper to identify men of that rank, but not the women. Occasionally men and women were lumped together in the record as *lavradors*, but few women were identified on their own as *lavradoras*, though undoubtedly they existed in substantial numbers.[127]

Portuguese people are generally known by their first names, with *Senhora* or *Senhor* attached to the first name in polite conversation. Likely this was the case in the early modern period as well, and for that reason first names are used throughout this study, except when the last name is preferable for clarification. Regarding family names, there was no standard practice in the choice of last names, and thus it was not unusual to find a wife, husband, and their two or three children all with different last names.[128] Sometimes a female version of a father's name was used for a daughter's last name – Francisca from Francisco, for example. The adoption of a family name through the maternal line was common in fifteenth-century Portugal, especially in cases of illegitimate birth.[129]

---

[125] The title of *cidadão* was also found in some municipal records in São Miguel, and in some notarized documents from other regions. See Lalanda, 'Os Municípios Micaelenses', 257–8; IAN/TT, Fundo Notarial (Lisbon), Caixa 2, no. 8 (1578), f.33v–34v; and ADE, Fundo Notarial, Domingos Pires (notary), Séries 232 (1595), f.64–65, for example.

[126] Cited in Júlia Maria Sousa Alves da Silva, *A Mulher em Gil Vicente* (Braga: Edições APPACDM Distrital de Braga, 1995), 84. As Barbara Todd has shown for early modern England, ideas of women's citizenship did not confer to women the civic offices opened to male citizens, but women took oaths of allegiance readily enough, especially when it was an essential element in protecting their economic interests. Barbara Todd, 'Written in Her Heart: Married Women's Separate Allegiance in English Law', in Tim Stretton and Krista J. Kesselring, eds, *Married Women and the Law: Coverture in England and the Common Law World* (Montreal and Kingston: McGill-Queen's University Press, 2013), 163–91.

[127] A poem celebrating the world of the *lavradora* is found in António de Villasboas de Sampaio (1629–1701), *Auto da Lavradora de Ayró* (Coimbra: Na Impressa da Universidade, 1841 [1678]).

[128] For a look at the Portuguese fluidity with surnames, and how the practice was adopted in Brazil, see Muriel Nazzari, 'The Waxing and Waning of Matrilineality in São Paulo, Brazil: Historical Variations in an Ambilineal System, 1500–1900', in Mary Jo Maynes, Ann Waltern, Birgitte Soland, and Ulrike Strasser, eds, *Gender, Kinship, Power: A Comparative and Interdisciplinary History* (New York and London: Routledge, 1996), 305–17.

[129] Rita Costa Gomes, *The Making of a Court Society: Kings and Nobles in Late Medieval Portugal*, trans. Alison Aiken (Cambridge: Cambridge University Press, 2003), 64. See also António Camões Gouveia, 'A linhagem ou o tempo da memória. D. Francisco Manuel de Melo e o nobre seiscentista', *Ler História* 18 (1990): 8 [3–24].

Some of the *perdões de parte* examined for this study made references to a financial settlement, or to legal costs and lost wages. The monetary system of early modern Portugal is complex and difficult to explain in modern terms, and for those reasons all references to monetary amounts were left in their original form. Starting in 1457, the monetary unit in Portugal was the *cruzado* and the *real*. Between the reign of D. Afonso V (r.1438–1481) and D. Sebastião (r.1557–1578), the *cruzado* was worth 253 to 500 *reais*. For most of the seventeenth century, the *cruzado* was valued at 400 *réis*. The plural for the *real* was *reais* until the reign of D. Sebastião, at which point it became *réis*. For simplicity, *réis* is used in this study for the plural of the *real*. The *real* was further broken down to smaller units, *vinténs*, *tostões*, and *meios-tostões*.[130] According to an English report from the 1620s, 1,000 *réis* was equivalent to 12 shillings and 6 pence.[131]

Records of wages paid to manual labourers attested to the challenges many encountered in making ends meet, especially women. In a royal decree from 1522 that determined the prices of certain goods, and the wages of a few types of workers for the purposes of taxation in Guimarães, the Crown ordered that a female day labourer, whether she was hired to hoe, thresh, or to work as an *espadeladeira* – a woman who beats or skutches flax or hemp – was not to earn more than 8 *réis* per day, plus meals. A male day labourer could not earn more than 12 *réis* per day, plus meals. Thus, according to this regulation, women engaged in agricultural work earned two thirds of men's wages, and neither a female nor male labourer earned enough in one day to buy a hand sickle or hoe, which the list priced at 25 *réis* and 60 *réis*, respectively, nor buy a chicken that cost 20 *réis*.[132] A woman could buy one *arrátel* of cheese that was priced at 8 *réis*, while a male day labourer who worked with a bricklayer or other trade earned a little more, 15 *réis* per day, plus meals.[133]

Sixty years later the city of Braga attempted to regulate the daily wages of women, and the registry of the municipal ordinance intimated that some women were not adhering to those regulations. On Wednesday, 21 June 1581, the municipal council decreed that female day labourers (*jornaleiras* in the title of the registry), or a woman worker (*mulher trabalhadeira* in the actual text), who

---

130 Almeida, *Aritmética como Descrição*, I: 172–7.

131 Anonymous, *The Anatomy of the English Nunnery at Lisbon in Portugal* (London: George Purslowe, 1622), f.10.

132 Eduardo de Almeida, 'Regimento de salários e preços de 1522 (para Guimarães)', *Revista de Guimarães* 40, no. 1/2 (January–June 1930): 62–3 [41–63].

133 Almeida, 'Regimento de salários', 152, 156. For food prices in other regions, see Fernandes, *Bibliografia do Distrito de Bragança*, 135–8; Meneses, *Os Açores*, II: 329–30; António dos Santos Pereira, *Vereações de Velas (S. Jorge, 1559–1570–1571)* (Ponta Delgada: Universidade dos Açores/Departmento de História, 1984), 28. Also see Olga Bettencourt, 'A Periferia das Pequenas Ilhas: o exemplo de São Jorge, a partir das Vereações de Velas (1559–1570–1571)', in *O Faial e a Periferia Açoriana nos Sécs. XV a XIX. Actas do Colóquio realizado nas ilhas do Faial e Pico de 10 a 13 de Maio de 1993* (Horta: Núcleo Cultural da Horta, 1995), 183–8.

earned a daily wage could not charge more than 12 *réis* per day plus food, or 20 *réis* 'sequo' (without meals), or else face fines of 1,000 *réis* and jail, half for the accuser.[134] Unfortunately the Braga records from 1581 did not indicate the prices for foodstuffs, except for olive oil, set at 20 *réis* per *quartilho* on Monday, 2 January 1581, and wine from other regions at 5 to 5.5 *réis*, local wine at 3.5 to 4 *réis* per *quartilho*, set on Wednesday, 30 August 1581. On Wednesday, 7 June, soap was priced at 30 *réis* per *arrátel*.[135] Further south, the municipal records from Viseu indicated that in 1601 beef cost 12 *réis* per *arrátel*, and a chicken cost 60 *réis* in 1605.[136] By mid-century, olive oil cost 33 *réis* per *quartilho* in Porto, and a chicken cost 120 *réis* in nearby Guimarães. Other essential items were also expensive, such as footwear, the prices for which were regulated by municipal councils. In June 1664, city officials in Porto established such a price list, and the cost for boots ranged from 480 to 1,800 *réis*, while shoes cost anywhere between 120 to 400 *réis*.[137]

Given the high cost of living, it is not surprising that some women ignored local regulations and attempted to charge more for their manual labour, as reported by the Braga municipal council. In fact, more people, especially urban dwellers, got into trouble with local ordinances than with actual state laws. The latter were generally linked to more serious crimes – those that led to a *querela* – and sometimes necessitated some formal resolution – such as a *perdão de parte*. Combined, these two sources provide the foundation for the analysis in the next two chapters which are organized by subject matter. Chapter 2 focusses on criminal cases that dealt with physical injuries, some of which caused death. The findings are organized into three major sub-topics: women who were attacked or attackers, death in the family, and women and orphans. The three sections shed light on the principal roles women juggled as they engaged in violence, or were confronted with violence that touched them directly or members of their families. Chapter 3 deals with cases related to sex crimes, particularly adultery, concubinage, and rape/defloration. The category of sex crimes warrants its own separate discussion because of the nature of those crimes which had a particular and personal effect on women, and women's and men's daughters. In both chapters the examples discussed highlight the ways in which crime and the road to forgiveness provided early modern Portuguese women a way to engage in important legal decisions that had long-term repercussions in their lives and that of their families.

---

134 Câmara Municipal de Braga (CMB), 'Acordos e Vreaçõens [*sic*] da Câmara de Braga', *Bracara Augusta: Revista Cultural de Regionalismo e História da Câmara Municipal de Braga* 24 (1970): 377 [284–435].

135 CMB, 'Acordos e Vreaçõens [*sic*]', 24, 325, 370, 390. The *arrátel* is a measuring unit equivalent to approximately 16 ounces; the *quartilho* is a liquid measurement of 0.6655 litre, or a pint.

136 Alexandre de Lucena e Vale, 'Livro dos Acordos da Câmara de Viseu, Actas de 1601–1605', *Beira Alta* 11 (Viseu, 1952): 233, 250 [225–54].

137 Arquivo Histórico Municipal do Porto (AHMP), *Livro de Vereações*, no. 52 (1649–1650), f.102v, and no. 58 (1662–1664), f.235v–236v; Arquivo Municipal Alfredo Pimento de Guimarães, *Livro de Vereações*, no. 1881 (1664–1670), f.111v–112v.

Chapter 2
Querelas and *Perdões de Parte* for Physical Injuries and Homicide

Escolácia Morena and her husband Manuel Taveiro were tenant farmers on a homestead called *Passo do Sagão* located behind the *Convento de Nossa Senhora do Espinheiro* in the district of Evora. The convent residents were likely the landowners in whose estate Escolácia and Manuel made a living, a living that included the raising of livestock. That livestock were in turn a source of a livelihood and a source of contention, for animals (and their owners) did not always respect the boundaries around individual plots of land. Whether or not Escolácia's husband was guilty of such a charge is not certain, but their neighbour Manuel Rodrigues had little doubt. On a hot summer day – Friday, 9 July 1666, to be exact – at around one or two o'clock in the afternoon, Rodrigues confronted Taveiro about the damage to the former's property caused by the latter's animals. Following that confrontation, Escolácia Morena and Manuel Taveiro's future looked very bleak.

Five days after the incident between the two Manuels, a local notary walked into Escolácia's home where he found her husband in such a state that necessitated the presence of a notary. Either Escolácia summoned the notary herself, or she had someone else do it for her; her husband was in no condition to do either. Upon his arrival, the notary set out to do the best he could do under the circumstances – he wrote up a pardon document that the victims granted to the perpetrator. Dated 14 July 1666, this *perdão de parte* indicated that during the argument of the previous Friday, Rodrigues gave Taveiro a few blows with a stick to the extent that Taveiro had some marks and bruises, and an injury to the head. The severity of those injuries was downplayed as Taveiro prepared to pardon the aggressor, but the injuries must have been serious indeed. Not only had Taveiro been bedridden for five days already, but the rest of the narrative pointed to a realization that the prognosis was not good, a fate to which the patient and his wife were resigned.

> And if God does not permit that the said her husband Manuel Taveiro [recover] and he dies of this injury and God takes him in such a case she of her free will and volition, without any constraint from anyone [she] pardons the said Manuel Rodrigues all culpability and penalty and damage that the said Manuel Rodrigues thus caused her with the death of the said her husband and from the said Manuel Rodrigues for her part [she] wanted nothing from him in any civil or criminal cause rather she pardoned him for the love of God as the Lord pardons her sins.[1]

---

1 ADE, Fundo Notarial, Manuel Galvão Bácaro (notary), Séries 722 (1666), f.110–110v.

The implication of this broad renunciation was that Escolácia and her husband had reached an understanding and appreciation of the situation. Taveiro's injuries were life-threatening, and no amount of vengeance against the culprit was going to change that. The practical solution was to broker an accord with the aggressor, who desperately needed a victim's pardon to deal with the repercussions of his actions, and the accord must have met the perceived needs of the surviving spouse.

The conflict between the two Manuels serves to illustrate some of the most common elements found in the source base for the present study, the *querela* or criminal accusation, and the *perdão de parte* or victim's pardon. First, both sets of documents showed that most crimes reported to authorities in early modern Portugal dealt with physical injuries committed by men against other men. Second, this example also showed that violence between men sometimes had wide-ranging ramifications, for themselves and their families. Third, any attempts to deal with the repercussions of that violence had serious implications for the integrity of the family property and its heirs or potential heirs. Thus, an injury to Manuel Taveiro was an injury to Escolácia Morena's well-being.

The incident that brought Escolácia and her husband to the record books started with a dispute connected to property, for the argument between the two Manuels ensued from damage to property (land) caused by another type of property (livestock), the result of which affected the overall property unit of Escolácia's household. Escolácia and her husband's pardon made no reference to a *querela*, an indication that perhaps the parties involved in the conflict had chosen not to alert authorities of the mishap. An injury or two could be overlooked between neighbours as long as those injuries healed, and some informal agreement proved beneficial to both sides of the dispute. Death was another matter altogether. In cases of homicide, an official inquiry would be held, and the culprit had to deal with the serious consequences – possibly the death sentence, likely exile to a Portuguese overseas post.[2] The culprit also had to compensate the victim, or the victim's heirs, for the immediate and future losses resulting from such a crime.

For this reason, one senses a certain urgency in the pardon from Escolácia and her husband. There was little time to spare, little time for protracted negotiations. Manuel Taveiro faced imminent death, Escolácia Morena faced imminent widowhood, and Manuel Rodrigues faced a criminal conviction for homicide. The victim's pardon would not stop the criminal process, but it could help the accused in an appeal for mercy, or for a reduced sentence.[3] As discussed in Chapter 1, the archival sources used for the present study – the *querela* and the *perdão de parte* – did not inform us of the ultimate outcome of the cases to which those documents referred, but one thing is certain: on paper, at least, the *perdão de parte* alleviated the guilt of the accused, by downplaying the hardships stemming from the criminal act, and by highlighting the victim's part in the whole affair.

---

2 Araújo, 'Cerimónias de execução pública', 177–8.

3 If an individual received a royal pardon prior to being officially accused, the judicial process could be terminated. *Ordenaçõens Filipinas*, Livro 5, Título 123, no. 6.

In his pardon, Manuel Taveiro acknowledged that his animals had done much damage to Manuel Rodrigues' land, that Rodrigues was provoked by the extent of the damage, and that Rodrigues was remorseful for having offended and molested Taveiro. Both wife and husband renounced all future claims and all laws that privileged them in these circumstances, and they begged His Majesty's justices not to arrest, persecute, or maltreat Rodrigues 'for this incident or death but to pardon his guilt'. In many ways, therefore, Escolácia and Manuel's pardon followed the formula typically found in other *perdões de parte*, particularly in the broad disclaimer, and in the central role that a woman had in the negotiations between culprit and victim. The details of those negotiations were conveniently concealed from the written record, but as it will be shown, a careful reading of these documents reveals that much more was at stake than the text purports. Escolácia's acquiescence was much more than formulaic.

This chapter focusses on a number of criminal cases that dealt with physical injuries, some of which led to the victim's death. Statistics from other parts of Europe show that crime was predominantly a male domain, and Portuguese historians have made similar discoveries for early modern Portugal.[4] The examples highlighted here confirm those findings, yet both the *querela* and the *perdão de parte* provide a unique window through which women's agency can be situated in an otherwise male-dominated sphere. The available sources offer an ideal mechanism with which to examine some of the wider ramifications of criminal activity through the experiences of those who often were left with the responsibility of cleaning up the mess created by their menfolk. Within their socially prescribed roles of wives and mothers, early modern Portuguese women had to contend with crimes committed by or against their husbands; harm done to or by their children; and, of course, the attacks to which women were personally subjected, or that they perpetrated themselves.

The cases examined in this chapter are divided into three categories of infractions. First, we look at women who were directly involved in physical injuries, either as victims or as perpetrators of those crimes. Second, we examine a number of cases that dealt with physical injuries causing death, the death of women, or the death of women's loved ones. For obvious reasons, a death precipitated greater official intervention, and the notarized documents related to homicide reflected the need for greater detail. Hence the cases of homicide are particularly invaluable for an analysis of women's input in the deliberations that led to a victim's pardon, and the implications that those deliberations had for the administration of common property. This question is especially evident when the homicide victim had minor children, and the last section of this chapter is dedicated to those crucial agreements made on behalf of those under the age of majority.

Before we examine those heart-wrenching cases of violence that led to a senseless death, we will look at a few examples of what was certainly a more common occurrence – arguments that led to some physical injury that in turn led

4 See discussion in Chapter 1.

to a *querela* and possibly a *perdão de parte*. While the homicide cases offer more riveting reading, the vast majority of conflicts led to relatively minor consequences. As Table 1.1 and Table 1.2 illustrate, most criminal denunciations were registered for physical injuries, as were most victims' pardons. Thus, these cases are arguably more representative of the types of conflicts women and men were more likely to experience, and the discussion starts with two examples of young women engaged in a common female occupation in many urban centres of early modern Europe, domestic service. The examples of the servant girls showed their vulnerability but also the support they had from parents and employers.

Domestic servants were generally unmarried, but as explained in the introductory chapter, a significant number of single women lived on their own in early modern Portugal. Undoubtedly there were various living arrangements that fit the socio-economic necessities of the unmarried woman, and two of the three cases examined here reveal what could have been common practice – unmarried sisters sharing accommodations and the manual labour to maintain themselves. However, the largest proportion of women who lived without a patriarch consisted of widows. The *querelas* and *perdões de parte* analysed here illustrate the ways those women presented themselves in an official forum.

As would be expected, in the *querela*, the complainant highlighted her innocence and the irrational behaviour of the aggressor; in the *perdão de parte*, the pardoner minimized the aggression and even hinted at her own minimal role in the confrontation. Not surprisingly, though, plaintiffs on either side of the spectrum depicted themselves as upstanding individuals, but both sets of records also showed that women were capable of retaliation, if only in reporting the incidents to the authorities. Whether the victims were young servants, single women of the age of majority, or mature widowed women, all victims of physical assault were attacked by people they knew, often neighbours, acquaintances, or relatives. Undoubtedly this was a factor in the ways events were presented and resolved. Some women and men did what they did because they could; some women and men attempted to negotiate and compensate because they had to.

The following discussion of physical injuries features two samples of disputes between neighbours and acquaintances, and two between siblings, a sample that serves to highlight the impact of conflict in the workplace, and closer to home. None of these cases related to physical assault made any specific reference to the costs involved in the judicial procedures that ensued, or to the out-of-court settlements that could have taken place, but such settlements were implicit in many of the *perdões de parte*, regardless of the stated arguments to the contrary.[5] It is difficult, for instance, to take the following victim's pardon dated 5 June 1754 at face value. On that day, Domingas Fernandes and her husband, José Fernandes, residents in the barracks of the castle of Castro Marim, where José was a soldier, granted a pardon to João Rodrigues Mascarenhas who had injured José during a

[5] For a discussion of the unseen costs of the judicial process, see Gay, 'Acheter la grâce'.

brawl. The injuries had been serious enough to warrant a notarized pardon, but the text suggested otherwise:

> João had not intended to injure him for they had always been and still were friends and it was he José who put himself at risk without warning João about what he José was about to do, nor did he José remember what transpired exactly and so could not know exactly on whom to place the blame, and since the incident happened like that [and] José and Domingas were Catholic and fearful of God they jointly stated that if the justices had cause to proceed with the case they [Domingas and José] asked and supplicated [the justices] not to punish the said João because he was innocent as declared above, [and] of their free will, without constraints, motivated by the truth and to relieve their conscience, they pardoned João forever for the said act and complaint, and José and Domingas and their descendants shall never have a claim regarding this incident against João or his descendants, and they wanted nothing from João or his descendants, not in law or otherwise because the incident happened fortuitously.

In fact, José's arm was 'accidentally' twisted and broken, and the arm had remained deformed, without any strength, with aches and pains during the lunar phases.[6] Such an injury would have hampered José's ability to be an effective soldier, and to do many other tasks necessary to earn a living, a living that was crucial to the survival of a household. Furthermore, such an injury could have cost the culprit between 10,000 and 12,000 *réis* for a royal pardon, depending on whether the arm in question was the left or the right (see Appendix 1). As a result of this injury, Domingas had a less productive husband, and their descendants' inheritance would be irretrievably affected. The statement at the end of the pardon wherein Domingas and José declared that they wanted nothing from the culprit was perhaps the most accurate reflection of their implicit agreement, for undoubtedly they were content with what they had already gotten.

As mentioned in Chapter 1, a crime victim was supposed to pardon the perpetrator without any pressure or inducement, and thus a financial settlement between the conflicting parties could be construed as an inducement from the accused for the accuser. For this reason the pardoner was encouraged to deny any influence from anyone except the almighty God whose motives could hardly be questioned. The pardoner also rejected any reference to future material gain because that could be interpreted as a bribe, and would undermine the aura of altruism behind the self-presentation of the good, honourable, and virtuous citizen who wanted nothing but peace on earth and glory in heaven. Yet, enough pardons referred to some form of financial arrangement to suggest that a lot more was at stake than a clear conscience, or that a clear conscience came at a price for the one who had rattled that conscience in the first place.

To get around the spirit of the law, financial arrangements were often framed in ambiguous terms that connected the payment to expenses incurred, not to

---

[6] Arquivo Distrial de Faro (ADF), Fundo Notarial (Castro Marim), Jacinto José dos Santos e Melo (notary), no. 1056 (1754), f.12v–13v. The arm ached 'com dores nas conjunções lunarias'. Some punctuation was added for clarity

personal profit.[7] The most commonly stated reasons for the acceptance of monetary payments were to cover medical and living expenses. Thus, one victim pardoned her attacker and claimed that 'she wanted nothing more from him than that he pay the person who treats her [injuries] and the essentials for her sustenance while she is healing'; one other, assaulted by a group of young men, indicated that 'if they pay the costs to the surgeon for his work in the treatment of the said injury and to the barber for the bleeding and an additional ten *tostões* for extra expenses in the healing of the said injury he will pardon them for whatever blame they could have in the said injury.'[8] Neither pardon stipulated the total amount of the compensation that the two victims eventually received, but a few other examples were found that specified the exact costs for medical services and for lost wages.[9]

A disruption to an individual's earning capacity had serious implications for that individual and for her or his dependents. One other study of victims' pardons in Portugal provided an example of costs that took into account the special circumstances of the judicial procedure. On 21 January 1608, João Pais granted a pardon to Francisco da Mota Rebelo, both from Vila Nova de Gaia (near Porto), with the condition that the latter pay all the costs of the judicial process, including the expenses incurred by the witnesses who had to travel from the municipality of Paiva, where the crime had taken place, and the costs owed to the scribe, for a total of 4,500 *réis*.[10] Such explicit details were rare, however, and most *perdões de parte* insisted that the parties had made peace and resolved their differences without any great difficulties, or the need for any undue incentive.

Under the pretext of an expansive act of generosity, victims of physical injuries often downplayed the incident and even accepted some of the responsibility for the infraction that led to their injuries. This rhetorical device was less common with cases for homicide, though one notable exception was found, as will be discussed later. Typically pardoners for a death were more reticent in their disclosures for they could hardly negate the severity of the injuries once the victim was dead, or was on her or his deathbed, as was seen with the case of Escolácia Morena and her husband at the opening of this chapter. As was shown, the victims did not negate the culprit's guilt, but rather they stressed the extent to which the misfortune was the result of provocation, that the culprit had some grounds for the attack, and that he regretted the results of that attack. Did Escolácia and her husband believe this? Doubtful. Did they truly pardon Manuel Rodrigues without any form of compensation? Equally doubtful.

---

7 One surprising find was a pardon granted to a wife and husband for insults and other injuries they had caused, upon their payment of 10,000 *réis* to the victim, seemingly as a straightforward form of compensation. See Arquivo Distrital de Viana do Castelo (ADVC), Fundo Notarial, Manuel Martins da Costa (notary), no. 4.32.4.2 (1648), f.22v–24.

8 ADP, Fundo Notarial, Po. 4, 1a Se, no. 47 (1656), f.96–96v; Po. 4, 1a Se, no. 39 (1648), f.55v–56v.

9 See, for example, ADP, Fundo Notarial, Po. 1, 3a Se, no. 42 (1572), f.37–39; Po. 4, 1a Se, no. 4–5 (1612), f.188v–189v; IAN/TT, Fundo Notarial (Lisbon), Caixa 2, no. 8 (1578), f.48–49.

10 Monteiro, 'A litigiosidade', 110.

In her work on pleas for royal pardons in early modern France, Natalie Zemon Davis examined the ways in which those pleas were crafted by supplicants who sought mercy for their misdeeds. In her analysis, Zemon Davis did not question the deeds that precipitated the supplications, but rather she deconstructed the cultural framework that engendered the narratives in those appeals.[11] The present study likewise deals with pleas for mercy from the Crown, but unlike the case in France, these pleas from early modern Portugal originated from those who were wronged, not from the wrongdoers. This is a significant difference. The *perdão de parte*, or victim's pardon, was a prerequisite for a culprit who wished to appeal a conviction, or a *possible* conviction. Note that Manuel Rodrigues had not yet been charged with any crime, let alone sentenced, but he clearly sought a documented pardon from Escolácia Morena and her husband before the latter expired. One can well understand Rodrigues' motivation for obtaining a pardon from his victims, but what could possibly have compelled the victims to such a seemingly generous gesture?

In Portugal, too, there was a cultural framework that generated the *perdão de parte*, and as the examples already demonstrated, a victim's pardon was often expressed in terms of Christian values of forgiveness. Nearly all *perdões de parte* assembled for this study made reference to the victim's desire to forgive the culprit as God would forgive the victim's sins. In the social context of the time period, in a very Catholic country such as Portugal, that was a laudable sentiment, and possibly even rang true for some of the pardoners.[12] There is no way to verify the sincerity of those assertions, but many of those pardons also contained elements of a more practical nature. In early modern Portugal, a good Christian turned the other cheek, and some of the offended did, once the offenders made amends.[13] Most victims' pardons barely alluded to this potentiality, while others were more upfront about the settlement. For instance, Graça Geraldes and Manuel Gomes, brother-in-law of Francisco Faria, Graça's late husband, granted a pardon on 12 January 1650 to the men they had initially accused of killing Francisco, after the accused paid the plaintiffs 12,000 *réis* (see Appendix 2). Hence, the socio-cultural principle that promoted forgiveness was enmeshed in financial and economic imperatives, the foundation for which was property ownership. The key to unravelling the *perdão de parte* is located in the legal codes that pertained to early modern Portuguese laws of inheritance.

---

[11] Davis, *Fiction in the Archives*, passim.

[12] Certainly confessors of the period were instructed to encourage their parishioners to recognize God's power of forgiveness. Maria de Lurdes C. Fernandes, 'As artes da Confissão: Em torno dos Manuais de Confessores do século XVI em Portugal', *Humanística e Teologia* 11 (1990): 68–9 [47–80]. See also Frei Heitor Pinto (1528–1584?), *Imagem da Vida Cristã*, ed., Alves Correia, 4 vols (Lisbon: Livraria Sá da Costa, 1940 [1563; 1572]).

[13] The practicalities of forgiveness were also debated in Protestant contexts. See, for example, Malcolm Gaskill, 'Reporting Murder: Fiction in the Archives in Early Modern England', *Social History* 23, no. 1 (January 1998): 26–7 [1–30].

Women and Inheritance

By law, family property in early modern Portugal was divided equally between wife and husband. Neither spouse could alienate the portion of the other spouse without her or his consent; upon the death of her husband the wife became head of her family and estate; and children of legitimate matrimony had equal rights of inheritance. There were, of course, numerous clauses and sub-clauses that had an impact on the ultimate division of assets. For instance, a testator could dispose of a third of her or his estate at will, and male primogeniture was well entrenched where the stakes were especially high, most notably among the nobility and aristocracy. Nevertheless, the law allowed for, and indeed maintained the precedent that female members of the family had a legal claim to family property.[14] As bona fide owners of property, women could also engage in property transactions that involved purchasing, selling, renting, leasing, and bequeathing, a practice that was well established already in the Middle Ages.[15] Women acted on their own, with their husbands, or on behalf of their absent menfolk, a phenomenon that became quite common especially along coastal communities where a significant percentage of the male population was away for long periods of time.[16]

In the books, at least, Portugal's laws of inheritance differed significantly from those in effect in some other European regions, most notably Florence where, insofar as property rights were concerned, 'Florence was the worst place to have been born a woman'.[17] Certainly Laura McGough argued that Tuscan women had fewer options than women in Venice, while another study that compared rights of inheritance in Portugal and in Italy proposed that in the latter case women were greatly disadvantaged.[18] There was, in fact, much variation across regions in

---

[14] *Ordenações Filipinas*, Livro 4, Título 80, 81, 82, 95, 96, 97.

[15] For some examples, see Maria Teresa Lopes Pereira, *Alcácer do Sal na Idade Média* (Lisbon: Câmara Municipal de Alcácer do Sal/Edições Colibri, 2007), 189–90.

[16] For a discussion of this phenomenon, see Amélia Polónia, '"Mulheres que partem e mulheres que ficam": O protagonismo feminismo na expansão ultramarina', *O Estudo da História* 4 (2001): 79–98. The challenges that women faced with absent husbands were not unique to early modern Portugal. See, for example, Margaret R. Hunt, 'The Sailor's Wife, War Finance, and Coverture in Late Seventeenth-Century London', in Tim Stretton and Krista J. Kesselring, eds, *Married Women and the Law: Coverture in England and the Common Law World* (Montreal and Kingston: McGill-Queen's University Press, 2013), 139–62.

[17] Samuel K. Cohn, Jr., *Women in the Streets: Essays on Sex and Power in Renaissance Italy* (Baltimore and London: Johns Hopkins University Press, 1996), 55. See also Thomas Kuehn, 'Daughters, Mothers, Wives, and Widows: Women as Legal Persons', in Anne Jacobson Schutte, Thomas Kuehn, and Silvana Seidel Menchi, eds, *Time, Space, and Women's Lives in Early Modern Europe* (Kirksville: Truman State University Press, 2001), 97–115; Christiane Klapisch-Zuber, 'The "Cruel Mother": Maternity, Widowhood, and the Dowry in Florence in the Fourteenth and Fifteenth Centuries', in Lorna Hutson, ed., *Feminism & Renaissance Studies* (Oxford: Oxford University Press, 1999), 186–202.

[18] Laura McGough, 'Women, Private Property, and the Limitations of State Authority in Early Modern Venice', *Journal of Women's History* 14, no. 3 (Autumn 2002), 40 [32–52]. See also Rebecca Jean Emigh, 'Property Devolution in Tuscany', *Journal of*

southern Europe and between the south and north of the continent. In Scandinavian countries, for instance, the laws generally protected rights of kinship to inherited properties. In Sweden, from the Middle Ages until the legislation was changed in 1857, no individual could sell or bequest land that had been inherited, for it belonged to the kin from whom the inheritance had originated. In Finland, too, inherited land was intrinsically connected to the kin group. Land for sale had to be offered first to kin, otherwise kin could demand for it back, an inheritance system that lasted until the late nineteenth century. Furthermore, in the seventeenth century the law in Finland determined that men reached their legal maturity at 21 years of age, whereas women never reached legal maturity unless they were widowed. Finally, in Norway the family estate was divided equally between surviving spouse and children, except for inherited land which was 'treated as separate property belonging to the lineage of each spouse ... the widow/widower had only a right to a lifetime use of the land, not ownership'.[19] As Aglaia Kasdagli has pointed out, in Naxos (Greece), 'the concept of absolute ownership hardly existed', for women or men.[20]

Women's rights to property ownership were also limited in the British Isles, particularly the rights of married women who, under English law, became economic and legal dependents of their husbands, but there, too, was room for negotiation. As Danaya Wright has shown, many women were savvy enough to employ informal methods to manoeuver around patriarchal codes.[21] Furthermore, Amy Erickson and others have found that legal disabilities that applied to married women's property

---

Interdisciplinary History, 33, no. 3 (Winter 2003): 385–420; Joanne M. Ferraro, *Marriage Wars in Late Renaissance Venice* (Oxford: Oxford University Press, 2001); Isabelle Chabot, 'Lineage Strategies and the Control of Widows in Renaissance Florence', in Sandra Cavallo and Lyndan Warner, eds, *Widowhood in Medieval and Early Modern Europe* (London and New York: Longman, 1999), 127–44; Jutta Gisela Sperling, 'Marriage, Kinship, and Property in Portuguese Testaments (1649–1650)', in Jutta Gisela Sperling and Shona Kelly Wray, eds, *Across the Religious Divide: Women, Property, and Law in the Wider Mediterranean (ca.1300–1800)* (London and New York: Routledge, 2010), 158–74.

[19] Maria Ågren, 'Individualism or Self-Sacrifice? Decision-Making and Retirement within the Early Modern Marital Economy in Sweden', 221–36, Anu Pylkkänen, 'Forming the Marital Economy in the Early Modern Finnish Countryside', 75–88, and Hilde Sandvik, 'Decision-Making on Marital Property in Norway, 1500–1800', 111–126, in Maria Ågren and Amy Louise Erickson, eds, *The Marital Economy in Scandinavia and Britain, 1400–1900* (Burlington: Ashgate, 2005). See also the collection of essays in Cordelia Beattie and Matthew Frank Stevens, eds, *Married Women and the Law in Premodern Northwest Europe* (Rochester: Boydell Press, 2013).

[20] Aglaia E. Kasdagli, *Land and Marriage Settlements in the Aegean: A Case Study of Seventeenth-Century Naxos* (Venice: Hellenic Institute of Byzantine and Post-Byzantine Studies, 1999), 262.

[21] Danya C. Wright, 'Coverture and Women's Agency: Informal Modes of Resistance to Legal Patriarchy', in Tim Stretton and Krista J. Kesselring, eds, *Married Women and the Law: Coverture in England and the Common Law World* (Montreal and Kingston: McGill-Queen's University Press, 2013), 240–63.

rights could and often were overridden by provisions in marriage contracts.[22] In her work on women in Sweden, Maria Ågren observed that although legislation in the eighteenth and nineteenth centuries changed to privilege husbands over wives in property matters, individual arrangements were often made to mitigate women's legal disadvantages.[23] Likewise, the legal restrictions in place in some Italian regions did not always translate into a rigid application of those restrictions. In her study of a number of marriage contracts and testaments in Italy, Anna Bellavitis found that, in some cases, husbands were prepared to make special arrangements to help their widowed wives to remarry. Bellavitis also observed that when matters of inheritance became litigious, women proved capable of working the law to their advantage.[24] Similarly, in her examination of women in late medieval Avignon, Joëlle Rollo-Koster noticed that there was a significant gap between legal theory and actual practice in the distribution of family assets. According to the legal prescriptions, male heirs were preferable, but due to a shortage of men, women made substantial gains in testamentary inheritance, a phenomenon also found among some elite families in early modern Portugal.[25] Moreover, a number of customary practices could exist within the same country, such as in Spain where

[22] Amy Louise Erickson, 'Property and Widowhood in England, 1660–1840', in Sandra Cavallo and Lyndan Warner, eds, *Widowhood in Medieval and Early Modern Europe* (London and New York: Longman, 1999), 145–63, and *Women and Property*; Elizabeth Ewan, '"To the Longer Liver": Provisions for the Dissolution of the Marital Economy in Scotland, 1470–1550', in Maria Ågren and Amy Louise Erickson, eds, *The Marital Economy in Scandinavia and Britain, 1400–1900* (Burlington: Ashgate, 2005), 191–206; Marjorie K. McIntosh, 'The Benefits and Drawbacks of *Femme Sole* in England, 1300–1630', *Journal of British Studies* 44, no. 3 (July 2005): 410–38; Sara Mendelson and Patricia Crawford, *Women in Early Modern England* (Oxford: Oxford University Press, 2003); Mary O'Dowd, 'Women and the Law in Early Modern Ireland', in Christine Meek, ed., *Women in Renaissance and Early Modern Europe* (Oxford: Four Courts Press, 2000), 95–108; Gordon DesBrisay and Karen Sander Thomson, 'Crediting Wives: Married Women and Debt Litigation in the Seventeenth Century', in Elizabeth Ewan and Janay Nugent, eds, *Finding the Family in Medieval and Early Modern Scotland* (Aldershot: Ashgate, 2008), 85–97.

[23] Maria Ågren, *Domestic Secrets: Women & Property in Sweden, 1600–1857* (Chapel Hill: University of North Carolina Press, 2009), especially chapter 4.

[24] Anna Bellavitis, 'Dot et richesse des femmes à Venise au XVIe siècle', *CLIO* 7 (1998): 91–100, and 'Women, Family, and Property in Early Modern Venice', in Jutta Gisela Sperling and Shona Kelly Wray, eds, *Across the Religious Divide: Women, Property, and Law in the Wider Mediterranean (ca. 1300–1800)* (London and New York: Routledge, 2010), 175–90. See also Sandra Cavallo, 'What Did Women Transmit? Ownership and Control of Household Goods and Personal Effects in Early Modern Italy', in Moira Donald and Linda Hurcombe, eds, *Gender and Material Culture in Historical Perspective* (London: MacMillan Press, 2000), 38–53.

[25] Joëlle Rollo-Koster, 'The Boundaries of Affection: Women and Property in Late Medieval Avignon', in Jutta Gisela Sperling and Shona Kelly Wray, eds, *Across the Religious Divide: Women, Property, and Law in the Wider Mediterranean (ca. 1300–1800)* (London and New York: Routledge, 2010), 38–50; Rosa, *O Morgadio em Portugal*, 165.

women's inheritance potential was significantly different in Galicia, Extremadura, Catalonia, and in the Basque region.[26]

Conversely, it would be inaccurate to assert that inheritance laws in early modern Portugal meant that Portuguese women enjoyed an unparalleled status. The sixteenth-century writer Rui Gonçalves contended that, by law, Portuguese women enjoyed greater privileges than their male counterparts, but his arguments were based on flattery rather than substance.[27] As other historians have pointed out, women's property rights were recognized in Iberia not because law makers acknowledged women's economic capacities, but rather because the women's family's property needed to be protected; that is why a woman's husband was not allowed to meddle with the wife's property which she had initially gotten from her natal family, and which property her natal family stood to inherit if the woman bore no children.[28] This concern is evident in the concession made by king D. João IV (r.1640–1656) to the Portuguese nobility who wished to preserve their family privileges by keeping their holdings intact. The decree of 2 May 1647 declared that the descendant of the first born, son or grandson, or other direct heir, including female, would take precedence in inheriting Crown holdings over the second son of the holder once deceased, and this in contradiction to the *Lei Mental* that excluded daughters and grandchildren.[29] While the change would certainly benefit a few daughters and granddaughters, the change was made not in recognition of women's rights but of the rights of the family.

A resolution ratified in 1435 by king D. Duarte (r.1433–1438), the *Lei Mental* aimed to consolidate the Crown's rights and prerogatives over those of the nobility, essentially giving the king the final say on the inheritance of property from royal donations. The three principal conditions that applied to the succession of royal grants were indivisibility, male primogeniture, and the possibility of the inheritance by the oldest daughter with royal approval.[30] While daughters of elite families were clearly disadvantaged by this legislation, the law left a window of opportunity that proved beneficial for some women. Two examples will suffice to illustrate this point. Alvaro da Silva, 3rd count of Portalegre, was succeeded by his granddaughter, Filipa da Silva (1550–1590), after receiving royal permission to bypass the *Lei Mental* which held that women could not inherit the father's titles

---

26 Poska, *Women and Authority*, 228–9.

27 Rui Gonçalves, *Dos privilegios & praerogativas q ho genero feminino tẽ por direito comũ & ordenações do Reyno mais que ho genero masculino* (Lisbon: Biblioteca Nacional, 1992 [1557]).

28 Cristina Segura Graiño, 'La Transición del Medievo a la Modernidad', in Elisa Garrido, ed., *Historia de las Mujeres en España* (Madrid: Editorial Síntesis, 1997), 226 [219–45].

29 José Justino de Andrade e Silva, *Collecção Chronologica da Legislação Portuguesa (1640–1647)* (Lisbon: Imprensa de F.X. de Souza, 1856), 62–3.

30 *Ordenações Manuelinas*, Livro 2, Título 17, and Livro 5, Título 3, no. 12, 13, 14; *Ordenações Filipinas*, Livro 2, Título 35, and Livro 5, Título 6, no. 13, 14, 20. See also Disney, *A History of Portugal*, I: 128, 237; Caetano, *História do Direito*, 513–15, 558; Carvalho, 'Condicionalidade sócio-cultural', 1073–5.

and feudal estates. Likewise, when Jorge de Lencastre, 2nd duke of Aveiro, died in battle in 1578, the dukedom was sought by his daughter, Juliana de Lencastre (1560–1636), and by his male cousin, Alvaro de Lencastre (1540–1626). After much argument from the two pretenders, the dispute was resolved by the king who had the two marry each other, and declared both of them 3rd dukes of Aveiro.[31] It is also worth noting that the *Infanta* D. Isabel Luísa Josefa (1669–1690), daughter of D. Pedro II (r.1683–1706) and D. Maria Francisca Isabel de Sabóia (1646–1683), was named heir to the Portuguese throne on 20 January 1674, but she died long before her reigning father.[32]

In the grand scheme of things, women's share of the royal piece of pie was smaller than the men's portions, but women's shares were not insignificant. In her study of royal grants to noblewomen in late medieval Portugal, Ivana Elbl pointed out that women generally received fewer grants than men, particularly in view of the fact that women were excluded from royal offices, but some women of the higher nobility could and did receive substantial royal grants, and those grants were often connected to the women's political involvement. Furthermore, Elbl concluded that the power exercised by noble women was a direct consequence of the laws of inheritance and property rights, for 'medieval Portugal explicitly acknowledged that women owned property in their own right and, once they had come of age, could dispose of it as they saw fit'.[33] The situation did not change in the early modern period.

Unlike their counterparts in many other European regions at the time, early modern Portuguese legislators were not compelled to tamper with the laws that governed property ownership. In fact, they left well enough alone, and they did that for two main reasons. One, because Portugal had a well-established sense of statehood, the borders of which remained relatively stable since the conquest of the Algarves in 1249, there was no urgency in the sixteenth century to consolidate and aggregate the territories for the sake of a newly emerging nation-state. Portugal as a country did not experience the birth pains of nation building in the early modern period to the extent that has been observed for other European regions, particularly in Protestant Europe.[34] Two, Portugal expanded its boundaries not at

---

31 Other interesting exceptions included the case of colonial Brazil, the territory of which was initially divided into 15 captaincies, the inheritance of which governing posts was not restricted by the rules of the *Lei Mental*. Marques, *História de Portugal*, 128, 346.

32 Maria Paula Marçal Lourenço, *D. Pedro II, O Pacífico (1648–1706)* (Lisbon: Círculo de Leitores e Temas e Debates, 2010), 192.

33 Ivana Elbl, 'Status and Agency: Royal Grants to Portuguese Noblewomen, 1438–1481', *Portuguese Studies Review* 13, no. 1/2 (Fall–Winter 2005/2007): 77 [61–114]; see also Jutta Sperling, 'Women's Property Rights in Portugal under D. João I (1385–1433): A Comparison with Renaissance Italy', in the same volume, 27–59. For a look at a list of recipients of Crown pensions in 1502, see Braamcamp Freire, 'Caderno da sisa da marçarya para 1502', *Archivo Histórico Portuguez* 2 (Lisbon, 1904): 21–6.

34 See, for example, Martha C. Howell, *The Marriage Exchange: Property, Social Place, and Gender in Cities of the Low Countries, 1300–1550* (Chicago and London: University of Chicago Press, 1998); Stanley Chojnacki, 'Daughters and Oligarchs: Gender

home but overseas, very far away from home, an enterprise that expended vast human resources, predominantly male humans. With so many men occupied in the long-distance business of empire building, it made little sense to limit women's access to and dealings with important matters at the home front.

The prescriptive and juridical literature of the period made a valiant effort to maintain a patriarchal stance, but patriarchy began at home.[35] With not enough patriarchs to go around, the exception became the rule. Despite the restrictions around large seigneurial land holdings noted earlier – with their concomitant honorary titles, offices, and privileges – which the *Lei Mental* attempted to reserve for the male line, Portuguese women enjoyed greater access to property ownership than most other women in early modern Europe.[36] All indications point to women's rights of inheritance as a key component that allowed them a wide berth in the economic sector, and in their involvement in accusations and forgiveness of criminal activity. The same rights that enabled women to manage what they owned also allowed them to launch complaints against those who trampled upon those potential possessions, and, conversely, to renounce those rights when necessary.

Property was at the heart of many of the agreements and disagreements that made the record books, especially landed property. Essentially, too few people had too much of it, but the masses held on to their rights of usufruct with tenacity. Land tenure in medieval and early modern Portugal was held under a system of emphyteusis or *prazo de três vidas* – that is, the contract was understood to encompass the lives of three holders, the father, mother, and child.[37] While the lease contracts between the landowners and the tenants emphasized the male head of the household as the first landholder, upon his death the wife took over the lease,

---

and the Early Renaissance State', in Judith C. Brown and Robert C. Davis, eds, *Gender and Society in Renaissance Italy* (London and New York: Longman, 1998), 63–86; Mary Murray, *The Law of the Father? Patriarchy in the Transition from Feudalism to Capitalism* (London and New York: Routledge, 1995); Erickson, *Women and Property*, passim.

[35] For an overview of the legal and philosophical tracts that dealt with Portuguese women and the law, see António Manuel Hespanha, 'O estatuto jurídico da mulher na época da expansão', in *O Rosto Feminino da Expansão Portuguesa, Actas I, Congresso Internacional (Lisboa, 21–25 de Novembro de 1994)* (Lisbon: Comissão para a Igualdade e para os Direitos das Mulheres, 1995), 53–64.

[36] In addition to the examples already cited, see also John A. Marino, ed., *Early Modern Italy* (Oxford and New York: Oxford University Press, 2002); Sandra Cavallo and Lyndan Warner, eds, *Widowhood in Medieval and Early Modern Europe* (London and New York: Longman, 1999); Howell, *The Marriage Exchange*; Tim Streton, *Women Waging Law in Elizabethan England* (Cambridge: Cambridge University Press, 1998); Elisa Garrido González, ed., *Historia de las Mujeres en España* (Madrid: Editorial Síntesis, 1997); Erickson, *Women and Property*, passim.

[37] Emphyteusis was a Roman landholding system that consisted of a perpetual lease, inheritable and alienable, called *emprazamento* or *prazo* in medieval and early modern Portugal.

not her son or any other male designate.[38] This would have been a concern for Escolácia Morena discussed earlier, for upon the death of her husband she would have been in a position to renegotiate her *prazo* with her landowners. Similarly, Manuel Rodrigues, the man who injured Escolácia's husband, was presumably a *prazo* holder as well, and his potential conviction could have had a negative impact on the other 'lives' attached to that *prazo*. Some crimes led to the loss of property by the apprehended and convicted criminal, and that potential loss had serious implications for the culprit's spouse or extended family.[39] Above all, it was this link to the loss of property, in all its guises, that brought women to the fore of the repercussions of crime. Women stood to lose, materially and otherwise, from the crimes that were committed primarily by men against men, and for this reason women were involved in petitions of various forms to protect their interests.

The extent to which crime and property were intertwined, at the *prazo* level, can be seen with an example from 22 April 1623, at which time the *Cabido* or church chapter in Coimbra dealt with a petition from D. Maria de Sá, wife of Manuel da Costa, regarding a tenancy (*prazo*) that she and her husband held in the district of Santa Clara. In her petition, D. Maria pointed out that she and her husband had been the first and second 'lives' of that property tenure, a property that had been held by her father. When the couple had renewed that *prazo* they had agreed to a clause in the contract that stated that if at any time any of the 'lives' committed a crime for which the individual's estate was confiscated, the *prazo* would be dissolved and returned to the church and *Cabido*, which was the seigneur of that property. Given that Manuel da Costa was at the time in jail, having been convicted by the Holy Office,[40] D. Maria asked the *Cabido* to renew the *prazo* for her, so that she would be the first 'life', but church officials denied her request, pointing out that such a change would be prejudicial to the third 'life', and for other 'particular reasons under consideration'. The crime that D. Maria's husband committed was not divulged in the petition, but the church clearly saw him as having undergone a social death; the record keeper referred to D. Maria as 'molher q foi', the same expression used for a widow.[41]

---

38 Isabel Maria Madureira Franco, 'As dinâmicas familiares e communitárias no couto de S. João da Foz (1449–1497)', in Luís Adão da Fonseca, Luís Carlos Amaral, and Maria Fernanda Ferreira Santos, eds, *Os Reinos Ibéricos na Idade Média: Livro de Homenagem ao Professor Doutor Humberto Carlos Baquero Moreno*, 2 vols (Porto: Faculdade de Letras da Universidade do Porto/Livraria Civilização Editora, 2003), II: 536 [529–38].

39 In certain instances, the law mandated that the appropriation of a culprit's property would not take place if the culprit had legitimate heirs. See, for instance, *Ordenações Filipinas*, Livro 5, Título 35, no. 7.

40 Portugal's Inquisition was established in 1536 and lasted until 1821. Known as the Holy Office of the Inquisition, the institution was first founded to deal with heretics, but over time became a formidable tool as the church persecuted dissidents, minority groups, and those engaged in what it termed deviant behaviour, such as sodomy, for instance.

41 Manuel Lopes de Almeida, *Acordos do Cabido de Coimbra, 1580–1640* (Coimbra: Coimbra Editora, 1973), 245–6. The expression 'molher que foi' translates as 'the wife that was' or 'the wife of the late', typically found in reference to the wife of the deceased.

While D. Maria was unsuccessful with her petition, another example showed that a woman managed to minimize her property losses due to her husband's criminal conviction. On 25 March 1538, the Crown absolved the Lisbon resident Ana Pires of the loss of 43,960 *réis*. The Crown had appropriated that amount as part of the penalty inflicted on Ana's husband, Pantaleão Fernandes, a ship pilot. Pantaleão was found guilty of stealing spices in the Azores from ships coming from India that belonged to the Crown, for which crime he was sentenced to four years of exile and to the loss of his half of his family estate. Ana petitioned the Crown, claiming that she was a poor woman with children who she had to maintain without her husband, who was leaving for his exile in India. The Crown agreed to let Ana keep her husband's share of the family assets.[42]

Compromise might not have been the order of the day, but it was taken into consideration on many occasions. Ideally, many thought, a man should be responsible for his family; in reality, many knew, every member of the family had to step in to make things work. In recognition of this reality, legislators took steps to protect those whose patriarch ran afoul, or was otherwise absent. The most obvious way to offer this protection was to allow women an equal share of family property, and to enact laws that prevented a husband from disposing of family assets without his wife's consent.

Law and practice were entirely different things, of course, and even legislators were aware that women could be intimidated to acquiesce to a sale of family property against their will. For this reason the Crown mandated that no husband could alienate immovable family property without providing notarized proof of the wife's consent, and that the consent was to be explicit not implicit, 'because often women, due to fear or reverence for their husbands let certain things pass quietly, not daring to contradict them, due to apprehension about some scandal or danger, that could happen to them'.[43] It is significant that the law in question attempted to protect wives from husbands, not the other way around. Seemingly there was no concern about women alienating family property without the consent of their husbands.

Women and men lived out their lives by doing what they could with the options available to them, sometimes in co-operation with one another, other times in open hostility, but survival depended on some form of negotiation and accommodation between the two. Feelings were hurt, tempers flared up, accidents happened, jealousies developed, animosities fermented, and violence broke out within and between families, neighbours, co-workers, and officials. Portugal had no shortages of laws to prevent trouble and to punish those who caused it, but, for some individuals at least, adherence to the prescriptive rules and regulations was problematic, and families had to deal with the troubles that befell upon them. A quarrel sometimes escalated, or a more serious offense was committed outright,

---

42 Ernesto Canto, ed., *Archivo dos Açores*, 15 vols (Ponta Delgada: Typ. Do Archivo dos Açores, 1883), V: 151–2.

43 *Ordenações Manuelinas*, Livro 4, Título 13; *Ordenações Filipinas*, Livro 4, Título 48.

and these conflicts occasionally precipitated a legal process that left a paper trail, or remnants thereof. The following discussion follows that trail to evaluate the extent to which women were embroiled in moments of conflict, and the strategies at their disposal to deal with the aftermath of those conflicts.

Women Attacked/Attackers

As already mentioned, the sample of *querelas* found for this study is not connected directly with the sample of *perdões de parte*. The denunciations dealt with complaints launched in Ponta Delgada, São Miguel (Azores), and no victim's pardon was located in Ponta Delgada to match with any *querela*.[44] While the *querelas* covered but one small region in one island, the victims' pardons were collected from a number of locations across mainland Portugal, with only a handful from the Azores. Still, the *querelas* and the *perdões de parte* discussed here are connected in a broader sense because each sample provided an example of how a case could have unfolded. Most victims' pardons referred to a *querela*, and the *querelas* from Ponta Delgada provided a fair representation of what other *querelas* would have looked like.

The *querelas* and the *perdões de parte* were also connected thematically. As seen in Table 1.1 and Table 1.2, the accusations and the pardons dealt with many of the same types of crimes, and both types of sources confirmed that most reported crimes were for physical injuries between men. What those numbers failed to show was the impact of those infractions on the victims themselves, and on their families and communities more broadly. A closer look at the details registered in the official denunciation or the victim's pardon allows us to delve into the options open for women who faced hardships that stemmed from crimes that at times had enormous consequences. The sources offer insights into women's strategies in dealing with trouble within the context of legal and cultural practices that made sense to women in early modern Portugal. The records sometimes revealed women in their work environments, telling us something about how they earned a living. Other times women were identified by their names only, seemingly autonomous beings who dealt with criminal matters that apparently mattered to them alone. Such examples were the exception, however, and even those exceptions were possibly the result of a scribe who was particularly succinct.

It must also be noted that the available sources are representative of the cases that were reported to officials, and that led to an official negotiated settlement. The victims' pardons especially must be seen in the context of successful negotiations, and thus the individuals who showed up in these records were arguably among those who felt a sense of entitlement, who had the conviction and necessary resources to persevere. Not everyone whose child was beaten dared to pursue the

[44] Admittedly, this lacuna could be a result of the difficulties I encountered during my initial visits to the district archives in Ponta Delgada, the consequence of which was that I was able to obtain only a fraction of the copies of notary documents I requested.

matter with the local authorities; not every servant stabbed during an argument made a public denunciation. Those who sought a legal recourse for their troubles, and whose brief statements survived, left us a few fragments that hint at what could have transpired, what was considered important to highlight, and what was imperative to conceal.

The Servant Girl

Maria Simões was a *moça* or young lass living in the household of the *almotacé* in Loulé where she was employed as a servant.[45] The pardon document that mentioned her name, dated 26 March 1608, informed us that among Maria's many tasks was fetching supplies, and one day she was sent to the house of Branca Rodrigues, wife of João Gonçalves, to get some soap. On its own, their encounter was unremarkable, one among countless mundane exchanges that went unrecorded, but something happened that day that triggered an argument that turned violent. Branca was arrested and jailed for giving the girl 'many slaps on the face and many blows, from which the girl was left with many bruises'. Upon seeing the girl in that condition, the girl's father and master together filed a complaint and denounced Branca to the authorities, and following the investigation by judicial officers, including the testimony of witnesses, the accused was found guilty of the charges and imprisoned. Two months later, though, the plaintiffs granted Branca a pardon because 'in fact the said girl Maria Simões was to blame for causing Branca to do what she did'.[46]

Not surprisingly, the pardon document did not reveal what exactly the girl had done to provoke Branca. Overflowing with incongruous reasoning, the text did not deny the beating to which Maria Simões was subjected, a young servant girl on an errand for her mistress, perhaps. Despite the rhetoric to the contrary, the pardon does not convince us that the girl was to blame for the attack or that her superiors believed it for a minute, for if that had been the case, there would not have been the accusation to judicial officials, the witness depositions, and the jail sentence, all of which was costly for the plaintiff or defendant, depending on the verdict.[47] The accused and her husband must have provided some form of compensation to appease the two men, one of whom was a city official. Perhaps some or all of that compensation went to Maria, but there is no way to confirm that because her point of view, if it was ever heeded, was not recorded. If adult women sometimes were defaced by their husbands' narratives, children's voices, too, were readily obscured by their adult superiors. Minors hardly made the notary's office, let alone the notary's page.[48] This is not to say that children were ignored, but as will be discussed later, parents and guardians looked after children's interests.

45 The *almotacé* or *almotacel* was the victuals officer, the price fixer, and regulator of weights and measures.

46 ADF, Fundo Notarial (Loulé), João Mendes (notary), no. 1–1-6 (1609), f.126–127v.

47 *Ordenações Filipinas*, Livro 3, Título 67.

48 For another example of an 'absent' daughter in her mother's pardon on her behalf, see ADF, Fundo Notarial, Manuel Pinto Ferraz (notary), no. M994 (1661), f.163v–164.

In the Branca Rodrigues case, the object of the attack was a female youth, but the dispute was resolved by adults. As a minor, Maria Simões was under the authority of her parents and of her employers. Both her mother and her mistress were not mentioned in the pardon document, but this type of absence applied to men, too. For instance, although Branca Rodrigues was identified through her husband, the record made no reference to his presence either during the attack or during the negotiated settlement that resulted in the *perdão de parte*. Partly this was a strategic manoeuvre to maintain a façade of a naturalized process of self-reflection on the part of the victim, and to downplay the process of negotiation with its implied pressures and possible bribes. Nevertheless, the fact that Branca's husband could be perceived to be absent from the entire business indicated that early modern Portuguese women, married or otherwise, were legally and socially capable of entering into contracts on their own. Still, following the conventions of the time, Branca was identified by her marital status only, whereas her husband was noted as a *tendeiro*, a hawker or shopkeeper, yet Branca, too, must have been involved in keeping that shop, for that was the context in which she got herself into some trouble.[49]

The case of Branca Rodrigues also indicated that while women were a minority among those involved in violent crimes, women were not immune to aggressive behaviour, including amongst themselves.[50] It could be argued that Maria Simões was particularly vulnerable as a young servant girl, but the record also showed that she was supported by her father and employer, the latter a city official who could have used his clout to pursue the matter and obtain a favourable resolution. Although Maria's age was not revealed, she must have been quite young for she was not named as one of the pardoners for the attack that she suffered, whereas another example was found of a servant whose initiative was acknowledged.

The Young Servant Woman

Although still considered a legal minor, Luzia granted a pardon on 4 March 1666, in which document the notary recorded that she was 22 years old, and who looked it by her demeanour, he explained. From Luzia's *perdão de parte* we learn that she had launched a complaint against Francisco Cardoso Manto because he mistreated her and injured her with a knife. The culprit was jailed and was sentenced, having been found guilty of the assault. After he was jailed, though, she reconsidered the situation:

---

[49] For an examination of the wife's contribution to a shop in early modern Rome, see Elizabeth S. Cohen and Thomas V. Cohen, *Daily Life in Renaissance Italy* (Westport and London: Greenwood Press, 2001), 33. See also Sandra Cavallo, *Artisans of the Body in Early Modern Italy: Identities, Families and Masculinities* (Manchester and New York: Manchester University Press, 2007), especially160–80.

[50] For an example of a woman accused of hiring two men to beat up another woman, see Rodrigues, 'Criminalidade e Violência', note 26.

> Given that he was a married man with a wife and children, and that to gain his freedom he would have to dispense of a lot of property which he did not have, and that if he injured her it was accidental, and he was moved by passion, provoked by words, she did not wish to accuse him and with this document [she] wished to pardon him.[51]

Luzia's pardon was written in the home of Francisco da Mota Rebelo and his wife, Maria da Silva, on Rua da Porta Nova in Porto, where Luzia was employed as a servant. While Luzia showed some autonomy by filing a complaint against the man who attacked her, the pardon also showed that she was not autonomous, for the pardon had to be ratified by her employers who were present at the drawing up of the document. Francisco signed the document, but since neither woman could write, they had Henrique Franklin, a surgeon, sign on their behalf. The surgeon's last name suggests that he was an English expatriate, or that he had some English parentage. Porto had a lively community of foreign merchants in the sixteenth and seventeenth centuries, predominantly Flemish in the earlier period, followed by French, English, and German, each of whom had its own *línguas* or interpreters. These officials had to make an oath of office at the municipal council, and the council in turn required that, in order for them to serve their offices, they had to be married in Porto. Although most of the foreigners in Porto were involved in the import and export trade, some of them practised other professions, such as medicine.[52]

The choice of the surgeon as a witness may be indicative that he was called upon to treat Luzia's injuries, the cost of which someone had to pay, probably the accused. If Luzia's master and mistress were part of the pardon process, they undoubtedly were part of the initial *querela* as well, and they would have known better than the young servant how to negotiate a deal with a desperate man in jail, with wife and children to consider. Luzia was recognized as the central pardoner in this case, but she was still a servant, under the age of majority, living with her employers. It is noteworthy that she was never given a last name, either because she did not have one,[53] or it was deemed unimportant by her superiors who most likely orchestrated the settlement with a man whose property was diminished somewhat in the process. Nevertheless, the unrecorded settlement could have been to Luzia's benefit, possibly in the way of a contribution to her dowry.

Many important elements of the victim's pardon were left unrecorded, most notably the inducements and pressures that must have been part of the process for at least some of the cases. None of the examples under discussion provided clear evidence to that effect, but in her study of *perdões de parte* in Vila Nova de Gaia in north-western Portugal, Isilda Monteiro uncovered a few cases from

---

51 ADP, Fundo Notarial, Po. 4, 1a Se, no. 56 (1666), f.178v–179. Some punctuation was added for clarity.

52 Francisco Ribeiro da Silva, *O Porto e o seu Termo (1580–1640): Os Homens, as Instituições e o Poder*, 2 vols (Porto: Câmara Municipal do Porto, 1988), I: 328–36.

53 The use of surnames among commoners was not the norm in the early modern period.

the second half of the eighteenth century that revealed the sources of pressures to which plaintiffs were subjected. In one case from 1777, for instance, the pardoned party admitted that some charitable people had convinced the injured parties to forgive the culprit. Another example from 1780 was especially revealing, from which document we learn that a young man forgave four other men who were related to each other, for having assaulted and injured him. Fifteen days later, the same young man appeared at the notary's office to annul that document, even though the pardon had been expressed in the greatest friendship between him and the four accused. In his annulment, however, he declared that he had only agreed to pardon the four because of a certain respected individual in the community who had put pressure on him to grant the pardon, and that he had agreed to it more in fear of this individual than for anything else. Finally, a woman conceded in a pardon document from 1675 that she granted the pardon as an obligation put on her by her confessors because, they informed her, to proceed with the case would have been detrimental for the accused.[54]

Single Women

Both Maria Simões and Luzia discussed above were young single women engaged in domestic service and living with their employers. This was a common phase in the lives of many poor young women in early modern Europe, but a significant number of single women in early modern Portugal lived on their own, were heads of their own households, owned property, and entered into legal contracts. Some of those single women shared accommodations, especially if they were sisters, as was the case with Catarina de Oliveira, Barbara de Oliveira, and Margarida de Penoas. All three sisters were identified as having reached the age of majority of 25 years, and they were probably single given that they were also identified as daughters of the late Francisco Dias. The three lived together and together they denounced Manuel de Araújo, worker, Manuel de Oliveira, shoemaker, his mother Ana de Oliveira, and her daughter Maria de Oliveira, for physical assault. In their *querela* the plaintiffs claimed that they were attacked in their own home on 13 June 1652. The invaders first threatened to set their house on fire, and then, with unsheathed swords, they told the three women that they were going to kill them, and they would have been killed, the sisters declared, had they not called out for the king ('se não chamavão pallavras del Rey'). Margarida de Penoas appeared to have received the brunt of the blows with the swords, as the scribe vouched for the three round bloody injuries on her right arm, each the size of a *vintem* coin, and another injury of half a palm long, on the same arm.[55]

Given the same last names of some of the accused and accusers, the dispute was probably between relatives, or, if not relatives, they were certainly not strangers, for the complainants allowed their attackers into their homes, at least initially.

54 Monteiro, 'A litigiosidade', 104–6, 110.

55 BPARPD, *Livro de Autos de Querelas*, f.176v–177.

The reason for the conflict was not recorded, nor do we know what the three sisters did to earn a living, but since all three were over the age of majority, they must have been engaged in something productive. Were the three sisters orphaned of both parents, or did the scribe merely note the late father's name due to conventional practice? He certainly followed a long-standing convention of identifying the two men involved in the conflict through their economic occupations, and the women through their kin relations.[56]

Occasionally women's work filtered through the records, as in the case of two other sisters, Catarina and Maria Rodrigues, residents in Estremoz, who initiated a *perdão de parte*. They initially filed a complaint against Manuel da Fonseca, a barber, who attacked them using a conventional weapon: his fists. As stated in their complaint, the previous September (1668), on a day when Catarina and Maria were sewing at home on Rua do Real, between seven and eight at night, Manuel and a companion attacked them with words and blows, from which one of the sisters ended up with two injuries, one on her face and the other above an ear, for which reason Manuel was arrested.

> But since the incident was accidental and based on a recent argument and previously they had been great friends and next door neighbours and there being between them a special friendship and the said blows and injuries had not caused any scars or deformities but a light scratch on the face and from everything she was healed and both [sisters] accepted that they were entirely to blame for the incident and that they caused it and they pardoned Manuel.[57]

The suggestion that Manuel acted with an unnamed accomplice ('con outro en sua companhia') was vague enough to insinuate that Manuel was not to blame for all of the harm, and perhaps none of it, for the sisters accepted responsibility for the attack that left but a little scratch on the face of one of them – the scratch being so insignificant that it was hardly necessary to identify the woman behind the scar. Odd as it may appear to the modern reader, this exercise was seen as an essential component of a public performance necessary to re-establish the social cohesion with neighbours that the dispute had damaged. In many ways this pardon resembled the *querela* discussed above by the three sisters attacked in their own home. In both cases the narrative metamorphosed the injuries and the sisters into one vague plaintiff. In the pardon document, we were informed that the two sisters were busy working at their sewing – an almost bucolic scene until it was shattered by an inexplicable bout of violence from their neighbours, but all was forgiven. The implicit understanding in the *perdão de parte* was that in order to forgive one also had to forget the details, the 'little scratch', the pain, fear, and humiliation. This collective amnesia served some internal purpose, the cost of which was not divulged in the archival record, but the individuals on both sides of

---

[56] For a number of discussions of this theme, see Bennett and Froide, *Singlewomen in the European Past*, passim.

[57] ADE, Fundo Notarial (Estremoz), Francisco Jorge (notary), Séries 23 (1669), f.79v–80.

the conflict had much to gain by forging some form of resolution to their conflicts. As Shakespeare's King Richard advised, 'Deep malice makes too deep incision: Forget, forgive; conclude, and be agreed'.[58]

In both cases that dealt with sisters living together, the sisters appeared to have been a source of support to each other in their construction of the events that led to the conflict in the first place. With or without that support, some women managed to negotiate a settlement with their aggressors, as exemplified by Margarida Lourença, a young single woman (*moça solteira*) who had enough confidence to venture on her own and go to a notary's office on 7 February 1650. In her statement to the notary Margarida declared that she lived in the Freguesia de São João de Lagos in Monção, near Viana do Castelo in north-western Portugal, and that her father was dead. The reference to her dead father was either a way to identify her, or a means to explain why she conducted this business alone, but legally she could act on her own because she declared to be over the age of majority. The reason for her visit to the notary's was to pardon Gregório Esteves and his sons, Francisco and Manuel, for attacking her. In her statement Margarida explained that the three men were her neighbours and friends, and that she was healed of the injuries that they inflicted on her. It stood to reason, therefore, that she should forgive them and forgo the rectification and reparations ('emenda e satisfaição') to which she was entitled. Per usual the victim vouched that she was under no pressure, yet Gregório Esteves, the patriarch who along with his two sons physically assaulted a lone young woman, was also at the notary's office – a rarity in these situations – and accepted the pardon, as if rejecting it was an option under consideration.[59] What Gregório accepted, in fact, were the terms of Margarida's pardon, terms that were left unrecorded on this folio, but were well understood by all present.

Although Margarida Lourença admitted that she had complained to the local judge, her statement made no reference to any of the three suspects being in prison. Indeed, Gregório Esteves' presence at the notary's office confirmed that he was at large, yet he needed the victim's pardon to deal with the pending case. This suggests that Margarida had been assaulted fairly recently, though ostensibly enough time had lapsed for her injuries to have healed. One gets the impression that Margarida was approached soon after her visit to the judge's office, and her neighbours were 'most desirous' ('bem querentes') for a peaceful resolution to their problems, undoubtedly to circumvent the judicial process that had barely begun. Undoubtedly they were also 'most desirous' to compensate Margarida in some form or another. Whatever transpired between them, the odds were not in favour of the defendants because essentially there were six male fists against two female. That was hardly an equitable equation, even if we take into account the reports by some writers of the time who lauded the exceptional robustness of women in northern Portugal.[60]

---

58 *King Richard II*, Act 1, Scene 1, in *The Complete Works of William Shakespeare* (New York: Avenel Books, 1975), 396.

59 ADVC, Fundo Notarial (Monção), Francisco Pereira de Araújo (notary), no. 5.7.1.6 (1649–1651), f.29v–30v.

60 See the discussion in Chapter 1.

The wording of these pardon documents had to follow a certain course that allowed for the record to be legally binding without implicating the accused too obviously, because that could be seen as an admission of guilt. From the plaintiff's point of view, the pardon had to contain enough substance that she or he could not be accused of having filed a false *querela*. The law was clear on this point: the person who launched a suit and lost the case had to pay all costs, damages, and losses incurred by the wrongfully accused. If the judge decided that the *querela* was filed deliberately and maliciously, under false pretences, the complainant would pay all costs in double, or even triple, depending on the severity of the malice. Furthermore, the legislation also informed judges that, under certain circumstances, if a pardon was granted to an accused after a *querela* was filed, but before the judicial inquiry had begun, the judge could dismiss the case. Margarida's attackers had much to gain by convincing her to pardon them as quickly as possible.[61] Likewise, Isabel Dias, 'a woman who is not married', granted a pardon on 19 October 1579 to the man who had attacked her just a few days earlier. In this case the document hinted at some motivating factors, for Isabel stated that she pardoned the culprit 'for other just and honest considerations', which were best left undisclosed (see Appendix 3).

Widowed Women

Other women without husbands were of course the widows, a group of women who conventionally were deemed amongst the most vulnerable in early modern Europe.[62] The sample examined here did not bear witness to widows' vulnerability, for the few who injured or were injured dealt with the problem as anyone else in similar circumstances. The evidence shows that some widowed women managed well enough on their own, including Caterina Ferreira, resident of Porta Nova in Porto. In 1653 Caterina received notice that Crown officials planned to pull down a dwelling she had in front of the new jail in Porto, a location where authorities wanted to enlarge the garrison. She agreed to the appropriation of her property only after it was properly evaluated, and she was paid 20,000 *réis* in compensation.[63] Still, the rhetoric of the vulnerable widow could be put to use, if necessary. The scribe determined how to record the information he received, but he was not immune to the constructs of those who dictated their stories before him. Enough filtered through that shows the art of crafting a narrative that

---

61 *Ordenações Filipinas*, Livro 5, Título 118 and 122.

62 For an examination of this theme, see Cavallo and Warner, *Widowhood in Medieval*, passim.

63 AHMP, *Livro de Vereações*, no. 54 (1653–1654), f.92–92v. For a look at a widow who tenaciously fought from 1639 to 1670 against the powerful Santa Cruz monastery in Coimbra over property rights, see Margarida Sobral Neto, 'Uma Mulher nas Malhas da Justiça Senhorial na Gândara do Séc. XVII', *Revista Portuguesa de História* 1, t.XXXI (1996): 529–53.

says something about the plaintiff's considered intention.[64] For example, in her *querela* of 7 April 1633, Catarina Luís, a widowed weaver, stated that she was at home when António das Pouvas entered her house and attacked her and her two daughters, after which attack Catarina went straight to the judge's house and filed an official complaint.

The scribe verified that Catarina had an open and bloody injury on her left arm, around the index finger, an injury that the plaintiff claimed needed the attention of a surgeon. To underline the unreasonableness of the aggression, Catarina stressed that it had happened while she was quiet and peaceful in her house, next to *Nossa Senhora da Natividade* – Our Lady of the Nativity, no less.[65] It is not clear from the narrative whether the Lady of the Nativity in question referred to a nearby church, or to an image of the heavenly Lady that the self-proclaimed peaceful Catarina had for company. Either way, the allusion was an effective tactic to set the scene of an innocent woman confronted with an unprovoked attack by a male intruder. Catarina also ensured that the scribe noted that she was a widow and a weaver, two identifying markers that helped to convey the message that she was without a husband to defend her, and that she was a responsible and respectable working woman, a woman who earned her living through an occupation acceptable for and often performed by women in early modern Portugal.[66]

It could be argued that single women and widows were targeted because they had no patriarch to protect them, but the evidence was insufficient to substantiate such a premise. These cases can also be interpreted in another way, for they revealed that lone women were not necessarily intimidated by those who attacked them, that some sought justice and were vindicated in one way or another, as the next example demonstrates. Indeed, if Gonçalo Fernandes attacked the widow Madalena Gonçalves because he feared no male opposition, he would have done well to control himself, regardless. Where his opponent could not match him in

---

64 For a discussion of the role of the record keeper and questions of agency for ordinary people, see Tommaso Astarita, *Village Justice: Community, Family, and Popular Culture in Early Modern Italy* (Baltimore and London: Johns Hopkins University Press, 1999), and Cohen and Cohen, *Daily Life*, passim.

65 BPARPD, *Livro de Autos de Querelas*, f.83v–84v.

66 Margarida Durães, 'Os Camponeses do Noroeste de Portugal. Família, Património e Cultura Material (Séculos XVIII–XIX)', in Mafalda Soares da Cunha and Juan Hernández Franco, eds, *Sociedade, Família e Poder na Peninsula Ibérica: Elementos para uma História Comparativa* (Lisbon and Murcia: Edições Colibri/CIDHUS/Universidade de Evora/Universidad de Murcia, 2010), 245 [235–54]. For references to *tecedeiras* or female weavers, and official attempts to regulate their work, see Artur de Magalhães Basto, ed., *Livro Antigo de Cartas e Provisões dos Senhores Reis D. Afonso V, D. João II e D. Manuel I* (Porto: Câmara Municipal do Porto, 1940), 178; António Cruz, *Os Mesteres do Pôrto: Subsídios para a História das Antigas Corporações dos Ofícios Mecânicos*, 2 vols (Porto: Edição do Sub-Secretariado de Estado das Corporações e Previdência Social/Empresa Industrial Gráfica do Pôrto, 1943), I: 4–7, 51; Pereira, *Vereações de Velas*, 221, 305; Maria Teresa Campos Rodrigues, ed., *Livro das Posturas Antigas* (Lisbon: Câmara Municipal, 1974), 25–6; Canto, *Archivo dos Açores*, XIV: 176.

muscular might, she made up in perseverance and tenacity. The conflict between the two began with an argument the widowed Madalena had had with Gonçalo's young daughter, also named Madalena, after which the girl told her father that she had been struck with a pitchfork and verbally abused by the widow. The opposing parties lived in the same Concelho de Gaia, in the outskirts of Porto, which facilitated the ensuing encounter between the widow and the young girl's father, an encounter that led to both sides hitting each other with pieces of wood, and the widow got the short end of the stick, so to speak: 'With a stick he brought with him the said Gonçalo Fernandes gave her some strikes one of which was on the head which resulted in her Madalena Gonçalves being injured with a small injury on the upper part of the head of very little danger'.

The widow Madalena denounced the father and daughter, and the two stood accused 'of the said beatings and injuries'. Two days after the incident, on 14 June 1661, 'as a good Christian', the widow Madalena felt remorseful and was ready to forgive, with one condition: Gonçalo had to pay for the medical treatment of Madalena's 'small injury', the cost of which was 2,000 *réis*, an amount he agreed to pay her in coin by St. Michael's day in September of that year, or else answer to the authorities. In return, Gonçalo also pardoned the widow Madalena for any responsibility she may have had in the words she said that led to the beatings, and he, too, wanted nothing from her. They pardoned one another and promised to live in peace and friendship from that day forward. They both pledged their respective properties and renounced all rights to any laws, privileges, liberties, and ordinances that could have allowed them to nullify the agreement.[67]

The devil is in the details, the old proverb goes, and this narrative is especially rich with tempting morsels. The injury to the widow's head was ever so small, yet it required medical attention at a significant cost; Madalena pardoned the father and daughter for the assault, but her generosity had a price and a time limit; the widow had only had some 'words' with the young Madalena, but in the latter's version of the incident, those words had been delivered with the aid of a pitchfork. Words, of course, mattered, and those that the older Madalena hurled at the younger girl and at the girl's father were ostensibly provocative enough to unleash a fit of passion that led to a physical injury, but Madalena Gonçalves was no fool. She only agreed that 'she may have had' some responsibility in the incident.

That qualification could have been important, in case the dispute was carried to the next level. If Madalena Gonçalves did not get her 2,000 *réis* by the following September, what were her options? According to a manual for notaries from the early nineteenth century, a victim's pardon could be granted with a condition, but even if the recipient of the pardon did not fulfil the conditions of the pardon, the pardon could not be revoked; the terms of a victim's pardon could be enforced only through civil court.[68]

---

67 ADP, Fundo Notarial, Po. 4, 1a Se, no. 52 (1661), f.211v–212v.

68 José Homem Correa Telles, *Manual do Tabellião, ou Ensaio de Jurisprudencia Eurematica* (Lisbon: Na Impressão Regia, 1819), 196.

Neighbours and Acquaintances

Whether they lived in large towns or small hamlets, most people interacted with friends, neighbours, and acquaintances on a daily basis. In turn, these were the same people with whom conflict arose most often. The *querelas* and *perdões de parte* examined for this study confirmed that, for the most part, plaintiffs and defendants knew each other, lived in proximity to one another, and worked side by side, either on the land or in town. In fact, this proximity was sometimes the source of contention when porous boundaries were not respected. We saw this with the case of Escolácia Morena and her husband discussed at the beginning of this chapter, and the same was true with the case of Maria Luís, resident of Lugar dos Fenais (São Miguel), wife of António Amaral. Luís had a plot of land in which she planted squash, and one day in early August she was horrified to find that all of her produce had been bitten and eaten by animals. The following day, 4 August 1648, this peasant woman found herself in the island's capital where she filed a complaint against Maria Ribeira, resident of the same place, wife of Francisco Pinheiro Pinto, who was absent at that time. In her *querela*, Luís alerted the authorities of the harm that was caused, not to her squash but to herself as a result of her attempts to deal with the encroachment on her property. She mentioned six other individuals in her statement, but Ribeira appeared to have been the main culprit in the attack.

Querelas were the means through which complainants voiced their woes, offering injured parties an opportunity to sketch the events according to their own point of view, a system that allowed for much creativity and ingenuity. Perhaps that was part of the point of the exercise; by providing people with a forum to grieve their ills, to unload their frustrations and have someone listen to their tales, the process validated the plaintiff for at least a brief moment. The *querela* provided a stage for re-enactment, and as every good actor knows, sometimes one has but one chance to make a favourable impression. Maria Luís prepared well for her audition.

In a calm, quiet, and peaceful manner, Luís informed the judge, she took some of the damaged squash and showed them to Ribeira who was nearby, and with equanimity Luís asked her neighbour how could she have let her animals cause so much damage to her plot, to which reasonable inquiry Ribeira and her companions attacked Luís, first with offensive words, and then with rocks and even some squash. The result of this confrontation was that Luís was injured, specifically on her right arm and on her leg which had a wound the size of an egg, for which the scribe vouched. Luís also claimed that she had many other injuries all over her body which the scribe could not substantiate for reasons of modesty ('pejo natural'), but the plaintiff was prepared to show them to him, if need be.[69]

Was hers an impulsive reaction that was regretted later? Many pardon documents made reference to an element of impetuousness that drove the plaintiffs to complain too readily, only to regret it later, or so the pardon insinuated. Brígida

---

69 BPARPD, *Livro de Autos de Querelas*, f.154–155v.

Gonçalves of Lisbon made such a claim in her *perdão de parte* dated 6 September 1588, with which she sought to remedy the results of an altercation she had had eight days earlier when in the Ribeira district of Lisbon, Brígida had had some words with Ana Pinheira. Both women sold fruit in the Ribeira, and the two women, who were also neighbours, argued over some fruit that they both had bought. Their heated words escalated to a physical confrontation, each woman resorting to her 'feixe de cavacos', or bundle of firewood, from which fight Brígida got an injury on her head over her right eye. At some point the women's husbands became involved as well in the confrontation, but a week or so after the incident Brígida and her husband came to realize that Ana and her husband were not at fault. The one stated condition to this pardon was that the accused pay their own expenses, and that if they were condemned, Brígida was not to pay anything toward their case and costs.[70]

Brígida and Ana's argument might have been an isolated event between them, but fractiousness was commonly associated with the *regateira* or market woman, and that association had a long history. In a session of 11 July 1390, for instance, municipal officials in Porto declared that *regateiras* were so audacious and unruly ('mal aforadas') that there was no way to control them, even if there were a victuals officer (*almotacé*) for each one of them. More than three centuries later, officials in the same town were still battling this seemingly persistent problem, ordering on 29 May 1738 that 'every *regateira* who fights with one another in the market shall pay one *tostão* for each time'.[71]

The notorious *regateira* was the source of much caricature in early modern literary works, typified in an anonymous play entitled *Auto das Regateiras de Lisboa* which began with a discussion by two *regateiras* about the lack of discipline in a female servant who was out on an errand. Upon the return of the servant, an argument ensued between the three women, the scene became erratic, and all three were arrested for being 'bravas e descompostas', argumentative and disorderly. While still in his office, the presiding judge overheard the clamour and guessed that it could only be from *regateiras*. One of the accused also admitted that she had already been in trouble with the law as a *regateira*. All ended well when the mistress begged the judge for a pardon, the servant begged the mistress for a pardon, and the friend asked the judge to pardon the servant, all of which the judge granted with careless speed.[72]

Not only did the play perpetuate the stereotype of women's garrulousness, it also ridiculed the concept of requesting and receiving judicial pardons with such relative ease. Some contemporaries cautioned the Crown to grant pardons with moderation, for there were concerns that clemency was exercised in an arbitrary

---

70 IAN/TT, Fundo Notarial (Lisbon), Caixa 4, no. 20 (1588), f.4v–5v.

71 A. de Magalhães Basto, ed., *'Vereaçoens' Anos de 1390–1395* (Porto: Câmara Municipal do Porto, 1972), 20, 363.

72 Silveira Bueno, *Auto das Regateiras de Lisboa Composto por um Frade Loyo Filho de hua dellas* (São Paulo: Edição Saraiva, 1969 [15??]). See also António Ribeiro Chiado (d.1591), *Auto das Regateiras* (Rome: Edizioni dell'Ateneo, 1970 [15??]).

fashion, and there were some grounds for those concerns, for the legislation on royal pardons contained a number of loopholes.[73] As mentioned in Chapter 1, an accomplice could receive a royal pardon without a *perdão de parte* if she or he helped authorities convict her or his partners in crime. In fact, legislators were prepared to grant a royal pardon to anyone who assisted judicial officials in the apprehension of a criminal, even if the individual who had helped in the arrest and conviction had not committed a crime. Wayne Johnston's fictional character, Deaco, 'granted universal pardons in advance and therefore made it impossible to break the law',[74] but unfortunately that had not been the result or purpose of the Portuguese legislation. At a time when the judicial infrastructure was poorly developed, the state depended on the assistance of the general public to maintain law and order, and one of the incentives for public participation was the reward of a royal pardon and a possible monetary payment of 30 *cruzados*. There were certain limitations placed on this generic royal pardon, but essentially an individual could possess a reprieve for up to four years of exile to Africa.[75]

This legal loophole begs the question as to why someone who had not committed a crime should want a royal pardon, and the answer lies in the value placed on such a certificate. At the very least, the recipient of this type of pardon could use it to deal with the repercussions of another violation. In essence, it was a credit that its holder could use against a criminal conviction in the future. More egregious still was the fact that the holder of a generic royal pardon could trade it away to a higher bidder. One notarized text showed that on 17 January 1503 two men, residents in Santarém, requested and received an official document (*instrumento de fé e certidão*) that proved their involvement in capturing a thief, though the text did not divulge what they planned to do with their certificate. More obvious was the petition dated 8 November 1511 from Pedro Pires, a *lavrador* in northern Portugal, whose narrative informed officials of the pursuit that he and his neighbours undertook to capture a notorious criminal, for which capture there was an additional reward of 100 *cruzados*. Since Pires was deemed to have put forth the greatest effort toward this end, he was given the royal pardon, but since Pires did not need the pardon, he granted it to Pedro Eanes who was at the time a fugitive for various crimes.[76]

Clearly, then, there were instances when the need for a *perdão de parte* was overridden by other considerations, but it is worth noting that the two cases noted above dealt with the apprehension of criminals who were from the outside of the

[73] Carvalho, 'Condicionalidade sócio-cultural', 1075–6; Hespanha, 'Da "Iustitia" à "Disciplina"', 314–15.

[74] Wayne Johnston, *A World Elsewhere* (Toronto: Vintage Canada, 2011), 46.

[75] *Ordenações Filipinas*, Livro 5, Título 116. This type of royal pardon was inapplicable in cases of making false testimony, or falsifying the royal stamp, for instance. *Ordenações Filipinas*, Livro 5, Título 52, 53, 54.

[76] IAN/TT, *Corpo Cronológico*, Parte 2a, Maço 7, Doc. 4, and Maço 29, Doc. 58, in Duarte, *Justiça e Criminalidade* (Document no. 105), 672–3, and (Document no. 109), 694–9.

communities where they were captured. Their cases were not representative of the majority of conflicts and disputes that individuals faced on a more regular basis. Local struggles often needed local remedies, and as the case of the two fruit sellers discussed earlier illustrated, a notarized pardon could be used to cement some kind of formal agreement between two adversaries who knew each other. Brígida and Ana lived and worked near each other, an arrangement that probably led to occasions of mutual assistance, and mutual animosities. Their dispute ostensibly erupted over some fruit, but what about the fruit? Did one undercut the other in terms of price or in dealings with the fruit suppliers? And why did their husbands get involved? The argument may have been based on some petty misunderstanding, resentment, or suspicion, but it could have led to some serious consequences. It was highly unlikely that either woman was in a position to move further afield and take up her trade somewhere else. For better or for worse, they were stuck together in the same neighbourhood, in the same marketplace. A negotiated settlement was a viable option, for neighbours and acquaintances, and for those with closer kinship ties.

Family Feuds

Not only did the majority of disputes occur between people who knew each other, some of the antagonists were related to one another. The family was the essential socio-economic unit for most people, but the family could also be the source of conflict.[77] If familiarity breeds contempt, the family unit provided the breeding ground for much discord, between spouses, parents and children, siblings, and other relatives. Not surprisingly, some of those conflicts were connected to the misappropriation of resources.

On 8 October 1613, Maria Vaz, widow of the late Domingos Afonso, walked with her son Bartolomeo to the home of António Mendes, shoemaker, who lived in the outskirts of Loulé in southern Portugal. The mother and son had an appointment with a local notary, and with António Vaz, *lavrador*, Maria's brother. The meeting place must have served as neutral ground for the two siblings, given their recent feud, and it was Maria who was the protagonist of this pardon document. In her statement, Maria claimed that about a month and a half earlier her son had had 'some words' with his uncle António over some 'farrobeiras' which Bartolomeo had stolen.[78] The dispute turned violent when the uncle assaulted the nephew, 'causing many bloody bruises', for which attack Maria filed a complaint against her brother. Maria had already appeared in court over this matter where she was

---

77 See, for example, J.R.D. Falconer, 'A Family Affair: Households, Misbehaving and the Community in Sixteenth-Century Aberdeen', in Elizabeth Ewan and Janay Nugent, eds, *Finding the Family in Medieval and Early Modern Scotland* (Aldershot: Ashgate, 2008), 139–50.

78 The stolen item may have been connected to 'alfarrobeira', a carob or locust-tree prominent in the Mediterranean. The locust bean (the pod resembles a locust) is edible and is commonly used in candy, liquors, and to feed cattle and horses. *Michaelis Illustrated Dictionary: Volume II, Portuguese-English* (São Paulo: Melhoramentos, 1961).

asked by the judge if she wanted to follow through with the accusation, but now, 'to avoid ill feelings and animosities that can result from these proceedings, it pleased her to pardon him'.[79]

Bartolomeo, of more than 14 years of age, also pardoned his uncle, and Maria Vaz agreed to her son's pardon. As her son's guardian, the mother had to acquiesce to her son's decision that had legal repercussions. Clearly Maria Vaz took the initiative to punish her brother for having harmed her son, and then took the necessary steps to resolve the potentially broader problem within the family. At some point there was one very angry mother and sister, one injured son and nephew, one possibly remorseful brother and uncle enmeshed in criminal proceedings, and a potentially distraught wife, sister-in-law, and aunt, if António was married. This rural family had some healing to do, though publically, at least, the siblings managed to resolve their differences in a fairly short period of time.

The opposite was true of a pardon that Gregório Domingos, a carrier of wheat in Lisbon, granted on 21 March 1587 to Diogo Afonso. In his statement Gregório claimed he had argued with Diogo, a *lavrador*, during which argument Diogo hit Gregório on the forehead with a scythe. Since Gregório was healed, the incident had been an accident, he and Diogo were friends, and Gregório was married to Catarina Afonso, Diogo's sister, it pleased Gregório to pardon his brother-in-law. Gregório's pardon did not stipulate whether Diogo was ever incarcerated for the assault, but Catarina Afonso must have had to contend with some competing emotions and loyalties. The conflict between the two men meant that Catarina had to deal with the possible devastating repercussions of her husband's head injury, an injury that had been inflicted by her own brother more than three years earlier.[80]

Another possible complication in the Gregório and Catarina household was that she was more implicated in the dispute than the document indicated. The pardon did not reveal the reasons for the argument between Gregório and Diogo, but Catarina, as wife of one and sister of another, was as likely to have been a participant in the dispute as not. In his study of the pardon document in early modern Spain, Francisco Tomás y Valiente rightly pointed out that the line between culprit and accomplice was sometimes imprecise.[81] Historians agree that most crimes were committed by men, but they also recognize that women were active participants in feuds and in aggressive and criminal acts. As Stuart Carroll has noted, women were 'troublemakers in their own right'.[82] In her study of women's

---

79 ADF, Fundo Notarial (Loulé), João Mendes (notary), no. 1–1-8 (1613) f.150–152.

80 IAN/TT, Fundo Notarial (Lisbon), Caixa 4, no. 18 (1587), f.115v–116v.

81 Tomás y Valiente, 'El perdon de la parte', 82.

82 Carroll, *Blood and Violence*, 246. See also Andrea Knox, '"Barbarous and Pestiferous Women": Female Criminality, Violence and Aggression in Sixteenth- and Seventeenth-Century Scotland and Ireland', in Yvonne Galloway Brown and Rona Ferguson, eds, *Twisted Sisters: Women, Crime and Deviance in Scotland Since 1400* (East Lothian: Tuckwell Press, 2002), 13–31.

networks among the Portuguese high nobility, Susannah Humble Ferreira has shown that 'women were indeed capable of orchestrating rebellion'.[83]

Family feuds, in particular, highlighted the agency of women both as peace-makers and peace-breakers, though it was not always easy to determine which was which. Often, though, some form of economic or financial offering – a transaction of property – served to broker a settlement. For instance, the inventory conducted on the estate of the noble António Gomes da Mata, concluded on 22 December 1644 in Lisbon, indicated that there was at least one family feud that had yet to be resolved at the time of D. António's death. One of the bequests he made was to his sister, D. Francisca Coronel, for 800,000 *réis*, but only on condition that she drop a claim that she had filed against him.[84] Similarly, in 1637 Isabel Fernandes of Terceira had no qualms reporting her son to authorities, accusing him of robbing her money, for which crime he was imprisoned. It is not clear how their feud was resolved, but it took approximately six years for the mother to grant her son a pardon.[85]

The gravity of the injury inflicted seemed to have had little bearing on the time that it took to grant a notarized pardon. Injuries that caused death were certainly amongst the most serious for the victim and the victim's family, as well as for the perpetrator and the perpetrator's family, but there was great variation between the time the crime was committed and the pardon was granted. As was seen with the example of Escolácia Morena and her husband, they granted a pardon five days after the potentially fatal attack. In the cases we will look at next, some people had to wait up to two decades for a *perdão de parte*.

Death in the Family

Because of the enormity of the crime, homicide cases warranted special consideration by everyone involved, and this was reflected in the documentation as well. Although the records showed that few women were killers or were killed, homicide by its very nature had broader implications for the family unit than most other physical injuries. For that reason, pardons granted for homicide tended to contain more details about the incident, more references to questions of inheritance, and more particulars about family members who had a claim against the perpetrator(s). These sources, therefore, are particularly rich for the study of women and their rights to negotiate for themselves and for their children. An examination of cases that dealt with the rights of 'orphans', for instance, shed

[83] Susannah C. Humble Ferreira, 'Agents of Political Change: Noblewomen in Portugal at the Turn of the Sixteenth Century', *Portuguese Studies Review* 13, no. 1/2 (Fall–Winter 2005/2007]): 121 [115–34]. For an example of a woman rebelling against church authority, see David Higgs, 'A *Beata* and Biography: Leonarda Rosa and Her Detractors, 1788–1794', in the same volume, 401–9.

[84] Godofredo Ferreira, 'Um Ricaço Lisboeta do Século XVII: Inventário de seus bens', *Estremadura: Boletim da Junta de Província*, nos 50/52 (January/December 1959): 13 [1–32].

[85] Cited in Corrêa, 'Aspectos da Criminalidade nos Açores', 554.

light on women as guardians and on girls under guardianship. The pardons for homicide revealed above all how women, as rightful heirs and administrators of their own property, took part in crucial settlements following the tragic loss of a member of the family, or, conversely, when a member of their family committed homicide.

Of the 224 victims' pardons analysed for this study, 39 were granted for cases of homicide (see Table 1.3), and these pardons were particularly revealing about the concerns of inheritance in early modern Portugal. The death of an individual meant different things to different people, but legally it resulted in the reshuffling of the distribution of family goods. When the death was of unnatural causes, another dimension was taken into account in that reshuffling: the potential material contribution that the deceased could have made to the family economy. Consequently, by law a person convicted of homicide had to make amends to all the victim's potential heirs. Since women were property owners in their own right, and were entitled to inherit as much as their menfolk, women showed up in these pardons in greater numbers than they did in cases of physical injury (see Table 1.4).

Because more physical violence occurred between men, more men were victims and perpetrators of injuries that caused death, and, consequently, women made up a disproportionate number of pardoners in homicide cases. Yet, while only one *perdão de parte* was located for a woman accused of homicide, the three *querelas* found that dealt with accusations of injuries causing death registered a total of 12 individuals implicated in those deaths, including three women (see Table 1.1). As already mentioned, on their own, the *querelas* and the *perdões de parte* are not representative of any discernible trend in criminal behaviour in early modern Portugal, but the discrepancy between the two types of records points to the need for caution in the interpretation of the statistical data. Unfortunately, the folios on which the three *querelas* for homicide were registered are in very poor condition, rendering an analysis of those cases very difficult. What can be ascertained is that the three cases dealt with the killing of three men, two of whom incurred fatal injuries during family brawls, and the women's participation in those brawls.[86]

Due to the deteriorated state of the *querelas* linked to homicide, the discussion of death in the family is based on the information contained in *perdões de parte* only. Women granted pardons to the killers of their husbands, fathers, sons, and brothers, but women were also called upon to pardon those who killed their womenfolk. Because the monetary compensation was not revealed in these cases, it is impossible to determine whether or not there was a gender differentiation between the amounts paid for the death of a female and that of a male relative. Homicide was taken seriously by all concerned, although occasionally the survivors betrayed mixed feelings about the departed.

---

[86] For the three *querelas* that dealt with homicide, see BPARPD, *Livro de Autos de Querelas*, f.131v–132, f.140v–141, f.159v–160.

The Unruly Woman

Madalena Pires might not have been very accommodating in her lifetime, but her death led to a lot of accommodation. A document that was both a pardon and a quittance, dated 4 September 1642, revealed that a Porto notary, a number of Madelena's relatives, three neighbours, and some witnesses met in Masarelos, in the outskirts of the city, at the home of Maria das Neves, widow of Manuel Luís. On the one side of the equation was Catarina Gonçalves, widowed mother of Manuel Alvares and Francisco Alvares, single young men ('mancebos solteiros'). On the other side, the group was substantially larger: Manuel Carneiro, Maria Manuel, Maria Carneira, Pascoal Martins, Manuel Martins, Manuel Fernandes, Maria Martins, Antónia Fernandes, another Maria Martins, Larsimão Luís, Antónia de Faria, Maria de Faria, Maria Correia, and Antónia Correia, all relatives in the second and third degree of Madalena Pires, the deceased.[87]

All those present declared that Madalena, their relative, had died in March of that same year, following a beating by Catarina Gonçalves' two sons. Madalena sustained a number of injuries from that beating, including a blow to her head inflicted with a measuring stick. This incident erupted during an argument ('palavras asidentais'), and the text indicated that Madalena was very fiery ('apaixonada'), full of rage ('cólera'), and that she gave full cause for what happened. Both brothers (Manuel and Francisco) were found guilty of this crime, but Manuel was judged to have given the fatal blow. Yet, Madalena's relatives claimed that despite her injury, she lived for a long time and only died because of her poor treatment of the injury. All were convinced that Madalena was responsible for the incident, and that she was careless ('desgovernada') in treating her injury which led to her death. Thus, in this case, a woman's fiery passion was used against her, whereas the two young men's heated emotions that led to the fatal injuries were normalized. As Kristi Gourlay has put it, 'both historical and literary evidence suggest that pre-modern Europeans considered anger, especially hot-blooded anger characterized by a loss of control or temporary madness, to be an acceptable response to affronts of honor', but less so for women, as Sarah Westphal has shown.[88]

The assembled family members gave the two brothers a full pardon because, they contended, Manuel Alvares was then a minor of 20 years, with no history of other crime. All nine female relatives had someone sign the document on their

---

87 In Spain, too, legislation demanded that, in cases of homicide, the victims' pardons be sought from relatives of the individual killed up to the fourth degree. Dios, *Gracia, Merced*, 331; José Luis de las Heras Santos, *La Justicia Penal de los Austrias en la Corona de Castilla* (Salamanca: Ediciones Universidad de Salamanca, 1991), 41.

88 Kristi Gourlay, 'A Pugnacious Pagan Princess: Aggressive Female Anger and Violence in *Fierabras*', in Lisa Perfetti, ed., *The Representation of Women's Emotions in Medieval and Early Modern Culture* (Gainesville: University of Florida Press, 2005), 137 [133–63]; Sarah Westphal, 'Calefurnia's Rage: Emotions and Gender in Late Medieval Law and Literature', in the same volume, 164–90. See also Kristine Steenbergh, 'Emotions and Gender: The Case of Anger in Early Modern English Revenge Tragedies', in Jonas Liliequist, ed., *A History of Emotions, 1200–1800* (London: Pickering & Chatto, 2012), 119–33.

behalf, while the five men made their crosses. Following the signatures, the notary registered an addendum, done the same day, in which Maria Manuel and her husband, João Gonçalves, plus Manuel Carneiro and his wife, Maria dos Anjos, stipulated that no one (in the family) would speak against the other (regarding this agreement) or else the ones who went against it would have to pay 100 *cruzados* to those who adhered to it, a stipulation to which everyone agreed.[89]

The addendum was done on the same day but probably later in the day because two of the four named in the addendum, João Gonçalves and Maria dos Anjos, were not listed among the first 14 relatives assembled. The actual motivations that propelled such an agreement were hidden in the gag order of the addendum, but the stated reasons for the pardon leaves little doubt that at least some of Madalena's relatives thought her to be a scold whose cantankerous disposition was to blame for her own demise. This could have been part of a strategy to minimize the incident for the benefit of the accused. Indeed, the document began with a declaration by Madalena's relatives that she had 'left this life', a euphemism that implied that she had chosen to leave, not that she had been killed. On paper, at least, there was no hint of sympathy for the victim, no allusion to compassion on earth or in heaven.

Sixteen relatives were prepared to condemn the victim, and release the accused, though there must have been some murmurs of dissension in the family, or concerns of possible discord in the future, necessitating an additional clause that imposed a hefty penalty to anyone who vocalized it. That dissension may explain in part why it took several months from the time of Madalena's death to the writing of the pardon document. Negotiations must have taken place between and within several branches of the victim's family, and the defendants. Regardless of how her relatives felt about her, Madalena's death meant that her relatives had to forgo that to which they were entitled as her heirs. The document did not reveal Madalena's marital status, but she was probably a single woman with some net worth, and depending on her age, that net worth could have potentially increased. Her heirs, therefore, stood to inherit more from her had she lived to a ripe old age. The law recognized this potential, and her relatives ostensibly renounced their rights to claim it.

On the other side of the equation, the pardon document was undoubtedly a relief to the two brothers accused of killing Madalena, and to their widowed mother, a woman who faced an uncertain future with a deceased husband and two incarcerated sons. In his examination of a petition from 1585 for a royal pardon in Castile, Luis R. Corteguera observed that the plea stressed the wide implications that such a pardon would have for the family. The petition in question was submitted by the mother of a culprit who had been sentenced to 10 years of exile and a hefty fine, and the mother argued that the pardon she sought would be as much of a benefit to her as to her son.[90]

---

89 ADP, Fundo Notarial, Po. 4, 1a Se, no. 33 (1642), f.150–151.

90 Luis R. Corteguera, 'Encuentros imaginados entre súbdito y monarca: historias de perdón y petición en la España de la edad moderna', in Riccardo Forte and Natalia Silva Prada, eds, *Tradición y modernidad en la historia de la cultura política. España e Hispanoamérica, siglos XVI–XX* (Mexico: Juan Pablos Editor/Universidade Autónoma Metropolitana, 2009), 31 [23–45].

It is not surprising that legal settlements with long-term implications sometimes led to disagreements between the would-be pardoners, but a *perdão de parte* would surely impress the judicial officials reviewing an appeal if it could be shown that the pardon had been granted unanimously by all concerned. There was also the possibility that the ones who did not adhere to it could still claim damages for their loss. One example from Vila Viçosa, in the district of Evora, showed that family unity was not always easily maintained. On 22 July 1631, Isabel Lopes and her daughter Beatriz Mendes agreed to pardon the man who had killed Isabel's husband and Beatriz's father. Isabel's son, Manuel Lopes, who was incarcerated at the time, had already signed the pardon document as well, but a second daughter, Bastiana Mendes, refused to adhere to the agreement ('não estava presente nem perdou').

In recognition of the tenuous status of this half-hearted pardon, the text was suspiciously brief, and the pardoners made no disclaimers and no pledges to honour the contract. We are left to wonder whether Bastiana was unable to forgive her father's killer because of some deep emotional wound, or because she believed that she was entitled to a lot more compensation than that pardon agreement promised. As a single woman and direct heir, Bastiana had to look after own her interests. Whatever her motivations, Bastiana's defiance could not have helped the accuser's appeal for clemency, nor her family's need to come to terms with the tragedy that befell upon them, or the possible reparations the family had negotiated.[91] A case from Spain showed that in 1649, in negotiations with the man accused of killing her husband, a widow 'pressed [the accused] for as much money as she could get to support herself and her children before she would grant him a private pardon'.[92]

While not ideal, the man accused of killing Bastiana's father could still proceed with his appeal to the Crown with the *perdão de parte* from some of his victims only, and hope that Bastiana would be convinced to reconsider her position at a later date. Crown officials were open to such reconsiderations, as seen in an order from the king dated 22 January 1465, with which officials in the high court were informed to issue a new pardon to two brothers who had killed two people, for which crime they had already received a royal pardon. The stated reason for the new pardon was that the two brothers had received more *perdões de parte* from people who had not been part of the first petition and pardon.[93] The additional pardoners, and the reissued royal pardon, offered the two brothers further guarantees that they would not be pursued by their victims' heirs.

Mothers and Daughters

It was one thing to have someone killed by a neighbour or acquaintance; it was quite another to have the victim and the culprit in the same family. In the latter case, emotions would be a lot more complex, and negotiations for possible

---

91 ADE, Fundo Notarial (Vila Viçosa), Manuel d'Oliveira (notary), Séries 90 (1631), f.95–95v.

92 Taylor, *Honor and Violence*, 203–4.

93 IAN/TT, *Chancelaria de Dom Afonso V*, Livro 8, f.78–78v, in Duarte, *Justiça e Criminalidade* (Document no. 26), 587–8.

compensation more critical. The alleged killer, too, was an heir to the individual killed, unless the accused was found guilty of the deed, in which case that right was nullified. Thus, much was at stake in resolving accusations and counter accusations, and dispelling rumours and suspicions. Not every judicial inquiry was measured by questions of inheritance rights, but ultimately that question came into the equation, and women were among those called to take a stand, on behalf of their parted kin and on behalf of their accused relatives. In their *perdão de parte* dated 19 February 1682, Antónia Martins, widow of the late Domingos Fernandes, and her daughters, Maria Rodrigues and Domingas Martins, all residents of Evora, made a declaration that is worth quoting at length because of the rich details it provided about women's lives, and their ability to affect change.

> In September of the previous year of 1680 Graça Martins died, wife of Manuel Gomes, inn-keeper, resident in this city at the Portas de Alconchel and daughter of the said Antónia Martins, and sister of the said Maria Rodrigues and Domingas Martins, and after she had been buried there was a false rumour in this city that the said Manuel Gomes her husband had been the cause of her death, for which reason the said deceased was exhumed by the justices, and because they found evidence of an injury, or a sign thereof, the justices had an inquiry from which her husband was charged [with the said death], but since [they] knew well of the incident and that he Manuel Gomes had no culpability in it, because the injury that was found on the deceased was not given to her by her husband, but was caused by a fall that the deceased had while still alive and long before her death, and had been an injury of little consequence, and her death was caused by an illness of a malignant fever that she caught from which she died, all of which they were well acquainted with their daughter and sister, and well informed of what caused her death and of the said injury as she herself told them of the said fall, and that she had never complained of her husband Manuel Gomes, on the contrary he never showed any malice toward her … for these reasons they pardoned the said Manuel Gomes for all and whatever culpability he may have had in the said death … because they knew that he was not to blame for the said death nor the source of any of it for it [the accusation] was due to false rumours going about in the city.[94]

There were enough inconsistencies in this pardon to raise questions about the integrity of the claims made by Antónia Martins and her two daughters. Of particular interest was the argument that Graça Martins incurred the suspected injury long before she had died, and that the injury was 'of little consequence', yet it left a mark long after the fact, and was still visible when her body was exhumed. Also perplexing was the claim that the husband was not to blame for his wife's death, yet his in-laws pardoned him for 'whatever culpability he may have had in the said death'. What the document revealed above all was that Graça Martins was dead and her surviving kin, mother and two sisters, had the power and authority to rescue the man accused of the alleged murder.

---

[94] ADE, Fundo Notarial, Manuel Galvão Bárcoro (notary), Séries 740 (1682), f.74–74v. Some punctuation was added for clarity.

Although their pardon might not have ensured a complete discharge for Manuel Gomes, the arguments put forth by his in-laws showed that they had some basis for doubting the rumours about his guilt. Yet, those rumours must have had some foundation to convince authorities to go to the lengths that they did to investigate the accusations. The husband had been charged following an inquiry, which would have included testimonials from neighbours and others with some connection to the couple. Indeed, the findings were enough to charge the widowed husband with his wife's death, but according to the in-laws' testimony, Graça was never subjected to any spousal malice. Judging by their assertions, Antónia Martins and her daughters were well acquainted with each other's lives, and Manuel's in-laws would have noticed if something was amiss. At the very least, the document indicated that a husband's mistreatment of his wife could have been used against him.[95]

While Antónia Martins and her two daughters used the *perdão de parte* to quell some rumours, another mother-in-law claimed that rumours were the source of her own suspicions. In the former document, the three pardoners were depicted as empowered women who took charge of a difficult situation. In the latter, the pardoner appeared almost desperate to get out of a difficulty she ostensibly created. Was this a result of different circumstances, or of different styles among scribes? Whatever the reason, the two examples serve to illustrate women faced with varying degrees of legal challenges, and the manoeuvres that they took to deal with those challenges. This second example, dated 6 April 1673 from Estremoz, indicated that Catarina Gomes, widow, had first alerted authorities that António Correia, her son-in-law, had killed her daughter, Inês Gomes, who had also been his wife. Subsequently, Catarina claimed that she was informed by certain persons that António was not culpable of Inês' death, and that she had accused him because of what enemies of his had told her. For these reasons, Catarina granted a pardon to António, and she agreed to the condition that if she ever reneged she would have to give him 200 *cruzados*, plus 30 *réis* per day to the person who worked on his case, from the initial citation to the final sentence, and all extra costs and damages.[96]

The reference to the significant monetary condition, imposed on the pardoner, can be interpreted in a number of ways, among which is that Catarina was utterly convinced of her son-in-law's innocence and wished to show it in no uncertain terms, or, alternatively, that her son-in-law worried about her doubts and needed an extra guarantee. Catarina Gomes filed the *querela* against the person she initially believed was responsible for killing her daughter, and the new information she received from 'certain persons' was suspiciously vague. It is noteworthy that nothing was stated about her son-in-law's devotion to his late wife, and the sense one gets from this agreement is that as the next of kin, Catarina was essential to António's chances for some plea bargaining with Crown officials. This *perdão de parte* has the hallmark of a legal renunciation for judicial purposes, not of a

95 For a discussion of some of the suspicions that could arise in connection to the death of spouses, see Gaskill, 'Reporting Murder', passim.

96 ADE, Fundo Notarial (Estremoz), Francisco Jorge (notary), Séries 25 (1673), f.5–6.

testimonial of personal relinquishment and heartfelt forgiveness. What motivated Catarina to withdraw her initial accusation, and grant a pardon to the very person she had accused, was unfortunately not divulged in the notarized document.

Women's Input, Near and Far

Catarina Gomes and Antónia Martins before her had each lost a daughter, and each had a crucial role to play in the destiny of their respective son-in-law. During such moments of crisis, the patriarchal façade that maintained a male-centred prerogative shifted, and even showed signs of stress. Catarina and Antónia were both widows, but that was not the reason for their intervention. Had their husbands been alive, they, too, would have been part of these pardons, along with their wives and children. The husbands even could have taken the lead in the process, or at least that was how the scribe would have presented the events. For instance, Alvaro Ramos was in Lisbon where on 16 September 1586 he found himself at the *Paço dos Tabeliães* (Offices of the Notaries) to initiate a written pardon. A *lavrador* from the outskirts of Viana do Castelo, Alvaro had travelled a long way to deal with a judicial process in the capital city that pertained to the death of his son, António Ramos. Alvaro may have travelled alone but he did not leave home empty-handed. He carried with him a legal document essential for the validity of the pardon he was about to grant to his son's killer. Prior to his departure, Inês Afonso gave Alvaro, her husband, her power of attorney with which he could act on her behalf.[97]

Inês did not go to the big city to meet with the big city notaries, but her contribution and entitlement were no less important. Public presentation mattered, but it was not everything. Women's history is all about dismantling the package cloaked in patriarchal rhetoric. What mattered most in these criminal cases that led to victims' pardons was the restitution to which the victims and their families were entitled. Given the social ideal of the early modern period that placed the man above that of the woman in all things material and spiritual, it is not surprising to find that a married woman usually had her husband take the role of public authority and decision making, but husbands were not always available. Sometimes they were dead, indisposed, or otherwise occupied or detained.

Maria da Costa of Porto, for instance, had to take the lead in a pardon process because her husband, Diogo António, was in jail. That was where she met him on 7 December 1635, and the visit had nothing to do with Diogo's incarceration, but rather Maria had to consult with her husband regarding a pardon for the death of their son, Frutuoso António, killed by Pantaleão Osório, Frutuoso's friend. Back at the notary's office, Maria met up with Domingas Antónia, her daughter, married to António de Azevedo, who was away. At this meeting Maria declared that she had a power of attorney from her husband with which to pardon Pantaleão, and thus in her name and on behalf of her husband, Maria da Costa agreed to pardon the accused, as did Domingas Antónia, the victim's sister, and Francisco Gonçalves, a

[97] IAN/TT, Fundo Notarial (Lisbon), Caixa 3, no. 16 (1586), f.100v–101v.

relative of theirs and of the deceased. This case showed yet again women engaged in a serious legal transaction while their husbands were 'absent'. While Maria had a power of attorney from hers, Domingas was seemingly capable of handling the affair on her own, as was their relative, Francisco.

All three in the notary's office agreed that Frutuoso's death had been accidental, and that the mortal injury the defendant inflicted on the victim had been in self-defence, for Frutuoso had raised a gun against the accused. The incident had happened when the two were in the company of others, merry-making and dancing to the music of a viola played by Pantaleão. Why Frutuoso had a gun with him, and why he was provoked to accost his friend with the gun, were elements not considered essential to include in the narrative. The pardoners preferred to highlight the lack of malicious intent of the accused, and the consensus of all those who stood to lose the most from the victim's death, emotionally and materially. The four pardoners renounced all rights to any future claims, and they asked the crown to pardon Pantaleão as well, for with this they would save the soul of the deceased.[98]

A record that attests to a tragedy can also reveal something about the social mores of the time. In the Frutuoso and Pantaleão case, the violence that led to a death erupted during a party, where people played music and danced. Perhaps alcohol was readily available, a factor which could have led to a fight that ended with a corpse.[99] What was the occasion for celebration? The pardon was written in early December but nothing was revealed about when Frutuoso actually died and whether or not death was instantaneous. Perhaps the fatal incident happened a month or so earlier, around November 11, 'Dia de São Martinho', a traditional feast day when the new wine of the season was first tasted.[100] Intriguing as they are, records that deal with criminal activity can lead to an overemphasis on outbreaks of violence and of sorrow. Such a premise perpetuates a view of the past as a dismal time, when people were downtrodden and miserable, but in fact some of those conflicts happened during happy times. Numerous accounts attest to instances of leisure activities that were communal in nature. For example, a report from Bragança in 1622 described the Jesuit celebration of the canonization of St. Francis Xavier, a celebration that was held in the public square next to the church. The highlight of the festivities was a *desafio* or lyrical duel that took place between representatives of the town of Vila Real and those of Bragança, to determine who had the best voices and tambourines, and the best dances and music.[101]

98 ADP, Fundo Notarial, Po. 4, 1a Se, no. 26 (1635), f.128–130v.

99 In fact, some studies show that alcohol was seldom a factor in violent crimes. See. for example, A. Lynn Martin, *Alcohol, Violence, and Disorder in Traditional Europe* (Kirsksville: Truman State University Press, 2009), 159–63.

100 I am grateful to my mother for telling me about this tradition that she remembers well from her younger days in Madeira, and the tradition has some historical precedence. Municipal council records from the early modern period make reference to the 'Dia de São Martinho' as the time when wine merchants could start selling their new wine. See, for example, AHMP, *Livro de Vereações*, no. 52 (1649–1650), f.108, for the minutes from the municipal session of Saturday, 30 October 1649.

101 Fernandes, *Bibliografia*, 175.

The *perdão de parte* discussed above also informed us that the pardoners believed that pardoning Frutuoso's friend would help Frutuoso's soul on its journey to the afterlife. Moreover, it provided a sense of closure, some peace of mind for the family who could rest a little easier knowing they did the proper thing. Perhaps they felt that Frutuoso would have agreed with their decision, especially since the family stated that his death had been accidental, and that he had been responsible for the accident – responsible but not reproached. It is worth noting the differences in tone between this pardon and the one by Madalena Pires' relatives, discussed earlier. Whereas that family pointedly blamed the victim for her demise and stressed that her misbehaviour was of long standing, Frutuoso's parents and other family members emphasized their sense of regret. Their disclaimer of any wrongdoing on the part of the accused did not reflect their frustration with the deceased, but rather the family's statement recognized the futility of the incident between Frutuoso and Pantaleão that led to such a tragic end.

Although different in tone, the documents that dealt with the deaths of Madalena and Frutuoso indicated that the respective families excused the perpetrators seemingly without any compensation. Sometimes we have to accept things at face value, while still maintaining a critical eye to distinguish between the possible and the probable. As noted in Chapter 1, attempts were made at the outset of this study to match the notarized victim's pardon with its corresponding royal pardon registered in the Chancelleries, but of the 224 *perdões de parte* collected, only six could be matched with their royal counterpart, and the case of Frutuoso's death was one of those matches. Pantaleão Osório received his royal pardon on 30 April 1636, and that document referred to the prerequisite *perdão de parte* that he had attached to his appeal to the Crown. The Crown agreed to pardon Pantaleão for the 'injury' that led to Frutuoso's death, at a cost of 20,000 *réis*. Did judicial officials have access to details about the case that were not spelled out in the victim's pardon noted above?[102]

Undoubtedly the appellant judges were privy to specifics that the culprit downplayed in her or his appeal, and the *perdão de parte* from Madalena's multitude of relatives, and the one from Frutuoso's smaller family were no exception; the documents met the needs of the respective applicants for circumscription. In neither case was there a mention of any minor children, a factor that must have facilitated the agreement between and among the parties noted in the records. As already shown, most pardons implicated more than the immediate victim and culprit, and the rights of children to inherit family property were recognized in these legal transactions. Whatever one person renounced or pardoned had an impact on a number of potential heirs on both sides of the equation. It was common, therefore, for parents to ensure that the interests of their offspring were well looked after in the negotiations for a *perdão de parte*, but what if the offspring *was* the culprit? We do not often see the transaction from the culprit's point of view, but one example was found that is poignantly revealing.

---

[102] IAN/TT, Chancelaria de Dom Filipe III, *Perdões e Legitimações*, Livro 12, f.166v.

The Sons of Women and Men

On 27 June 1642 a notary visited Inácio de Gouveia, a prisoner in the local jail, so that Inácio could ratify a document. Inácio was from Coimbra but was incarcerated in Porto for killing Manuel Ferreira, son of Maria Ferreira and brother of Maria dos Anjos. For his crime, Inácio had been condemned to exile, and his parents, Isabel Figueira and António de Gouveia Ribeiro, also from Coimbra, had made a settlement with the two Marias to compensate for their loss. The notarized document presented to Inácio was a *consentimento e outorgua*, or consent and authorization, a document with which Inácio accepted all the conditions of the settlement made by his parents and his victim's family, and with which he renounced all claims and rights to contest the agreement, and relinquished all future claims to any family property. The particulars of that settlement were not recorded in this *consentimento*, but the wide-ranging implications were understood. Inácio signed the document, witnessed by another prisoner and the notary's assistant. Death sentences came in a variety of forms.[103]

Although not explicitly stated, Isabel and António disinherited their son, and used his portion of the family estate to pay for his crime. The law allowed for such measures under certain circumstances, and in this case, the heir accepted responsibility for his actions and agreed to his own disinheritance.[104] The notarized settlement between Isabel, António, and the two Marias – ratified by Inácio – allowed for a look behind the scenes. It epitomized what surely happened in some form or another before many, if not most, victims granted pardons to their perpetrators. This settlement was the equivalent to the 'new information' or 'certain considerations and conveniences' to which many pardons referred. What motivated Inácio to relinquish that to which he was entitled? Possibly he hoped that with this arrangement he would obtain a *perdão de parte* from his victim's mother and sister, facilitating his appeal for a reduced sentence. As it stood, both families had lost a son.

Inácio's case illustrated the precarious balance that some families had to maintain as a consequence of a criminal act. We do not know how and why Inácio killed Manuel, but the result was a tragedy for at least two households. The case also showed that although the crime was committed by one man against another man, four other people – three women and one man – had to deal with the aftermath in some very concrete terms. Crime, like inheritance, had less to do with the individual than with the family to which the individual belonged, and the two – crime and inheritance – were intricately connected in early modern Portugal. The former impinged on the latter; the latter mitigated the former.

---

103 ADP, Fundo Notarial, Po. 4, 1a Se, no. 33 (1642), f.111v–f.112v.

104 The law allowed for parents to disinherit their children under certain circumstances, such as when a daughter under the age of majority had sex with or married a man without parental consent (a similar prohibition did not exist for sons), when the child inflicted injuries on the parents (physical or verbal), if the child was involved in witchcraft or in heresy, and so forth. For further details, see *Ordenações Filipinas*, Livro 4, Título 88.

Women and Orphans

The road to mitigation between crime and property was a slippery slope, especially in connection to the rights of legitimate children. Inácio, discussed above, was a young adult legally capable of rescinding his entitlement, but in cases that involved minors, negotiations for pardons were more complex. As we saw with the *querela* filed on behalf of Catarina da Ascenção examined in Chapter 1, the wishes of the child's dead mother were cited in a criminal accusation pertaining to the alleged theft of that child's inherited property. Had Catarina's father wished to grant a pardon connected to that accusation, he would have had to consult and get the approval of the local authorities. The *querela* launched by Catarina's father did not label her an orphan, but technically that is what she was. In early modern Portugal, minors (under 25 years of age) were considered orphans once one of their parents was dead. Legally, this was true whether the dead parent was the mother or the father. Legislators recognized that the widowed father was holder of *patria potestas*, but the rule of the father was not absolute and in fact was arguably a social convention. Because most men named in the *querelas* or *perdões de parte* were not identified by their marital status, we do not know if some of them were widowed, but a few examples were found that showed a motherless child labelled an orphan despite the existence and presence of a father. At stake was the protection of the minor child's interests and rights of inheritance, and neither parent was legally deemed adequate to act on this alone. A third party, usually a Crown official called *Juíz dos Orfãos*, or orphan judge, was considered a more disinterested party in terms of a child's financial well-being.[105]

The legal requirement to have an orphan judge represent minor children was not followed consistently, particularly if the children were already adolescents. The legislation conferred certain adult privileges to children of an advanced age: a girl aged 12 years or more, and a boy aged 14 or more, could make decisions along with their guardians; those younger of either sex had to have a public trustee act on their behalf.[106] Undoubtedly there were cases of children who were coerced by their guardians, or whose interests were ignored, but the victim's pardon provided a mechanism to protect minor children. There is no way to know how many individuals availed of that protection, but the *perdão de parte* that dealt with very young 'orphans' was especially revealing about the fundamental link between the pardon and the relinquishment of property. Furthermore, because more women were widowed than men, these documents also highlighted women's roles as protectors of their children's rights. The last examples examined in this chapter showed that physical injuries, especially those that were fatal, had enormous and far-reaching ramifications that touched on the rights of even the unborn.

---

[105] *Ordenações Filipinas*, Livro 5, Título 102 and 135.

[106] *Ordenações Filipinas*, Livro 3, Título 41, no. 8.

The Poor Orphan

We do not know if Manuel Fernandes, resident of Estremoz, was a father or even married, but legally he was responsible for a small child whose best interests he had to seriously ponder in 1666. With that purpose in mind, on 7 May of that year Manuel visited the local notary's office in his role as guardian of Maria, orphan girl, daughter of the late Maria Rodrigues and her husband Luís Martins. Manuel presented to the notary a copy of a judicial ruling that gave him license and authority to grant a pardon to Francisco de Sande de Vilalobos for his culpability in the death of António Martins, uncle to the orphaned child and brother of her late father, a copy of which sentence was included in the text of the pardon. In fact, this document was no ordinary pardon, but a 'pardon and relinquishment of an accusation and obligation', the obligation that by law the accused had to compensate the plaintiff. In his sentence, the orphan judge explained the reasons for his ruling, and that ruling revealed much about the legal conundrum inherent in the pardon process, particularly for individuals of modest means.

The first item that the judge had to consider was the petition from Manuel (the guardian) and Francisco (the accused), both of whom requested that Manuel be given authority to give this pardon to Francisco on behalf of the minor and orphaned Maria. In his petition, dated 3 April, Francisco stated that he had been accused of the death of António Martins, his servant, for which he (Francisco) was released on bail, and the accused outlined two reasons for his petition. One, the deceased had no father or mother, nor another relative who could make any further accusation or claim against him (Francisco), except for a niece of four or five years of age, daughter of a brother of his (the deceased), the guardian of whom was Manuel Fernandes, the orphan's uncle, her late mother's brother. Two, since Manuel (the guardian) was poor and could not afford to pursue the legal case, he (the guardian) had decided to pardon Francisco. Thus, Francisco asked the judge to give the orphan's guardian permission to grant this pardon.

The second item the judge had to deal with was the appointment of the *Licenciado* João Pereira Fidalgo, a lawyer, to investigate the case and to act as public trustee for little orphan Maria. In his report, dated 9 April, the *Licenciado* concluded that the orphan was very poor and thus had no resources with which she could launch a formal accusation. With this report and the assent of the court-appointed trustee, the judge made his decision, stressing once again the poverty of the orphaned child and her lack of means to pursue her uncle's killer. On 4 May the judge signed the license to allow for the pardon to go through.

With the judge's permission in hand, Manuel Fernandes, on behalf of the orphan Maria, and of his own free will, pardoned Francisco de Sande de Vilalobos. In the document, Manuel stressed that he pardoned Francisco for the love of God, because the minor orphan did not have the means with which to make an accusation for the death of her uncle, and Manuel made all the necessary pledges on behalf of Maria's estate. The *Licenciado* was also present, and when the pardon was drawn up, he declared that, on her behalf, her guardian could grant this pardon to the supplicant. Maria's trustee signed the pardon, while her guardian made a cross. Nothing was said about the cause of death of António Martins, or about the presumed innocence of the accused killer. That was not the point of the exercise. The point was to create a paper trail showing that due process was followed on behalf of a poor orphaned girl. In the process we learn that it was legally acceptable for an accused to avoid prosecution if the surviving heir was too poor to cover the costs of a legal procedure. Her best hope was that her one living relative, her guardian and uncle Manuel Fernandes, enjoyed good health for many years, and continued to support her at least until she could earn her keep.[107]

While this *perdão de parte* made little Maria's future a little more precarious, the pardon did not clear the accused entirely. Even if Francisco de Sande de Vilalobos obtained his release through this pardon, he still could have faced an accusation for the same crime from orphan Maria once she became of age. The law granted her that right, as the *Ordenações Filipinas* (1603) outlined:

> If a person is acquitted in a case of homicide, and the relatives of the first degree, or the second degree were not notified, [if] the deceased does not have relatives in the first degree, and some of those who were not notified want to accuse [her or him] afterward, or the one acquitted notified the Guardian, or Trustee of an orphan who was entitled to accuse, the said Guardian, or Trustee did not accuse, and then the said orphan wanted to accuse [her or him], or when a person has a pardon from us [Crown], having received a pardon from the Guardian of an orphan who was entitled to accuse; it is well that, in the said cases where the relatives were not notified and as well, the male orphans up to the age of twenty-four years, and the female up to the age of twenty-two, can accuse [her or him] anew, as if [she or he] had never been acquitted, or as if [she or he] had never received a pardon, in as much as, that they accuse first.[108]

In reality, though, the likelihood of such an appeal was not very great. The same law indicated that if a case was reopened and the accused was cleared of all charges, the accuser had to pay all costs in duplicate, and all losses and damages that the accused suffered in the process. Still, Tomás y Valiente found one example in Spain of a father of a victim of physical assault who intervened even after his daughter had granted a pardon to the accused. The father claimed that he had learned that in the addition to the beatings, the accused also had had sex with his daughter, and thus the father asked that he be allowed to be a complainant as well, and his request was granted. For this reason, writers of legal treatises argued that all interested parties had to be part of the pardon.[109]

Little orphan Maria was clearly from a disadvantaged socio-economic group, and the law could not change that. Since she had little to inherit – the argument went - she had little to lose from the death of her paternal uncle and the pardon by her maternal uncle. Still, it is significant that several men had to go through the

---

[107] ADE, Fundo Notarial (Estremoz), Francisco Jorge (notary), Séries 20 (1666), f.65v–68.

[108] *Ordenações Filipinas*, Livro 5, Título 130, no. 1.

[109] Tomás y Valiente, 'El perdon de la parte', 77–9.

motions of justifying the surrender of her rightful claim, minuscule as it was. Little Maria was of course not only lacking in material wealth but also in kinship ties. She had but one impoverished uncle left to represent her, whereas children of the elite would generally have a lot more weight behind them, from blood relatives or otherwise. As will be seen with the next two examples, the legal process to deal with crime and property matters connected to poor or rich minors was ostensibly the same, but the long-term effects at the material level were significantly different.

The Wealthy Orphan

If little Maria survived to adulthood she did so through hard work, in all likelihood as a domestic servant, starting at a very young age. Certainly she did not have the resources to enjoy a prolonged childhood as the children in the next example were positioned to experience.[110] The latter, too, lived in Estremoz, and a pardon document from 17 November 1677 also affected their lives. By then, Maria would have been approximately 15 years old, and she could have been aware of this powerful family, maybe as an employee in their elite household. This second pardon from Estremoz features *Dona* Maria de Castro, widowed lady of the late Gaspar de Lemos de Vargas; her daughter, *Dona* Camila, 17 years old, for whom *Dona* Maria was the guardian; and *Dona* Inês de Castro de Vasconcelos, widowed lady of the late Gaspar da Mota Mascarenhas, guardian of her son of seven years of age, Gaspar de Lemos. Also present at the home of *Dona* Maria, where the notary went to meet the elite ladies, was João Pereira Fidalgo, identified as a lawyer and trustee for minors, the same functionary who had dealt with little orphan Maria's case. Same town and same court official, and both pardons dealt with a homicide and the interests of minor orphans, but the similarities ended there. Whereas little Maria and her guardian lacked the resources to pursue the accused more than a decade earlier, there is no reason to believe that such would have been a concern for the above-named children and their guardians.

In their pardon, the two adult women, acting for themselves and as guardians of their minor children, stated that 20 years earlier, as far as they remembered, there had been a duel in which Rui de Lemos Sagalo was injured. Rui was the stepson of *Dona* Maria, half-brother of *Dona* Camila, brother-in-law of *Dona* Inês, and uncle of her son, Gaspar. Within days of this injury, Rui died, after which there was an inquiry in Estremoz, and António Pereira de Melo, resident in Evora, was denounced for being one of the 'padrinhos' – that is, a witness or a second at the duel.[111] But since António had been a particular good friend of Rui, and was not implicated in his death, D. Maria and D. Inês, on their behalf and on behalf of their minor children, forgave António for all the culpa linked to Rui's death.

---

[110] For a discussion of the varying types of childhood, depending on the wealth of families, see Mendelson and Crawford, *Women in Early Modern England*, especially Chapter 2.

[111] Duels were prohibited in early modern Portugal, and the harsh penalties against the practice applied to those who assisted in the duel, as well. *Ordenações Filipinas*, Livro 5, Título 43.

The trustee for minors also agreed with the contents of the pardon, and on behalf of the pardoned (António), the notary was presented with a judgement from the orphan judge, in which document a reference was made to a petition from António to the orphan judge. As was the case with little Maria, this petition showed that António requested assurances that the minor children could legally grant this pardon, and so the judge nominated a trustee for minors and gave him judicial jurisdiction to act on behalf of those minors. The two mothers, as guardians of their minor children, responded favourably to António's petition. With the acquiescence of all interested parties, the judge granted António license to seek a victim's pardon. On behalf of herself and as guardian of her daughter, *Dona* Maria signed her full name, *Da Maria de Castro Salboa*, as did her daughter, *Da Camila de Lemos e Castro*, and *Da Inês de Castro e Vasconcelos*. The document gave no explanation for the 20-year lapse between the fatal incident and the granting of the pardon.[112]

We do not know what happened to António Pereira de Melo after he was denounced, but given that he sought a victim's pardon 20 years after the fact showed that his status was still uncertain after all that time. Perhaps he had been a fugitive and wished to return home. The tone of *Dona* Maria and *Dona* Inês' pardon suggested that the wealthy could more afford to prolong the dispute if it was to their advantage. Alternatively, there could have been other factors that had an impact on the final outcome, including the two women's widowhood. Since *Dona* Maria's stepson had died 20 years earlier, it is possible that he had been killed before his father had remarried, and before *Dona* Inês had married the victim's brother. The one hint for this hypothesis is that both women had younger children, one a 17-year-old daughter, and the other a seven-year-old son. Perhaps the defendant had tried but was unsuccessful in his bid to obtain a pardon from the two patriarchs, the father and the brother of the deceased, but once they died, their respective wives were more approachable because they had less of an emotional investment in the original catastrophe. Nevertheless, both women and their children had a vested interest in the broad renunciation that the *perdão de parte* implied. As guardians of their children, the two women yielded significant power and authority regardless of the input from the orphan judge. The appointment of an orphan judge was not dependent on the gender of the surviving parent or guardian.

The conventions that had surviving parents act on behalf of their minor children was followed by widows and widowers alike, but their guardianship did not preclude the intervention of the orphan judge or a court-appointed trustee for 'orphans'. This was true whether the surviving parent was a mother or a father as seen in a *perdão de parte* from Porto dated 5 April 1657, granted by João Dalpoim da Silva, *Fidalgo da Casa de Sua Majestidade*. As a knight of the royal household, D. João was certainly deemed responsible enough to act on behalf of his six children, all from Viana do Castelo: Bernardo Dalpoim de Abreu, Paulo Coelho da Silva, Jerónimo Dalpoim da Silva, *Dona* Feliciana da Silva, *Dona* Isabel da

---

112 ADE, Fundo Notarial (Estremoz), Francisco Jorge (notary), Séries 28 (1677), f.128–131.

Silva, and *Dona* Lianor da Silva.[113] But in order to grant this pardon that affected the children, D. João had to obtain a license and authority from the orphan judge, which license he presented to the notary. D. João also had a power of attorney from *Dona* Madalena Prego, his mother-in-law and grandmother of the minor children, and another one from *Dona* Antónia da Silva, a nun in the monastery of Santa Ana in Viana do Castelo, daughter of *Dona* Madalena and the children's aunt. Interestingly, the notary deemed it necessary to stipulate that the respective powers of attorney were 'feitas e assinadas por suas letras' – both women had signed their names to the documents in question.

With all the necessary documentation in hand, on behalf of himself, the six children, and the two women, D. João pardoned Baltesar Coelho da Silva and his son Alvaro Coelho da Silva, *Fidalgos da Casa de Sua Majestade* (knights of His Majesty's household), residents in Vila de Amarante. Baltesar and Alvaro were at the time in the prison of the *Relação do Porto* (Court of Appeal in Porto), having been sentenced to death, and to the confiscation of all their property. Both men had been found guilty of killing *Dona* Luísa da Silva, daughter of *Dona* Madalena Prego, sister of *Dona* Antónia da Silva and of *Dona* Maria da Silva, deceased. The latter was the late wife of João Dalpoim da Silva, and mother of the minor children. Thus, D. João was a widower with six minor children, and he represented a number of individuals in a pardon granted to the killers of his sister-in-law, a woman killed by two men very close to her: Alvaro had been her husband and first cousin; Baltesar had been her father-in-law and uncle.[114]

Although the pardon document did not reveal the particulars surrounding the murder of *Dona* Luísa da Silva, and of the ultimate fate of her murderers, it showcased yet again the extent to which the victim's pardon was part of a complex system that encompassed rights of inheritance, the rights of which necessitated additional judicial protections in the case of minor children. Even little orphan Maria discussed earlier had rights to inherit from an uncle who had been killed, though due to her poverty her rights were extinguished by her guardian and court-appointed trustee. It is possible that her guardian made an out-of-court settlement on her behalf with the accused killer before agreeing to grant a pardon. It is also probable that the deceased uncle had little property for little Maria to inherit. On the other side of the spectrum, the six minor children of the widowed knight were clearly part of a wealthy and powerful family whose members had no financial constraints to prevent them from pursuing a lawsuit against the convicted murderers of their kinswoman.

The example of the six noble children also showed that a court-appointed trustee was necessary to advocate for the children's portion of any legal settlement, whether they were poor and orphaned of both parents, or 'orphans' with one wealthy and powerful father. True, in the pardon document discussed above, the *fidalgo*'s children were called minors, not orphans, but that was a mere question of semantics, again, for the purposes of maintaining a patriarchal stance. The lines

113 The document indicated that the six children were minors between the ages of 12 and 14, which was highly unlikely, unless there were sets of twins or triplets.

114 ADP, Fundo Notarial, Po. 1, 4a Se, no. 147 (1657), f.207–208.

between widows' 'orphan' children and widowers' 'minor' children were blurred and often inconsequential. The widowed knight in Porto had to deal with similar officialdom, and obtain the same licenses, as the two widowed ladies in Estremoz, and the socially inferior guardian of orphan Maria. The law that aimed to protect the rights of inherited property applied to rich and poor, young and old, male and female. As the next example illustrates, the law even applied to the unborn, a stipulation that once again gave women another avenue through which they exercised their legal rights on behalf of their future children.

The Unborn Orphan

The archival evidence showed that women and children were more likely to lose a spouse or parent, or some other family member, due to violent acts committed by men rather than women. Ironically, though, one of the most intriguing examples found of women exercising their rights as pardoners, and of their roles as guardians of their children, was connected to two pardons granted in Angra (Terceira), to a woman accused of homicide. Catarina Pacheca, *dona viúva* or widowed lady of the late Constantino Machado, received her first pardon on 14 March 1603 from João Pamplona de Miranda, in which document João declared that he was 'moved by this holy time and that we are in Lent and the said Catarina Pacheca is his relative and she has many children it pleased him to pardon her'. At the same time, he withdrew all denunciations and accusations he had made against Catarina for the death of his brother, António Pamplona de Miranda. Two days later, on 16 March 1603, from her apartment in the Castelo São Cristovão, Filipa Frois, widowed lady of the late António Pamplona de Miranda, also granted a pardon to Catarina for any role that Catarina may have had in the death of Filipa's husband. Filipa was also moved by 'the love of God our lord and for the holy time in which we are [presently]'.[115]

The circumstances of the death of António Pamplona de Miranda, and the evidence against Catarina Pacheca in causing that death, are not known, but her household was certainly struck with its share of troubles. Three years before Catarina received her two pardons, her son also received a pardon related to another homicide, and this earlier pardon shed light on some particularly intricate details about the rights of 'orphan' children. Beatriz Gonçalves, widowed lady of the late António Fernandes, granted a pardon on 23 September 1600 to Pedro Pacheco, identified as son of Constantino Machado. In her statement Beatriz claimed that back in May her husband was found in the bush, dead from some injuries inflicted on him. At the time Beatriz filed a denunciation and accusation against Pedro, but 'due to the uncertainty of the case and other considerations and inconveniences', she was prepared to pardon him.

An ordinary pardon would have ended there, but this was no ordinary case. Further to her renunciation of any claims against Pedro for any damages owed her, Beatriz stated that she had petitioned the local judge to inform him of her doubts regarding Pedro's culpability in her husband's death, and the costs involved in

[115] BPARAH, Fundo Notarial (Angra), no. 3 (1602–1603), f.94v–95v, f.100–100v.

the legal process. More importantly, Beatriz told the judge that given that upon the death of her husband she had been pregnant, and still was at the time of her petition, she requested that André Fernandes de Cea, city procurator, be named trustee of the posthumous child that she carried in her womb ('postumo que no ventre trazia'). The judge acquiesced and ruled that André be the *procurador ao posthumo*, or procurator of the posthumous child.

A posthumous child is a child born after the father's death. The Portuguese Civil Code in effect in the twentieth century still referred to the *curador do ventre* or 'trustee of the womb', the person who looked after the interests of a posthumous child. According to the law, such a child was entitled to all inheritance rights as long as it was viable at birth and lived for at least 300 days from the date of the father's death.[116] It was in this context that Beatriz sought to ensure that her pardon was legally binding because her decision had an impact on the inheritance potential of the baby she carried; as an unborn 'orphan', her child needed a third party to act independently on its behalf.[117] For this reason André, 'procurator of the posthumous', also granted Pedro a pardon.[118]

This extra precaution was deemed necessary because a sole parent could ostensibly make decisions contrary to the interests of minor children. Given that the unborn child's representative was named by its mother, the exercise was more of a formality than an intrusion by the authorities to curtail her rights. As seen in the example discussed above of the six minor children, their widowed father also had to provide a third party who represented the interests of his children. The victim's pardon, therefore, was not a simple transaction between those who were directly subjected to and those who committed violence, most of whom were men. The victim's pardon is a unique venue through which to study the broader ramifications of a gamut of conflicts that confronted families and individuals. Women were not the majority of pardoners, but they were involved in *pardoning* in a significant way. Historians have started to question the archival record from the early modern period in new ways, by looking beyond the *noun* as an identifier of what people *were*, and finding instead the *verb* as a descriptor of what people *did*. Such methodological tools allow for a more inclusive historical analysis, an analysis that reveals more fully the multi-faceted activities of women and men in pre-modern Europe.[119]

---

116 *Lello Universal: Novo Diccionário Encyclopédico Luso-Brasileiro*, 2 vols (Porto: Lello & Irmão Editores/Propietários da Livraria Chardon, 1938), II: 746.

117 For the law that dealt with claims of a false pregnancy, and the related inheritance rights following the death of the pregnant woman's husband, see *Ordenações Filipinas*, Livro 5, Título 55. For an example of a widow accused of falsifying her pregnancy, see Rosa, *O Morgadio em Portugal*, 167–8.

118 BPARAH, Fundo Notarial (Angra), no. 1 (1600), f.123–124v.

119 I was fortunate to participate in some fascinating discussions around the 'verb' in women's history that took place at the 'Gender and work in early modern Europe' workshop, Stockholm, Sweden, 10–11 May 2012, organized by Maria Ågren; and again at the 'Women's work across time and space: foundations for comparison in pre-census Europe' workshop, Glasgow, Scotland, 11–12 September 2014, organized by Alex Shepard. I am grateful to all the participants in those workshops for their engaging feminist analysis, and for stirring the pot of women's history.

Beatriz's pardon referred to 'other considerations and inconveniences', and one suspects that that vague statement was at the heart of many pardons, a euphemistic expression that covered a gamut of possibilities. It pointed to the likelihood of an out-of-court settlement, such as the one we saw with the case of Inácio, his parents, and Inácio's victims. Beatriz's case also highlighted the ramifications of violent acts for women and their children, in some cases 'orphaned' before they were born. Although fatherless from birth, Beatriz's child would be born into an elite family, and consequently live a different life than that of the little orphan Maria noted earlier. Death of a parent or relative was undoubtedly devastating for all families implicated in the tragedy, but the economic impact was greater for some than others. It is worth remembering, after all, that little Maria's dead uncle had been killed by his own master, a factor that could have entered into the application of the law. The law was one thing, and justice was quite another.

In his analysis of 'el perdon de la parte' in early modern Spain, Tomás y Valiente observed that because the agreement recorded in the victim's pardon could be seen as a confession of guilt by the accused, the culprit had to be careful about the wording of the pardon sought from the victim. Even the willingness of the accused to pay for reparations could be interpreted as an avowal of her or his responsibility; for this reason, the majority of victims' pardons pretended that they had been granted for free. Nevertheless, Tomás y Valiente concluded that although the majority of those documents stressed the appearance of 'gratuidad', the victim's pardon was negotiated in monetary terms, even if it was written to appear otherwise. One way this payment was camouflaged was through the use of such expressions as the accused had been 'of great help' or 'of good service' to the plaintiff. The need to have the victim's pardon appear to have been a benevolent act on the part of the plaintiff had to be balanced with the need of some culprits to have proof of payment. The idea was to avoid the likelihood that the pardon granted to the accused be used against the accused. The extent to which negotiations took place before the victim's pardon was written up can be seen in the case that Tomás y Valiente found of a woman who settled for half of what the sentence had ordered be paid to her by the culprit.[120] An even less plausible scenario was discovered in another study of a pardoner who offered to pay the expenses for medical treatment needed by the individual he was pardoning.[121]

Although the *perdão de parte* and its antecedent, the *querela*, dealt with critical steps in the operation of criminal law in early modern Portugal, neither set of documents indicated how the law was actually implemented in each case. Portuguese legislation promoted a hierarchical application of laws and punishments according to the individual's rank and status, and the *querela* and *perdão de parte* hinted at such social hierarchies in the ways people self-identified, or the scribes identified them. As already seen, the documents made distinctions between a widowed woman ('mulher viúva') and a widowed lady ('dona viúva'). Those of the nobility, especially, were dutifully noted with their titles, *Dona* for

[120] Tomás y Valiente, 'El perdon de la parte', 61–71.

[121] Silva and Cardoso, 'Escrituras de perdão', 189–90.

women, *Dom* for men. Note that the three *donas* in the case discussed earlier about a duel signed their names *and* titles.

Commoners, for their part, were registered by their names only, but the records showed that commoners, too, cared to differentiate themselves from those they considered beneath their dignity. This attitude was particularly conspicuous in a *querela* that Ana Gomes filed on 18 September 1629. Ana was a prisoner in Ponta Delgada's city jail when she filed a complaint against Tomé Rodrigues, the jail guard. In her complaint Ana stated that she was 'a woman of good repute' and that she was scandalized by the mistreatment she had received from the jail guard. Ana petitioned the local judge, and he sent a scribe to take down her statement, in which statement Ana declared that Tomé had beaten her with a bull's pizzle, in front of the other female prisoners.[122] The scribe vouched for the numerous black and bloody marks on Ana's body, including on her arms, legs, and buttocks (see Appendix 4).[123]

Ana was incarcerated for an undisclosed infraction of her own, but she maintained a certain distance from her cell mates, a position that was compromised by the humiliation the jail guard inflicted on her. As Elizabeth Cohen has shown, questions of honour were important to the socially marginal as well as the elite.[124] Adherence to one's rank or station was an important component of early modern societies, an element of social capital that was rigorously safeguarded by women and men alike. Our last example of 'orphans' and inheritance rights highlighted this concern, and the determination of one irate mother intent on protecting her interests which were intricately connected to her son, the heir apparent to the family estate.

The Orphan Gone Astray

Cecília Ramalha de Queiros believed that her son was in danger, the reasons for which she knew only too well, the source of which she was determined to terminate. In her *querela* dated 11 April 1644, Cecília was identified as *dona viúva* or widowed lady of the late Manuel Lopes Anriques, a title associated with members of the upper ranks, and the crux of her concern was a breach of the proper social order. In effect, Cecília appeared before the *Ouvidor Geral*, or Crown magistrate in Ponta Delgada, 'to accuse and denounce the defendants [daughters] of the widow of [the late] Manuel Alves Cardoso *físico* [physician]'. This latter widow was never identified in the record, and for good reason. Although she was certainly part of the problem, the real source of contention for the plaintiff was the widow's daughters, 'Maria de São João who now calls herself Maria Alves de Sousa and other daughters called Amaral and more single daughters *que por nome*

122 The Oxford English Dictionary defines pizzle as 'a penis of an animal, esp. a bull (formerly used as a whip)'.

123 BPARPD, *Livro de Autos de Querelas*, f.66v–67v.

124 Elizabeth S. Cohen, 'Honor and Gender in the Streets of Early Modern Rome', *Journal of Interdisciplinary History* 22, no. 4 (Spring 1992): 597–625. For a look at a Portuguese noble's sense of honour, see Gouveia, 'A linhagem ou o tempo', passim.

não percam. This expression showed up in the manuscript on several occasions, seemingly in reference to people whose names were unknown, or perhaps deemed unimportant at that moment.

Cecília's account was convoluted and betrayed a frenzy that perhaps befitted her agitated state of mind, or the work of an extremely sloppy scribe, or a bit of both.[125] Regardless, the report implied that the unidentified widow had so many single daughters that naming them all would be tedious. The impression that the plaintiff created was that the case concerned a household of a multitude of unruly women, where the late physician's tools of the trade were perhaps being tampered with, for Cecília stated that the reason for her denunciation was that these women were publicly known for being witches and sorceresses ('bruxas e feiticeiras') who gave concoctions and potions ('caldos e beberagens') to people, to do good to some, and evil to others. And evil they had committed, not to Cecília herself, but to João Carvalho Benavides, her son, making him lose his mind with foods and broths 'in the bed where he slept'. It is unclear whether those foods and broths were applied in his bed, or if he showed signs of losing his mind while he slept in his bed after having consumed the foods and broths. Either way, Cecília stressed that her son was deranged to the point that he claimed he wanted to marry the defendant, Maria de São João, even though she was known for being a public woman and a witch. According to Cecília, this showed that the accused gave her son broths and potions, which he acknowledged, but he said that the broths did him good. Thus, lamented the mother, he accepted that which made him lose his mind. Such an attitude was incomprehensible, she argued, for her son was a minor, and a good student, and a nobleman.

To Cecília, her son's acceptance of the situation was proof of his delirium and of the women's guilt in causing that delirium, for a man of his social position would never stoop so low, if he were in his right mind. To substantiate her claim, Cecília presented those women as renowned users of love potions, insisting that the accused were accustomed to giving men drinks with certain ingredients to make men want them, and, consequently, those women unsettled ('descasar') married men, and took their sons from their mothers, offending their lineage in the process.

> And with the said potions [they] kill men and create a public scandal as they did to Manuel de Galhegos and Dionisio de Oliveira and Mateus de Morais a student cousin of the plaintiff and they locked a male child ['menino'] in an oven to do witchcraft and potions which child was found and seen by some persons with many bloody cups.

[125] For instance, the accused were erroneously referred to as 'crelosas'. The term 'querelosa' (female), 'quereloso' (male) or 'querelante' refers to an accuser or plaintiff, whereas the accused or defendant is the 'querelada' (female) or 'querelado' (male). The scribe ought to have known the difference, yet he confused the terms throughout the document, unless he purposely took down Cecília's words, verbatim.

Cecília finished her account by referring to a specific royal ordinance, found in the 'Livro Quinto Titolo Terceiro', which stated that those who committed villainous crimes would get serious penalties ('penas gravissimas').[126] It is not clear whether she came up with this reference on her own, or if she was coached by someone well versed in the law, but Cecília was literate enough to sign the document, a rarity for women in early modern Portugal. She also went to the justices well-armed with 'evidence', including the names of more than 20 witnesses, of whom at least 13 were women, some of whom were anonymous, *que por nome não percam.*[127]

This *querela* document did not refer to Cecília's son as an 'orphan', but as we have seen, the law considered him an 'orphan'. As a minor, he was still under his widowed mother's authority, an authority she exercised to influence the company he kept, especially female company. Her account revealed much about the wrath of an angry mother who was outraged at the alleged manipulation of her son by some cunning women, to the detriment of her family's social standing, a position she was ready to defend with unmitigated vigour. Cecília's narrative also showed that women were not a homogenous group joined together in their struggles against a common patriarchal enemy. Cecília's enemy at the time of her *querela* was an uppity woman who allegedly seduced a young nobleman with conventional tricks of the trade, potions and whatnot. For good measure, the widowed mother associated Maria de São João with witchcraft and all its accoutrements, including the sacrificial baby in the oven and the bloody cups. These were serious allegations and there was little doubt that *Dona* Cecília would not be taken seriously by authorities. The *Ouvidor Geral*, too, was from the elite, and he would have understood the dangers implicit and explicit in this *querela.*[128]

* * *

All the cases discussed in this chapter dealt with criminal acts that significantly affected women and children. The cases provided some insight into the accommodations that those crimes precipitated, as individuals and families attempted to protect their interests. As daughters, sisters, wives, and mothers, women were an integral part of those negotiations that had an impact on their property and of that of their dependents. *Dona* Cecília was another matter. Although she claimed that a crime had already been committed, her real fear was what loomed in the future if the course of events remained unchecked. For Cecília, the worst crime was yet to happen, the potential nuptials – and the property

126 Cecília's account in fact referred to the *Ordenações Filipinas*, Livro 5, Título 3, which deals with witchcraft, and that section specifies that those involved in the activities she described could face the death penalty.

127 BPARPD, *Livro de Autos de Querelas*, f.129v–131.

128 For a study that examines superstitions about women and their mysterious potions, see Benedita Araújo, *Superstições populares portuguesas: contribuição para um estudo* (Lisbon: Edições Colibri, 1997), 60.

transfers that those nuptials entailed – between her noble son and a woman of the lower ranks with seemingly even lower morals.

Cecília's *querela* referred to a motley crew of women involved in diabolical rituals, but as the only woman clearly identified, Maria de São João, alias Maria Alves de Sousa, was the widow's true nemesis and the target of the denunciation. By pointing out that the defendant had changed her name, Cecília underscored Maria's duplicity, a 'public woman' donning a new identity to ensnare an unsuspecting young man of such high quality that only witchcraft could have led him astray. One can well imagine the *perdão de parte* that this case would generate, if *Dona* Cecília could ever be compelled to such magnanimity. Such a pardon would undoubtedly impose a non-negotiable condition on Maria: leave the young man, and leave the island.

The accusation of witchcraft was a clever calculation on the part of *Dona* Cecília because the allusion to Maria's unbridled sexuality could have been insufficient for a conviction.[129] Sex outside of marriage was generally not prosecuted in early modern Portugal, unless it was connected to explicit sexual crimes such as rape, seduction, adultery, or concubinage, or unless a woman 'did it with more than one man' – that is, women who were associated with prostitution.[130] A man faced prosecution for 'doing it' with any man, but the sexual double standard that privileged men – especially men of privilege – was entrenched in law and in practice.[131] There was no legal or social penalty against a man who 'did it' with more than one woman, unless his actions threatened the integrity of a household, his or another man's. As will be shown in the next chapter, sexual crimes had a greater impact on women because of women's vulnerability to sexual assault, unwanted pregnancy, and accusations of adultery. Nevertheless, the sources indicated that the vagaries of life necessitated much compromise and negotiation.

Both samples of documentation used for this study – the *querela* and the *perdão de parte* – provided a few examples with which we can examine the constraints and options open to women faced with a sexual crime committed against

---

[129] There was no witch hunt per se in early modern Portugal, but witchcraft was punishable. See José Pedro Paiva, *Bruxaria e superstição num país sem 'caça às bruxas', 1600–1774*, 2nd ed. (Lisbon: Notícias Editorial, 2002).

[130] In fact, the legislation focussed on those who kept brothels, or aided women to 'harm themselves', and not on prostitution per se. *Ordenações Filipinas*, Livro 5, Título 32 and 33. For a discussion of some popular views on prostitution as depicted in the plays of Gil Vicente, see Kathryn Bishop-Sánchez, 'Por detrás das alcoviteiras: prostituição e libertinagem na obra de Gil Vicente', in *Gil Vicente 500 Anos Depois: Actas do Congresso Internacional realizado pelo Centro de Estudos de Teatro da Faculdade de Letras da Universidade de Lisboa*, 2 vols (Lisbon: Imprensa Nacional – Casa da Moeda, 2003), I: 9–24.

[131] For a discussion of sodomy laws in early modern Portugal, see Francis A. Dutra, 'Sodomy and the Portuguese Nobility: The Case of Dom Filipe de Moura and His Circle', in Harold Johnson and Francis A. Dutra, eds, *Pelo Vaso Traseiro: Sodomy and Sodomites in Luso-Brazilian History* (Tucson: Fenestra Books, 2007), 165–94.

themselves, or against their female kin. These examples serve to highlight the unique position of early modern Portuguese women vis-à-vis questions of crime and forgiveness at a more personal level than the other criminal cases already discussed. Any focus on women, sex, and crime runs the risk of perpetuating the idea of women's victimization, but these cases also provide an opportunity to see women's ingenuity in the face of adversary.

Chapter 3
Querelas and *Perdões de Parte* for Sexual Crimes

In an account of his travels through northern Portugal in the mid-sixteenth century, Doctor João de Barros recollected the story of a woman who told him that she had been sentenced to hang for a 'shameful and immoral' crime, but when she approached the gallows she prayed to the Glorious Virgin to help her. The authorities hanged her and returned next day to take down the corpse, only to find the woman still alive. Stupefied by what they saw, the authorities asked the hanging woman what had happened, and she told them that the Virgin Mary had appeared and held up her body so that she would not die. Cutting the noose right off would have been more efficient, but a woman at the end of her tether was not likely to complain. Nevertheless, a new hearing was held and the woman was sentenced again, this time to perpetual exile in São Tomé, but the boat in which she was to sail could never leave port as long as she was on board, again ostensibly due to the Virgin's intervention. The woman, whose identity the author did not reveal, was eventually released.[1]

The doctor also did not reveal the nature of the 'shameful and immoral' crime that the unidentified woman had committed, but chances are that he referred to adultery, for female adultery was subject to the death penalty. Yet, as the story revealed, sometimes that severe penalty was mitigated by certain circumstances, and not miraculous circumstances alone. At the terrestrial level, the occasional pardon could be just as effective. In addition to female adultery, other sex-related crimes were punishable by death, including rape, incest, and sodomy, but with the exception of the latter, few of those convicted of sex-related crimes were executed.[2] This chapter looks at a number of cases that dealt with sexual crimes and examines the strategies available to women accused of wrongdoing (adultery and concubinage), and women as accusers of harm inflicted on them (concubinage and rape).

Of the 224 victims' pardons collected for this study, only 25 dealt explicitly with sexual crimes: 11 for rape/defloration, 10 for adultery, and 4 for concubinage. In the sample of 94 *querelas*, there were 3 cases of concubinage and 9 of rape/defloration, for a total of 12 judicial complaints of sexual crimes. This is a very

---

1 (Dr.) João de Barros, *Geographia d'entre Douro e Minho e Tras-os-Montes* (Porto: Bibliotéca Pública Municipal do Porto/Tipografia Progresso de Domingos Augusto da Silva, 1919 [1549?]), 115–16.

2 Correia, 'A Evolução Histórica'; Hespanha, 'Da "Iustitia" à "Disciplina"'; Ramos, *Violência e Justiça*; Ribeiro, 'Convívios difíceis'; Araújo, 'Cerimónias de execução'.

small sample from an already small corpus. The low number of *perdões de parte* and *querelas* related to accusations of sexual crimes could be a sign that those crimes were not considered a problem in early modern Portugal, or that sexual crimes were not reported, or that such crimes were not dealt with at the notary's office. According to the royal ordinances, there were some sexual crimes that were not pardonable, such as sodomy and bestiality. Those cases were usually dealt with by the Inquisition, but even with that ominous machine there was room for negotiation.[3]

The more plausible reason for the scarcity of references to sexual crimes, in the notary and judicial records, is that, in cases of rape in particular, there was a low rate of reporting the assault. Some statistics from the late twentieth century showed that only about 10 per cent of women who had been raped reported the attack to the police, largely because many women feared being re-victimized in the process.[4] As will be discussed later, the cultural understandings for rape in the early modern period were different from those of the twentieth and twenty-first centuries, and historians continue to struggle with the terminology of the time.[5] Whatever term used, though, remaining silent must have been an option for more than a few women, then as in now.

Even a cursory look at the number of cases related to rape or defloration (see Table 1.1 and Table 1.3) reveals a significant disconnect between the two sources. The random sample of victims' pardons comes from various districts in Portugal, and spans from the sixteenth to the eighteenth centuries, yet only 11 *perdões de parte* were located related to rape/defloration. The *querelas*, for their part, cover a period of approximately 20 years, and dealt almost exclusively with the Ponta Delgada district, yet this small sample contained nine accusations of rape/defloration. Moreover, one other study of *querelas* from Ponta Delgada in the eighteenth century showed that of the 667 denunciations recorded during that period, 111 were for rape/defloration.[6] In the absence of other supporting documentation, it appears that the vast majority of accusations of this sort did not lead to an official victim's pardon.

Despite the small number of cases found that were linked to sexual crimes in the sixteenth and seventeenth centuries, this topic warrants its own discussion because of what these cases tell us about women as women. In Chapter 2 women were examined as pardoners and as those who were pardoned for crimes that

---

3 For a look at the Inquisition and sexual deviance in early modern Portugal, see the collected studies in Harold Johnson and Francis A. Dutra, eds, *Pelo Vaso Traseiro: Sodomy and Sodomites in Luso-Brazilian History* (Tucson: Fenestra Books, 2007).

4 See, for example, Janice Du Mont and Deborah Parnis, 'Judging Women: The Pernicious Effects of Rape Mythology', *Canadian Woman Studies/les cahiers de la femme* 19, no. 1/2 (1999): 102–9.

5 For a discussion of the challenges with determining the social meanings of rape in the early modern period, see Elizabeth S. Cohen, 'The Trials of Artemisia Gentileschi: A Rape as History', *Sixteenth Century Journal* 31, no. 1 (Spring 2000): 47–75.

6 Rodrigues, 'Criminalidade e Violência', Table 1.

happened most often to and between men. The examination of the cases about physical injuries and homicide showed the extent to which women could and did negotiate *along* with their men in areas of common interest. That equation existed less with sexual crimes. Women were accused of adultery by their husbands, never the other way around, for male adultery was considered a sin, not a crime; women were raped by men, not the reverse; and in cases of keeping a brothel or living in concubinage, the laws were ostensibly the same for women and men, but those laws were applied unevenly. Even when the law caught up with the male adulterer, concubine, or brothel keeper, the socio-economic repercussions those men faced were not the same as those that awaited women for similar crimes. The most obvious differences were that men were never labelled whores, and men did not get pregnant. In the early modern period, biology, with a generous dosage of social constructs, was a significant determinant in many women's lives.

Within the context of state legislation as well as some church and municipal accounts, the *querelas* and the *perdãos de parte* that dealt with sexual crimes are evaluated here to highlight the specificity of some women's experiences. The *querela* sample showed women as accusers (rape and concubinage), and accused (adultery and concubinage). In the *perdão de parte*, women were found as pardoners (rape) and sometimes as the pardoned (adultery and concubinage), and in both accounts we get glimpses into some of the social mores of the time, and how women negotiated around those borders. Through the prism of a few cases of adultery, concubinage, and rape or defloration, this last chapter examines crimes that had a greater impact on women than men, and raises some questions particular to women's lives. The examples showed that women were not necessarily defenceless against their aggressors, and that commonly women were defended by their families. The sources also showed that in the social, economic, and political climate of the sixteenth and seventeenth centuries, there was a great need for a lot of compromise and accommodation, between women and men, and among family members and neighbours.

Women and Adultery

In his discussion of marriage, the sixteenth-century Portuguese cleric Frei Amador Arrais lamented that too many marriages were initiated for carnal pleasures, a sin that he associated mainly with lecherous husbands. In fact, he insisted that if husbands loved their wives properly, there would be no adultery, and he was particularly critical of male adulterers, pointing out that 'the day that a married man decides to become an adulterer, and to engage with another woman, on that day he starts a fire on his honour, estate, house, and puts his life and person at great risk'.[7] The cleric clearly perceived that there was a serious social problem with married men engaged in adulterous affairs, but the archival evidence does

---

7 Frei Amador Arrais, *Diálogos*, Fidelino de Figueiredo, ed. (Lisbon: Livraria Sá da Costa, 1944 [1589?]), 265–8.

not support such a view.[8] As Tables 1.1 and 1.2 indicate, only 10 cases of adultery were found among the pardons, and none in the *querela* sample.[9]

The church maintained that adultery was a grievous sin for both women and men, but historians have detected some inconsistencies in the ways those ideals were upheld. For instance, the most renowned Portuguese Jesuit priest, Padre António Vieira (1608–1697), delivered a sermon in which he indicated that women and wine were the most powerful entities in the world because both were the ruin of men.[10] Moreover, a study of Spanish women's petitions to church authorities for separation from their husbands showed that the church considered applications under two reasons only: abuse and adultery, and the latter option was open only to cuckolded husbands.[11] There was, of course, no option of a divorce in Catholic Europe, but in certain Protestant regions, where women had an outlet, they used it, as in the case of early modern Norway where, according to one study, the second most common reason cited for divorce was adultery, and women were at least half of the plaintiffs in most regions examined.[12]

The situation in early modern Portugal appeared to have been more conservative around questions of adultery. In questions of sexual deviance in general, there was an ideological double standard that favoured one sex over another, and this ideology was especially pronounced in the laws that dealt with unfaithful spouses. As one historian has explained, Portuguese legislation on adultery in the early modern period followed two distinct influences, one from Roman law, and the other from canonical law. In Roman law, adultery was a violation of the conjugal law, that is, in the exclusivity that the wife owed to her husband in sexual relations. At the core of this sentiment was the guarantee of the paternity of the children born in matrimony, and, thus, adultery could only be committed by a married woman and her lover, not by a married man and a single woman. In canon law, adultery was a violation of conjugal fidelity, and thus both parties could commit adultery. In Portugal's royal ordinances, the definition of adultery followed the Roman law, in that adultery by the husband was not punished, and the offended husband was authorized to kill the adulterous

---

8 Some literature of the period also stressed the need for conjugal fidelity, especially that of husbands. Maria de Lurdes Correia Fernandes, '(Re)Constructions des Images du Couple dans la Péninsule Ibérique aux XVIe et XVIIe Siècles', *Histoire Economie et Société* 21, no. 2 (2002): 133–44.

9 A study that looked at 667 *querelas* from the eighteenth century found only seven cases related to adultery. Rodrigues, 'Criminalidade e Violência', Table 1.

10 António Soares Marques, 'A Mulher nos Sermões do Pe António de Vieira', *MATHESIS* 2 (1993): 130 [121–41].

11 Edward J. Behrend-Martínez, '"She Wanted to Be Her Own Master": Women's Suits against Impotent and Abusive Husbands in a Spanish Church Court, 1650–1750', Ph.D. Thesis (University of Chicago, 2002), 87.

12 Hanne Marie Johansen, 'Marriage Trouble, Separation and Divorce in Early Modern Norway', in Maria Ågren and Amy Louise Erickson, eds, *The Marital Economy in Scandinavia and Britain, 1400–1900* (Burlington: Ashgate, 2005), 177 [175–89].

wife and her lover, but not the other way around. There was no such thing as a cuckolded wife.[13]

While state legislation condemned adulterous wives more than adulterous husbands, it is worth noting that the relevant sections in the *Ordenações Manuelinas* and the *Ordenações Filipinas* are both entitled 'Do que dorme com molher casada' – on he who sleeps with a married woman – and the opening statement in that section declared that 'We establish that all men who commit adultery with a married woman, and who is known for being a married woman, that he die for it', unless the man in question was of a higher station than the injured husband, in which case the Crown reserved the right to determine the fate of the (male) adulterer. If the order in which legal clauses were listed can be said to be indicative of anything, one could argue that at the forefront of the legislators' concerns was first, that men not corrupt other men's wives, and second, that the hierarchical superiority of some men over other men and women be maintained.[14] Aside from this preamble, though, the remainder of that section on adultery, which consisted of an additional eight clauses in the *Ordenações Manuelinas* and 10 in the *Ordenações Filipinas*, dealt more directly with the legal penalties to be imposed on an adulterous wife.[15]

The legislation also stipulated that only a husband could accuse his wife of adultery, and that if she was found guilty of the charge, she and her lover faced the death penalty.[16] The husband could also pardon his wife for the alleged adultery, and in such a case the wife's lover was not to be killed but exiled instead. In the early sixteenth century, the law indicated that the guilty lover would be exiled perpetually to São Tomé unless the injured husband had not accused him, in which case judicial officials would take up the accusation and exile the culprit for 10 years to some place in Africa. If the husband pardoned his wife's lover, the latter would be exiled for seven years to Ceuta. The change in Portugal's overseas colonization priorities was reflected in the legislation compiled in the early seventeenth century

13 Hespanha, 'Da "Iustitia" à "Disciplina"', 339; Rodrigues, 'A Guiné nas cartas', 403.

14 A study of laws on adultery in early modern Spain showed that legislators were concerned with the need to confine men's sexuality. Edward J. Behrend-Martínez, *Unfit for Marriage: Impotent Spouses on Trial in the Basque Region of Spain, 1650–1750* (Reno and Las Vegas: University of Nevada Press, 2007), 83, and his more recent article, '"Taming Don Juan": Limiting Masculine Sexuality in Counter-Reformation Spain', *Gender & History* 24, no. 2 (August 2012): 333–52.

15 *Ordenações Manuelinas*, Livro 5, Título 15; *Ordenações Filipinas*, Livro 5, Título 25. For an examination of the *Ordenações Manuelinas* as they applied to women, see Maria Joana Corte-Real Lencart e Silva, 'A Mulher nas Ordenações Manuelinas', *Revista de História* 7 (Porto, 1993): 59–79. For a review of the Portuguese laws on adultery in the fifteenth century, see Amélia Andrade, Teresa Teixeira, and Olga Magalhães, 'Subsídios para o Estudo do Adultério em Portugal no Século XV', *Revista de História* 5 (1983–1984): 93–129.

16 In Spain, too, most accusations for sexual crimes had to be filed by the victim or a relative. Pablo Pérez García, *El Justicia Criminal de Valencia (1479–1707)* (Valencia: Generalitat Valenciana, 1991), 91–4.

whereupon the same penalties were applied to the adulterous (male) lover, except that the perpetual exile was to Brazil.[17] Undoubtedly the circumstances of the adultery determined the fate of the accused, though those circumstances were seldom outlined in the archival record. For instance, among those who received financial assistance from the Casa da Misericórdia in Ponta Delgada between 1608 and 1609 were two men who had been found guilty of 'the same case' of adultery. Nothing else was revealed about that case, but authorities must have deemed it so villainous that they punished both men to perpetual exile in the galleys.[18]

The section on adultery in the *Ordenações Filipinas* also differed somewhat from the earlier compilation in the way legislators outlined the penalty for the adulterous woman. The wording of the clause outlined that a woman accused of simple adultery faced a 'civil death', whereas if she willingly left her husband with her lover, or committed adultery with someone in her husband's household, she faced a 'natural death' – that is, in the first case, she would be fined and exiled, and in the second she would be executed. It is also worth noting that if the accusation proved false, the wife was entitled to her husband's property.[19]

In another section on adultery, legislators outlined the legal means with which a husband could kill his adulterous wife and her lover, whether the husband caught the couple in flagrant adultery or not. The law permitted for a husband to prove the accusation of adultery after the fact, with the usual exceptions concerning men who enjoyed a rank above that of the injured husband. If the husband was successful in proving the charges, he still faced a penalty of exile for a period to be determined by the judges, for a maximum of three years. If the accusation proved to be false, the murderous husband faced the death penalty.[20] This would have been of little consolation to a wife who had already been killed, unless there was some miraculous intervention.[21]

---

17 São Tomé is a small island at the far eastern edge of the Gulf of Guinea, off the coast of Gabon, Africa, where the Portuguese established a settlement in the 1480s, primarily with Portuguese men who had been exiled. Disney, *A History of Portugal*, II: 110–11. Ceuta is a Moroccan port city captured by the Portuguese in 1415.

18 Arquivo da Santa Casa da Misericórdia de Ponta Delgada, *Receitas e Despesas*, Livro no. 190 (1608–1609), f.124–126v. The Casa da Misericórdia was a charitable institution, found in most urban centres in early modern Portugal, and one of its mandates was to provide assistance to poor prisoners. For a look at the Misericórdia more broadly, see Isabel dos Guimarães Sá, *Quando o rico se faz pobre: Misericórdias, caridade e poder no império português, 1500–1800* (Lisbon: Comissão Nacional para as Comemorações dos Descobrimentos Portugueses, 1997).

19 See *Ordenações Filipinas*, Livro 5, Título 25, no. 1, editorial footnote 4, for an interpretation of the 'civil' and 'natural' death; clauses no. 7 and no. 8 for the reference to property rights in cases of the wife's adultery.

20 *Ordenações Manuelinas*, Livro 5, Título 16; *Ordenações Filipinas*, Livro 5, Título 38; Caetano, *História do Direito*, 563–4.

21 For one such story, see Luís dos Anjos, *Jardim de Portugal em que se da Noticia de alguas Sanctas & outras Molheres Illustres em Virtude* (Coimbra: N. Carvalho, 1626), 308–19.

Despite these legal concessions available to cuckolded husbands, it is difficult to gauge the number of men who exercised their prerogative. The priest Rafael Bluteau delivered a sermon in Lisbon in 1723 denouncing the practice, claiming that any hint of conjugal infidelity had led to the sharpening of the dagger, and that some men viewed it a point of honour to kill women.[22] No statistic has been found to substantiate the claims made in that sermon, though the occasional notorious case was well documented. One of the most renowned examples was the case of Isaac Eliot, a French surgeon living in Lisbon who was accused of homicide in 1731, and sentenced to death on 13 January 1733. He had killed his 16-year-old wife and a cleric who he claimed had been engaged in adultery together. The problem was that Isaac had killed his first wife for adultery as well, and suspicions arose about his intentions to kill his two wives for their dowries, especially in light of the fact that he had arranged for the cleric to visit his wife. For his troubles, Isaac was hanged, as was one of his male servants, while two female servants were condemned to public whippings and to serve in the galleys, presumably for being accomplices.[23]

One other option available for the injured husband was to file an official accusation against his errant wife for adultery, and subsequently to grant her an official pardon with all the magnanimity he could muster. Ignoring or condoning the offense was not an option. Female adultery was considered so abhorrent that the offended husband who chose to disregard the infraction risked being punished along with his errant wife. The *Ordenações Manuelinas* and the *Ordenações Filipinas* legislated that if it could be proven that a husband permitted the adultery of his wife, both spouses would be whipped in public while each wore a garland of horns ('capelas de cornos'), and both would be exiled to Brazil. As for the wife's lover, he faced perpetual banishment to Africa, even if the cuckolded husband chose to pardon the two accomplices.[24] In Spain, the penalty for complacent cuckolded husbands ('cabrones consentidos') was public humiliation and 10 years in the galleys.[25]

The husband could also pardon his wife's lover for the injury caused to his honour, a delicate situation given the nebulous implications in such a decision, and the legislation that penalized disinterested cuckolded husbands. This was especially problematic if the adultery had been committed with 'aleivosia', that is, under exceptionally duplicitous circumstances. Dina Catarina Duarte Alves found one example from the town of Óbidos of a man who pardoned the accusation of adultery against a judge who had committed adultery with his wife, 'com aleivosia por serem grandes amigos' – the judge had been particularly deceitful for the

22 Cited in Araújo, 'Cerimónias de execução', 178.

23 Araújo, 'Cerimónias de execução', 199–201. The report did not explain how the women would be employed in the galleys. While in prison, Eliot composed a text in pamphlet form, *Oraçam que Compoz Isaac Eliot Na Sua Prizam*, 1733.

24 *Ordenações Manuelinas*, Livro 5,Tituto 15, no. 8; *Ordenações Filipinas*, Livro 5, Título 25, no. 9. See also Correia, 'A evolução histórica', 93.

25 Alloza, *La vara quebrada*, 201.

plaintiff and defendant had been great friends.[26] The pardon document said nothing about the wife's fate, but Alves also found an example of a man who paid a hefty fine of 35,000 *réis* for a pardon he obtained for the crime of adultery.[27] Again, the pardoner would have been the injured husband, not the injured wife of either party. As will be shown later, the only time a wife could have made a legal claim against her philandering husband would have been in a case of flagrant neglect of the family household, such as when a husband was involved in concubinage.

Overall, then, the law clearly aimed to punish those who had disgraced a husband, not a wife, though the pardon system allowed for some softening of the harsh penalties in the books. Under Portuguese legislation, a husband's pardon to his adulterous wife and her lover released the accused from the death sentence. Indeed, the law stipulated that once a judge received a notarized pardon from the husband for an adulterous wife, the accused wife was to be released from jail immediately, but only in cases of 'simple adultery'. If the accusations of adultery involved sex with kin or with an infidel, the accused woman still faced the prohibitions connected to those 'sins'.[28] While the anecdote that opened this chapter indicated a certain cultural loophole for the occasional 'shameful and immoral act', an earlier tract written by the same author pointed out that a wife's adultery injured her husband more than if his daughter had been raped, more than if someone had knifed him to death, more than if he had lost all his property, and more than the death of all his children.[29] Perhaps the doctor's views had mellowed over time.

All 10 *perdões de parte* found that dealt with adultery consisted of accusations made by husbands against their wives or their wives' lovers. Because so few details were provided about the source of the accusation, there was no way to know whether or not the plaintiff had just cause for his complaint, the response of the accused, and the long-term effect on the parties involved. The very existence of a pardon document tells us that there was some form of reconciliation, something was worked out and agreed to, due to emotional bonds or other pulls, possibly monetary pulls. In his instruction manual for notaries working on pardon documents, José Homem Correa Telles reminded the scribes that the pardon granted by a husband to his wife for adultery had to be done in front of a judge. Furthermore, it was advisable for the husband to affirm in the written document that the pardon was freely given, for it would be improper to gain financially from this type of injury. The predicament was that a husband was not supposed to be his wife's panderer.[30]

26 Alves, 'Violência e perdão', 121. The law stipulated that a judicial official who had sex with a female plaintiff or defendant would lose his office and be exiled for one year. *Ordenações Manuelinas*, Livro 5, Título 20, and *Ordenações Filipinas*, Livro 5, Título 20.

27 Alves, 'Violência e perdão', 139.

28 *Ordenações Manuelinas*, Livro 5, Título 15, no. 2; *Ordenações Filipinas*, Livro 5, Título 25, no. 2.

29 (Dr.) João de Barros, *Espelho de Casados* (Porto: Imprensa Portugueza, 1874 [1540]), p. ix verso.

30 Telles, *Manual do Tabellião*, 165.

Whatever the incentive, at some point during the judicial process the accuser was convinced to forgive or to at least go through the legal motions of granting an official pardon; perhaps due to the intervention of family members, friends, or the local priest; perhaps due to a financial offer by the alleged lover or his family and friends; perhaps due to the pleas of the accused wife and his own conscience. None of this is for us to know, but whatever the motivations and insinuations, the accusation of adultery could be devastating for the accused even if forgiven, especially for the woman who could be stigmatized for life by friend and foe.

Society was also ambivalent toward husbands who were deemed too forgiving.[31] A collection of anecdotal stories circulated in the Portuguese royal court in the sixteenth century included several that ridiculed cuckolded husbands, and that ideological pressure continued well into the eighteenth century, if not beyond.[32] A reflection on love in the eighteenth century, written by the Portuguese writer Júlio Dantas, contained a chapter on 'maridos cucos' or cuckolded husbands, in which chapter the author revealed that the phenomenon merited some colourful terminology. A 'cuco' was a husband of an unfaithful wife; an 'ante-cuco' was a man married to a woman who had been with another man before marriage, but who behaved appropriately once married; a 're-cuco' was a man whose wife had had other men before him, and who continued to have other men; a 'chiscismelro' was the husband who knew of his wife's infidelities and did not care; a 'ribeirinho' was the husband who consented and even accommodated his wife's lovers; and an 'assombrado' was a husband who came close to being a 'cuco' but escaped it by a miracle. The source for these distinctive terms was not provided in the text, and may be more representative of the author's fanciful pen than of a widespread cultural phenomenon. Still, as Dantas pointed out, the problem of cuckolded husbands was considered so great that the Marquis de Pombal (1699–1782), Chief Minister for King D. José (r.1750–1777) issued a decree on 26 September 1769 to combat the great public disturbance and the rise in numbers of depressed husbands. In essence, the decree prohibited the custom of hanging horns ('chavellos') at night on the doors of people's homes.[33]

The fact that there was no such anxiety over cuckolded wives speaks volumes. As Laura Gowing has shown for early modern England, women's adultery and men's adultery were entirely different things.[34] A man's adultery could be perceived to damage his wife, financially and emotionally, but he would never be accused of 'whoredom' but rather of maintaining a woman who was labelled

---

31 For anxieties in early modern France about men who were too forgiving of their wandering wives, see Muchembled, *Le Temps des Supplices*, 141.

32 Mário Justino Silva, *O rei e os nobres: Imagens do quotidiano nos 'Ditos Portugueses Dignos de Memória' (século XVI)* (Cascais: Patrimonia Historica, 2004), 85–6.

33 Júlio Dantas, *O amor em Portugal no século XVIII* (Porto: Livraria Chardron, 1916), 215–16.

34 Laura Gowing, *Domestic Dangers: Women, Words, and Sex in Early Modern London* (Oxford: Clarendon Press, 1998), 93–6.

a 'whore'. In his study of women and litigation in early modern England, Tim Stretton found that wives and husbands accused each other of adultery in almost equal numbers, but the double standard that favoured male infidelity persisted, and accusations by husbands against wives were much more damaging to those wives than vice versa.[35]

It was always the woman's sexual impropriety that was an issue, not the man's, even if he were married. A wife's adultery, on the contrary, was viewed as a direct threat to a husband's ability to govern his household, and dishonoured his character and reputation. Because a wife was not supposed to control her husband, his waywardness was not a blemish on her character, but hers was on his. This was true in early modern London and in early modern Ponta Delgada. One archival example was found that showed a man's concerns about his reputation. In a *querela* filed on 9 July 1644, Miguel Alves Quaresma complained that while he was making a citizen's arrest, the culprit swore at him and called him a cuckolded buck-goat ('cabrão e cornudo').[36] As is well known, this double standard was widespread in early modern Europe, of long standing, and historically linked to questions of inheritance and men's needs to control the legitimacy of their offspring – a concern that conveniently left out the children they sired out-of-wedlock.

Similar to other pardons, the ones that dealt with adultery provided some intriguing hints about what was culturally acceptable and what was best left unsaid. A particularly acute case of circular reasoning was found in a *perdão de parte* that dealt with adultery. Melchior Barbosa had initially filed a complaint against Martinho da Cunha for committing adultery with his (Melchior's) wife, Isabel da Costa. During a confrontation between the two men, Martinho injured Melchior, which resulted in a second *querela*. Upon some reflection, Melchior came to admit that Martinho was not guilty of the first offense, and since the second was connected to the first, Martinho was innocent of the physical injuries as well. This convoluted reasoning was further complicated by Melchior's avowal that Martinho was innocent of the charges, and thus Melchior was compelled to pardon Martinho for the guilt that Martinho could have had. That, at least, was the way the previously injured husband presented his resolve, but this case offered further examples of the inconsistencies and contradictions inherent in the pardoning process (see Appendix 5).

By law, a victim's pardon had to be sanctioned by all immediate heirs or their representatives, but cases of adultery were seemingly exempt from this requirement. Thus, when Isabel's husband pardoned the man he accused of committing adultery with her, and those who injured him in the process of those accusations – technically – Isabel's acquiescence should have been included in the pardon document, but in such cases, the less said the better. Her name was barely mentioned in the long text which also revealed nothing about her fate. Isabel was probably in no position to bargain and negotiate in such a public forum regarding such a publicly-charged crime. A woman who faced an accusation of adultery

[35] Stretton, *Women Waging Law*, 195.

[36] BPARPD, *Livro de Autos de Querelas*, f.133–134v.

became *persona non grata*. Conversely, a husband of an unfaithful wife had the prerogatives of patriarchy to support his injured pride. Because only a husband could accuse his unfaithful wife, only a husband could make a claim against those involved in the alleged adultery, or a disclaimer to that effect.

Enough vague language was used to camouflage some inconspicuous element that led to the visit to the notary's office, but invariably the pardoner in adultery cases presented himself as a righteously injured man, but that the right thing to do, onerous as it might have been, was for him to forgive and forget. It is doubtful that he or the accused could do either, at least in the short term, but stating it might have been an important first step, an especially crucial step if the estranged couple was resolved to stay together. Such a scenario was sketched in a notarized record dated 30 April 1605, at which point Miguel Gomes, *trabalhador* or labourer, granted a pardon to his wife, Domingas Pinheira. Undoubtedly Domingas also worked for a living, but that was not what the scribe noted in the notary document, a document that pointed out that Domingas was in jail in Ponta Delgada (São Miguel) because her husband had accused her of adultery. Subsequently Miguel had a change of heart, and 'since he had lived with her as God wished it', he forgave his wife and asked His Majesty's justices not to proceed against her but to release her, 'for he was ready to receive her and to lead a marital life with her as God commanded'.[37]

Sometime after his accusation against his wife, Miguel moved to another island, Terceira, possibly to distance himself from his wife's alleged crime, which included 'adultery and other things'. In his pardon Miguel did not claim that his wife was innocent, but rather that 'he had received other information about her', an innocuous statement that presented him as a reasonable man who was willing to live according to a higher power. Miguel's declaration resonated with the rhetorical devices discussed in the previous chapter, and his carefully-crafted statement implied that there was some settlement behind the scenes to his satisfaction. Unfortunately Miguel's original complaint was not found, but chances are that Domingas had to deal with the repercussions of the accusation long after her jail term. Still, one could argue that Miguel had been generous, at least on paper, whereas other plaintiffs displayed a more limited generosity.

Breaking the Marriage Vows

Maria Moreira, for instance, was pardoned on 25 October 1594 for having been unfaithful to her husband, Pedro Rodrigues Leão, a soldier in the castle of Viana do Castelo. In his account Leão claimed that Maria had married him with words in the present tense ('por palavras de presente'), according to the Holy Mother Church, and the Sacred Council of Trent, but she committed adultery against him with another soldier named Pedro do Campo. Leão's pardon did not indicate when he first launched the *querela* against his wife, nor what prompted him to withdraw it, except for the usual formulaic explanations. Ostensibly for no other reason than to clear his conscience, Leão pardoned 'the said Maria Moreira the said adultery

---

37 BPARAH, Fundo Notarial (Angra), no. 4 (1604–1605), f.169–169v.

and all other errors that she had committed against him, her husband, sinning against the laws of matrimony'. Despite all those errors that Maria committed, Leão asked that she be freed from prison where she was, without any further legal procedures, but on condition that upon her release they remain separated.[38]

It is worth noting that Leão outlined the ways in which he and his wife had been married, and made specific reference to the requirements established by the Council of Trent (1545–1563). In the church visitation to the church of Sant'Ana in Lisbon in 1570, the religious authorities found that many parishioners were still ignorant of the decree from the Council of Trent regarding what constituted a proper marriage. Apparently too many people were living together having exchanged 'promises in the present' and believing that such an exchange was adequate. Authorities ordered the local priests to continue to announce from their pulpits the proper rules about marriage so that no one could claim ignorance any longer.[39] No less challenging for church officials was educating its own representatives. At a church visitation in Braga in 1565, a servant testified that he had heard the local priest ridicule a young woman for wanting to confess too much. The religious authorities also were told that some *lavradores* claimed that they did not have to pay church tithes to abbots who were involved in mortal sins.[40] Such a boycott could have proven inconvenient for certain priests. During a church visitation to her parish in 1620, Catarina Carvalho, a 30-year-old widow, complained of the local priest who had asked her if he 'could put his hands on her secret parts'.[41]

The reference to the Council of Trent in his pardon document showed that Leão had been well coached, or that he actually had some awareness of the church's position on the proper procedure for a marriage to be considered valid. By the late sixteenth century the procedure was to involve more than the uttering of 'words in the present tense', though the church usually recognized such unions while encouraging couples to formalize their vows in the presence of a priest. Maria Moreira and Pedro Rodrigues Leão must have been living together, for Leão clearly stipulated that the two were to remain apart despite the notarized pardon. Did Maria consider herself married to Pedro, or was she ready to move on to another lover, also named Pedro? Given that the two men vying for Maria's affections were soldiers in the same fortress, there must have been some serious

---

38 ADVC, Fundo Notarial, Heitor de Barros (notary), no. 4.32.3.1 (1594), f.372v?–373? (pagination approximate).

39 Luís F. Farinha Franco, 'Um Livro de Visitações à Igreja de Sant'Ana de Lisboa (1570–1598)', *Boletim Cultural* 79/80 (Lisbon, 1973/74): 73–4 [61–90].

40 Cartório Dominicano Português, *Livro da Visitação que se [a Inquisição] fez na Cydade de Braga e seu Arcebispado [1565]: Bartholomaeana Monumenta IV* (Porto: Arquivo Histórico Dominicano Português/Movimento Bartolomeano, 1974), 16, 46.

41 Maria de Deus Beites Manso and Maria Margarida Caeiro, 'A Visitação de Francisco Cardoso de Torneo aos Açores (1618–1620) (Contribuição em torno de alguns processos)', in *O Faial e a Periferia Açoriana nos Sécs. XV a XIX: Actas do Colóquio realizado nas ilhas do Faial e Pico de 10 a 13 Maio de 1993* (Horta: Núcleo Cultural da Horta, 1995), 520 [515–21].

intervention and pressures from authorities to have this problem resolved. It is not known whether or not Maria's alleged lover also had to be pardoned, but, not surprisingly, the two witnesses to this notarized document consisted of a *Comissário de Sua Majestade* (royal agent) and a military officer.

On the one hand, the condition that Leão imposed on Maria appeared to have been fairly benign; on the other hand, she could have had difficulty setting herself up on her own. In her husband's pardon Maria was identified as a *portuensa*, the female version of *portuense*, or someone originally from Porto, a city south of Viana do Castelo, and the distance between Maria and her kin could have made her more vulnerable. Her alleged moral lapse would have been public knowledge, particularly after her husband made a public complaint about it. The notoriety resulting from such a scandal would render matters difficult for all parties involved, though some were seemingly prepared to move on and let bygones be bygones.

Inappropriate Gifts

This, at least, is what seemed to have transpired on 19 November 1582 when Diogo Fernandes, shoemaker, resident of the district of São João in Lisbon, visited the *Paço dos Tabeliães* (Offices of the Notaries) to have a pardon drawn up. His pardon had two parts, for Diogo had much to complain about, and to reconsider. During the *oitava* (church festival of eight days) at Christmas time of the previous year (1581), at the tower of São Pedro in Lisbon, Diogo had had a quarrel with Gaspar Dias, 'homen baço' (dark skinned), also a shoemaker. During that fight Diogo was stabbed with a knife on the head and on the left hand, for which injuries he filed a complaint. In that complaint Diogo had also accused Gaspar of having relations with his (Diogo's) wife, a complaint Diogo filed as well against his wife, Margarida Fernandes. These were two serious accusations, but Diogo had changed his mind on both counts.

First, the stab wounds had healed without any scar or blemish, and it was foolish to ruin a perfectly good friendship over such a minor skirmish.

> Given that Diogo has respect for Gaspar and they had been good friends, and they ate and drank together, and there was a lot of good affection between them, and the argument had been over words that they had, and for other just and honest considerations but principally for the love of the Senhor Deus who pardoned his sins, and also because he [Diogo] had been the aggressor and responsible for the said fight, he pardoned Gaspar for the said injury and of all blame for the said fight, of his free will.

Second, there had never been any adultery, or maybe just a little bit, hardly worth mentioning.

> As for the *querela* against the said his wife, claiming that she had dealings with Gaspar Dias … he [Diogo] said that he had based his accusation on false information and because he was still vexed for the said injury, but not because his wife had any culpability in this, for he knew and knew with certainty that his

> wife was not involved with the said Gaspar Dias, for these reasons and others that moved him [Diogo] said that he also pardoned his wife and the said Gaspar Dias for the said *querela* and adultery which had no basis.

Benevolent he may have been, but Diogo Fernandes had his pride and there were limits to what he could tolerate. To avoid future misunderstandings, the kind that led to the 'false information' noted in his statement, Diogo granted this pardon to Gaspar on one condition: Gaspar was not to send any more earrings ('arrecadas') to Margarida Fernandes, Diogo's wife, nor speak with her for whatever reason. The document further stipulated that Diogo granted this pardon to Gaspar because of their friendship, but if Gaspar did not adhere to this important condition of the pardon, Diogo would renew the complaint against him for adultery. Both witnesses were shoemakers as well, who vouched for Diogo's identity and possibly intervened to bring a peaceful solution to a problem between two guild members.[42]

In Margarida's case, the term 'adultery' may have been used to hint at some impropriety but not necessarily at illicit sex. Perhaps Gaspar Dias, her alleged lover, was only guilty of giving Margarida some jewellery, an inappropriate gift for a married woman, but not illegal in itself. Regardless, the accusation had been launched, necessitating a pardon to seal the peace process. Still, Diogo's pardon to Gaspar included a condition that begs the question of Margarida's fate, and in fact highlights her vulnerability. If Gaspar persisted in his interest in Margarida, Diogo would withdraw the pardon, presumably to both, because by law a husband could not accuse one and not the other.[43] As already mentioned, the law also did not allow for a pardoner to withdraw a pardon, but perhaps Diogo and his notary felt that the threat would serve to keep Gaspar at bay.[44] Whatever Diogo's motives, the sexual double standard of the time left Margarida in a precarious position. In cases of sexual relations, two women fighting over one man could inflate his ego; two men fighting over one woman could deflate her reputation.

In the two previous examples, the accused, Domingas Pinheira and Maria Moreira, were jailed following their respective husbands' accusations of adultery. Presumably there had been a judicial inquiry in both cases, and each woman had been found guilty of the charges, precipitating the need for a pardon. The fact that Domingas' husband was willing to take her back would help her cause, but both she and Maria Moreira still faced possibly hefty fines for their crimes. Who would pay those fines? Would the money come from the wife's portion of the family assets, would the forgiving husband cover the legal costs, or was the bill split between the two? These were among the particulars that possibly were negotiated prior to the signing of the *perdão de parte*. As for Margarida Fernandes, her pardon did not indicate her whereabouts, but if her husband had to pardon her, she must have

---

42 IAN/TT, Fundo Notarial (Lisbon), Caixa 2, no. 12 (1582), f.6v–7v. Some punctuation was added for clarity.

43 *Ordenações Filipinas*, Livro 5, Título 25, no. 4.

44 Telles, *Manual do Tabellião*, 196. For an example of a royal pardon granted and later withdrawn, see Coates, *Convicts and Orphans*, 105.

been charged and jailed as well. It took her husband nearly a year to recognize his error based on 'false information', enough time for an arrest and a conviction, and enough time for the offering of incentives to sway his inclination.

These cases of adultery showed the extent to which matrimony was a double-edged sword for some early modern Portuguese women. Marriage was considered a sacrament and married women generally enjoyed higher status and social security than single or widowed women. Yet, an accusation of adultery – deservedly or undeservedly – placed women at the mercy of their husbands' whims. In some respects, therefore, Maria Moreira was arguably in a better position at the end of her ordeal, at least from an emotional and psychological point of view. Although she had to deal with her husband's imposed separation, and the hardships that such ostracism entailed, Maria was free of his emotional claims on her. Domingas and Margarida, for their part, would always be indebted to their husbands' generosity, and have to contend with the occasional reminder thereof. At a more concrete level, all three women risked the loss of their assets, for the law decreed that a woman found guilty of adultery forfeited her share of the family property, if she were executed for her crime, a factor that would have been a concern for the woman's heirs.[45] It is doubtful that forgiving husbands forgave that, too. More likely, the question was raised during negotiations for the *perdão de parte*, and agreements were reached that benefited the pardoner and saved the pardoned from a worse fate.

A Death Sentence

That worse fate included the death sentence, which was what befell on Catarina Varella of Vila Fronteira, in the district of Evora. The pardon from Garcia Gonçalves, Catarina's husband, illustrated the most extreme consequences of adultery cases. Instead of pardoning his wife's alleged lover, Garcia killed him, an act that landed him in jail, for that is where he was found on 16 August 1560. On that day the notary went to the church prison (*aljube*) in Evora to meet up with the prisoner Garcia who wanted a pardon document drawn up for his wife. Garcia's pardon revealed that he had filed a criminal accusation against her for the adultery that she had committed with António Pires, deceased, killed by Garcia for that very reason. Catarina, in the meantime, had been condemned to death, but Garcia was ready to forgive her

> for the said death for which she was condemned in the said sentence and also pardoned her of any other guilt, debt, damages, or any obligation, and he wanted nothing from her nor wanted to accuse her any further for the adultery mentioned in the sentence, and he asked His Majesty's justices not to proceed against her for he forgave her freely.[46]

---

45 *Ordenações Filipinas*, Livro 5, Título 25, nos 6 and 7.

46 ADE, Fundo Notarial, Fernão de Arcos (notary), Séries 38 (1560), f.92v–93v. Some puncuation was added for clarity.

Although his pardon could have saved his wife from the gallows, Garcia was not ready to admit that Catarina was innocent, let alone that he was ready to live with her as husband and wife. That was an admission that he could never make, even if it were true, because then he risked being accused of killing an innocent man. Catarina's death sentence suggested that there was strong evidence against her, and Garcia's incarceration also implied that he awaited his departure for the possible three years of exile that the law imposed on husbands who killed their adulterous wives or their lovers. Granting Catarina a pardon was likely a calculated move on the part of the injured husband, for it would impress judicial officials when he appealed his own exile. Since his wife was found guilty of adultery, Garcia had nothing to lose and much to gain from a convicted wife, despite his avowal that he wanted nothing from her.[47]

Garcia's act of revenge looked to have been unusual, for most injured husbands chose a less severe course of action.[48] The nature of the pardon document naturally lends itself to this conclusion, for a pardon would not be granted by those bent on retaliation. The absence of court transcripts means that the hypothesis cannot be proven one way or another. Nevertheless, the remnants that exist do not point to an open season on adulterous wives and their lovers. What was more probable was a settlement of some kind, such as the one that Gaspar Fernandes agreed to on 10 December 1595. At a meeting with the notary and other witnesses in the home of Francisco Freire Serrão, *cavaleiro* and *cidadão* of Evora, Gaspar pardoned Pedro Mendes, a married man, of all culpability that Pedro had or could have had in the complaint and denunciation (*querela e denunciação*) that Gaspar made for having found Pedro with his (Gaspar's) wife. This accusation had been made to the outside judge of Evora, but Gaspar retracted the accusation and wanted nothing from the accused, for Gaspar pardoned him for the love of God, a statement that was repeated three times in the short narrative.

Whether Gaspar was coached by anyone, or influenced by anything in particular, was not revealed, naturally. Indeed, the absence of particulars made this pardon especially suspect. Gaspar did not explain the reasons for his initial suspicions nor for his subsequent change of heart, and the defendant, Pedro Mendes, was also present at the meeting, who accepted and signed the document. It is curious that the alleged adulterous wife and the wife of the accused remained anonymous in the record. Furthermore, the presence of the accused at the signing of the document showed that he had a direct role in the negotiations of this transaction. His own signature pointed to the perceived need for extra caution, to safeguard the best interests of the defendant or plaintiff, or both.[49]

---

[47] For a discussion of the husband's potential material gains in cases of female adultery, see Caetano, *História do Direito*, 563–4.

[48] A study of accusations for adultery and other sexual crimes in the fifteenth century showed that many defendants chose a form of self-imposed exile, from which place they later appealed for a royal pardon. See Andrade et al, 'Subsídios para o Estudo do Adultério,' especially. Table 2.

[49] ADE, Fundo Notarial, Domingos Pires (notary), Séries 232 (1595), f.64–65.

A Sentence of Exile

While Gaspar Fernandes' pardon did not identify his wife, the one by António Aires, a *lavrador* from Vila Pouca de Aguiar, did not identify his wife's lover. Written in a notary's office in Lisbon on 30 March 1579, the pardon granted to Isabel Garcia revealed that António had accused her of adultery to the justices in Vila Pouca de Aguiar, where a sentence was rendered against her. An appeal had been filed and was sent to the *Casa da Suplicação*, the High Court of Appeal in Lisbon. In the meantime, 'for the love of the Lord God, and for the days of Santa Conceição', António was willing to forgive his wife, and he 'relinquished the sentence and the writs ['autos'] ... on condition that the said Isabel Garcia leave for the island of São Tomé and remain there forever'.[50] Isabel had been found guilty of the charges of adultery in her hometown, but she had appealed her case to a higher court. A pardon from her husband undoubtedly helped her appeal, but the condition imposed by her husband was a harsh sentence in itself, a life-sentence of exile to a remote island off the coast of Africa, where life would be arduous at best, if she ever survived the voyage. Her best hopes lay in a successful plea to the Crown, though women had fewer grounds on which to base their appeals.

Timothy Coates found an example from 1513 of a man who had been exiled for the murder of his wife, but then had the sentence removed 'in light of his services to the Crown'. It is not known whether or not the murdered wife had been suspected of adultery, but regardless of the circumstances of the case, the accused benefited from a system that favoured convicted men over convicted women. Indeed, Coates noted that 'the Crown was not only merciful but also quick to acknowledge services rendered to it'.[51] Since women had fewer opportunities to render such services, women had fewer opportunities to enjoy the benefits, particularly in the general pardons granted to those who committed themselves to military expeditions. Thus, if Isabel Garcia was sentenced to perpetual exile overseas, her chances of escaping her fate were minimal.

Although a small sample, the six adultery cases examined here illustrated that there was a wide range of possibilities on how those cases were handled. António Aires chose to condemn his errant wife, Isabel Garcia, to perpetual exile; Garcia Gonçalves pardoned Catarina Varella's death sentence, but killed her lover and had his wife exiled for life; Diogo Fernandes pardoned Margarida Fernandes and claimed her innocence, as well as that of her alleged lover, though the latter was to cease contact; Gaspar Fernandes pardoned his wife's lover, but had nothing to say about his unidentified wife; Pedro Rodrigues Leão pardoned Maria Moreira

---

[50] IAN/TT, Fundo Notarial (Lisbon), Caixa 2, no. 2 (1579), f.56–57. On two occasions the scribe erroneously identified Isabel Garcia as Isabel de Aguiar, crossing out his mistake at one point. It is not clear which days of 'Santa Conceição' are referred to in this pardon written in March. The day of the 'Immaculada Conceição' is presently celebrated in Portugal on December 8.

[51] Coates, *Convicts and Orphans*, 104, 107. For similar findings, see Corrêa, 'Aspectos da Criminalidade nos Açores', 550.

but insisted that their estrangement was permanent; and Miguel Gomes forgave Domingas Pinheira and was prepared to take her back. This was the least that each document revealed, but it was enough to show the difficulties with broad generalizations about the laws on female adultery and the social mores that dictated how those laws were applied.

Undoubtedly some men killed their wives, for adultery or otherwise, and some very powerful men found ways to escape judicial and social censorship. For instance, the Duke of Bragança had his wife the duchess executed in 1512 under suspicion of adultery. He was able to free himself from the criminal investigation by providing a hefty sum of money to finance the Portuguese military expedition to Morocco in 1513.[52] As one Portuguese historian has pointed out, no one ostracized the duke following his assassination of his own wife.[53] A powerful man had powerful allies, and the law, created to uphold the privileges of the powerful, preserved the double standard between men and women, rich and poor.

The archival examples examined here dealt with accusations of adultery filed by common men, not men who saw themselves above the law. A record from the seventeenth century showed that a man from Porto Santo in the Madeira Archipelago was disinherited once he was convicted of killing his wife, for which crime he was ultimately executed.[54] It is not known whether that husband had suspected his wife of adultery, but his execution revealed that killing a spouse was not tolerated by authorities, particularly in cases that involved people of the lower echelons, of which he was certainly a member. Moreover, as the following example illustrates, concerns over possible adulterous misconduct could, in the face of limited options, result in some creative solutions.

A Dubious Compromise

On 16 May 1638, the notary Frutuoso Bravo Moguemes went to the local jail in Viana do Castelo to conduct business with two prisoners. For reasons unknown, Domingos Gonçalves Cerqueira and Susana Correia, his wife, were in jail in Viana do Castelo at the same time, and it was during their incarceration that they made peace. They summoned a notary and he proceeded to record their entente in the form of a *perdão de parte* from Domingos to Susana. In his pardon, Domingos stated that he had accused and filed a complaint against his wife, Susana, for adultery, but he had been misled and enticed to accuse Susana, and lately he had become better informed of the truth and knew her to be innocent. With this pardon

---

52 Saraiva, *História de Portugal*, 160.

53 Joaquim Romero Magalhães, 'O Pano de Fundo', in José Mattoso, ed., *História de Portugal: No Alvorecer da Modernidade*, 8 vols (Lisbon: Editorial Estampa, 1997), III: 487 [485–9].

54 *Arquivo Histórico da Madeira: Documentos Históricos da Ilha do Porto Santo, Série Transcrições Documentais 2*, Maria Favila Vieira da Cunha Paredes, trans. (Funchal: Secretaria Regional do Turismo e Cultura/Direcção Regional dos Assuntos Culturais, 2005), 31.

Domingos declared that he desisted from the accusation, confessed that she was not guilty, and even if she were, he pardoned her. Domingos did not reveal the identity of Susana's alleged lover, nor who or what misled him to the initial accusation, but his willingness to forgive regardless of those unidentified enticements was clearly linked to his other projected gains. The narrative is somewhat convoluted but worthy of a lengthy quote for the richness of the details it provides.

> … and the said Susana and Domingos confirmed that they wanted to lead a life together ['fazer vida ambos'], and in case that there was any trace of consanguinity between them, they both stated that they wanted a papal brief from Lisbon, so that while he Domingos was in jail she Susana obliged herself to provide him with the necessary means, and thus reconcile one with the other … and he stated that he would not ever take from his wife's property more than [what was needed] to sustain himself, for she his wife would provide him with sustenance for all necessities which included food, drink, clothes, and shoes as [she would] to her husband, and this was understood [to be in effect] during her lifetime, for after her death he could do what he wanted with her properties.[55]

While the other pardons for adultery contained scant information, this account was layered with hints and insinuations, not least of which was the question about the legality of their marriage, forcing them to seek a church dispensation. If the marriage was judged to be invalid, could Susana be accused of adultery anyway? The question may have occurred to Domingos, for he tried to deal with that possible outcome by stating that Susana would support him for the rest of her life 'as she would to a husband'. What she was to provide for him was detailed enough, but the costs of that daily maintenance were not specified, though he promised not to take more than was necessary, the gauge for which was left wide open. Domingos signed the document and Susana had someone sign it on her behalf, an indication of her commitment and acquiescence to their agreement noted in a pardon ostensibly for her benefit. Why would Susana acquiesce if she were not guilty of something? Willingly or not, Susana was going to support Domingos out of her own pocket, a pocket that he would take over upon her death. Indeed, this document was less about adultery and more about a financial arrangement between two people whose relationship was dubious at best. Susana had the financial resources that Domingos coveted, and by pardoning her he took out a life insurance, with dividends.

Despite the law on adultery that privileged husbands, no notarized document was found with a reference to a husband having killed or attempted to kill his adulterous wife. If men were killing their wives indiscriminately, as the priest noted above decried, one would expect to find some evidence that at least a few of those husbands would need a pardon from their in-laws. The evidence, sparse and contradictory as it is, points to resolutions that did not result in bloodshed, even when adultery occurred under particularly egregious circumstances. For instance, Mor Gonçalves' husband, Nuno Martins, committed adultery with her

55 ADVC, Fundo Notarial, Frutuoso Bravo Moguemes (notary), no. 4.32.3.24 (1637–1639), f.147–148. Some punctuation was added for clarity.

own mother in 1480 in Graciosa, for which crime Mor's father granted Nuno a pardon on condition that Nuno leave their home island for Faial, though the fate of the adulterous mother and the betrayed daughter is less clear.[56]

The theme of a raging husband intent on killing his adulterous wife makes for titillating drama, especially if the wife proves to be innocent, as seen in Shakespeare's *Othello*, for instance. Outside the theatrical world, husbands bent on revenge were fewer than some classical texts purported. Scott Taylor, for example, found a verifiable disconnect between the literature of Golden Age Spain and contemporary attitudes toward cuckolded husbands killing their wives.[57] In France, Stuart Carroll found that revenge on the cuckolder was applauded more than the killing of an adulterous wife.[58] In Portugal, too, there was some preference for accommodation rather than retaliation. These examples demonstrate that the ideal patriarchal family was occasionally disrupted at its core, and this was true in cases of adulterous husbands, as well. As already mentioned, no victim's pardon was found of a wife pardoning her adulterous husband, but popular culture provided some examples that a man's adulterous affair could also cause him great harm.

The Adulterous Hero

One sensational account of adultery worthy of some examination comes out of the romanticized story of D. Paulo de Lima Pereira (1538–1589), *fidalgo* and military leader of the Portuguese campaign in India. Written by Diogo do Couto (1542–1616), the biography explained that at a younger age, 'when the sensual appetites rule the most', D. Paulo committed 'some mischief of the flesh', including with married women. One of those married women, whose beauty – the author informed the reader – was the root of the problem, was married to a very wealthy man, and one day the cuckolded husband was alerted of the liaison and surprised the couple *in flagrante delicto*. The wife tried to escape through a window and crashed to the ground, where her husband finished her off, while her lover made his escape. At this point the biographer highlighted D. Paulo's warrior qualities in great detail, as the noble valiantly fought off the household servants who tried to restrain him for their master. Still, the cuckolded husband filed a *querela* against D. Paulo for committing adultery with his wife, and D. Paulo had to escape further afield. His friends tried to plead his case, but the best they could do was to get him a pardon with the condition that he leave Goa, which he did. He ended up in

56 Cited in Rodrigues and Martins, 'A Construção de um Espaço', 77.

57 Taylor, *Honor and Violence*, especially chapter 6. See also Luis R. Corteguera, 'The Painter Who Lost His Hat: Artisans and Justice in Early Modern Barcelona', *Sixteenth Century Journal* 29, no. 4 (Winter 1998): 1023–42. For some examples of honour killing in early modern Spain, see Abigail Dyer, 'Seduction by Promise of Marriage: Law, Sex, and Culture in Seventeenth-Century Spain', *Sixteenth Century Journal* 34, no. 2 (Summer 2003): 440–41 [439–55].

58 Carroll, *Blood and Violence*, 238.

Hormuz where eventually, nearing his forties, he settled and married D. Beatriz, the 18-year-old daughter of a Portuguese noble family stationed in Hormuz.[59]

Still D. Paulo was unsatisfied with his refugee status, and so he returned with his young bride to Goa to attempt to lift his sentence of exile, but since this was breaking the condition of the pardon, he kept himself hidden, while many high-level people, including the viceroy, other nobles, and religious leaders attempted to renegotiate the terms of the original pardon with the injured husband, but the latter refused to budge. The stalemate continued for a while until one day D. Beatriz approached the injured cuckolded husband at the local monastery, where she fell at his feet, in tears, and begged him to pardon her husband, in honour of Christ's blisters, because her husband was an outcast, and she well knew the reason for everything, but for the love of Christ she begged him for forgiveness for her husband's wrongdoing. Seeing the woman so disconsolate at his feet, the man whose name was never mentioned in the narrative (nor was his late wife ever properly identified), responded to D. Beatriz that for the love of Christ, as she asked, he would pardon her husband, but he asked that he never encounter that husband nor pass him on the street where he lived.[60]

Couto presented D. Paulo as a hero of the Portuguese overseas project, and included the narrative of the adulterous affairs as more proof of D. Paulo's prowess and adventurous spirit, but in the process the author betrayed his hero, for in fact D. Paulo was more coward than noble. First, he escaped while he let his lover take the fall, literally; second, he hid while his wife did his bidding with the injured husband. Nowhere in the story were we told that D. Paulo was regretful for his actions, or that he needed his wife's forgiveness for his past misdeeds, though he certainly was indebted to her for the less restrictive pardon he received at last. Predictably, D. Beatriz's intervention was described not in heroic terms but couched in quintessential female humility.[61] The two principal women in D. Paulo's story represented the classical dichotomy of bad/good women, while D. Paulo remained the hero of the narrative, a hero who caused a great deal of trouble and was troubled in return, but whose reputation remained seemingly unblemished. The narrative fit well with the social ideal for men of the upper ranks, but underneath the bravado was the reality – the necessity for a victim's pardon and the unsung role that a woman played in obtaining it.

---

59 Hormuz is a small island in the Gulf of Hormuz, located between the Persian Gulf and the Gulf of Oman, settled by the Portuguese in 1506, and taken by the English in 1623.

60 Diogo do Couto (1542–1616), *Vida de D. Paulo de Lima Pereira Capitam Mor de Armadas do Estado da India* (Lisbon: Na Officina de Jozé Filipe, 1765), 118–24.

61 A collection of stories dedicated to the wife of the viceroy in India typifies the idealized virtues associated with women of the upper ranks, virtues that included honour, obedience, and chastity. Gonçalo Fernandez Trancoso, *Primeira, Segvnda e Terceira Parte dos Contos e Historias de Proveito, e Exemplo, Dirigidos a Senhora Dona Joana D'Alburquerque, molher que foy do VisoRey da India, Ayres de Saldanha* (Lisbon: Antonio Alvarez, Impressor, 1608).

Although this had not been the author's intention, Couto's account of the noble's (mis)adventures highlighted the unstable ground on which patriarchy was built, particularly when one patriarch threatened another patriarch's turf. In the case discussed earlier about Susana and Domingos, we also saw that the husband was not always the man of the house, or that the man of the house was not necessarily the principal provider. The agreement between Susana and Domingos was in fact a reversal of the ideal patriarchal marriage which held that the husband build the nest and the wife maintain it. The ideal was for a man to keep a woman, not the other way around. In early modern Portugal, as elsewhere, each member of the couple contributed to the establishment and the operation of the household, and there is little doubt that the wife worked as hard as the husband. This was especially true among the labouring populace, but ideologies persisted that men's contributions were more substantial, and this stance was promoted in real terms through the customary higher wages for male labourers. Yet, the agreement between Susana and Domingos revealed that a husband could be dependent on his wife for sustenance and all other necessities. Other studies have shown that elsewhere in Europe patriarchy manifested itself in a variety of ways, and by necessity had to be malleable.[62]

The example of Susana and Domingos also illustrated some of the misconceptions about what constituted a valid marriage in the early modern period. Those misconceptions sometimes led to accusations of adultery, bigamy, or concubinage. Although the Council of Trent outlawed informal marriage arrangements in Catholic Europe, and ruled that a marriage was valid only if it was officiated by a priest at the church, in front of witnesses, following the banns, the church had to remain vigilant well into the seventeenth century and beyond. In fact, as Emlyn Eisenach has shown in her study of Verona, for a long time church condemnation did little to change the attitudes toward and the practice of concubinage, especially among commoners.[63]

In Portugal, too, the practice continued long after the Council of Trent's directives on the sanctity of marriage. In his examination of the records from the church visitations to the Bragança district in the eighteenth and nineteenth centuries, Belarmino Augusto Afonso noted that the sin/crime that came up more frequently was connected to concubinage and women bearing children out of wedlock. While several witnesses testified to the scandalous behaviour of the accused, one particular single mother was not a concern to her neighbours because she behaved appropriately otherwise. It was not the act of unlawful or immoral fornication itself that upset certain parishioners, but rather the flaunting of it, such as the case of a single woman who paraded her new-born son up and down the village; or the two sisters who lived scandalously, having children and leaving

---

62 See, for example, DesBrisay and Thomson, 'Crediting Wives'; Falconer, 'A Family Affair'; O'Dowd, 'Women and the Law'.

63 Emlyn Eisenach, *Husbands, Wives, and Concubines: Marriage, Family, and Social Order in Sixteenth-Century Verona* (Kirksville: Truman State University Press, 2004), 136–42.

them at the 'roda de Vinhais'; or the married man who had been chased by a few women who threw stones at him because he had been at the home of a single woman, Ana, where he had spent more than 20 hours.[64] Perhaps two hours would have sufficed.

Still, the church was not without its influence, particularly among those who depended on the institution for spiritual guidance, and for their livelihood. For instance, church officials in Coimbra dealt with a petition on 9 April 1607 from Catarina Henriques, in which petition she asked the church chapter for a donation to help her daughter get married. The church agreed to grant her 2,000 *réis* for her daughter's marriage, but officials notified Catarina that the money would not be handed over until her daughter was properly married in the church. On 6 March 1619 the church bureaucracy dealt with another petition from Catarina, when again she made a request on behalf of her daughter (never identified in the record). Catarina was the *varredeira da Sé* or sweeper of the main church in the diocese (cathedral), and she asked that her daughter be her successor in that post. Officials agreed to grant Catarina's daughter the office of *varredeira* upon the death of her mother, trusting that the daughter would be diligent in doing the cleaning as her mother had been.[65] Presumably Catarina's unidentified daughter had been properly married by then and was leading a model life of a married woman, otherwise the church would not have awarded her the *officio de varredeira*. The economic rewards must have been an incentive for some to follow church-sanctioned marital practices, but not everyone adhered to church prescriptions. Most cases brought to the attention of authorities dealt with single people living together, but some married men, too, were accused of engaging in what was termed 'public concubinage', a practice deemed detrimental to their wives and children, and to the moral fabric of society at large.

Women and Concubinage

By law, a married man could be punished for concubinage, but only if this caused great scandal and if he favoured the concubine to the detriment of his own family. A married man who had sexual relations with another woman, but did not provide her with all her living necessities, was legally not engaged in concubinage, even if the relationship resulted in offspring. Church officials, however, condemned both men and women for concubinage, and consequently some civil authorities were influenced to sentence married men with simple adultery in cases of sexual relations with single women.[66] In reality, though, the double standard was applied

64 Belarmino Augusto Afonso, 'Livros de devassa e etnotextos', *Sociedade Portuguesa de Antropologia e Etnologia* 25 (Faculdade de Ciências do Porto, 1985): 350–53 [347–58]. The 'roda de Vinhais' was a turn-box commonly found in the wall of a foundling hospital, an institution that looked after abandoned babies whose upkeep was financed by the municipality.

65 Almeida, *Acordos do Cabido de Coimbra*, 119, 223.

66 Hespanha, 'Da "Iustitia" à "Disciplina"', 340.

by both church and state, as seen in the promulgation from church authorities in Madeira, a promulgation that clearly viewed women as the source of the problem of concubinage. In that church decree, all male adulterers and male concubines were ordered to return to their wives and follow a proper life; if after three warnings they continued in their sinful ways, the female concubines would be banished.[67] In Spain, too, female concubines were more severely punished than their male concubines or cohabitors.[68]

Women and men faced accusations of concubinage, but the sexual double standard spread across secular and religious lines. For instance, a royal decree that the University of Coimbra enacted on 19 September 1538 warned students that if any concubine or other 'suspect' women were found in their lodgings, the women would be imprisoned and fined 1,000 *réis*, but the students themselves did not face the same harsh penalties.[69] The same discrepancy was entrenched in cases of concubinage that involved clerics, and the practice was of long standing. The town charter granted to Lisbon in 1217, for instance, stipulated that if any cleric was found fornicating with a public woman, the *mordomo* or church warden was not to arrest him, but that he could arrest the woman if he wished; similar sentiments were registered in the twelfth-century charter for Povos (Vila Franca de Xira), located between Lisbon and Santarém.[70] While these examples come from the more permissive Middle Ages, vis-à-vis the sexual infractions of the clergy, the cleric's concubine continued to be subjected to harsher penalties in the early modern period.

The royal ordinances of the sixteenth and seventeenth centuries left the cleric involved in concubinage to be handled by church authorities, but the law declared that any woman kept by a cleric would be subjected to a number of penalties. For the first offense, women faced fines of 2,000 *réis* and a year of exile from their town; for the second offense, the women paid the same fine and were exiled for a year further afield, outside their bishopric; for a third offense, they were publicly whipped and exiled outside the bishopric for an indefinite time period, to be determined by the Crown. The law provided an outlet, however, for women who were accused of concubinage could avoid all penalties if they married or entered the religious life. The caveat offered some room for negotiation, a way

---

67 Maria Margarida Castro Neves Mascarenhas Caeiro, 'Concepções da vida e da morte na Madeira entre 1580 e 1640: alguns contributos para a história das mentalidades do arquipélago', in *Actas III Colóquio Internacional de História da Madeira* (Funchal: Centro de Estudos do Atlântico, 1993), 578 [575–83].

68 Renato Barahona, *Sex Crimes, Honour, and the Law in Early Modern Spain: Vizcaya, 1528–1725* (Toronto: University of Toronto Press, 2003), 95–6.

69 Mario Brandão, ed., *Documentos de D. João III*, 4 vols (Coimbra: Universidade de Coimbra, 1937), I: 114.

70 Câmara Municipal de Lisboa, *Documentos do Arquivo Histórico da Câmara Municipal de Lisboa: Livros de Reis*, 8 vols (Lisbon: Câmara Municipal de Lisboa, 1957–1964), I: 5; Ma Filipa de Meneses Cordeiro, 'Foral de Povos – 1195', *Boletim Cultural* no. 1 (Câmara Municipal de Vila Franca de Xira, 1985): 151 [149–75]. For Viana do Castelo, see Pe Sérgio Augusto Gonçalves Pereira, 'Foral dado por D. Afonso III a Viana', *Arquivo do Alto Minho* 8, Tomo II (1958): 15 [7–19].

to find alternative solutions to the perceived challenge to the social order. Not surprisingly, negotiations manifested in a number of ways, including incidences of corruption that resulted in bribes for those who were in a position to launch accusations of concubinage. For this reason legislators stipulated that no one was allowed to accept or offer payment for the withdrawal of such an accusation, or pay a fine of 20 *cruzados*. It needs be reiterated that all of these conditions and penalties applied to the woman accused of living in concubinage with a cleric, not to the cleric himself, who was barely mentioned in the respective legislation. Indeed, secular authorities were not permitted to harass the guilty cleric, unless they had been instructed to intervene by the religious superiors.[71]

Not only was there a gendered component to the laws on concubinage, there were also clear distinctions between the elite and the commoner accused of living in concubinage. As already mentioned, the law also condemned male concubines, and in fact addressed the problem first and foremost at the royal court. A courtier was not allowed to have a concubine in court, otherwise he faced a fine according to his station. In addition to a year of exile from court, any man with the rank of *cavaleiro* or higher, paid 20 *cruzados*, a squire paid 10 *cruzados*, and the lower ranked man paid 5 *cruzados*. As for their female concubines, they, too, were banished from the royal court for a year, and paid 2,000 *réis* for the infraction. Furthermore, if the women were tradeswomen, such as bakers or hucksters, they were henceforth banned from practising their trade in the royal court or in Lisbon.[72] Note that the female concubine was not distinguished along categories of social station because she was presumed to be of the lower ranks. For this reason the women were fined a similar amount to what was inflicted on the lower-ranking male concubine-keeper, although the woman was further punished by losing her means of making a living.

The legislation differentiated between social ranks and between the marital status of those engaged in concubinage. Although often women were targeted, by far the most severe penalties for concubinage applied to married men. For the married male concubine, a first offense merited three years of exile to Africa and a pecuniary penalty of one fortieth of his estate separate from his wife's portion; the pecuniary amount was doubled for each subsequent offense of the same nature. The female concubine of a married man was also punished more harshly than the concubine of a single or religious man. For her first offense, she was whipped publicly, paraded through town with a noose and a public announcement ('baraço e pregão'), exiled to Castro Marim for a year, and levied a fine of half of what her married male concubine had to pay, with the doubling of this amount for subsequent accusations.

It is difficult to gauge which of the two accused were worse off, for the public humiliation was akin to a social death, but the exile overseas was also sometimes fatal due to the perils of high-seas travel and living conditions in overseas posts. The lower pecuniary penalty for the woman was undoubtedly due to a recognition

---

71 *Ordenações Filipinas*, Livro 5, Título 30 and 31.

72 *Ordenações Filipinas*, Livro 5, Título 27.

that a woman kept by a married man was likely to have little revenue or possessions of her own. Indeed, the law indicated that if an unmarried woman was kept in concubinage by any man, including clerics, and she ran away with any items stolen from her concubine-keeper, she was not liable to any persecution. Undoubtedly this clause served as a disincentive for men to enter into concubinage, and not as a form of protection for the hapless female concubine. Still, it could be argued that women who were desperate to leave their lovers did not need to fear the law if they absconded with goods that legally belonged to the rejected lovers. The only exception to this rule was that if the concubine lover was a married man, his wife could sue his female concubine for anything she took from the husband, or for any gift given to the concubine by the errant husband.[73]

As was the case with concubines of clerics, a female concubine of a married man also had the option of averting the legislated punishments by getting married or by entering a religious institution. Once again, though, the legislation of the period implied that some women were ingenious in finding ways to manipulate the law to their advantage. The problem was apparently more pronounced in Lisbon, where authorities suspected that some concubine women claimed to have married men from afar just to have the pretext that they were married. They then attempted to use their married status as a protection against accusations of concubinage, but the law ordered officials to verify those cases, and that if the alleged husbands had been absent for up to two years, and their whereabouts were unknown, the women in question were liable to persecution. Authorities were cautioned, however, not to proceed against women whose husbands were squires or of a higher station, a clause that allowed the upper ranks to deal with their marital problems in private and avoid public scandal.[74]

While the law had much to say about adultery and concubinage, historians have no way to gauge the extent to which either phenomenon was practised, how the laws were applied, and the social costs of these behaviours that were deemed deviant by state legislators and church leaders alike. The pulse of the general population cannot be measured by the admonitions of a select few, however almighty they were placed, but given the concerns with the proper administration of family property noted earlier, it is safe to hazard that the more property was at stake, the greater the perceived need to control women's sexuality, and the wider the spectrum for men's. More than a double standard, it was a hodgepodge of standards that overlapped depending on the individual's social, economic, and marital status. In this regard, Portugal did not deviate from the rest of Europe. As Maria R. Boes has stated, while regional differences were sometimes significant, a double standard – if not a multi-standard – was the norm in the application of the law in early modern Europe, with gender and socio-economic status ranking high on the list of determining factors.[75]

---

73 *Ordenações Filipinas*, Livro 5, Título 28 and 29; *Ordenações Manuelinas*, Livro 5, Título 25 to 28.

74 *Ordenações Filipinas*, Livro 5, Título 28, no 7.

75 Maria R. Boes, 'Women and the Penal System in Frankfurt am Main, 1562–1696', *Criminal Justice History: An International Annual* 13 (1992): 61–73.

The laws reflected these hierarchies and the contradictions within the law codes reflected the difficulties law makers and law keepers faced in promoting ideologies that were inherently inequitable and untenable. Prohibitions against sexual activities outside the normalized codes were especially challenging to maintain because those activities could occur in the most private and secret places, and it was difficult to catch someone 'at it' under most circumstances. For women, who risked getting pregnant and whose offspring had to be cared for and ultimately could inherit family property of significant proportions, the clandestine sexual encounter was perceived as particularly troublesome. Yet pre-marital sex occurred more frequently than authorities deemed appropriate, as shown in the high rate of illegitimate births in certain regions. Portuguese researchers found that while in southern Portugal only 2 per cent of children were born out of wedlock – a European norm – the rates of illegitimacy in northern Portugal ranged between 10 and 15 per cent. The high figures for the northern region have been explained as a result of a sex ratio imbalance in the north due to a high concentration of men who migrated to Brazil.[76]

Even more contradictory was the example set by the Portuguese Crown. In his study of justice and criminality during the reign of King D. Afonso V (r.1438–1481), the historian Luís Miguel Duarte found a record from Santarém, dated 27 March 1471, in which the Crown gave a woman named Leonor a license to continue to make her living in *mancebia*, or concubinage/prostitution, free of harassment from officials. In her appeal to the Crown, Leonor maintained that she made her living with men at the royal court and outside of it, but that she did not want a pimp nor to give her money to any other person. She also pointed out that she was not a concubine of clerics or friars or of married men, yet she was being arrested for the latter, so she sought and obtained this document which gave her some protection because she refused to give her money to the bailiffs, who she claimed persecuted her maliciously. The document stated that from that day forward she could not be arrested, imprisoned, or accused of being a concubine of a cleric or friar or married man, nor of having a pimp, unless authorities could provide two witnesses to that effect. The document implied once again that bailiffs were harassing her because she refused to pay them off.[77]

The case of Leonor showed that a conventionally marginalized woman could manoeuvre her way through a system that was set up to hinder her illicit line of work, but it is perhaps no coincidence that she was identified as a 'judia castelhana', or a Castilian Jew. Possibly the law could be more tolerant of Leonor's seemingly deviant activities because of her status as an outsider. What could be expected

[76] Isabel dos Guimarães Sá, 'As crianças e as idades da vida', in José Mattoso, ed., *História da Vida Privada em Portugal: A Idade Moderna*, 4 vols (Lisbon: Círculo de Leitores e Temas e Debates, 2011), II: 89 [72–95]. For Lisbon, see Teresa Rodrigues, *Cinco Séculos de Quotidiano: A vida em Lisboa do século XV aos nossos dias* (Lisbon: Edições Cosmos, 1997), 96–7.

[77] IAN/TT, *Chancelaria de Dom Afonso V*, Livro 16, f.56v, in Duarte, *Justiça e Criminalidade* (Document no. 50), 606.

from an infidel from the other side of the border? Yet the Crown was flexible when it was convenient to indulge in flexibility. Four years after Leonor received her special license, the king sent an order to officials in Guimarães that flaunted the laws against concubinage even further. The order provided 12 years of unrestricted license for whichever concubine attached herself to Lourenço Afonso de Andrade, schoolmaster in Guimarães. Lourenço was no ordinary schoolmaster, for he was also chaplain of the Duke of Guimarães, the king's nephew. To ensure that everyone involved understood the implications of this order, the document stated that this license was in effect even though it was contrary to the legislation of the realm.[78]

The special licences granted to Leonor and to Lourenço were issued almost a century before the Council of Trent and the Catholic Reformation, after which authorities became more restrictive with cases of concubinage, but the perceived problem persisted, and the legislation reflected the inconsistencies between ideology and reality. This inconsistency was particularly acute in the section of the royal ordinances that dealt with the rights of daughters and sons to disinherit their parents. A daughter could disinherit her mother if the mother had 'carnal knowledge' with the daughter's husband or the daughter's male concubine ('barregão'), who had kept and maintained the daughter. Likewise, a son could disinherit his father if the father had 'carnal knowledge' with the son's wife or with the son's female concubine ('barregã') he had, or previously had kept and maintained. The significant distinction in the clause was that the son could still have a concubine while he was married, while the reference to the daughter's concubine was in relation to someone who had kept and maintained her in the past. Furthermore, the legislation took for granted that it was the man who kept a concubine woman, and the concubine woman who was kept by the concubine man. A woman could be kept but she was not a keeper, and as a married woman she was only supposed to be kept by her husband.[79]

Although the above-noted ordinance on inheritance and concubinage was found in the *Ordenações Filipinas* of 1603, it was clearly a remnant of former times, and it is doubtful that the law was implemented as a matter of course in the sixteenth and seventeenth centuries. Still, those ordinances were in effect, and, given the regularity with which authorities were confronted with the problem of concubinage, a fair segment of the population deemed it as an accepted form of human relations. Secular and ecclesiastical authorities prosecuted concubines, but it is difficult to gauge whether or not those prosecutions were effective deterrents. Part of the problem was that the laity and the clergy were dealt with in separate courts, and this practice did little to ensure consistency in the ways cases were handled, and in the perception of fair treatment among all sinners. For instance, Francisco Lopes, single, and Maria Rodrigues, also single, were both in the Porto jail in September 1572 for concubinage, though under different circumstances.

78 In Duarte, *Justiça e Criminalidade* (Document no. 71), 621.

79 *Ordenações Filipinas*, Livro 4, Título 89, no. 2. A parent could also disinherit a child for having sexual relations with her or his concubine. *Ordenações Filipinas*, Livro 4, Título 88, no. 10.

Francisco's partner, Maria Afonso, would have been charged with the same crime of concubinage, while Maria Rodrigues' partner, a cleric, was handled by the church, and subsequently did not face the same dire consequences.[80]

Women and the Clergy

The town charters noted above revealed that both church and state shared a preoccupation with sexual misconduct, and that both institutions targeted women in their endeavours to curb the problem. In the late fifteenth century, Portuguese church officials attempted to regulate the clergy by imposing sanctions on those living with concubines, but those sentiments, too, betrayed an ideological prejudice. The cleric was living *with* a concubine, not *as* a concubine himself. Given such a premise, it is not surprising that the church ultimately aimed to punish the priest's companion and not the priest. There were some attempts to curb priests as well, through the imposition of fines, withdrawing of privileges, and excommunication, but none of these threats led to any substantive changes in the behaviour of the clergy. Consequently, the church asked the Crown to apply certain penalties on the women instead, and as mentioned above, the Crown complied. The church also decreed that women who at the time of their death were concubines of clerics would not be buried in sacred ground, and any cleric or anyone else present at her burial would be excommunicated. For those women who repented of their sin and entered marriage or a convent, their royal pardon would be honoured by the church, as long as they did not return to their former sinful lives.[81]

Despite those efforts, the church had an uphill battle. One Portuguese study looked at 269 royal pardons granted from 1481 to 1485 and found that 154 or 56 per cent of those pardons were granted to women who had been concubines of clerics. In one of those pardons a reference was made to the belief that 'a woman will never know love unless she has a cleric for a lover'. Apparently some women saw clerics as more sensitive men, and a relationship with them was a means for women to escape from the conventional conjugal obligations where procreation was essential for the family lineage, though clerics and their concubines also had children. Indeed, some priests openly acknowledged their offspring and even employed their children to assist with church services on Sundays.[82]

The extent to which the combination of male cleric and female concubine was a perceived problem can be seen in a law from 1401 which attempted to curtail clerics. In its preamble, legislators noted that many clerics and friars kept women in their homes and paraded them through town. Worst still, those women

---

80 The two prisoners obtained powers of attorney to deal with their cases, dated 29 August 1572 and 5 September 1572, respectively. ADP, Fundo Notarial, Po.1, 3a Se, Livro 43 (1572), f.37–38v, f.47v–48.

81 Queirós, 'Theudas e Mantheudas', 41.

82 Leandro Alves Teodoro, 'O comprometimento moralizante dos sínodos portugueses entre os séculos XIV e XV', *Portuguese Studies Review* 21, no. 1 (Summer 2013): 10–13 [7–18].

were dressed and adorned so well, and so much better than the wives of the laity, that many women refused to accept legitimate husbands and preferred to live with clerics and friars as their concubines. Over and over the church was urged to punish the clergy with excommunication, suspensions, and other penalties, but some church leaders responded that those penalties were ineffective if the monarch did not impose temporal penalties on the women.[83] Apparently this was still a concern in the seventeenth century as a marriage manual advised husbands to minimize the encounters between their wives and priests.[84]

Part of the problem stemmed from the fact that many clerics had female servants, and often those female servants became concubines of clerics, or were accused of the practice. To safeguard against false accusations, the Crown legislated that clerics could have live-in servants as long as the clerics were more than 60 years old, and the servant women more than 50. Problems arose, nonetheless, as exemplified by the royal pardon dated 23 January 1483, granted to Catarina Rodrigues, a 60-year-old single woman, resident of Lisbon. Catarina had been accused of being the concubine of Alvaro Fernandes, a vicar of 80 years of age, also of Lisbon, for which offense she had been condemned to one year of banishment from the capital. She petitioned the Crown for a pardon, seemingly not because she was innocent, but rather she argued that she had been serving the exile sentence for six or seven months already, and as she was poor, and of that advanced age, and weak, she asked the Crown to lift the remaining time left in her banishment, to which the Crown agreed for a payment of 500 white *reais* for the *Arca da Piedade*.[85] Again, Catarina Rodrigues was accused of concubinage, not her vicar concubine.

The perceived anxieties with concubinage were part of a broader problem that the church had imposing its authority.[86] The church visitation in 1570 to the parish of Sant'Ana in Lisbon is a case in point. At that time, officials established a list of individuals engaged in concubinage, and of the 25 identified names, 15 were women. The registry also included another list of those who were guilty of not attending to religious services on Sundays and holy days, and the first part consisted of 29 women, nearly all identified as *tripeiras* or tripe-mongers, plus four of their female servants who were not identified by name, and one lone male, a market gardener who provided the *tripeiras* with water on Sundays and holy days. Yet another list of those guilty of failing to attend church services contained 19 names of fleecers, three of whom were women, all of whom were also reprimanded for blasphemy. Finally, officials ordered the following to appear

---

[83] Queirós, 'Theudas e Mantheudas', 37, 40–42; Caetano, *História do Direito*, 565.

[84] D. Francisco Manuel de Mello, *Carta de Guia de Casados*, 2nd ed. (Porto: A 'Renascença Portuguesa', 1923 [1651]), 100.

[85] Queirós, 'Theudas e Mantheudas', 42, and her Appendix no. 25.

[86] The problem was exacerbated by an inadequate number of clergy to offer guidance to the population at large, a problem that was especially acute in larger cities. See Amélia Polónia, *O Cardeal Infante D. Henrique, Arcebispo de Évora. Um prelado no limiar da viragem tridentina* (Porto: Fundação Eugénio de Almeida, 2005), 98–9.

before the Church Visitation within eight days: Ana Lopes and Tomé Lopes, a pair of siblings who lived in front of Roque Leitão, and other women who lived in the premises of Francisco Sodre on Rua de Martim Vaz, possibly to deal with accusations of prostitution.[87]

Given the moral laxity in the parish, a follow-up was deemed necessary, but the new findings were not encouraging. Records from the church visitation in 1571 showed that religious practices had not been improved very much, and that indeed church doctrine had not been taught properly. The church thus ordered that sinners and curates alike be fined for their lapses. Officials also issued another registry of couples living in concubinage, and imposed hefty fines on four of those couples who had been warned the previous year. Another list of 'women who work on Sundays and holy days' was concocted, and that list contained the names of 21 identified women and one woman's husband. Of those 21 women, 11 had been on the list the previous year. On the one hand, the church could claim some success in convincing a few parishioners to abandon their sinful habits; on the other hand, there were more women who did not honour the sanctity of the Sunday church service, and a new batch of couples living in concubinage, some of whom were women and men married to others.[88] Nor was the problem unique to that parish or to that time period. A social history of the town of Cuba in the eighteenth century showed that the residents of that area circumvented church doctrine in a number of ways, most notably by engaging in adultery and prostitution, and in practising contraception. Furthermore, the parishioners generally kept their devotional rites at arms-length, and even denounced the local priest for invading their privacy in the confessional.[89]

Both the church and state could be harsh in its pecuniary penalties to wrongdoers, yet that threat did not deter everyone from doing whatever was necessary to survive. The tripe-mongers noted above had to clean the tripe whenever fresh tripe was available, including on Sundays and holy days. They might have purposely disregarded religious doctrine, or they might have been pressured by economic necessity. The same could be said of individuals accused of concubinage, individuals motivated by emotional needs and the lack of resources to seek other accommodations. Yet fines were serious enough. A list of prices for royal pardons from the early sixteenth century indicated that a pardon for concubinage could cost between 2,000 and 3,500 *réis* (see Appendix 1). That was a substantial amount for most people, especially for women of the lower ranks; a survey of Lisbon done in 1552 noted that domestic servants earned 2,000 *réis* per

---

87 Franco, 'Um Livro de Visitações', 77–80.

88 Franco, 'Um Livro de Visitações', 85–9. For examples of people who flaunted church rules and chose to live in co-habitation in Galicia, Spain, see Poska, *Women and Authority*, 79–81.

89 Amília Salvado Borges, *Homens, Fazenda e Poder no Alentejo de Setecentos: O Caso de Cuba* (Lisbon: Edições Colibri, 2000), 194–5. Cuba is located in the district of Alentejo, just north of Beja.

year, plus room and board.[90] In Spain, too, the average fine for concubinage was six ducats for first-time offenders, which equalled to one year's rent for some.[91] It is impossible to determine the extent to which the phenomenon of concubinage was widespread, but parishioners had reason to be cynical of the view from authorities. For instance, during a church visitation in 1708, in Soure, the church official found that even the outside judge had a young single woman kept outside of town, but within his jurisdiction.[92]

Overall, the evidence was inconsistent and inconclusive. Even arguments about women being targeted more than men need some qualification.[93] On 2 December 1640, the new Portuguese king, D. João IV (r.1640–1656), sent word to Crown officials in the Algarve to be more diligent with the problem of male concubines, and clerics, and married men who were engaged in scandalous behaviour by living with single women.[94] The Spanish king before him, too, found that matters had gotten out of hand, in response to which on 20 October 1632 the Crown sent out a plea to its subjects, stating that the realm had endured great losses at sea and in military campaigns because God was unhappy with the laxity with which people were conducting their lives. Consequently, the Crown urged justice officials to be especially diligent in punishing 'public sins' and to be fair in the administration of justice, protecting widows, orphans, and the forsaken, and to follow through with their complaints and finding remedies for them, for in this way maybe God would once again favour the (Iberian) kingdoms.[95]

The king was not alone in linking human misbehaviour with God's wrath. In Catholic Europe, the idea of good works on earth for salvation in heaven reigned supreme, and officially Portugal was a very Catholic country, but the exigencies for a proper Christian life, expounded by ecclesiastical and secular leaders alike, were not easily adhered to, and lapses into 'public sins' were not easily curtailed. For early modern Portuguese women (and some men), accusations of sexual misconduct could lead to serious repercussions, but often those repercussions could be mitigated through some formal and informal negotiations. Negotiations were sometimes protracted, though, as in the case of Brites Lourenço of Terceira who received a royal pardon for concubinage in 1650. In her petition to the Crown, Brites indicated that she had already spent two years in jail, and had been too

---

90 Brandão, *Grandeza e Abastança*, 70.

91 Barahona, *Sex Crimes*, 118.

92 Joaquim Ramos de Carvalho, 'Confessar e devassar: a igreja e a vida privada na época moderna', in José Mattoso, ed. *História da Vida Privada em Portugal: A Idade Moderna*, 4 vols (Lisbon: Círculo de Leitores e Temas e Debates, 2011), II: 39 [32–57].

93 In certain regions, the public purging of sexual sins sometimes targeted women. See, for example, Gordon DesBrisay, 'Twisted by Definition: Women Under Godly Discipline in Seventeenth-Century Scottish Towns', in Yvonne Galloway Brown and Rona Ferguson, eds, *Twisted Sisters: Women, Crime and Deviance in Scotland Since 1400* (East Lothian: Tuckwell Press, 2002), 137–55.

94 Andrade e Silva, *Collecção Chronologica (1640–1647)*, 9.

95 Andrade e Silva, *Collecção Chronologica (1627–1633)*, 251.

ill to fulfil the one-year sentence of exile off the island.[96] As is often the case, nothing is known about the other parties in the evidence presented against Brites, but a sample of accusations related to concubinage is examined here to explore the phenomenon at the micro level, and to highlight the inconsistencies in the accusations, as well as the exigencies that occasionally necessitated a retraction of those accusations.

The Concubine's Pardon

Because accusers in early modern Portugal were typically awarded half of the pecuniary penalties inflicted on the accused, local officials and members of the general public had an incentive to report and launch complaints against their neighbours for concubinage. Some of these same accusers could in turn be motivated to grant the accused a *perdão de parte*, as seen in an example dated 17 August 1657 when João de Oliveira, the bailiff in Porto, granted a pardon to Jerónima Martins, widow, resident of the Freguesia de São Martinho do Campo, Concelho de Refóios. João had initially denounced Jerónima for concubinage, and 'through his diligence she was finally sentenced and condemned to pay him 2,000 *réis*, and to one year of exile outside the city and district'. Content with the monetary payment, João was prepared to pardon Jerónima's exile so that the royal senate could pardon her exile as well.[97]

This scenario is worth reconstructing, in as much as possible. A judicial official accused a woman of breaking the law by living in concubinage; the woman was found guilty of the charge, and sentenced; that same official was rewarded for his 'diligence' and received half the pecuniary penalty the woman was condemned to pay; the official then granted the woman a *perdão de parte*. How was the bailiff a victim of Jerónima's concubinage? It could be argued that, on the grand scheme of things, he was victimized by the harm his community was subjected to by the lax morals that Jerónima's crime represented, but that was highly unlikely. There was nothing altruistic about this matter, though certainly there was plenty of room for scheming. The bailiff stood to gain by denouncing Jerónima, and this case exemplifies the extent to which the *perdão de parte* was a tool through which people negotiated settlements. As already shown, to pardon was not necessarily to forgive, but rather to forgo that to which a victim – or another interested party – was entitled. As the accuser, the bailiff was an interested party in this case because by law he was entitled to half the penalty imposed on the accused, monetary or otherwise. Indeed, that was how he earned his living. Thus, he was owed half of Jerónima's exile or its equivalent. Jerónima negotiated with the bailiff for his portion, received his *perdão de parte*, and was set to negotiate the Crown's share of that equivalency. Interestingly and significantly, the bailiff's pardon said nothing about Jerónima's repentance and avowal to change her living arrangements. That would be her argument when she appealed her case.

---

96 Cited in Corrêa, 'Aspectos da Criminalidade nos Açores', 553.

97 ADP, Fundo Notarial, Po.4, 1a Se, no. 48 (1657–1658), f.8.

The Wrongfully Accused

The same system that allowed for an accuser to pardon the accused also permitted the accused to pardon the accuser. This measure was necessary because not all accusations were favourable to the accusers. For instance, Mariana Segurada, single woman, and Filipe Teixeira, tailor, residents of Evora, granted a pardon to the local bailiff who had erroneously denounced them for 'ilicita conversação' or illicit conversation – a euphemism that was associated with concubinage, or nearing that dangerous zone of sexual deviance that was just one step removed from more serious delinquency. The case had been judged by the *Supremo Senado da Relação* (Supreme Court), and the court condemned the bailiff to a two-year suspension of his office ('vara de correição'), as well as to pay for all costs, losses, and damages the two accused incurred in the process, including personal days ('dias pessoais') – that is, days they lost of work while dealing with the charges. For reasons not stipulated, Mariana and Filipe

> pardoned the said António de Sousa de Faria all the part and right that they have in the said suspension of the said office of bailiff of corrections, to which the said António de Sousa de Faria was condemned according to the *Sentença da Relação* for the said time of two years, and likewise they pardoned him of all culpa, loss, damage, and injury that the said António de Sousa de Faria caused them due to the said denunciation, and they wanted nothing from him, civil or criminal.[98]

From a case of a seemingly overzealous official we learn that not all accusations were successful, and that the wronged defendants were entitled to some compensation, including the possible loss of daily wages. Although the record did not indicate how Mariana earned a living, the court ruling recognized that she, too, incurred financial losses through the disruption to her work day. Since she and Filipe were vindicated, we can presume that their lives returned to normal, but the effects of an accusation, however false, could linger for a long time. As a single woman, Mariana would be particularly vulnerable to sexual innuendo that blemished her reputation, a reputation she needed to safeguard in order to work as a domestic servant, for instance, or to attract an honourable match in matrimony.[99] Yet the case also illustrated that men, too, could be affected by accusations of sexual impropriety, albeit in a different way. If Filipe was single, and romantically unattached, he likely received some winks and nods of approval from his mates; if he was married, he had to deal with possible doubts and suspicions from his wife, and in-laws.

Mariana and Filipe had been able to fight an accusation of concubinage at the local level, but some couples were forced to appeal their cases to a higher court,

98 ADE, Fundo Notarial, Manuel Galvão Bárcoro (notary), Séries 734 (1677), f.63–63v. Some punctuation was added for clarity.

99 For an overview of the status of the single woman in early modern Europe, see Bennett and Froide, *Singlewomen*, passim, and Vollendorf, *The Lives of Women*, 148.

even if they maintained their innocence. The best defence against an accusation of concubinage was proof of matrimony, a certificate of which Domingas Jorge and João Rodrigues received from their local priest, and which they attached to their petition to the Crown. From the royal pardon they received we learn that the couple had been rounded up during a 'devassa dos amancebados', or general inquiry into concubinage, held in Setúbal in 1630 by the district magistrate. In fact, they argued, they had been preparing to get married, and the Crown accepted their arguments by granting them a pardon on 20 June 1631, seemingly without the customary fines. The pardon was worded in a way that pointed to a marriage that had been precipitated by the judicial troubles that befell upon Domingas and João, but, for early modern Portuguese authorities, the end justified the means. The accused were married and all was well, at least on paper.[100]

The Would-Be Concubines

As was often the case with accusations of concubinage, Domingas and João claimed that they had been reported to authorities by their enemies, a claim that cannot be verified, though by its very nature, the public inquiry encouraged individuals to come forth and denounce their neighbours, friend or foe.[101] The system was open to false accusations, or to accusations that had more to do with personal gain than with public outrage. Hints to this effect were found in a *perdão de parte* issued in Porto that suggests that the accusers manipulated the system to their own advantage. In their pardon dated 6 December 1633, Pedro Gonçalves, tailor, and his wife, Maria Martins, residents of Rua da Lada in Porto, stated that they had denounced and requested an inquiry against Domingos António who at the time of their denunciation was a single man. This initial accusation led to a dispute, and Domingos injured Pedro at the *Feira de Arnelas* (a public fair) on St. Michael's Day in 1629. Thus, Domingos was initially jailed not for concubinage but for having injured Pedro during a fight about the alleged concubinage.

Whether or not Maria Martins and her husband orchestrated the whole thing is not for us to know, but at the time that the pardon document was drafted, Maria Gonçalves, the prisoner's wife, met the accusers at the notary's office and gave them 6,000 *réis* in coin, 'for this quittance, and to assist with the costs of this legal procedure' that the plaintiffs incurred. In recording her presence, the notary identified Maria Gonçalves as a resident of Melrois, 'esposada que disse ser de Domingos António' – that is, who claimed to be married to Domingos, also of Melrois. Such a statement raised doubts about the marriage that took place between Maria and Domingos, the notary deliberately indicating that she claimed to be married to Domingos, as opposed to merely identifying her as 'wife of', per usual.[102]

---

100 IAN/TT, Chancelaria de Dom Filipe III, *Perdões e Legitimações*, Livro 21, f.287–287v.

101 Afonso, 'Livros de devassa', 349.

102 ADP, Fundo Notarial, Po.4, 1a Se, no. 23 (1633), f.259–260.

The severity of Pedro's injuries was not indicated, but he and his wife received a substantial amount from the defendant, possibly more than they stood to gain if the initial accusation of concubinage had been proven in court. It took them four years to recognize that Domingos was a poor man, that he was not to blame for the injuries inflicted on Pedro, and that he had done the right thing by marrying Maria Gonçalves; or, more likely, it took that long for the defendants to raise the funds to pay off the plaintiffs. An accusation cost time and money to the accused, especially if she or he ended up in jail and had to hire someone to deal with the legal case. An accusation of concubinage also put a strain on a relationship. Maria and Domingos were propelled to get married, but such a step was impossible when one of the concubines was already married.

A Concubine Husband, and the Husband's Concubine

We do not know when Beatriz Guarda of Evora married João Moreiro, but a *perdão de parte* dated 13 April 1545 showed that the marriage had been troubled for some time. Part of those marital problems were undoubtedly connected to the fact that Beatriz's husband was living in concubinage with Bertoleza Veiga, for which infraction the local *alcaide* denounced João and Bertoleza for being 'barregueiros públicos', or living in concubinage. The complaint against her husband had been made in September 1542, and on 13 April 1545 Beatriz was prepared to pardon her husband for 'all the wrong, harm, injury, and offense' that he had caused by this incident and 'she did not wish to accuse him nor demand anything of him, not civil or criminal'.[103]

As already mentioned, a married woman had no legal recourse against a philandering husband, but the law could intervene if a married man was deemed to be negligent of his duty to his family by engaging in concubinage. In such a case the injured wife could play a key role in the judicial process, particularly once the conviction had been handed down against the errant husband. Thus, Beatriz's husband needed her pardon to deal with his legal case, though negotiations for her acquiescence must have been laborious given that it took almost three years for her pardon to materialize. Beatriz's husband needed a pardon from the bailiff, as well, for the bailiff was the primary accuser. A *perdão de parte* from the injured wife was a formality that provided the appearance of a reconciliation between the spouses, and that ostensibly the 'barregueiro' husband had mended his ways.

In cases of a philandering husband, the law recognized that the abandoned wife was in peril, but patriarchal ideals deemed it inappropriate for the wife to accuse her husband of concubinage or adultery-by-any-other-name. Men had the legal if not social prerogative to philander all they wanted, as long as their philandering did not undermine the family economy. It was one thing for João Moreiro to have an illicit relationship with Bertoleza Veiga; it was quite another for him to live with her and, in the conventional patriarchal mindset, maintain her. This meant that Beatriz Guarda, wife, was deprived of that maintenance: emotional, sexual,

[103] ADE, Fundo Notarial, no. 6 (1545), f.24–24v.

and material. There was little she could do about the first two, but the law provided Beatriz a way to protect her rights to the latter.

This pardon showed that there was some recourse for women with husbands who neglected their marital duties. Unfortunately for Bertoleza Veiga, Beatriz's husband's concubine, the pardon did not extend to her, and the fate of that single woman remains unknown. In fact, the state of Beatriz and João's marriage was also precarious, regardless of the resolution that the wife's pardon implied. If he had to be charged and sentenced in order to desist from his concubinage (presuming that he desisted), João must have been a reluctant husband, at best. This is not to say that João could ignore the charge of concubinage – the need for his wife's pardon is proof that the charges were serious, and could prove costly. One royal pardon was issued on 3 March 1610 to a man accused of engaging in concubinage with two women, for which pardon he had to pay 6,000 *réis*, double the fine listed in the *Regimento dos Perdões* (See Appendix 1). The justifications for the amounts charged for royal pardons were not revealed, though, and it is noteworthy that Domingas Luís, too, had to pay 6,000 *réis* for the royal pardon she received on 13 March 1579, despite the extenuating circumstances connected to her concubinage. As she explained to authorities, her male partner's wife had left him fourteen years earlier and was believed to be dead, but she still had been sentenced to two years of exile for that illicit relationship.[104]

No example was found of a wife confronting her 'barregão' husband directly, but one other option for wronged wives was to denounce the husband's female companion, instead. In that case, it is difficult to ascertain which woman faced a more uncertain future, as revealed in a *perdão de parte* written up in Lisbon on 12 March 1582. In an unusually long and detailed pardon document, Maria Gonçalves declared that she had denounced Beatriz de Paiva for being a concubine kept and maintained by Maria's husband, Baltasar da Costa.[105] In that denunciation, Maria also claimed that her husband had beaten her, from which she had head injuries, and that Beatriz had been the source of the attack. Maria filed her complaint in February, and Beatriz was in the local jail as a result, but a month or so later, Maria was better informed.

In a detraction steeped with ambiguities and contradictions, Maria declared that she had been wrong all along: Beatriz was not involved with her husband; her husband had not beaten her because of Beatriz; if her husband had beaten her it was due to some marital problems and her husband was stressed; Maria's husband had turned against her but not because of Beatriz; even if Beatriz had been the cause of the beating, Maria pardoned her because it was the time of Lent; Maria's injuries were healed and left no scar; because Beatriz was innocent of the charges, Maria paid Beatriz for the losses she incurred in her incarceration; Maria pardoned Beatriz on condition that Beatriz pay for her own costs and losses.

---

104 IAN/TT, Chancelaria de Dom Filipe II, *Perdões e Legitimações*, Livro 28, f.239–239v; Chancelaria de Dom Sebastião e Dom Henrique, *Perdões e Legitimações*, Livro 33, f.218–218v.

105 IAN/TT, Fundo Notarial (Lisbon), Caixa 2, Livro 12 (1582), f.61v–62v.

In her attempt to downplay the incident, Maria Gonçalves betrayed the desperation of a woman likely badgered by a violent husband to acquiesce to this legal procedure that may have helped another woman who was charged with a serious offense. It is not clear if the husband was also charged with concubinage or with beating up his wife, but the 'differences' between them could not have improved during this ordeal. The domestic scene was turbulent and probably remained so for a long time, and the conflict was well known outside the matrimonial bedchamber. Among those gathered at the notary's office was Domingos Dias, one of Maria's servants, who made a cross on the document, vouching for his mistress' identity, while the illiterate Maria had someone sign her pardon on her behalf. Whatever the outcome of this case, whatever costs to her honour and purse, Maria had at the very least alerted authorities of a wrong she perceived had been caused against her. Furthermore, as already seen with the Beatriz Guarda case, had Maria's husband been charged with concubinage, he would have needed her pardon as well. One Portuguese study noted the example of a man who received a royal pardon for concubinage on condition that he pay a fine, and the stated justification for the plea was that his wife had forgiven him and his concubine had already died.[106]

Renato Barahona found an example in Spain of a husband who blamed his mistreatment of his wife on the misbehaviour of his mistress.[107] In Maria Gonçalves' pardon, she blamed her husband's mistreatment on herself. Either way, the abusive husband was seemingly blameless for his attacks, and adulterous behaviour. Even allowing for the rhetorical conventions of the victim's pardon, the case of Maria Gonçalves highlighted the great divide between a pardon and forgiveness. The first was necessary for judicial purposes, the second for peace of mind; sometimes both were essential for survival. The outcome of the turmoil that led to Maria's pardon is unknown, but it is not inconceivable that the troubled marriage continued till its bitter end. In her work on Frankfurt am Main, Germany, Maria Boes found some compelling examples of women 'forgiving' their abusive husbands. Women who had been victims of their husbands' criminal behaviour, or whose husbands had been convicted of incest with their own daughters or sisters, plea bargained for a milder sentence for their convicted husbands. Women did this, Boes noted, because they needed to be practical instead of emotional; the punishment imposed on their husbands had a direct effect on their own lives.[108]

The example of Maria Gonçalves underscored the risks that a woman faced if she confronted her adulterous husband. It is impossible to gauge the prevalence of married men engaged in concubinage, but the risk of the husband retaliating must have been enough of a threat to deter some women from seeking redress. After all, Portuguese law allowed for husbands to discipline their wives and children.[109] It is also worth noting that the best that Portuguese law allowed for women to deal with their husbands' unfaithfulness was for wives to accuse the women with whom

---

106 Rodrigues, 'A Guiné nas cartas', 404.

107 Barahona, *Sex Crimes*, 102.

108 Boes, 'Women and the Penal System', 69.

109 *Ordenações Filipinas*, Livro 5, Título 36.

the husbands were unfaithful. Such a practice served patriarchal ideologies well, for wives were not encouraged to deal with the culprit head-on, but instead to go around the back door. This way a wife did not disturb the husband's authority, and the problem was turned into a woman's quarrel. As mentioned earlier, Laura Gowing found in her study of women and slander litigation in early modern London that in cases of men's adultery, wives were more inclined to verbally attack their husbands' mistresses than actually confront their cheating husbands.[110] The head injuries that Maria Gonçalves received from her adulterous husband go a long way to explain the reasons for that phenomenon.

Although Maria Gonçalves retracted her accusation against Beatriz de Paiva, her husband's concubine, Beatriz still faced a legal procedure that was not in her favour. Some Portuguese studies showed that in cases of concubinage between two secular people, there was a gender bias in the application of the law. Of the 197 royal pardons granted to residents of the Azores Archipelago during the reign of D. Sebastião in the sixteenth century, several were awarded to married men while only one was given to a woman.[111] As already mentioned, one of the major drawbacks of the royal pardon collections was that the surviving records represented the successful pleas only, not the number of accusations nor the number of unsuccessful pleas. There is no way to know whether those married men's concubines were also apprehended and whether they, too, applied for a royal pardon.

The discrepancy in the records raises questions of an inequitable application of the law, or an inequitable distribution of resources with which to deal with the judicial process. At some very concrete level, women were disadvantaged in the financial costs of concubinage. Three examples of royal pardons for concubinage from 1627 showed that two female plaintiffs and one male paid 4,000 *réis* each for their respective pardons, but in actuality this pecuniary penalty was a harsher sentence for women because most of them earned substantially less than men and thus would have had less access to that amount of money.[112] Karen Jones, too, found that English authorities generally imposed similar penalties to women and men for fornication or adultery, but men had greater financial resources to pay to have their penalties commuted.[113]

My own findings were insufficient to determine whether or not the single woman was disadvantaged in the eyes of the law vis-à-vis her married concubine lover. Given that legislators and church leaders were above all intent on protecting the integrity of the matrimonial unit, it is highly probable that the 'other' woman would be deemed more blameworthy, but the evidence under discussion here does not reflect those views. The only two *querelas* found in connection to concubinage

---

110 Gowing, 'Language, Power', 34.

111 Braga and Braga, 'A criminalidade nos Açores', 532.

112 IAN/TT, Chancelaria de Dom Filipe III, *Perdões e Legitimações*, Livro 18, f.346; Livro 19, f.107v–108.

113 Karen Jones, *Gender and Petty Crime in Late Medieval England: The Local Courts in Kent, 1460–1560* (Woodbridge: Boydell Press, 2006), 144–7.

showed two married men and two single women accused simultaneously. As a precedent to the victim's pardon, the *querela* shed light on the arguments that were deemed pertinent to each case, and the social values that precipitated the accusations. Both *querelas* were launched by the same *alcaide* of Ponta Delgada, though they were filed two years apart and dealt with two different concubine couples. Indeed, the two cases underlined the disparate conditions under which individuals were involved in what was termed concubinage. The first example implied that both parties were equally complicit in the relationship; the second hinted at trickery if not treachery on the part of the married man. In both accounts, moreover, the *alcaide* focussed on the man's wrongdoing, an indication that for the *alcaide*, at least, the errant husband was especially culpable of a grave crime/sin.

In the first *querela* under discussion, the *alcaide* stressed the concerns of the neglected wife, a rhetorical device used to show that as a public official, his duty was to maintain the public peace rather than to profit from the process. Thus, ostensibly with little regard for his own personal gain, on 12 August 1630 the *alcaide* filed an accusation against Manuel Mendes, master of his own ship, and Maria Guerra, single woman, for living in concubinage. Apparently the relationship between Manuel and Maria had been going on for several years, and it is not clear why the *alcaide* chose to proceed against them at that junction, but he was compelled to report that two days earlier to the denunciation, Manuel had returned to Ponta Delgada from a trip to the island of Terceira, and upon his return he did not go to his wife as he ought to have done, but rather he went to Maria's place where 'he changed his clothes and whatnot'.

Although the text pointed to the injured wife, she was never identified, and the only other detail revealed about Maria Guerra was her nickname, the *bisquainha*.[114] The denunciation stressed instead that Manuel's misbehaviour had caused great scandal in the neighbourhood, and that 'according to the ordinances of this realm there are great penalties for any married man who engages in concubinage and for the woman who was with him'. Interestingly, this *querela* was three to four times longer than most of the complaints filed by ordinary people, partly because the *alcaide* named 13 witnesses, six women and seven men, plus his guarantor and the details of the surety that was arranged with that guarantor, an indication that the *alcaide* was well armed to proceed with this case (see Appendix 6).[115] The *querela* did not provide any indication about the outcome of the criminal procedure that inevitably ensued, but the *alcaide* must have won his case, as otherwise he would have been reticent about committing himself to another similar suit. That he did, with equal fervour, against another married Manuel and a young woman seemingly ensnared in a dangerous web of deceit.

[114] The nickname suggests that she had some roots to the region around the Bay of Biscay along northeast Spain.

[115] BPARPD, *Livro de Autos de Querelas*, f.69v–70v. Another accusation of concubinage was filed by a judicial official on 9 February 1650, but the text ended with the stipulation that the *querela* was invalidated. BPARPD, *Livro de Autos de Querelas*, f.166v–167.

Ana Mendes, the Reluctant Concubine

On 7 September 1632 the *alcaide* of Ponta Delgada, António Pereira de Castro, denounced Manuel Dias, *o gadelha*,[116] to the outside judge, declaring that a man in his position of *alcaide* was obliged to attempt to check the evil deeds that occurred in the city, for they were offensive to God as well as to the republic. He initiated this *querela* because, the *alcaide* explained, with little fear of God and the scandal among those who knew of it, Manuel, a married man, was engaged in 'illicit conversation and concubinage' with Ana Mendes, daughter of (the late) Pedro Jerónimo, an orphaned girl, the girl being a resident in the outskirts of the city, in a secluded and depopulated place.

> Manuel had publicly dishonoured the said girl and impregnated her, and one time had her abort ['fazella mover uma vez'] against the wishes of her mother and without her [the mother] knowing of it, [Manuel] having her [the girl] kept and maintained ['theuda e mantheuda'], of which there was clamorous gossiping, and since similar cases do not go unpunished, and to prevent evils in the republic which are what destroys it, and to serve as an example to others, he [*alcaide*] asked and requested that the judge accept this *querela* that he [*alcaide*] presented in truth, according to the information he had on the said Manuel Dias and Ana Mendes.

Although the *alcaide* insinuated that Ana Mendes was a victim of the married man's ruses, he launched the accusation against the two. The implication was that while Ana was vulnerable because she was young, fatherless, and isolated from neighbours, she must have consented to the relationship at some point for she was 'kept and maintained' by Manuel. The relationship, in fact, had gone on long enough to elicit gossip in the community. That, at least, was the *alcaide*'s public presentation of the case. Ana's mother thought differently.

Ana Mendes, the Rape Victim

Three days following the registration of the *querela* discussed above, Maria da Costa, widow of the late Pedro Jerónimo, and her daughter, Ana Mendes, residents in the outskirts of the city, went to the home of the *Licenciado* António Pinheiro de Seabra, outside judge of Ponta Delgada. The two women came before the judge to complain against and denounce Manuel Dias Gadelha, *hortelão* or market gardener. In her statement, Maria da Costa declared that she was an honoured widow, and that she had under her care in her house ('das portas a dentro') her daughter, Ana Mendes, the plaintiff, an orphaned lass ('moça orfã'), a young woman ('donzella') for honour and marriage, living outside the city in a secluded and depopulated place, far from neighbours. It came to happen, the widow explained, that the

116 In this *querela* the third name appeared as a nickname, which according to the *Novo Michaelis Dicionário Ilustrado Português Inglês* refers to 'a tuft or mop of hair, long tousled hair, tangled hair, or mane'.

accused befriended one of Maria's sons who worked for Manuel in his gardens, and using that friendship as subterfuge, Manuel entered her house, on a day while Maria da Costa was away in the town of Ribeira Grande.

> He [the accused] entered her house where the plaintiff, her daughter, was in the remote and secluded place, and he forced her and dishonoured her and took her honour and virginity and impregnated her, with which he committed a serious crime, for which reason they asked the judge to take their complaint against the defendant for rape, treachery, and betrayal ['força aleivosia e treição'] because of the friendship which got him to enter the house.

In her narrative, the widow sketched a picture that highlighted the vulnerability of her young daughter, left alone in a secluded homestead, and the deceitfulness of the accused, 'a married man without fear of God nor of His Majesty's justices', who assaulted the fatherless girl. The widow urged the judge to 'proceed against him, and to condemn him to the most severe punishments that according to the law he deserved and were imposed on those who committed similar crimes and offences'. To Maria da Costa, her daughter had been tricked into allowing her brother's friend and master into the house, and then was raped by a man who did not fear either God or king. To add to the element of deceit and treachery, Maria maintained that the assault happened when she was out of town, a factor that pointed to the premeditation behind Manuel's ill-intentioned visit to the girl's home. Both mother and daughter took the oath, but since Ana was a minor, the judge appointed a public procurator, Cosme da Rocha, to act on her behalf, and Cosme made an oath on the Holy Scriptures as well. The judge accepted their petition and the scribe added that the two plaintiffs declared that the defendant dishonoured the plaintiff Ana Mendes the previous May while she was alone; her mother being away, she opened the door to him and he forced himself on her. The scribe, Gregório Sanches, signed for both women.[117]

Seen together, the *querelas* by Maria da Costa and the *alcaide* confirmed and contradicted one another. The mother and daughter's narrative contained nothing about concubinage or an abortion, but their text hinted at the latter for the accused 'committed a serious crime' with the girl's pregnancy.[118] Nevertheless, the core of their complaint was the treachery of a devious family friend and his sexual assault of an unsuspecting girl. Nowhere in their text was any suggestion that the underage girl was complicit in this affair. In fact, although Maria da Costa and Ana Mendes appeared together before the judge, and Ana was identified as the plaintiff in their *querela*, the narrative was written entirely from the mother's point of view. In the process, the widow stressed the minority status of the girl, and thus the girl's incapacity to act on her own, in any circumstances.

---

[117] BPARPD, *Livro de Autos de Querelas*, f.77–78v. Some punctuation was added for clarity.

[118] For the legislation on abortion, see *Ordenações Filipinas*, Livro 1, Títuto 73, no. 4; on pandering, see *Ordenações Filipinas*, Livro 5, Título 32. See also Correia, 'A evolução histórica', 93, 100.

The *alcaide*, for his part, maintained that the two participants in the dishonourable affair were equally guilty of consorting with one another in concubinage, albeit through the machinations of a devious married man. As would be expected, the state representative's interpretation of events differed from that of the distraught mother, but the inconsistencies merit some reconsideration. Why did Maria da Costa launch her *querela* three days *after* the *alcaide* launched his? More importantly, why did Maria not accuse the culprit till four months after the assault? In an attempt to untangle this conundrum, we will begin with those elements on which the two *querelas* agreed: the girl was dishonoured or raped; the girl was underage and fatherless (orphan); the girl was impregnated; the girl's mother did not know or consent; the culprit was a married man.

From the widow we learned that the assault on her daughter took place sometime in May. When did the mother first learn of it? It is possible that Ana did not tell her mother of the incident until the girl could no longer hide her burgeoning belly, out of fear, shame, or under pressure from the culprit. It is also possible that once she learned of the incident, the widow attempted to negotiate a settlement with the culprit. Given that the accused was a married man, the two women could not have sought a forced marriage for the victim, but rather some sense of justice, and hopefully some monetary compensation as well. But then the local *alcaide* made a public denunciation, and Maria da Costa was obliged to register her own complaint on behalf of her daughter to offset the damage that the official's *querela* could cause that very daughter. Still, there was the nagging problem of concubinage, asserted by the *alcaide* but to which the mother made no response. Ironically, the two *querelas* listed several of the same witnesses, some of whom the *alcaide* expected to confirm his suspicions, and, conversely, the widow chose to defend her and her daughter's honour.

An accusation of concubinage was a serious matter for the accused and accuser. As we have seen, an official who failed to prove his case was liable to pay damages and costs. The system was set that way because the early modern state lacked the infrastructure to engage in actual police work. Consequently, the state depended on the general populace to alert authorities of a crime, to which denunciations the authorities responded, investigated, and ruled accordingly. People were in fact encouraged to report criminal activity with the promise of a share of the fines and penalties imposed on the guilty culprits. Individuals denounced crimes committed against themselves or others, but to avoid malicious accusations, the state required that third parties supply a surety for their claims. A victim who launched a *querela* for a crime to which she or he had been subjected had to pledge her or his estate to cover the court costs in case of a negative verdict; anyone else not implicated directly in the crime could also file a complaint, but in that case the third party had to provide an additional guarantee, a surety of up to 20,000 *réis*.[119]

Public officials could also initiate judicial complaints, but the *alcaide*, for example, had to provide a guarantor and surety with each *querela* he filed for cases

---

[119] *Ordenações Filipinas*, Livro 5, Título 117, nos 6 and 7.

from which he stood to gain, and the penalties imposed on concubines belonged to the chief *alcaide* or his deputies.[120] And so it was with António Pereira do Castro, the *alcaide* in Ponta Delgada who registered two *querelas* for concubinage, one in 1630, discussed earlier, and another in 1632 that implicated Ana Mendes and her widowed mother, Maria da Costa. In the latter *querela*, another *alcaide* named Manuel de Lemos offered a *fiança* (surety) and agreed to be that *alcaide*'s guarantor and principal payer, according to the royal ordinance. António needed a surety to cover his expenses if he lost his case against Manuel and Ana. In other words, the *alcaide* must have had some basis for his accusation, enough to convince someone to guarantee his endeavour.[121]

Given the timing of Maria da Costa's *querela*, one senses that hers was an act of desperation, compelled by circumstances beyond her control. This does not necessarily negate the veracity of her claims against Manuel Dias Gadelha, but how long could the mother have remained ignorant of her daughter's predicament, a daughter who was accused of being 'kept and maintained' by a married man? The degree and duration of that 'maintenance' is unclear, but both *querelas* against Manuel were unequivocal about his corruption of young Ana. Alternatively, Maria da Costa and the *alcaide* could have been in collusion, agreeing together to pursue the culprit according to the legal and social prescriptions assigned to them. The mother's *querela* reinforced the judicial agent's case, and while his narrative implicated Ana in the accusation of concubinage, the mother's arguments stressed Ana's youthfulness and vulnerability, attributes that were meant to arouse the sympathy of the presiding judge. The crux of both *querelas* was that Manuel took advantage of a naive orphan girl, and in the mother's account in particular, these extenuating circumstances accentuated Manuel's villainy.

If the accusations proved true, Manuel was guilty of some serious crimes (treachery, rape, abortion, concubinage), and of the betrayal of his wife who remained anonymous in the records, but who would feel the impact of the calamity that befell upon her household. Her husband Manuel, if found guilty, would have to pay, in one way or another, and his punishment would not be his alone. The unidentified wife had to contend with the public notoriety that her husband's criminal behaviour incited, and the diminution of the family property, even if only his share was subjected to the judicial penalties and costs. Ana, too, risked a penalty for concubinage, and even if her sentence was mitigated by the circumstances of the case, it is possible that she was left with a psychological or social scar that would take some time to heal. We will never know for certain whether Ana was raped or seduced, but often those lines were blurred. Given the social position of the young woman, and the duplicity of the older married man, true consent on her part was highly improbable.

---

120 *Ordenações Filipinas*, Livro 1, Título 74, no. 17; Livro 3, Título 92; Livro 4, Título 59; Livro 5, Título 117, no. 6.

121 BPARPD, *Livro de Autos de Querelas*, f.75v–76v.

The *querela* introduces an injury and some context under which the injury occurred, but, on its own, it leaves the case suspended in some obscure recess of archival documents, with little clue about how the complaint was resolved. In the case of the *querelas* found in the Ponta Delgada regional archives, some of the registries had marginal annotations, most of which confounded more than clarified the situation. Not all *querelas* contained these annotations, but the two that pertained to Ana Mendes included some marginal notes that raised further questions. In the *alcaide*'s text, someone wrote on the margin that the accused was dead. In the widow's *querela*, a marginal note was indecipherable because the folio was damaged, and another note indicated that the defendant was free per sentence by the outside judge. Since neither of these annotations was dated, the chronology of the two insertions cannot be determined. In any case, the postscripts said nothing about the ways the three women most affected by one man's sexual offenses went on to live their lives.

Rape and Defloration

Unlike concubinage and adultery, in which women's participation and responsibility were highlighted in Portuguese legislation, rape was seen as a crime committed by men against women, though women were not necessarily excluded from some obligation. To begin with, women were expected to come forth after the violation in a very public way. In certain regions, the custom in the Middle Ages was for the 'mulher forçada', or raped woman, to go immediately following the assault to the nearest village or town, tearing at her hair, howling, and telling everyone she encountered along the way that so-and-so raped her, naming him if she knew his name, and if not, providing identifying marks. When she reached the town or village where there was a judge, she was to go directly to him, tell him all about the incident, and file an accusation on the manner in which she was raped, and the place where it took place. Likewise, she was to tell all those she encountered along the way the identity of her rapist, and in that manner she would prove the rape.[122] Thus, the onus was on the woman to make a spectacle and attract the public gaze, an ordeal that compounded her terror and humiliation, a process that undoubtedly succeeded in silencing many rape victims.

In the law books, rapists in early modern Portugal faced severe penalties. The legislation stipulated that any man, regardless of rank or station, who 'forcibly slept' ('forçosamente dormir') with any woman of any rank or station, would die for it, though in some cases the death penalty first had to be approved by the Crown before it could be executed. The same penalty was imposed on those who helped in any way with the said 'força', either directly or through some other means. Furthermore, even if the 'forçador' married the woman after the fact, with her full consent, he could not escape the death penalty. Seduction and abduction from the parents' or guardians' home were subject to heavy penalties, as well, with exile to Africa for the elite culprit, and death for the plebeian. The death penalty

122 Caetano, *História do Direito*, 384–5.

was imposed on any culprit who abducted a woman in the presence of and against the expressed wishes of her parent or guardian.[123]

Legislators attempted to regulate even what might be termed consensual sex, for any man who entered someone's home to have sex with a virgin or an honest widow was liable to pay the woman's dowry. In this case there was some room for negotiation for the law stipulated that if the man with such intentions wanted to marry the woman with whom he had 'slept', and if she agreed to the marriage, and the host in whose house the offense took place was in accord with the marriage, and was willing to forgive the intruder, the penalties were null. Thus, the offense was not just the seduction of a woman, but also the intrusion into someone else's domain. The woman could consent all she wanted, but if the sexual act took place while she was under someone's care, her consent alone was inadequate to release the male lover of any future liability. At issue here was the curtailment of indiscriminate goings-on that could impinge on the honour and reputation of the hosting party. True, such a law insinuated that a woman was not a free agent in terms of her sexuality, but in the context of the early modern period, such reasoning made sense. A wrong committed against an individual could not be separated from the consequence that wrong could cause the family or broader community.

Of primary concern to legislators, therefore, was to maintain the integrity of a household, and not necessarily a male-headed household only. Note that in the Ana Mendes case, both the *alcaide* and Ana's mother stressed that Manuel had acted without the widowed mother's knowledge, and thus without her consent. To underscore this point, Maria da Costa indicated that Manuel's assault of her daughter took place while Maria was out of town, away when her legally-sanctioned authority over her children was violated. In Maria's account, not only did her daughter Ana not consent; her daughter was in no position to consent.

In fact, according to the law, consensual sex under any circumstances, with a virgin or an honest widow, placed a man under obligation of marrying the woman, if she and he desired it, or to pay her dowry. Those who could not pay the dowry – the amount to be determined by the judge according to the social station and wealth of her father – would be exiled to Africa, with the plebeian man also receiving a public whipping. Drafted in the later Middle Ages, Portugal's national ordinances reveal a number of assumptions on the part of the jurists who framed those early laws, not least of which was the premise that only 'a virgin or an honest widow' merited compensation for a man's sexual deceit. Such an argument was founded on an understanding that only 'a virgin or an honest widow' stood to lose her eligibility for marriage, and that financial payment toward a dowry would go a long way toward minimizing her losses.

Interestingly, the legislation stipulated that a culprit faced the death penalty for the rape of a woman of whatever rank, though no evidence was found of a woman of 'ill repute' who launched a complaint of sexual assault. On the contrary, all female plaintiffs – whether as the accusers or the pardoners – depicted themselves as honourable women, or were depicted as such by their representatives. Nearly

[123] *Ordenações Manuelinas*, Livro 5, Título 14 and 23; *Ordenações Filipinas*, Livro 5, Título 16, 18, and 23.

all cases of sexual assault or defloration included some reference to the young woman having been kept well-guarded, behind closed doors, up to the point of the treachery of the accused. It is doubtful that many girls or women were or could have been kept secluded and guarded to the extent that these narratives suggested - for such seclusion was impractical for most - but the allusion and illusion served their purposes. The victim was a good girl, and thus undeserving of the harm that she suffered. Ironically, in most reported cases that indicated where the sexual assault or defloration took place, that place was often the victim's home. By implication, a woman attacked outside those prescribed 'safe zones' was deemed less worthy of compassion and compensation.[124]

The surviving documentation for cases of rape or sexual assault against women in its many manifestations was problematic in a number of ways. First, the terminology of the period offers a challenge to our modern-day sensibilities.[125] There was no word for rape, per se, but rather several euphemisms were used such as to 'force' a woman, 'sleep' with a woman using force, and deflower or rob a woman of her virginity. Second, it is difficult to gauge the social meaning and experience of rape in the distant past without imposing our current values on such an emotionally charged issue. The terminology of the period tells us something about the prevailing attitudes toward a crime that was enmeshed with cultural, religious, and economic assumptions about the victim and the perpetrator, attitudes that some have argued remained constant until the late eighteenth century, if not beyond. Third, it is worth remembering that the few cases of sexual assault that made the official record say nothing about the almost daily acts of sexual harassment to which many if not most girls and women were subjected.

One Portuguese study concluded that in cases of 'deflowering', women were 'artless and defenceless', but that generally it occurred by consent; the denouncement took place because the young woman was abandoned and the promises of marriage not fulfilled. Another study found that the perception of women's agency in matters of sexuality changed over the course of the early modern period. Whereas prior to the 1770s a woman had up to a year after the 'desfloração' took place to file a complaint, afterwards only women of under 25 years of age had that long to file a complaint, because in the new legislation women were seen as less fragile in terms of their sexuality, and more as an active subject. In fact, as discussed in Chapter 1, the legislation in effect in the early modern period stipulated that all *querelas* had to be registered within a year and

[124] The ideal of women kept behind closed doors has been promulgated in a variety of media, including through proverbs. See Elisa Maria Lopes da Costa, 'História, Memória e Sabedoria: Tempos e "Ditos que se dizem" em algumas ilhas açorenses', in *O Faial e a Periferia Açoriana nos Séculos XV a XX. Actas do IV Colóquio* (Horta: Núcleo Cultural da Horta, 2007), 436 [431–59].

[125] For a discussion of the difficulties with the language in legal codes about rape, see Christopher Cannon, 'Chaucer and Rape: Uncertainty's Certainties', in Elizabeth Robertson and Christine M. Rose, eds, *Representing Rape in Medieval and Early Modern Literature*, (New York: Palgrave, 2001), 255–79.

a day of the incident. This meant that women had up to a year from the day of the assault to make an official claim to 'demand their virginity', and their claim would not be heard once the year had passed, except in cases of women under the age of majority and who had a valid reason for not filing the complaint within the time limit. The legislation underwent some changes in the course of the eighteenth century, most notably in 1775 when a law was passed that removed marriage as a means through which cases of rape could be resolved.[126]

Of the nine *querelas* found that dealt with sexual offenses, three involved married men, including the case of Ana Mendes already discussed. The sex accusations against single men typically claimed the accused took the young woman's virginity and honour, and reneged on promises of marriage. The claims made against married men differed in this regard for marriage was clearly not an option. In one or two cases the wording of the *querela* intimated that rape was the charge, while in others the wording was more ambiguous. For instance, after João Pereira, apothecary, called the maiden Lúcia with deceitful words to his own house, when his wife was not at home, and took Lúcia's honour and virginity, there was little doubt of the nature of his sexual assault, at least in the minds of Lúcia and her mother.[127] The context of that dishonouring was significantly different than that as reported by Margarida Fernandes who filed a complaint against Gaspar Carvalho for dishonouring her with promises to take her as his wife. In her own statement Margarida explained that this had happened in September past, and that she was dishonoured until Christmas, with the same promises of marriage, in a dark place where they would be seen by nobody; not even her mother was aware of it.[128] Through the filter of the scribe's input one gets the impression nonetheless that Lúcia was attacked by a duplicitous married man, whereas Margarida was a willing participant in her clandestine encounters with Gaspar, albeit under the impression of a more long-term commitment. The remainder of this chapter is dedicated to a discussion of sexual crimes committed by men against women.

In addition to the nine *querelas* already mentioned, there were also 11 *perdões de parte* connected to sexual assault or defloration (see Table 1.3). As was the case with the *querelas*, the victims' pardons also showed that crimes of this nature involved primarily a single woman who accused a single man, but there were some notable exceptions. In Evora, a young woman and her uncle filed a complaint against a single male for having raped her and beaten the uncle, and the uncle ended up granting a *perdão de parte* to the accused for the beating, but the niece was not included in the agreement – that is, the victim's pardon did not deal with

---

[126] *Ordenações Filipinas*, Livro 5, Título 23, no. 2; Alves, 'Violência e perdão', 107; Ribeiro, 'Convívios difíceis', 43.

[127] The denunciation was filed on 3 September 1646. BPARPD, *Livro de Autos de Querelas*, f.148–148v.

[128] In this accusation of 23 May 1646, the scribe carelessly recorded and mis-recorded the names of individuals, including in reference to Margarida Fernandes who he also called Margarida Ferreira, and by identifying her mother as Maria da Victoria and Victoria da Costa. BPARPD, *Livro de Autos de Querelas*, f.138v–139v.

the sexual assault.[129] Also in Evora, the married couple Josefa Rodrigues and Luís Gomes granted a pardon to a single man who had beaten and attempted to rape Josefa ('querendo a forçar').[130] Further north, in Porto, Francisca André granted a pardon in July 1577 to two men, Jorge Manuel and Manuel Baltazar, for robbing her of her honour and virginity.[131] Unfortunately, the document in question was too damaged by ink bleed to enable any further scrutiny, and thus it cannot be known whether the two men were involved in the same incident, or whether this was a case similar to the example Abigail Dyer found in Spain of a woman who used the argument of 'seduction of a virgin by promise of marriage' against two men, two years apart.[132] To conclude this chapter on sexual crimes, three *querelas* and three *perdões de parte* were examined more closely to highlight the cultural and legal imperatives that supported those claims, and the underlying principle behind those claims – financial restitution for the harm committed.

Ignoble Conduct

Agueda de Carvalho went to the outside judge on 13 January 1645 to launch a complaint with her father, Afonso de Oliveira de Vasconcelos, as her companion, or perhaps more accurately, as her chaperone and master of the household to which she belonged. Agueda was not identified as a minor, but she was rendered invisible in her denunciation against Francisco Rodrigues, son of André Gonçalves. Parental support for a troubled daughter would make an impression on the judge, especially if the father, as head of the household, took an active and public role in defending his offspring, and Afonso was such a father. In fact, Agueda's *querela* was written entirely from the father's point of view as he outlined the depth of deceit to which he (and his daughter) had been subjected:

> He [Afonso] being a noble man and related to nobles of this island [São Miguel], Francisco entered his house fraudulently ['aleivosamente'] ... in pretence of friendship for her [the] plaintiff, and with treachery and betrayal, with words that he had communicated to her of marriage, he solicited the said his daughter and took her honour and virginity, having had with her carnal knowledge ['copia carnalmente'] for three years, she being a noble and honourable woman without having any reputation with anyone except the defendant.[133]

The father reiterated that this was 'a scandalous and serious incident' that needed to be remedied, the remedy being matrimony. At a time when marriage was the principal avenue for respectability, there was much at stake for a spurned

[129] The pardon was dated 2 December 1629. ADE, Fundo Notarial, Manuel d'Oliveira (notary), Vila Viçosa, Séries 87 (1629), f.101–102.

[130] The pardon was dated 23 December 1608. ADE, Fundo Notarial, Felicio de Béça (notary), Séries 337 (1608), f.86v–87v.

[131] ADP, Fundo Notorial, Po.1, 3a Se, no. 59 (1577), f.168v–170.

[132] Dyer, 'Seduction by Promise', 448–9.

[133] BPARPD, *Livro de Autos de Querelas*, f.135v–136v. Some punctuation was added for clarity.

lover, and for the honour of the family as well, as Afonso's testimony intimated. Still, Afonso said nothing about Agueda having been tricked or forced into 'carnal knowledge' with Francisco, nor that the sexual encounters had taken place without the father's knowledge or approval (the wife and mother of that household was not mentioned). Francisco's ignoble behaviour, therefore, was not that for three years he had pre-marital sex with Agueda, but that he no longer cared to contract the promised marriage. In early modern Portugal, that was a crime.

If Francisco were found guilty of the charge, he would face two possible options: marry Agueda or compensate Agueda financially. As a noble woman, she expected to marry well, although her chances were dimmed somewhat by this scandal. According to the social and legal mores of the time, Agueda's problems could be abated with an increased dowry. In certain circumstances, honour could be bartered, and Agueda's father was prepared to engage in some tough negotiations. Indeed, the father's claim to his noble status was not corroborated by any insertion in the registry of a title appropriate to his professed station, nor was his daughter given the title *Dona*. The vast majority of *querelas* found in Ponta Delgada dealt with ordinary folk, and the few individuals of higher rank were properly identified as such. Perhaps Agueda's family was of the middling sort with noble pretensions, and her traitorous lover took advantage of those pretensions akin to scenes portrayed in Molière's *Le Bourgeois Gentilhomme*.[134]

Parents in the Dark

Afonso took charge of his daughter's *querela*, seemingly on his own, but the lack of reference to his wife and Agueda's mother was in no way indicative that women could not take on a public stance against a wrong done to themselves or their children. In the patriarchal world of the sixteenth and seventeenth centuries, the male lead in a legal case would have been considered ideal, but, as with most ideals, this ideal did not always materialize. The absence of the husband or father was significant for the plaintiffs in these suits, as it was used to underscore the vulnerability of the women and hence the distinct culpability of the men who took advantage of the situation. It was as if the behaviour of such men was especially heinous and cowardly. In fact, as we have seen, the dishonouring of young women was considered particularly vile if it occurred while either parent was away, a notion that rendered the unsupervised female especially helpless. Whether the plaintiffs believed this or not is another matter. As a rhetorical device, the argument fit the social conventions that posited parental approval as a keystone in the maintenance of social morality. Maria da Costa and her daughter Ana Mendes, discussed earlier, stressed this point in their *querela*. Ana's father was dead and

[134] For a historical account of a commoner with pretensions of nobility, and who behaved accordingly with a woman he seduced and deceived, see James S. Grubb, 'Piero Amadi Acts Like His Betters', in John A. Marino and Thomas Kuehn, eds, *A Renaissance of Conflicts: Visions and Revisions of Law and Society in Italy and Spain* (Toronto: Centre for Reformation and Renaissance Studies, 2004), 259–78.

her mother had gone on an errand to another village when the culprit approached Ana, left alone at home.

Similarly, Maria do Rego emphasized that her parents were not at home when the accused dishonoured her. In fact, the patriarch, João do Rego, was absent from the island on 17 January 1634 when Maria and her mother, Catarina Fernandes, denounced Manuel Fernandes Manganejo, son of Manuel Fernandes Manganejo.[135] Portraying herself as a virtuous young maiden, living under the roof of her father and mother for marriage, without having a reputation with anyone, Maria claimed that the accused came to court her ('a namorar della') for a significant duration:

> For five years he entered the house of her father, day and night, and she sustained him in all that she could, continuing in the said friendship with his promise to marry her, and both making an oath between them to that effect, one day the defendant slept with her carnally and her father was not at home nor her mother, and he dishonoured her and impregnated her all under the outward pretence that he would marry her, now he withdrew from her and has gone to another [woman] and did not want to fulfil what he had [promised] to her.

Catarina supported her daughter's claim, telling the judge that the accused committed treachery by entering her house without her knowing and while she and her husband were away, a claim that stressed the duplicity of the accused. Note that Maria did not profess to having been coerced by Manuel, but rather that 'it' had happened clandestinely while her parents were away. On the surface this argument seems a *non sequitur*, for Manuel was not likely to ask the parents' permission to have sex with their daughter. Maria declared that the sexual act took place during her parents' absence in order to maintain her parents' honour and thus her own. Honourable parents did not allow daughters to engage in pre-marital sex, but while they were away, a misguided daughter could succumb to the wiles of a man who had promised to marry her. Manuel, in fact, had been a welcome guest at the family home – at the father's house, it need be stressed – for five years, welcome day and night, behaving appropriately until that one fateful day. Again, the problem was not that Manuel had sex with Maria. The problem was that he had sex with the promise to marry her, and then left her pregnant for another woman.

The text betrayed a tone of desperation by two women who found themselves in a very difficult situation. The plaintiff even declared that her mother was her legal guardian in the absence of her father, though Maria admitted that she was of age of majority of more than 25 years.[136] Even if the relationship with Manuel had started while she was still a minor, the pregnancy presumably happened

---

135 Some text is missing from these folios because the top right-hand corner is ripped off, but the scribe clearly noted the same name for the father and son.

136 For the themes of absent husbands and fathers in early modern Portuguese literature, and the opportunities this opened up for women, see Maria Isabel Rodrigues Ferreira, 'Tipos femininos em Gil Vicente: um olhar pela sociedade das descobertas', 127–9, and Isabel Carita, 'A mulher que fica – dois exemplos vicentinos', 131–5, in *O Rosto Feminino da Expansão Portuguesa, Actas I, Congresso Internacional (Lisboa, 21–25 de Novembro de 1994)* (Lisbon: Comissão para a Igualdade e para os Direitos das Mulheres,1995).

more recently, given that there was no indication that the child had been born. Whether willingly or not, Maria do Rego faced an uncertain future as an unwed mother, and she hoped that authorities would intervene and maybe alleviate, at least temporarily, the hardships ahead. On the left margin of this entry another scribe noted, clearly in different ink and different writing, that the accused had been released by the outside judge, but nothing was written about the date and conditions of that release.[137]

The two cases examined above dealt with two young women, Agueda and Maria, each of whom had enjoyed a relatively long courtship, three and five years, respectively. They also willingly engaged in sexual relations with their respective partners, Maria ostensibly only once, just enough to get pregnant. In both cases the *querelas* did not denounce the sex itself but rather the relinquishment of a promise of marriage under which conditions the women agreed to have sex. That, at least, was what the plaintiffs claimed, a strategy that spoke to the law and social mores of early modern Portugal. In his examination of church visitations in Soure in the early eighteenth century, Joaquim Ramos de Carvalho found an example of a woman who made a successful complaint to church officials once she heard of the banns that announced the marriage of her intended husband with another woman. Josefa Espírito Santo contended that she had allowed José Rodrigues 'to do as he pleased with her' with the understanding of a future marriage between them, an understanding that was corroborated by witnesses who testified to the social parameters of such relationships.[138] Sex outside of marriage was inadvisable but not illegal; reneging on a promise of marriage was another matter.

At stake for most of the plaintiffs was the loss of a potential husband, a man who had allegedly promised marriage in return for sexual favours. Some of the narratives indicated that there had been sexual assault of young women, but in the majority of *querelas* of this kind the intent had been to resolve the problem through matrimony, regardless of how the relationship began. There was one important exception to this general rule: when the culprit was a married man.[139] In such a case the accused was considered particularly treacherous, as were those perceived to have assisted him.

Treacherous Man, Treacherous Woman

Ana do Rosário was implicated in a *querela* launched on 22 August 1650, but it is doubtful that she had any say in the way the case was presented to the outside judge in Ponta Delgada. In fact, she was not even present when the complaint was filed, for her father, Manuel Vaz, resident of Rosto do Cão, alone outlined how

137 BPARPD, *Livro de Autos de Querelas*, f.94–95. Some punctuation was added for clarity.

138 Joaquim Ramos de Carvalho, 'As sexualidades', in José Mattoso, ed., *História da Vida Privada em Portugal: A Idade Moderna*, 4 vols (Lisbon: Círculo de Leitores e Temas e Debates, 2011), II: 96 [96–129].

139 Marriage was also out of the question when the accused was a member of the clergy.

Filipe Fernandes dishonoured and deflowered Ana who he, Manuel, had guarded virtuously at home for honour and marriage, without a reputation with anyone, except the defendant.[140]

> Filipe had been courting her ['a namorar e della'] for a year more or less, entering night and day in the home of Maria Martins, wife of Roque Fernandes Homem, also resident of Rosto do Cão ... and [the defendant] tricked her [Ana] and with treachery dishonoured her and took her honour and deflowered her in the house of Maria Martins ... and he [Manuel] accused and denounced also the said Maria Martins for having allowed her house to be used for this purpose and being the cause of his daughter being dishonoured and discredited ['desonrada e desautorizada'] which he [the] plaintiff would rather lose five hundred *cruzados* than to have happen.

In this rare case, a woman was counted among those charged with aiding a man in the rape of another woman (see Table 1.1). Manuel did not contend that Maria participated in the actual act, but he argued that she facilitated the encounter by providing a venue where the deed took place, or deeds. Thus, while denouncing the actual perpetrator, Ana's father also blamed a female neighbour for being an accomplice in his daughter's disgrace, pointing out that Maria used her house as an 'alcouceiro' or bawdy house. The plaintiff, for his part, portrayed himself as 'an honourable man who had always maintained his house as is publicly known with much honour and virtue'.

Manuel's *querela* contained several other curious details worthy of further examination, including the reference to a 'courtship' that existed between Filipe and Ana, a courtship that had been going on for about a year. Had Manuel been unaware of this for the entire time? If so, how vigilant was he as a head of a household? He also claimed that Filipe entered Maria's house night and day, giving the impression that Ana, too, was at the neighbour's night and day. Such an admission was inconsistent with Manuel's claim that he ran a house with much 'honour and virtue'.

In the *querela* filed by Maria do Rego, discussed earlier, the accused was said to have entered her father's house 'day and night' as a means to show the extent to which the defendant was already a part of the family, as a betrothed would be. In the present case, the plaintiff used the term 'night and day' to underline the degenerate nature of the goings-on at Maria's house. Nevertheless, doubts remain about Manuel's intentions and possible collusion, for he admitted that he knew that something had been going on for about a year, something that involved his daughter Ana, the neighbour Maria, and the culprit Filipe, a married man, the latter revelation almost an afterthought. Although the subject of an alleged plot of intrigue and corruption, Ana was objectified in her father's *querela*, an official complaint that denied her any agency, ostensibly for her own good. Manuel Vaz left his mark

---

140 'Pera onra e cazamento recolhida e vertuosa das portas para dentro sem ter fama con pessoa algua'. BPARPD, *Livro de Autos de Querelas*, f.169v–170. Some punctuation was added for clarity.

at the end of the document after having named four women as his witnesses, all residents in the same area in the outskirts of Ponta Delgada, and after having ordered his own copy of the document. One wonders about Manuel's reference to 500 *cruzados* and whether that would have been his price for a daughter's virginity.

Given Filipe Fernandes' marital status, there was no question of forcing him to marry Ana do Rosário. The more likely scenario was that armed with a copy of his own fully registered *querela*, Manuel Vaz proceeded to negotiate a financial settlement with the accused. The patriarchal tone of this *querela* suggests that such a settlement would meet Manuel's needs for retribution and restitution, seemingly with little regard for the actual victim, Ana, though we cannot know of their private conversations. As already mentioned, the legal culture of the time was intent on preserving the integrity of the family unit. As head of his household, Ana's father had the legal and social prerogative to represent his daughter, and his public stance was probably appreciated and applauded by the daughter, the family, and the community at large.

In most accusations of sexual misconduct marriage was put forth as an ideal, but that ideal, too, was a malleable tool as events unfolded and compromises were made. Sometimes a *querela* did not even raise the question of marriage, even if the accused was single, as in the case of Agueda Bantes who simply told the island official on 14 June 1641 that 'Manuel Marques had deflowered her and taken her virginity … and many times had had "copia carnal" with her from which she had had children, and five months ago he left her, plaintiff, and she accused him.'[141] Several children were born out of wedlock, and wedlock was seemingly never a question. Yet, the accused was liable for the maintenance of those children, at the very least.

According to the royal ordinances, fathers of illegitimate children were first and foremost responsible for raising those children, because the law recognized the financial costs that such a responsibility entailed. If the father did not have the means to raise those children, the burden fell on the mother, or on other relatives, before the local charities were called for assistance. The mother was expected to nurse the child for three years, however, so by implication she looked after the child for those three years, with the financial support of the father.[142]

> And if the child is not born out of a legitimate marriage, be it natural, or spurious, and of whatever other manner, the mother shall maintain the upkeep of the child in milk for the [first] three years, and all other expense, in the said period, as well as after, shall be done at the expense of the father, as has been said of the legitimate child.[143]

As was the case with the other *querelas* discussed in the previous chapter, the ones related to sexual misconduct pointed to the initial registry of a complaint,

141 BPARPD, *Livro de Autos de Querelas*, f.124–124v.

142 *Ordenações Filipinas*, Livro 1, Título 88, no. 11.

143 *Ordenações Filipinas*, Livro 4, Título 99; *Ordenações Manuelinas*, Livro 4, Título 68.

not to the veracity of the circumstances that led to those complaints, nor to the outcome of the judicial investigations that ensued. The process cost money for the accuser and the accused, depending on the judge's verdict, so it was unlikely that many people launched *querelas* for frivolous reasons, or that the accused took the denunciations lightly. Undoubtedly some complaints were resolved informally, out of court, while others led to a more formal agreement in the form of a *perdão de parte*. The last three cases that will be examined in this chapter come from that corpus of documentation. The sample consists of one example of a woman who granted a pardon in her father's presence, one of a woman with her mother, and one of a woman with her extended family – in the latter case, the extended family of the accuser and the accused. The three examples are not necessarily representative, but each offers a glimpse into the possibilities open to women faced with exceptionally difficult times in their lives.

Honour Restored

On 17 April 1578, Margarida da Silva and her father, Gonçalo Pires de Vilasboas, residents of Rua Chã in Porto, met a notary at the home of Doctor Simão de Medeiros, just down the street from their house. The reason for this meeting was to conclude a pardon document that Margarida and Gonçalo were prepared to give to Bento da Costa Brandão, also resident of Porto, whose power of attorney had been granted to the host to act on his behalf. In their pardon, Margarida and Gonçalo attested that they had filed an accusation with the local justices against Bento for dishonouring Margarida and taking her virginity. According to their testimony, there had been some promises of marriage made by Bento, but he later reneged, wanting to marry someone else. As fate would have it, Margarida had no sufficient proof of Bento's promises ('por ventura não ter provas suficentes'). For this reason, and for other just causes ('por outros justos respeitos'), of her free will, with no pressure from anyone else, and with her father's consent, from this day forward and for always, Margarida released Bento of any promises and assurances that he may have made to marry her, even if they (the promises) had been sworn, and she freed him to marry whomever he wished, and freed him from any obligation he may have had to her in this regard.

Margarida also forgave Bento for having dishonoured her and for taking her virginity and honour. In compensation for the dishonour, she was satisfied with the payment of 20,000 *réis*, in nickel and silver coin ('tostões e tostões de prata'), which Margarida counted in front of the notary; her father concurred the amount was correct, and she put away the money. Thus she granted Bento this pardon and her father also agreed to renounce all future claims related to this case and freed Bento of any further obligation. Two witnesses and everyone present signed the document, except for Margarida who did not know how to write, her brother Pantaleão da Silva signing on her behalf.[144]

---

[144] ADP, Fundo Notarial, Po.1, 3a Se, no. 62 (1578), f.115v–117.

Margarida clearly had her family's support in her conflict with her former lover, a factor that must have weighed heavily in her favour. That Bento was willing to pay her such a substantial amount of money to restore her 'honour' suggested that there was enough evidence of his earlier intentions, despite Margarida conceding that there was no proof of his promises. Margarida may have been a willing participant in the sexual encounters with Bento, but that had been part of the courtship that was supposed to lead into marriage. Bento broke the verbal contract, and the law insisted that he make amends. Margarida's pardon was proof that he had done the honourable thing with a dishonoured lass, whose monetary settlement could perhaps aid a prospective suitor to overlook her former misfortunes and indiscretions.

While Margarida da Silva attended that crucial meeting at the neighbour's house in the company of her father, another Margarida – Margarida Fernandes – conducted her transaction with her mother. Neither record revealed the identity or existence of the missing parent, presumably because either parent's presence was deemed socially acceptable to formalize the negotiated arrangement. As will be shown, in the case of the second Margarida, the compensation was significantly different from what Margarida da Silva received, an indication perhaps of the differences in negotiating skills of the plaintiffs and defendants, the resources with which the defendants could expect to contribute, and the social standing of either party. Neither text provided an explanation for the amounts of the settlement, but there was a wide spectrum of possible reparations.

In their study of 83 *perdões de parte* from one notary's office in Porto in the second half of the seventeenth century, Hugo Ribeiro da Silva and Susana Cardoso found that the financial settlements recorded for sexual assault varied widely, and the reasons for those variations were not disclosed in the documentation. Custódia da Rocha, a single woman, received 14,600 *réis*; Mena, single, received 30,000 *réis*; and Isabel, also single, who was impregnated as a result of the rape, received 20,000 *réis* for herself, and 15,000 *réis* for her parents.[145] Yet a sentence rendered in Lisbon on 20 December 1524 ordered that the man accused of raping Catarina da Câmara, resident of Madeira, pay her 100,000 *réis* for her marriage, in addition to 22,572 *réis* in court costs.[146] That case must have dealt with particularly egregious circumstances, for another study of royal pardons granted to residents of Portalegre in the first half of the sixteenth century showed that the amount of restitution to victims of a variety of crimes ranged from 370 to 20,000 *réis*.[147]

Historians have shown that reparations imposed by judicial officials depended on the gravity of the crime and the social position of the victim. Undoubtedly those factors also played a role in the negotiations at the local level. Furthermore, the ability to obtain that reward depended largely on the power of the victim's

---

145 Silva and Cardoso, 'Escrituras de perdão', 177. The documents did not provide last names for Mena and Isabel.

146 IAN/TT, Núcleo Antigo, *Livro da Receita do Mestrado de Cristo*, no. 558, f.39v, in Duarte, *Justiça e Criminalidade* (Document no. 123), 740.

147 Braga, 'A criminalidade em Portalegre', 76.

family. In his study of royal pardons in early modern France, Jean-Pascal Gay noted that widows and unmarried women were especially vulnerable in this regard. He found an example of a widow's daughter who had yet to receive her portion of a reparation 10 years after the award was made, and another example of an individual who had yet to make his payment 20 years after the fact, and only followed through once the king himself intervened.[148]

It is possible that the system operated differently in early modern Portugal. Each royal pardon registered in the chancelleries concluded with a certification of payment of the imposed penalty, presumably of the entire amount and not just the Crown's portion. For example, João Rodrigues, resident in the district of Guarda, was accused of raping Beatriz Fernandes, 'mulher solteira', or single woman. Having received her pardon, João petitioned the Crown and was granted a royal pardon on 16 August 1634, for a fine of 3,000 *réis*, the payment of which was registered at the bottom of the document, along with the scribe's signature.[149] In the case of the agreements that led to the *perdão de parte*, it is reasonable to expect that the majority of the accused would have fulfilled the conditions of their settlements because they needed that document to deal with their judicial cases. Indeed, most of the *perdões de parte* examined for this study gave the impression that victims visited their local notary once they had been compensated per some prior agreement, often camouflaged as 'some considerations'.

Occasionally the record left a trace that negotiations had broken off, as in a document dated 31 January 1646, at which point Domingas Luís and her husband, Gaspar Macedo, residents of São João da Foz, outside of Porto, were seemingly prepared to grant a pardon to Domingos Carvalho da Cunha, who had been accused of stabbing Domingas on the arm. The document ended abruptly, a blank space was left on the folio, and the next folio contained the phrase, 'não se outourgou' – not granted. Something must have happened to stop the process, literally in mid-sentence, and that something might have been connected to another *perdão de parte*, written up five days earlier, in the same office by the same notary, in which document Anastácia de Freitas, also resident of São João da Foz, pardoned the same Domingos for a beating he had inflicted on her. This document was complete and signed by the notary and witnesses, including one who signed on behalf of Anastácia. Still, following the signatures, the scribe added, undoubtedly at a later date, 'não se outorgou' – the agreement was cancelled.[150]

Not only were Domingas and Anastácia assaulted by the same man, the incident that led to their injuries was possibly connected, and the reasons for their abandonment of their respective pardons likewise must have been related to similar concerns. We know that the notary involved in those transactions did not suddenly die or fall gravely ill, for he continued to write documents long after this impromptu interruption. Given that the notary left a blank space on the unfinished pardon from Domingas, there had been some expectation on the part of the

---

148 Gay, 'Acheter la Grâce', 241–2.

149 IAN/TT, Chancelaria de Dom Filipe III, *Perdões e Legitimações*, Livro 22, f.326.

150 ADP, Fundo Notarial, Po.4, 1a Se, no. 36 (1646), f.158–159v.

notary that the text would be completed at a later date, but that future date never materialized. Something must have happened to stop the parties from continuing with a settlement that at some point they had agreed to, and likely that something was connected to the defendant's inability or unwillingness to acquiesce to the terms of the agreements. Because the *perdão de parte* was commonly issued locally, in the presence of family members, neighbours, acquaintances, or local dignitaries who acted as witnesses and provided sureties, the accused were under a lot of pressure to meet their obligations. This was especially imperative in cases of sexual offenses that resulted in pregnancy.

Parental Responsibility

As mentioned above, the particulars of Margarida Fernandes' *perdão de parte* differed in a number of ways from those mentioned by the other Margarida discussed earlier. For starters, Margarida da Silva lived in the city, whereas Margarida Fernandes and her mother, Maria Afonso, lived in the Aldeia de Roibas, Freguesia de São Martinho, in the district of Porto. On 6 March 1573 the mother and daughter travelled to the city to meet with the notary at a house on Rua das Flores, residence of the *Licenciado* Gaspar Gonçalves, *cidadão*. In the case of this Margarida, she met her adversary face to face at the *Licenciado*'s house, for Gonçalo Rodrigues, *lavrador*, from the same locality as the two women, was also present at the meeting. The purpose of their meeting was to conclude the terms of a pardon document in which Margarida and Maria declared that they had launched a formal accusation with the city judge against Gonçalo for dishonouring Margarida and taking her honour and virginity, the consequence of which was the following agreement:

> The said Gonçalo Rodrigues had to give her [Margarida] 6,000 *réis* in coin and 10 *alqueires* of dry grain of corn and rye, and as for the child with which she was pregnant from him, Gonçalo Rodrigues, she Margarida Fernandes would raise it and sustain it at her expense for the first year, and from that day forth he, Gonçalo Rodrigues, would take the said child to have, raise, and maintain as his own child [at his expense] and the payment of the said money paid at the making of this [document], the sum of 4,000 *réis*, and the 2,000 *réis* on the next day of St. John the Baptist [24 June] of this present year, and the grain he will give her half when she gives birth and the other half at the time he has to pay her the said 2,000 *réis*.

In the presence of the notary and other witnesses, Gonçalo paid Margarida the 4,000 *réis* which she counted and accepted as correct payment. Gonçalo also agreed to pay the remaining 2,000 *réis* of good silver coin in June, and the grain as stipulated, and to take the child after its first year and to feed and raise the child as his own. Gonçalo placed his properties as collateral to guarantee his commitment to this agreement, and his guarantor for the remaining payment, in cash and in kind, was Gaspar Dias, another *lavrador*, resident of the same *aldeia* or hamlet, who was also present. Gaspar vouched for the money, grain, and child, for which he used his properties as collateral, and Gonçalo and Gaspar relinquished all laws and privileges that might have invalidated this document. If Gonçalo and Gaspar reneged on the payments as stipulated, they would have to pay all costs and expenses that Margarida could incur in the process. Margarida and her mother agreed that, upon full payment, they would relinquish their complaint and wanted nothing more of Gonçalo, nor would they make any future claim against this incident. Mother and daughter, once fully paid and satisfied with Margarida's restored honour, pardoned Gonçalo, and they asked His Majesty's justices not to prosecute him, and Gonçalo and his guarantor agreed to pay any costs and expenses that Margarida might incur otherwise.[151]

Bento da Costa Brandão paid Margarida da Silva 20,000 *réis* to release him from any further commitment to her, but Gonçalo Rodrigues could not have made such an arrangement with Margarida Fernandes. Bento's occupation was not recorded, but we know that Gonçalo was a *lavrador*, and perhaps he was unable to raise that much money. More importantly, his crime had an added dimension that had immediate and long-term implications that were less obvious in the Bento case. Gonçalo was going to be a father, and he had to accept parental responsibility, either willingly through an agreement with Margarida, or forcibly through the arm of the law. Once apprehended, Gonçalo, if found guilty of the charge, and without the *perdão de parte*, risked exile and his property confiscated to cover judicial expenses and to compensate the victim.

The two Margaridas were clearly assisted by their respective parents in the negotiations for the settlements with the men who had dishonoured them. Nothing was mentioned in either document about the age of either Margarida, because that was unnecessary for this stage of the process. In both cases there had been an official *querela*, and it was at that point that the plaintiff would have described herself (or been described by a parent) as a *donzela*, a young maiden living under the protection of her patriarch or matriarch, and so forth, as shown with the examples analysed earlier. In their respective *querela*, each Margarida was the victim seeking justice; in their *perdão de parte*, they found justice in the form of compensation. Although the document was called a victim's pardon, there was little evidence of an actual act of forgiveness. Rather, each Margarida *released* her respective culprit from any further material obligation. The emotional debt would last a little longer.

In many ways, therefore, the Portuguese *perdão de parte* was a financial settlement the likes of which were found in other parts of Europe, including France. Carol Loats uncovered examples in the Paris archives that echo many of the sentiments and strategies noted in the Portuguese samples. One case from the Paris archives, dated 25 January 1548, showed a woman who agreed to raise the baby after the man who had impregnated her made a financial payment at the outset, and agreed to provide more financial assistance for the following two years. A second case, dated 18 June 1540, was also resolved with a financial payment

151 ADP, Fundo Notarial, Po.1, 3a Se, no. 45 (1573), f.73v–75v. An 'alqueire' is a measuring unit, equivalent to approximately 8.4 litres. Some punctuation was added for clarity.

after the female plaintiff filed a complaint against a man for 'defloration and fleshly copulation', and for reneging on promises of marriage. In both instances the defendants also had to provide guarantors to ensure that the promised obligation would be honoured.[152]

The cases from early modern Portugal were typically more ambiguous. The pardons from the two Margaridas were unusual because they both stated outright some of the particulars of the arrangement, while most victims' pardons were vague in that regard, and the reasons for the difference remain a mystery. Although issued five years apart, both documents were written in the same notary's office in Porto, and thus the explicitness of the document could have been a result of the influence of the notary. Given this notary's penchant for details, therefore, it was noteworthy that Margarida Fernandes' account said nothing about a promise of marriage. The tone of the narrative suggested that Gonçalo raped Margarida, for which reason she filed a complaint and ultimately came to accept the best possible forms of compensation under the circumstances – a monetary payment and enough grain to sustain her for a while, as she had to care for an unwanted child. It is possible that Margarida would come to feel affection for that baby, but the harsh realities of having an extra mouth to feed meant that the father had to take responsibility of raising it. A child would also lessen Margarida's mobility if she were to seek employment as a domestic servant, for instance, and lessen her marriageability. Gonçalo was probably single as well, although the document did not stipulate it. Either way, he had to make plans to raise a one year old, a child that might not have been welcome by a present or future wife, although there, too, there could be room for negotiation and compromise.

Three Women and a Baby

Maria Fernandes was a single woman who lived with her widowed mother in a small parish called Freguesia de Sampaio de Solda, in the district of Vila dos Arcos, located in Portugal's northern interior, along the Lima river. She lived with her mother and was identified in the record as the daughter of Gonçalo Gonçalves, deceased, and of his wife, Maria Fernandes, but the younger Maria was old enough to engage in a legal transaction on her own. It is not known if she left alone, or what mode of transportation she used when she departed her village, but on 4 July 1646 the young Maria Fernandes went to the office of Manuel Martins da Costa, notary, at Rua Nova da Santa Ana in Viana do Castelo. The purpose of her visit was to have a pardon document drawn up, in which document she stated that two to three months earlier, more or less, she had complained to the corregidor of the district. Her complaint had been against João Gonçalves, a married man, who subsequent to her report to the authorities had been imprisoned in the public jail of Viana, for the reason that he took her honour and virginity. The resolution of this

[152] Cited in Monica Chojnacka and Merry E. Wiesner-Hanks, eds, *Ages of Woman, Ages of Man: Sources of European Social History, 1400–1750* (London and New York: Longman and Pearson Education, 2002), 55–7.

case involved the input of some men, and three key women, whose 'words' are worth quoting at some length.

> From this she had a baby girl called Maria who was four months old, more or less, and after his arrest, the said João Gonçalves, she the plaintiff had a pang of conscience and to alleviate it she declared that the said accused prisoner did not owe her anything for her virginity nor for having impregnated her and making her have a child by him, thus … [she] requested that the authorities not proceed with the said accusation, and in case it was necessary she granted him a pardon and quittance for the said virginity, as long as the said João Gonçalves take, raise, and sustain the said baby girl Maria as his daughter, the responsibility for which she the supplicant from this day forward and for always is exempt, per agreement with the relatives, [the] father and brothers of the said João Gonçalves and her plaintiff, with which she was satisfied and of her own volition, and of the said João Gonçalves she wanted nothing at all and she asked His Majesty's justices to release him and to be benevolent and charitable in giving him his freedom.

As Maria's statement indicated, other parties were involved in the settlement she accepted, and some of them were also at the notary's office that day, including Francisco Gonçalves, father of the prisoner João Gonçalves, as well as Domingos Gonçalves and João Rodrigues, Francisco's son and son-in-law, respectively, of the same village. All three stated that they pledged themselves and their properties as a guarantee that João Gonçalves (prisoner) and his wife, Maria Fernandes (yes, that makes three Maria Fernandeses, and one baby Maria), accepted the baby girl Maria, and would raise her, feed her, and treat her as they would their other children of legitimate matrimony – that is, not as a bastard child. They remained obliged to do this until the child reached a suitable age ('idade conveniente'), to which they promised and obliged themselves and all their assets, movable and immovable. Also present were António Fernandes, shoemaker, resident of Viana do Castelo, and João Fernandes, his brother, another shoemaker, resident of Ponte de Lima, brothers of Maria Fernandes (plaintiff). They in turn had a power of attorney from their mother, Maria Fernandes, widow, resident of Freguesia de Sampaio de Solda, and they made a statement as well.

> On behalf of the said their mother they approved and ratified this pardon document and quittance as stipulated above, and of the said prisoner, João Gonçalves, not now nor at any other time would she [the plaintiff's mother] ask nor demand anything in relation to the said *querela* that the said Maria Fernandes, her daughter did, nor of what she [the plaintiff's mother] could do against the said prisoner regarding all the injury, rights, and cause that she had and could have against him, all of which she defers and pardons him and from him she wants nothing at all.

As mother of an unmarried daughter who had been raped and impregnated by a married man, the widowed Maria Fernandes had a legal claim against the culprit, yet she rescinded that right through a power of attorney that she granted to her two sons. The statement made by António and João was clearly written to represent the mother's sentiments, not theirs. It was not a question of the male members of the family handling the affair, but rather a choice made by the mother who probably did not feel comfortable going into town for that occasion. Still, she and her daughter lived in the same village as the accused and his family, and one wonders how neighbourly relations would continue thereafter. It is curious that mother and daughter demanded nothing of the accused but that he raise the child. There could have been an unrecorded monetary payment as well, but the document made no such allusion.

If questions can be raised about the emotional impact the incident had on the two women who pardoned the prisoner, some of the same questions could be asked in relation to his family, and his wife in particular. Maria Fernandes, wife of João Gonçalves, prisoner, was also present at the notary's office on that fateful day, and her consent to the agreement between her in-laws and the plaintiff was duly recorded.

> She said that she consented and was very happy that the said her husband adopt ['perfilhasse'] and leave all of his share of the [family] property to the said baby girl Maria, and give it to the said [child] for life for her training, for they have no sons or daughters from their marriage, [while] her [the wife's] portion of the assets remains free for her [the wife] to do as she wishes.

All agreed to this contract and its terms and conditions, accepted all stipulations, and the notary accepted it on behalf of the absent widow Maria Fernandes. The notary's assistant signed the document, registering in writing that he 'signed on behalf of the two Marias Fernandes', while of the other eight men involved, only António could sign his name. The others made their crosses, including the three witnesses, identified by the notary, who found it necessary to note next to one particular sign that it was from 'Francisco Gonçalves, father of the prisoner'.[153]

Out of one act of violence, several lives were afflicted immeasurably, including that of the new life whose existence stemmed from that very act. How this scenario played out in a small rural community is impossible to know, but the terms under which the plaintiff granted a pardon, acquiesced by her mother, and approved by the defendant's wife, showed in no uncertain terms that women were implicated and engaged in legal decisions that had long-term effects for themselves and their families. They were not necessarily the only peace makers in their communities, but because most violence was committed by men, women were disproportionately affected by and responsible for dealing with the turmoil perpetrated by their fathers, husbands, sons, and brothers.

Margarida Fernandes and Maria Fernandes, single women, each filed an accusation against a man for 'taking her honour and virginity', and the term has been interpreted in the discussion above as 'rape' because it could have been rape, and probably was. The terse tone of the documents indicated that both women had been sexually assaulted, victims of a horrific act that was best not to dwell

---

[153] ADVC, Fundo Notarial, Manuel Martins da Costa (notary), no. 4.32.4.1 (1645–1647) f.76–78. Some punctuation was added for clarity.

on at the notary's office. The only way to move forward for both of them was to deal with the immediate consequences of those rapes, the women's pregnancies. Admittedly, the 'taking of one's honour and virginity' was ambiguous enough that its meaning was open to interpretation: did the 'taking' take place through force or with consent? We know that marriage was not an option, particularly in the case that involved a married man.

Because neither document revealed anything about when, where, and how it happened, the historian is left with a ponderous 'it' that can never be truly explained. What we can ascertain is that there was some negotiation that took place prior to the meeting with the notary, and Maria Fernandes' pardon provided some hints about the possible duration and complications of those negotiations. Maria granted her pardon on 4 July 1646, at which time she indicated that she had alerted authorities two or three months earlier about the sexual assault. That would have been April or May 1646. Maria also indicated that she had had a baby girl from that sexual assault, and that the baby girl was four months old. That would mean that the baby was born sometime in February or March 1646, which means that the baby was conceived sometime in May or June 1645. What all these approximate dates demonstrate is that Maria did not publicly denounce the man who 'took her honour and virginity' until long after the fact, sometime after the baby was born.

Why wait all that time? Again, Maria Fernandes, single woman, could not have been hoping to negotiate a marriage with a married man. The most likely answer was that there were protracted negotiations between the parties and possibly those negotiations stalled, prompting Maria to get the authorities involved. With their son, brother, and husband in jail, the clan from the other side managed to propose or accept a workable solution, an agreement as stipulated in the victim's pardon, or perhaps one that included further monetary compensation that was left unrecorded. Despite it all, the three Maria Fernandeses appeared to have maintained some dignity in the process, but in particular the wife of the accused must be given credit for rising to the occasion. A seventeenth-century catalogue of famous and illustrious women in Portugal highlighted the example of a woman who was so virtuous that she even loved her husband's 'bastards', but those would have been fatuous words to the practical women named in this archival account.[154] The married Maria Fernandes was willing to help raise her husband's ill-begotten child, and she might even have come to appreciate the infant in her childless home, but this Maria could also differentiate between business and family harmony. There was no messing with her property.

At that junction in her life, the four-month baby was the most vulnerable of all the Marias identified in this pardon document. How would she be treated by her adopted mother, rapist father, and extended family? How much would her family tell her about the circumstances of her birth? How long would she be supported by a family that pledged to look after her until she reached a 'suitable age'? And how would she be viewed in the village where everyone knew everything? Given

154 Anjos, *Jardim de Portugal*, 233.

that her birth mother was from the same village, would there be some contact and reconciliation, perhaps some affection from that side of the family, despite it all? As was the case with most pardon documents, this one concentrated on the practicalities of economic necessities and left the emotional bonds and scars to be dealt with outside the notary's office. No facet of the tragedy could be erased or undone, and all that was left was to deal with the consequences and move forward. Fields and animals had to be tended, meals had to be made, clothes had to be mended. For a while, at least, those daily tasks were undoubtedly performed with some heavy sighs, followed by especially earnest bedtime prayers, if not curses. Because the two families arrived at a resolution that was as honourable as possible under the circumstances, personal and social reconciliation was possible as time moved on, but the single Maria Fernandes likely moved on more literally. A move to either Viana do Castelo or Ponte de Lima, where she had a brother for some moral support, would have offered her an opportunity to rebuild a life for herself.

The road of pragmatism was followed out of necessity, and especially by those who could least afford the costs of a long judicial battle, in early modern Portugal and elsewhere. In a study of 650 cases found in ecclesiastical courts in Florence in the seventeenth century, the authors concluded that although the plaintiffs presented their arguments in terms of honour, their main concern was to get the fathers of their illegitimate children to recognize their paternity.[155] Even when there was no child, a young woman could be persuaded to settle out of court, depending on the resources at her disposal to pursue the case any further. One particularly telling example was found by a Spanish historian of a rape case that involved a young female servant and a 16-year-old male youth in Colomera, in the district of Granada. On 13 February 1588, Inés Pérez filed an accusation against Francisco López, claiming that 11 days earlier, while she did the washing in an outlying area, Francisco attacked her and 'corrupted her and took her virginity'. Her attacker also told her that if she said nothing to anyone about the incident he would marry her.

Two witnesses testified to Inés' credibility and honourable reputation, as well as to her condition after the attack and her bodily injuries, and Francisco was arrested, although he denied everything. Three days later, on 16 February, Inés (with her father's permission) granted Francisco a pardon, in which document she made the usual disclaimers: this was to clear her conscience; despite her earlier accusation the truth was that he tried to force her but that she managed to fight him off and so he did not succeed; she was doing this of her free will; she did not want anything from him; she asked His Majesty's justices to pardon him as well.[156] Unlike the examples found in the Portuguese notaries, the file on Inés

---

[155] Sandra Cavallo and Simona Cerutti, 'Female Honor and the Social Control of Reproduction in Piedmont between 1600 and 1800', in Edward Muir and Guido Ruggiero, eds, *Sex and Gender in Historical Perspective* (Baltimore: Johns Hopkins University Press, 1990), 73–109.

[156] Aurelia Martín Casares, 'La violencia contra las mujeres en al siglo XVI: un caso de violación en la provincia de Granada', *Arenal: Revista de Historia de las Mujeres* 4, no. 1 (January–June 1997) 160–62 [149–62].

Pérez contained many of the crucial elements with which to reconstruct a case: the report from the judicial officer, witness depositions, the statement from the defence, the petition from the trustee for the accused, and the victim's pardon. Still, many questions remained about what happened to Inés while she did her washing that compelled her to file an accusation, and withdraw it three days later. The depositions from the witnesses indicated that Inés had been dishevelled and bloody. Despite the victim's pardon, and all the extra documentation connected to it, this file hinted more at a resignation than a resolution.[157]

This is not to say that Inés' alleged rapist was automatically free of the charges, or got away with 'it' any more than João Gonçalves noted earlier. Even with the victim's pardon in their hands, João and Francisco were forced to deal with a judicial process that had been initiated against them. Other sources from Spain, France, and Italy showed that often victims of sexual crimes received some compensation, and that authorities sought to punish men who either raped or had sex with women under false pretences.[158] On the one hand, Malcolm Greenshields found an example in France from 1660 indicating that, following the instructions from a judge, a 40-year-old bachelor was seized by a group of men, taken to the local priest, and forced to marry a widow he had impregnated.[159] On the other hand, James Casey found a case of a man in Spain who in 1682 made a declaration in front of a notary that despite the sentence by the church court, he had not promised marriage to Inés de Llamas, and although he would marry her in order to be released from prison, he wanted it known that he was doing so under duress.[160] One can but wonder at the outcome of those forced arrangements.

To be sure, there were ways to manipulate the system, and some people had to be creative to get around patriarchal rules, those imposed by the state or by the church. A notarized document dated 4 May 1715 showed that Manuel João Magar, *lavrador*, and his daughter Agueda, single, granted a pardon to Frutuoso Mendes, all residents of Póvoa de Varzim on the northwest coast of Portugal. The text indicated that on 4 August 1714 the father and daughter had launched a

---

[157] For a discussion of the judicial inequities in cases of rape in eighteenth-century Madrid, see Fabio T. López-Lázaro, *Crime in Early Bourbon Madrid (1700–1808): An Analysis of the Royal Judicial Court's Casebook* (Lewiston: Edwin Mellen Press, 2008), 247–56.

[158] Tomás A. Mantecón Movellán, 'Mujeres forzadas y abusons deshonestos en la Castilla moderna', *Manuscrits* 20 (2002): 161 [157–85]; Greenshields, 'Women, Violence', 187; Joanne M. Ferraro, 'The Power to Decide: Battered Wives in Early Modern Venice', *Renaissance Quarterly* 48, no. 3 (Autumn 1995), 495 [492–512]; Beatrice Gottlieb, 'The Meaning of Clandestine Marriage', in Robert Wheaton and Tamara K. Hareven, eds, *Family and Sexuality in French History* (Philadelphia: University of Pennsylvania Press, 1980), 49–83; Dyer, 'Seduction by Promise of Marriage'.

[159] Greenshields, *An Economy of Violence*, 104. For another example of a man who was confronted with a mob of men to force him to marry a young widow, see IAN/TT, Chancelaria de Dom Filipe I, *Perdões e Legitimações*, Livro 3 (1580–1582), f.63v.

[160] James Casey, *Family and Community in Early Modern Spain: The Citizens of Granada, 1570–1739* (Cambridge: Cambridge University Press, 2007), 141.

complaint against Frutuoso for taking Agueda's honour and virginity, for which crime Frutuoso was condemned to marry Agueda despite the fact that the two were related in the third and fourth degree. For this marriage to take place the couple had to appeal to the church for a dispensation, and so the accusers granted this pardon so that the accused could be free from the charge and marry Agueda.[161] Could this have been a ruse to get the church to allow the prohibited marriage?

It was an imperfect system, but from the point of view of a desperately pregnant, unmarried woman, the 'forced' marriage option was preferable to the situation in certain Protestant regions in northern Europe where women who had been raped, or who became pregnant out of wedlock, were potentially punished for fornication.[162] Where authorities were intent on maintaining a social order based on a strict code of moral behaviour, severe penalties were sometimes imposed on those suspected of deviating from the norm, despite the circumstances of that perceived deviation.[163] In other regions, marriage was recognized as a viable tool with which to uphold a prescribed social order, and thus certain practices were devised that allowed individuals to work toward that end. Undoubtedly an untold number of women and men arrived at informal solutions to their difficulties, but some resorted to a judicial process for those solutions, and the Portuguese chancelleries attest to a pattern that sometimes worked. A man had sex with a woman, without her consent (rape) or under false pretences (deceit), and the woman insisted he return that which he was not entitled to take or receive. Such a man, if found guilty, either restored her honour through a financial payment, or through a financial and emotional commitment, which was what matrimony entailed. It is tempting to think that some form of affection led to the latter option, but the records made no such allusion, for that was not the point, at least not as far as the law was concerned. For instance, Ana Gonçalves pardoned Pedro Gonçalves for taking her honour and virginity, once he married her, for which reason the Crown was pleased to pardon Pedro, once he paid 3,000 *réis* (see Appendix 7). The arrangement met some basic needs for the newlyweds, and for society at large.

According to the available evidence, women were more likely to be the victims of male sexual duplicity and aggression than the other way around. The result of that duplicity and aggression meant different things to different women, but,

---

161 Flávio Gonçalves, 'Documentos Avulsos sobre a Póvoa de Varzim no século XVIII', *Boletim Cultural Póvoa de Varzim* 27, no. 2 (1990): 585–6 [585–607].

162 Raymond A. Mentzer, 'Morals and Moral Regulation in Protestant France', *Journal of Interdisciplinary History* 30, no. 1 (Summer 2000): 1–20; Michael F. Graham, 'Women and the Church Courts in Reformation-Era Scotland', in Elizabeth Ewan and Maureen M. Meikle, eds, *Women in Scotland c.1100–c.1750* (Linton: Tuckwell Press, 1999), 187–98; Merry E. Wiesner-Hanks, *Christianity and Sexuality in the Early Modern World: Regulating Desire, Reforming Practice* (London and New York: Routledge, 2000), 81.

163 Men, too, were punished for fornication under that strict code of moral behaviour. See, for example, Maria Kaspersson, 'Prosecution and Public Participation – the Case of Early Modern Sweden', in Richard Mc Mahon, ed., *Crime, Law and Popular Culture in Europe, 1500–1900* (Portland: Willan Publishing, 2008), 102–3 [96–117].

at the very least, a child out of wedlock meant an economic burden for the vast majority of single women, and authorities at all levels attempted to intervene for the sake of the child, if not the woman. The evidence shows that, in Portugal as elsewhere in pre-modern European, attempts were made to ensure that men accept responsibility for parenthood, in some form or another.[164]

***

Legislators at all levels, ecclesiastical and secular alike, attempted to regulate and prohibit a wide spectrum of behaviours that were deemed harmful and contrary to the social order that they wished to maintain. In the process, that social order privileged a select few and perpetuated inequities for and among the rest. No law could guarantee the safety and security of any individual, and, conversely, no prohibition could be said to represent the cultural understanding and common experience of any significant number of people, let alone all of them. Many of the documents chosen for this study dealt with questions of criminal activity, but the criminal act each record referred to was often but a veil through which we detected other crucial elements about the lives of some early modern Portuguese persons.

The victim's pardon offers a particularly fascinating avenue to evaluate women's contributions to conflict resolution in a pre-modern society. True, the examples gathered for this study represent but a fraction of the ways in which people resolved their differences, a fraction that can never be measured, yet the personal pardon was important for some individuals, even long after the infraction took place. Enough people believed in the process to go through the motions, to incur the costs of a notarized document to deal with their troubles. The perils that some women faced as sexual beings were among those troubles settled through a *perdão de parte*. Some of those perils were considered serious enough that they were highlighted in popular stories, morality stories that portrayed troubled women with an outlet, even if those women occasionally had to rely on the miraculous intervention of a friend or two. We saw this with the story at the opening of this chapter which outlined how the 'Glorious Virgin' rescued a woman at the gallows. One other story was found that testifies to the perseverance of this popular tradition, and illustrates that the Virgin Mary was not the only celestial being to intervene on behalf of 'fallen women'.

During his travels through Santarém in the seventeenth century, the French priest François de Tours saw a special crucifix kept by the Benedictine Brothers, on which cross Christ's right arm was detached from the cross and the body was curved, the reason for which had become legend. Once upon a time, the French visitor was told, a young shepherd was busy looking after her flock of sheep when a *fidalgo* made overtures, promising to marry her. For a long time she refused him,

164 Sara M. Butler, 'Maintenance Agreements and Male Responsibility in Late Medieval England', in Anthony Musson, ed., *Boundaries of the Law: Geography, Gender and Jurisdiction in Medieval and Early Modern Europe* (Burlington: Ashgate, 2005), 67–83.

but since he insisted so vehemently, she took him to a chapel and had him promise in front of the crucifix to marry her, which he did, and he also eventually got her pregnant, but, alas, refused to marry her. She launched a complaint against him, but the *fidalgo* told the judges that he had never promised to marry her, and so the case was dismissed. In desperation, the young woman begged the judges to accompany her to the chapel where the promise had been made, and they agreed. At the chapel the young shepherd took the crucifix down and asked the crucified Lord if it were not true that the *fidalgo* had promised to marry her, at which point the right arm on the crucifix detached itself and the body inclined toward the young woman, as proof of her story. The judges ordered the *fidalgo* to marry her.[165]

One can well imagine what a useful husband the *fidalgo* would have made, especially at shearing time, but the Santarém miracle must have been widely known for it was recounted by several travellers, including the Italian cleric, Juan Bautista Confalonieri, who visited the area 100 years prior to the French priest. In his version of the story, Confalonieri said that this incident had occurred about 300 years earlier.[166] What do these stories tell us about women and society in early modern Portugal? If nothing else, the stories speak to the enduring quality of oral histories, and that some of those moral tales did not always denigrate women. The stories tell us that women who committed 'shameful' acts were not necessarily damned – the biblical Magdalena was proof of that. The tale of the young shepherd is especially intriguing because of what it did not reveal: nowhere in the narrative was there a sense of blame or judgement against the shepherd. It was not a warning to young women against the perils of pre-marital sex; it was a warning against deceitful men who attempted to renege on their false promises.

The story of the deceived shepherd can also be juxtaposed against other popular depictions of rape, as exemplified in the seventeenth-century fictional work of the Dutch writer, Jacob Cats, for instance. In his collection of stories, entitled *The World's Beginning, Middle, and End Encapsulated in the Wedding Band, and its Touchstone*, written in 1637, Cats narrated a tale in which a knight raped two women, and at the knight's trial, the author depicted the rapist in sympathetic terms while practically ignoring the two female plaintiffs.[167] It is noteworthy that in both accounts, the miracle in Santarém and the Dutch tale, a knight was the sexual predator and the victims of his deceptions and violations were women of the lower ranks. Both cases revealed stereotypical ideas promulgated by some writers of the period that plebeian women were fair game for men of the elite, but

[165] Tours, 'Voyage du P. François', 498–9.

[166] Jose Guerra Campos, 'Viaje de Lisboa a Santiago en 1594 por Juan Bautista Confalonieri', *Cuadernos de Estudios Gallegos* 19 (1964): 197–9 [185–250]. See also Joaquim Veríssimo Serrão, ed., *Viagens em Portugal de Manoel Severim de Faria, 1604–1609–1625* (Lisbon: Academia Portuguesa da História, 1974), 89–90; Angel Sanchez Rivero and Angela Mariutti de Sanchez Rivero, eds, *Viaje de Cosme de Médicis por España y Portugal (1668–1669)* (Madrid: Centro de Estudios Historicos, 1933), 310.

[167] Amanda Pipkin, *Rape in the Republic, 1609–1725: Formulating Dutch Identity* (Leiden and Boston: Brill, 2013), 83–6.

the two stories also hinted at some possible cultural ideas about women engaged in pre-marital sex.[168] In the Portuguese example, the young woman was vindicated; in the Dutch example, one of the women eventually got her man, but both women were initially ignored and essentially ridiculed. Two examples are insufficient for any meaningful comparisons, but further research may reveal some significant regional variations of this theme.

While the shepherd story was based on anecdotal evidence, one other account was retrieved from the archives that relates to the question of women's capacity to seek redress from men of the upper ranks. Francisca Pires, resident of the Concelho de Felgueiras (northern Portugal), single and orphan, was able to negotiate a settlement with a *Cavaleiro da Casa del Rey* (a noble member of the king's household) after he 'took her honour and virginity' and impregnated her. The amount that Francisca received as compensation cannot be verified due to the frailty of the document, but in her notarized statement dated 25 October 1575 she declared that she was satisfied with what he paid for her honour, and that she was prepared to look after the child until a stipulated date (difficult to decipher), after which the father would raise the child as his own. Rare as these arrangements might have been, they serve to highlight the idiosyncrasies of an early modern worldview that allowed for such possibilities.[169]

The archival findings analysed for this study pointed to difficulties in the lives of a few women whose troubles were recorded in some truncated fashion. From these remnants we learned that some women were accused of adultery, and faced serious consequences as a result; others were accused of living in concubinage, and had to deal with possible exile and heavy fines; still others were made false promises in cases of seduction, or were raped in other cases. We cannot say that these were common occurrences because the records were insufficient for determining the prevalence of incidents found in those very records. On the surface, these examples objectified women; at some level women were victims, women to whom something happened, the consequences of which they had to contend with, make do. A scratch on that surface disturbed that facile view. Women's sexuality could most definitely be used against them, to hurt them, and to cause great havoc in their lives, but as the examples examined in this study showed, some women had the capacity to act, not just react. If men who were assaulted, stabbed, and sometimes seriously wounded, were not seen as mere victims, why should women?

In matters of sex in the early modern period, it is difficult to determine the extent of women's agency, particularly in cases of 'deflowering', or 'dishonouring', or 'promises of marriage'. In the end, perhaps the context of the encounter or assault mattered less – at a practical level – than the result of that encounter or assault. Circumstances not well recorded created a problem; sometimes the vital part of

---

168 According to 'The Art of Courtly Love', penned by Andreas Capellanus (fl. ca.1170–1190), a knight should not hesitate to take a peasant woman at his convenience, using force if necessary. Cited in Jacqueline Murray, ed., *Love, Marriage, and Family in the Middle Ages: A Reader* (Peterborough: Broadview Press, 2001), 91.

169 ADP, Fundo Notarial, Po.1, 3a Se, no. 52 (1575), f.99–100.

the story for both sides – the implicit understanding of reparations – was worthy of a written record, the *perdão de parte*. As we have seen, often even the specifics of the reparations were not elaborated, because it was well understood. The parties involved in the dispute were not strangers; they did not need to explain that which was self-evident to everyone concerned. In his discussion of the pardon document in early modern France, Pierre Braun arrived at similar conclusions. He cautioned about the need to place those documents in their proper historical context, and to pay attention to what was not said, 'le non-dit, le sous-entendu' – that is, that which was implied, or was an innuendo. Braun found that through a close reading of the nuances the historian could detect that the silences were deliberate in order to conceal that which was inconvenient to report, or, conversely, that the silences were matter-of-fact, and there was no need to state the obvious.[170]

Unfortunately, the difference between deliberate and disinterested omissions was not always discernible. Thankfully for the historian, occasionally a case came along when the parties felt it necessary to leave nothing to chance, or as little as possible. The best example of this is the *perdão de parte* of the three Maria Fernandeses. That document was explicit about that which was only implicit in the majority of victims' pardons, and in the process, that document contained many of the essential ingredients on which the present study was based. It was not an unusual case; it was unusually complete.

First, the case of the three Maria Fernandeses showed women at their most basic social roles: single, daughter, sister, wife, mother, and widow. Second, and most importantly, the record revealed how women were involved in the crucial arrangements necessary to resolve conflicts that had wide-ranging ramifications far beyond the culprit and the immediate victim. This victim's pardon underscored the inter-dependency between family members, between neighbours, between women and men, and between men and men. The culprit was in jail, and his father, brother, and brother-in-law came to his rescue while his wife acquiesced to a settlement that had an enormous impact on her life. Out of one violent act a baby was born. Aside from the emotional trauma – not to be dismissed – there was the fundamental problem at the doorstep: who was going to raise the baby, and pay for all the costs of her maintenance? In this regard, the other *perdão de parte* discussed earlier that involved Margarida handing over her baby to Gonçalo was glaringly incomplete. It is doubtful that Gonçalo would have been able to raise that one-year-old on his own, yet Margarida's pardon left those arrangements for Gonçalo's clan to figure out.

What precipitated the parties in the Maria Fernandes case to lay out all the terms and conditions of their agreement? It was unlikely due to the input of the prisoner, but one can well imagine his wife insisting on some clarification from the start. Maria Fernandes, wife, did not have the heart, or courage, or opportunity, or

170 Pierre Braun, 'La Valeur Documentaire des Lettres de Rémission', in *La Faute, la Répression et le Pardon: Actes du 107e Congrès National des Sociétés Savantes, Brest, 1982*, 2 vols (Paris: C.T.H.S./Comité des Travaux Historiques et Scientifiques, 1984), 208 [I: 207–21].

inclination to desert her traitorous husband,[171] but there was one thing not open to negotiation: her property. Maria Fernandes, single, could have made claims on her rapist's property, but she apparently renounced those rights, perhaps for the sake of her new-born daughter. Julia Rudolph has argued that in seventeenth-century English political theory, property law and rape law were linked because the rape of a woman was seen as an offense against a man's property.[172] I propose that in early modern Portugal property law and rape law were linked in a fundamentally different way: women who were raped had means for redress because of women's capacity *to own property*.

[171] Studies of other parts of Iberia indicate that women's pleas for annulments were successful for a limited number of reasons, most notably impotency and consanguinity. Francisco Javier Lorenzo Pinar, 'La mujer y el Tribunal Diocesano en Zamora durante el siglo XVI: divorcios y nulidades matrimoniales', *Studia Zamorensia* 3 (1996): 77–88. See also Behrend-Martínez, *Unfit for Marriage*, passim.

[172] Julia Rudolph, 'Rape and Resistance: Women and Consent in Seventeenth-Century English Legal and Political Thought', *Journal of British Studies* 39, no. 2 (April 2000): 162 [157–84].

Chapter 4
Conclusion

Not one wet eye around
Her lonely little grave
Said, 'He was out of line girl,
You were not to blame'.[1]

It is possible that, at some point, Catarina Antónia had had some affection for Domingos Jorge, but by 1 April 1656, when they met at the notary's office on Rua da Ourivesaria de Prata in Porto, she was more likely confronted with mixed feelings, at best. The daughter of Isabel Gonçalves and the late António Gonçalves, Catarina was a 'moça solteira', a single young woman who lived in the village of Bouça in the parish of Paranhos, where she raised two small children, Pedro and Maria. The children were the result of a relationship she had had with Domingos, a *lavrador*, resident of the village of Aguedo, in the same parish.

This snapshot into the lives of Catarina and Domingos came to us through an archival document entitled 'quitação que levaria de criação de duas crianças' – that is, a quittance that lifted the obligation for the raising of two children. The quittance was granted by Catarina to Domingos following some negotiations between them that were not recorded but the result of which led to a financial settlement to which both acquiesced. Catarina had been raising the children on her own and she demanded that Domingos contribute to their upbringing. In addition to the money that he had occasionally given her already, they agreed upon a final payment of 8,000 *réis*, a sum that released him of all further responsibility to her and the two children. Catarina had agreed to accept the first payment of 5,000 *réis* in silver coin, which amount was placed on the notary's buffet, picked up and counted by Catarina in front of the notary and witnesses, with the remaining 3,000 *réis* to be paid one month later.

This quittance was drawn up at the final payment of the remaining debt, and with it Catarina vouched, for herself, her children, and her heirs, that Domingos could never again be pursued for child support. Both parties were content with the agreement once it was read to them, and they signed – that is, someone signed on Catarina's behalf because she did not know how to write, while Domingos made a cross, vouched by the notary. It is not known how long their relationship lasted or why it ended, but it is noteworthy that the unwed mother had the legal recourse to obtain some form of compensation, a financial contribution to assist with the expenses of raising two children. How she was viewed by her community is less clear.[2]

1 Joni Mitchell, 'Not to Blame', *Turbulent Indigo* (Reprise Records/Warner Music Canada, 1994). The song reflects on a case of assault of a woman by her male partner.

2 ADP, Fundo Notarial, Po.4, 1a Se, no. 46 (1656), f.187v–188.

The steps that took Catarina and Domingos to the notary's office were not recorded, but undoubtedly some negotiation took place prior to the registration of the official and formal document. The archival record that brought them to our attention was not a pardon document, but in granting a quittance Catarina essentially forgave Domingos for a debt that no monetary amount could erase: the emotional and social responsibilities of fatherhood. Because he was identified by his occupational title and not by his marital status, we cannot know whether Domingos was legally available to take on those responsibilities, nor do we know if either one of the parties wished that he would. Catarina seemingly settled for the practical solution and was prepared to continue to raise her children on her own. As Merry Wiesner-Hanks has reminded us, 'money leaves far more traces in the records than love'.[3]

Catarina's fate, and that of those many others whose troubles left a trace in the records, must be left to our imaginations. There was a mechanism in place that some used to grieve the ills with which they were afflicted, and in early modern Portugal, the official mechanism in place was the *querela*, the accusation of a crime to a judicial official, and the *perdão de parte*, the official retraction of the accusation written up by a notary. Catarina would not have had to launch a *querela* against Gonçalo, and later grant him a *perdão de parte*, because seemingly no crime was committed. They were in a relationship; it ended, but due to the two children they produced together, there were some long-term obligations that needed to be settled. In hindsight, their notarized agreement looks almost progressive. Certainly some single mothers in the twenty-first century could do worse.

For people enmeshed in more serious disputes, especially those stemming from or resulting in criminal acts, an option was to alert officials of the problem through the *querela*. For some accused of a crime, a possible strategy was to seek a *perdão de parte*, a pardon from the victim in order to negotiate for a lighter sentence or full remission from the crown. The number of people who exercised this prerogative can never be known, but the ritual offered a workable solution to the legal problems that some people faced. Maybe for a few individuals it was the ritual that mattered most, a form of public acknowledgement that some harm had been caused, some pain had been endured, and that some remedy – however illusive – was necessary. The ways that most *perdões de parte* were written up suggested a congenial approach to resolving conflict, a conflict that had, for the most part, ceased to matter. But it mattered.

The victim's pardon insinuated that the two sides implicated in the conflict had arrived at some agreement, but we have no way of knowing the depth of the reconciliation, and whether relations between the two conflicting sides were eventually normalized. Feelings hurt as well as bodies, and some wounds have long memories. The potential for long-lasting resentment, suspicion, and apprehension was not necessarily erased with a few words written on a piece of paper. Yet people had to resolve their differences in some form or another because the alternative

[3] Merry Wiesner-Hanks, *The Marvelous Hairy Girls* (New Haven and London: Yale University Press, 2009), 126.

was untenable. Undoubtedly the majority of disputes, great and small, between families and within families, did not result in documentation that survived for our perusal, but enough evidence exists to demonstrate some of the possible acts of misbehaviour, and some of the paths taken to correct it, or make amends.

Few victims' pardons portrayed the culprit as repentant, but that was partially a symptom of the document. As we have seen, the *perdão de parte* was a sanitized account of a crime and as such it was more a recognition of the misdeed than reconciliation between the feuding parties. Yet, some version of 'I am sorry' must have occurred in order for the parties to have summoned the notary public; some acknowledgment of wrongdoing must have been uttered or understood to have been uttered, however reluctantly, however tightly-pressed the lips. This would have been especially critical in altercations between people who knew each other, who lived in close proximity, who worked together or shared a trade, or who were related to one another, and this applied to the majority of cases found in the archives. Few acts of violence were attributed to total strangers, and indeed, a good portion of the recorded conflicts involved family members.

Both sets of archival documents used in this study – the *querelas* and the *perdões de parte* – represented a performance by individuals involved in conflict. The *querela* consisted of a dramatic rendition of an incident, where a victim of a crime portrayed her or himself in the most favourable light, painted the accused in predictably negative terms, and lamented the consequences of the reported incident in hyperbole. In essence, the *querela* offered a victim a forum to disclose an offense in all its gory detail.[4] Conversely, the *perdão de parte* offered the offended a means to conceal the out-of-court settlement she or he had reached with the offender. In one the performer was centre stage, re-enacting a well-rehearsed script; in the other the players were still on stage, but the curtains had been drawn, and we barely got to hear their murmured assents and discontents. Fortunately some *perdões de parte* left a crack or two through which we could get a glimpse into what unfolded behind the scenes. Ultimately, though, the *perdão de parte* was a cautious dance around a minefield of pain and humiliation paved over with a sheen coat of an undisclosed compound – some form of compensation.

Behind the theatrics of the *querela*, and the illusions of the *perdão de parte*, lay real people who had undergone real suffering, the measure of which is immeasurable. In early modern Portugal, the best gauge to determine the potential losses that occurred through criminal acts was associated with the tangible world of property ownership, and this was evident in some of the more detailed *perdões de parte*. As has been shown, the victim's pardon was more of a financial agreement than an altruistic selfless act of forgiveness. Behind the stylized accounts of piety and magnanimity lay a tacit understanding of some material concession. To some extent the laws enacted at a certain time and place can be said to represent the values of that society, or at least the values of a segment of that society whose interests were protected and entrenched in the legislation. If this is true, then a

4 For a look at the role of theatricality in criminal investigations, see Gaskill, 'Reporting Murder', passim.

segment of early modern Portuguese society had a relatively pragmatic approach to crime, sexual or otherwise. The common saying, 'You do the crime, you do the time', would not fit well in early modern Portugal. A more accurate proverb for that era would be, 'You do the crime, you pay the dime', or as many coins deemed appropriate for the reparations.

Through the *perdão de parte*, the victim(s) renounced all present and future claims against the perpetrator, and this renouncement applied to the claims of all future heirs as well, claims that had potentially enormous implications for the inheritance rights of even the unborn. The stated motivations for granting the pardon were often couched in religious sentiments, as an act of faith and a sense of moral obligation, but while some pardoners were undoubtedly motivated by religious feelings, the justifications elaborated in most victims' pardons lacked credibility. Too often the text of the victim's pardon was unconvincing, but maybe its intent was not to convince. Maybe it was enough for judicial authorities to see some evidence, however thinly veiled, however precariously worded, that there had been some attempt at reaching a resolution. The ways the pardons were written down say less about the conviction of the pardoner, and a lot more about the interception of the pardoned on how a certain phrase should be worded, or about the commitment of the notary to the process.

If the *perdão de parte* did not reflect the victim's private dilemmas, it said even less about the other parties who were injured in the process. Most victims' pardons were silent about the effects of the crimes on the defendants and their families. On the one hand, the victim's pardon was an asset for the perpetrator of a crime, but it also could be a liability to her or his assets, and a potential loss to the perpetrator's household and heirs. The *perdão de parte* was concrete proof that the victim released the perpetrator of any further responsibility because the defendant had already met that responsibility. On the other hand, some form of forgiveness had to come from the family and friends of the culprit, for acts of violence invariably had ramifications for their well-being as well. How did a wife deal with a husband accused of raping a woman?[5] How did a mother continue to love a son convicted of homicide? The victim's pardon said little about the remorse of the perpetrator of a crime because, from a legal point of view, the *perdão de parte* was to contain no evidence of an avowal of guilt. Francisco Rodrigues Lobo, a Portuguese writer in the seventeenth century, commented on the extent to which an individual who received a favour, or was saved from misery, would feel a prolonged sense of indebtedness, gratitude, and obligation toward the benefactor.[6] Shakespeare's Portia believed otherwise:

---

5 For an example of a wife who refused to join her husband in exile after he was prosecuted for sodomy, see João José Alves Dias, 'Prohibited Sex in Portugal in the Sixteenth Century: An Approach', in Harold Johnson and Francis A. Dutra, eds, *Pelo Vaso Traseiro: Sodomy and Sodomites in Luso-Brazilian History* (Tucson: Fenestra Books, 2007), 59 [49–61].

6 António Manuel Hespanha, 'Les autres raisons de la politique: l'économie de la grâce', in Jean-Frédéric Schaub, ed., *Recherche sur l'histoire de l'état dans le monde ibérique (15e – 20e siècle)* (Paris: Presses de l'Ecole Normale Supérieure, 1993), 79–80 [67–86].

> The quality of mercy is not strain'd;
> It droppeth as the gentle rain from heaven
> Upon the place beneath: it is twice bless'd;
> It blesseth him that gives and him that takes;[7]

Was such a noble outcome possible without an acknowledgement of wrongdoing by the wrongdoer? The sample of *perdões de parte* examined for this study hinted at but overall was equivocal about heartfelt remorse by the defendant, and in most cases one sensed a veritable distance between the public display of reconciliation and the private experience of the pardoning process. This was especially palpable in situations where the parties involved in the dispute operated from unequal terms of reference, such as the case of the young servant Luzia, discussed in Chapter 2. She had been physically assaulted by a male neighbour who used a knife to injure her, injuries that appear to have necessitated medical help, yet, through the intervention of her mistress and master, Luzia granted a pardon to the culprit. Given her dependent status on her employers, it is possible that the young woman was encouraged to acquiesce to the agreement, willingly or not, with or without any sign of compunction from the perpetrator. A genuine apology was unlikely by the powerful; genuine forgiveness was impossible by the dis-empowered.

Some members of society were expected to compromise more than others as a matter of fact. In her review of the literature of Renaissance Spain, Aurelia Martín Casares found that in the writings about marriage, especially, some authors stressed women's submission to the idea of a peaceful home, and that the vices and wickedness of husbands were never to detract or deter women's patience, whose mission was always to pardon their husbands and accept the suffering as part of life. In his *Espejo de la perfecta casada*, for instance, Fray Alonso de Herrera argued that there was greater strength for wives to pardon than to avenge, and great strength in suffering. Another male Spanish writer promoted the example of the honour of pardoning by referring to Saint Monica, mother of Saint Augustine, who while married for 30 years endured the misery of her marriage.[8] Such notions served patriarchy well, in Iberia and elsewhere in pre-modern Europe, but they did not go unopposed. Some women (and a few men) were cognizant of the need for the patriarch to make amends, as seen in a satirical collection of women's opinions and folk beliefs from the fifteenth century, largely from the region of Flanders and Picardy. The collection featured a fictional female character who presented as gospel that 'a man who beats his wife for whatever reason, will never obtain the mercy of the Virgin Mary, in spite of all the prayers he may say, if he has not first obtained his wife's forgiveness'.[9]

---

[7] *The Merchant of Venice*, Act IV, Scene I, in *The Complete Works of William Shakespeare* (New York: Avenel Books, 1975), 222–3.

[8] Martín Casares, 'Las mujeres y la "paz en la casa"', 240–41.

[9] Madeleine Jeay and Kathleen Garay, eds, *The Distaff Gospels* (Peterborough: Broadview Press, 2006), 83.

Be that as it may, the only hints of begging for forgiveness in the Portuguese victim's pardon came from the victim who often addressed the intended audience – crown officials – with great signs of humility on behalf of the accused. The implication in the *perdão de parte* was that the culprit was sorry, but because of the need to minimize the harm that the culprit had caused, the victim often accepted responsibility for the circumstances that led to the infraction, and insinuated that in fact the culprit did not have much to be sorry about. Significantly, though, this rhetorical device was not used in cases of sexual assault. No example was found that the woman took the blame for having been raped, or deflowered, or dishonoured through the loss of her virginity. A woman could grant a notarized pardon to the man accused of such crimes, but there was no call for pretending that it was anything but a legal resolution.

For the sake of the harmony in the family, and survival in the community, certain social pressures were put on some women and men to acquiesce to a *perdão de parte*. How many of those victims' pardons found in notary collections were the result of coercion? We will never know, but that potential cannot be ignored. A list of Portuguese epigrams collected in the late eighteenth century included some references to popular views about justice, and one epigram indicated that there was justice in heaven, to which the response was: that explained why there was so little of it on Earth. Another epigram referred to the social pressures to pardon, and that only a wicked person would choose to refuse.[10] This theme was addressed by other authors, including in the poetry of the Italian writer and courtesan, Veronica Franco (1546–?):

> Should I go on fighting you?
> I hear that he's considered vile
> Who, begged forgiveness, fails to grant it.[11]

The purpose of this study was not to show the extent of violence in early modern Portugal, but rather to show how some forms of violence were expressed, and how some women and men dealt with the wrongs that befell upon them. If it is true that a person's true character can best be gauged during a time of crisis, the sources analysed here portrayed a few of those individuals with an uncanny ability to fashion their stories, and to negotiate and reconcile as needed, at least on paper. Both women and men were involved in criminal activities, as perpetrators or victims, as forgivers or forgiven. As it has been argued, while the majority of crimes were committed by men against other men, their violence had an inordinate impact on the female members of the families to which the perpetrators and

---

[10] Miguel do Couto Guerreiro, *Epigrammas Portuguezes* (Lisbon: Na Officina Patriarcal, 1793), 191, 367; see no. XXXVI, 'Manda-se-nos perdoar: / A regra tem excepção; / Porque eu devo dar perdão / A qualquer que me aggravar; / Mas a mim, se sou máo, não'.

[11] Cited in Carol Cosman, Joan Keefe, and Kathleen Weaver, eds, *The Penguin Book of Women Poets* (London: Penguin Books, 1980), 118.

victims belonged. The case that involved the three Maria Fernandeses, discussed in Chapter 3, represented women's experiences with crime par excellence: victims certainly, but also resourceful and survivors despite the odds.

Combined, the *querelas* and the *perdãos de parte* are useful tools for the study of early modern Portuguese women because both sets of records reveal women's agency in the criminal and legal spheres that were publicly presented as the affairs of men. While these cases cannot be said to represent the experiences of most ordinary women, the texts contained some ordinary details about women's lives. Occasionally the texts informed us that arguments, or fights, or more serious tragedies took place while women worked on the fields, at the local market, in local shops, or at home where most of the family's sustenance was produced. The archival records used in this study showed that disputes broke out, some of which led to serious harm, but the records also testified to more joyful events. Many women courted, got married, and gave birth, events that often led to some small celebrations. Women also had some occasion to partake in community and religious festivities, where they would sing and dance, but few women could play a musical instrument; they were more apt with the mortar and pestle.

Some women were members of urban trades, such as weavers, and enjoyed some form of public recognition for their work.[12] Overall, though, women were largely responsible for the mundane, for which they received little acknowledgement or remuneration. This observation was reflected in Gil Vicente's play of 1523, *Auto de Inês Pereira*, which began with the protagonist lamenting about all the household chores she had to do while other women were free to come and go as they pleased.[13] It is doubtful that the playwright saw many women (or men) roam about freely, but one seventeenth-century literary nun of Portuguese origin was prepared to give women a lot of credit. In an examination of the sonnets written by Sor Violante del Cielo (born in Lisbon in 1607 as Violante Silveira de Montesinos), Gwyn Fox contended that Sor Violante privileged the female over the male in her work, and in fact came to the defence of women's contributions in society by depicting the Virgin Mary as 'a rallying symbol of female agency and independence and, above all, of power

[12] For the place of women in the festivities of urban processions, see Filipe Themudo Barata, 'Organizar a Procissão nos Finais do Século XV. O lugar de cada um e do grupo na cidade', in Hermínia Vasconcelos Vilar and Maria Filomena Lopes de Barros, eds, *Categorias sociais e mobilidade urbana na Baixa Idade Média. Entre o Islão e a Cristandade* (Lisbon: Edições Colibri/CIDEHUS – Universidade de Evora, 2012), 187–94; for a look at women's identification with civic offices and urban crafts in late medieval Portugal, see Arnaldo Sousa Melo, 'Women and Work in the Household Economy: The Social and Linguistic Evidence from Porto, c.1340–1450', in Cordelia Beattie, Anna Maslakovic, and Sarah Rees Jones, eds, *The Medieval Household in Christian Europe, c.850–c.1550: Managing Power, Wealth, and the Body* (Turnhout, Belgium: Brepols Publishers, 2003), 249–69.

[13] Francisco Torrinha Augusto C. Pires de Lima, ed., *Farsa de Inês Pereira de Gil Vicente* (Porto: Domingos Barreira – Editor, 1941 [1523?]), 38–9.

and dominance … in Sor Violante's determination … it is the woman who holds the upper hand'.[14]

The archival records did not confirm Sor Violante's optimism, but the evidence showed that due to the nation's laws of inheritance, some early modern Portuguese women had their hands on things criminal and the proceeding negotiations that those incidents generated. Still, it must be reiterated that Portuguese women's rights to property ownership did not translate into a more egalitarian society than was found elsewhere in Europe. Patriarchy was alive and well in early modern Portugal; circumstances just forced it to accommodate as needed. Some women were mistreated, and some mistreated back. For many, things could have been better; for some, the situation could not have been worse. Occasionally women had to take care of business beyond their daily grind, and that business took them to the notary's office, where they looked after their interests, their families, their properties. While many *perdões de parte* appeared relatively benign, others pointed to what could be a summation of some women's attitudes as they faced serious conflicts with personal and financial repercussions: you can break my heart and you can break my hymen, but hands off my soul and my soil.

Such a sentiment was not unique to Portuguese women or to the early modern period. When Silona Calverie of Marseille sought a separation from her husband in 1424, she highlighted the physical abuse she had endured from her husband, but above all, she sought the recovery of her property.[15] Indeed, the present study did not attempt to show that early modern Portuguese women were unusually independent, but rather that they could and did act independently when necessary; legally, they could; financially, they sometimes had to; culturally, they managed as well as possible under the circumstances. At the heart of those acts of independence was the necessity to deal with property in its many manifestations, and the possibility of gain or loss of assets was fundamental to the renunciations explicit and implicit in the *perdão de parte*.

In more modern times, the inherent suspicion that a woman is at the centre of an intriguing scandal or drama is reflected in the popular saying: *cherchez la femme*. For early modern Portugal, it would be more accurate to say: *cherchez la femme avec la terre*. It was women's ability to inherit, own, buy, sell, or bequeath property that gave them a voice in the negotiations to settle a dispute, in the ability to grant a pardon, and ostensibly forgo that to which they were entitled. The *perdão de parte*, when analysed closely and in connection with other documents, did not show women's autonomy, but instead highlighted the inter-dependence of women and men; for too long the dependence of the former has been taken for granted while the independence of the latter has been exaggerated.

---

14 Gwyn Fox, *Subtle Subversions: Reading Golden Age Sonnets by Iberian Women* (Washington, DC: Catholic University of America Press, 2008), 98–101.

15 Susan McDonough, 'She Said, He Said, and They Said: Claims of Abuse and a Community's Response in Late Medieval Marseille', *Journal of Women's History* 19, no. 4 (2007): 39–40 [35–58].

* * *

Growing up I often heard my mother tell of how my father as a young man wanted desperately to leave Madeira, to escape the abject poverty to which he was born, hungry to emigrate to some place where he stood a chance of improving his lot. He finally got the opportunity he sought, but in order to have the sponsorship for migratory work approved, he needed a guarantor, and my mother proudly recounted how it was her father who provided that guarantee. One day, as I pored over the piles of archival documents I had collected over the years, the penny dropped: what did she mean *her father* provided the guarantee? A visit to the village archives confirmed my suspicions. The guarantee in question contained a pledge that had an impact on the little plots of land my maternal grandparents had up the rugged mountains on the northern coast of Madeira, property that belonged to both spouses, and so the written document contained both their names and their thumb prints, because neither grandparent could read or write.

My mother's retelling of that transaction speaks volumes about the power of memory, the insidious character of patriarchy, and the challenges for women's history. She always spoke of *her father's* house, *her father's* land, and his fig trees, and his apple cider, and whatnot, even though in reality all of it belonged to her mother, as well. That was understood, but for the sake of appearances, in order to maintain a façade of the supremacy of the patriarch, the culture promoted a public discourse that placed the man of the house perched on top of that house and everyone associated with it. He was the rooster, and nobody better say otherwise, or else. Or else what?

There were and are consequences to this ideological practice, not least of which is the erasure of women's history from the public consciousness. At worst, such ideological premises could and did lead to some serious harm, including to my maternal grandmother, as illustrated in another of my mother's stories. One day, she recounted, my grandfather returned home late at night after having stopped at the local tavern. He found his wife already in bed, but he demanded that she get him his supper. She told him to serve himself, to which response he pounded on her, giving her a beating the likes no one had ever seen. As a result of that assault, my grandmother was bedridden for several weeks. None of this made the archival record, and the archival records that have survived from the early modern period do not contain the many collisions of this sort that happened in families, the very institution to which women were supposed to be dedicated for life. For some, it was a life sentence.

The archival record also does not narrate the informal and internal dialogue that took place after such collisions. In the case of my grandmother, the story continued, there was some consequence to my grandfather's violent outburst. The following morning, upon hearing about the incident, my grandmother's sister stormed down to the house, and in a stupendous outpour of anger, she gave her brother-in-law a piece of her mind, threatening him that if he ever did such a thing again she would report him to the authorities, a tirade he apparently listened to in dismal silence. In the end, said my mother, it was her father who had to deal with the consequences of his outrage because, due to the injuries he inflicted on his wife, he had to do without her contribution to the household economy for nearly a month. A rational explanation for an irrational act.

Traces of how that married couple, and couples further back in the past, reconciled after such difficult situations are not easily found in archival documents, but the search occasionally yields some remnants that point to certain possibilities. An examination of women *trouvères* found that there were songs, called *chansons de malmariée*, voiced by women that specifically addressed the laments of unhappily married women, whereas there was no equivalent song for unhappily married men.[16] But men had their reasons to lament, too, at the end of the day. The story of the three Maria Fernandeses is a case in point. Maria Fernandes, wife, had to live with the grief her husband caused her; he had to live with his conscience. My clearest childhood memory of my maternal grandmother is from the day that she died. As she lay on the bed, my grandfather used his hand to wave away the flies from her face, and I looked at him in astonishment, wondering, 'Why is he crying?'

---

16 Wendy Pfeffer, 'Constant Sorrow: Emotions and the Women Trouvères', in Lisa Perfetti, ed., *The Representation of Women's Emotions in Medieval and Early Modern Culture* (Gainesville: University of Florida Press, 2005), 126 [119–32].

Appendix 1
List of prices (in *réis*) for royal pardons (*Regimento dos Perdões*), 18 June 1517, Lisbon

1. Item – [prisoner] escape from open space 300 – [prisoner] escape from enclosed space 400
2. Item – [female] concubine of cleric, first time 2,000
3. Item – [female] concubine of married man 3,000
4. Item – [male] concubine, married 3,500
5. Item – [female] concubine of [male] courtier 2,000
6. Item – [male] courtier who has a [female] concubine 2,500
7. Item – simple [female] adultery 3,000
8. Item – [female] adultery with departure 5,000
9. Item – injury to the head 1,000
10. Item – body injury with spear 1,000
11. Item – body injury without spear and no scarring 800
12. Item – [injury to] finger on right or left hand 3,000
13. Item – body injury with scarring 2,000
14. Item – deformity to right hand 10,000
15. Item – deformity to left hand 8,000
16. Item – deformity to right foot 8,000
17. Item – deformity to left foot 6,000
18. Item – [injury to] toe of right or left foot 1,000
19. Item – deformity to the right arm 12,000
20. Item – deformity to entire left arm 10,000
21. Item – deformity to entire right leg 12,000
22. Item – fracture to right or left eye 7,000
23. Item – cutting of the nose 4,000
24. Item – cutting off the entire ear 2,000
25. Item – various
26. Item – to lift a year of exile overseas 4,000
27. Item – to cause grief to Our Lord and Our Lady 1,500
28. Item – for renouncing God 2,000
29. Item – removal of exile to asylum 3,000
30. Item – removal of year of banishment from a town and its vicinity 2,000
31. Item – removal of year of banishment from small open areas 1,200
32. Item – woman who sleeps with her first [male] cousin 3,000
33. Item – [man who sleeps] with wife's sister 3,000
34. Item – pardon for theft of items valued up to 3,000 *réis* shall cost double the value of the amount stolen

35. Item – [jail guard who allows] escape of prisoners 2,000
36. Item – escape of prisoners 1,000
37. Item – [causing a] fire with a license 500
38. Item – a beating ['pancadas'] 3,000
39. Item – a beating of an honest woman 4,000
40. Item – resistance to a gate-keeper 2,000
41. Item – breaking of municipal corral 2,000
42. Item – slap on the face ['bofetada'] 2,000

Source: Instituto de Arquivos Nacionais/Torre do Tombo, *Maço 2 de Leis*, no. 49, f.1–8, in Luís Miguel Duarte, *Justiça e Criminalidade no Portugal Medievo (1459–1481)*, 2 vols, II: 726–32 (Lisbon: Fundação Calouste Gulbenkian, 1999) (Document No.118)

Notes

This code represents the items on the list in the order of appearance, and contains the prices that supplicants had to pay for a royal pardon, according to the crimes for which they were sentenced. The numbers on the left column have been added for clarification.

Item 2 has a note on the original copy indicating that the fee would double each additional time the female concubine of a cleric was caught committing the same crime, and similar conditions applied to many of the other fees. In some cases the crown allowed authorities to use their discretion in determining whether or not the fees should be increased, depending on the rank of the individuals, and other factors. Most of the items on the list had further explanations, including the regional variations in the application of these fees, and the situations under which crown authorities could grant pardons without crown approval, but those explanations were deemed too lengthy to be included here.

Item 25 did not refer to any specific crime and the cost of its pardon, but rather it provided a lengthy note regarding certain circumstances under which a pardon may or may not be granted, including in cases where the culprit knew the victim, yet the monarch reserved the right to grant such pardons as it pleased, and according to the prices it deemed appropriate. The note also reiterated that authorities were allowed to increase the costs for any pardon depending on the wealth of the supplicant, or ability of the supplicant to pay more, 'for wealthy supplicants should suffer more in their finances than they did in their bodies'.

Item 31 indicated that if supplicants for these pardons were in prison, having been sentenced, they could be pardoned once they received the *perdão de parte* from their victims. If there was no pardon from the victim, the exile would not be pardoned until at least a third of the time in exile had been served, and this applied to those who were in or out of jail.

Item 36 had a note explaining that this reduced cost applied to a prison guard who requested a pardon for the escape of prisoners (under his guard), whose prisoners escaped without any malice or great negligence (on the part of the guard), and who could show that he had received a pardon from the victim (*perdão de parte*), in cases when the prisoner or prisoners did not deserve death or exile. In particular, this reduced fee for a royal pardon applied to guards and bailiffs in regions that did not have a jail, and to municipal councillors who were obliged to accompany prisoners transferred from one municipality to another, and who sought a pardon once their prisoners escaped, as long as the escape had happened without malice or great negligence on the part of the supplicants.

Item 37 referred to those who had a license to use fire for clearing, for instance, but the fire caused some damage; those who committed the same infraction but without a license to use fire in the first place had to pay 1,000 *réis* for a royal pardon, though the fees could increase depending on the location of the fire, the amount of damage caused, and the status of the supplicant.

Item 39 provided that a pardon for the beating of other women who were not of the same 'quality' cost 2,000 *réis*.

Item 42 stated that authorities could grant this pardon without permission from the crown if the slaps were given to a plebeian; from a plebeian to a rank above, the pardon needed to be sanctioned by the crown. Likewise such pardons needed the crown's approval if the slaps on the face occurred in Lisbon or in Madeira.

Appendix 2
Victim's pardon (*perdão de parte*) from Manuel Gomes and Graça Geraldes, widow, from Barcelos, to João Lourenço and more associates, 12 January 1650, Monção

[f.24] Be it known those to whom this pardon factum, or through whatever means by right exists elsewhere, see that in the year of the birth of our lord Jesus Christ of one thousand six hundred and fifty years on the twelfth day of the month of January, in this town of Monção and residence of me, notary, there in my presence and of the witnesses identified below appeared present, and grantors, Manuel Gomes and Graça Geraldes, widow of the late Francisco de Faria, residents of the town of Barcelos. And by them it was said that they as brother-in-law and wife of the said Francisco de Faria, who had been a soldier in the Castelo de Castro Loureiro, [they] initiated an accusation for his [Francisco's] death, for [someone] killed him in the Lugar de Torre in this district, for which death were found guilty João [f.24v] Lourenço the younger, and Pedro Rodrigues Palaço, and Bento Afonso, and Manuel Afonso, and Bastião Afonso, and Pedro da Rocha, and João Rodrigues the younger, and Francisco Vidal, and Francisco Ferreiro, and João Francisco, and Francisco Esteves, and Francisco Vaz, all from the said Lugar de Torre, Freguesia da Relva, in this district. And since they, grantors, had been informed of how the incident of the said death occurred, and found that the above-mentioned did not have any guilt in it, and they [grantors] acknowledged it, and for this reason they pardoned freely all the above-mentioned, and they [grantors] did not want their part from them [defendants]. And in case that they [defendants] had any guilt, they [grantors] pardoned them because they [defendants] gave them 12,000 *réis* in coin, and [the grantors] are satisfied, which money they received in the presence of me, notary, and [the] witnesses to this act. And in case that for reasons of restitution, which they renounced, or through some way [they] wanted to accuse again or join the justices, they [grantors] cannot do it, and before they be heard [by justices] they [grantors] return the said 12,000 *réis* with an additional 12 [thousand] in penalty, and everything [is] voided. And [the money] was handed over with which they [grantors] accepted as being advanced, and thus they stated and declared. And standing as witnesses [were] André Velho de Azevedo, *cavaleiro*, professed person of São Bento de Avis, and Reverend Manuel de Lanções, both of this town, persons recognized by me, notary, who said they recognized the grantors Manuel Gomes and Graça Geraldes to be who they claimed to be. And on behalf of her who does not know how to write according to what she said, signed [f.25] the said André de Azevedo, and standing more as witnesses [were] João Pereira, son of

Gonçalo Rodrigues de Caldais, of this town, and Tomé Lourenço from above the fountain of this district, [and] that all signed with the grantor Manuel Gomes. And I, Francisco Pereira, notary, wrote it and declare that they further said, the grantors Manuel Gomes and Graça Geraldes, that in case of a sentence of the *Relação do Porto* [Court of Appeal in Porto], the said [defendants] come out guilty, condemned [to pay] them [grantors] any [portion of a] punishment in money, they [grantors] want nothing at all of it because with the said 12,000 *réis* they were well satisfied, witnesses the above-mentioned, the above-mentioned notary wrote it.

[four signatures: André Velho de Azevedo, Manuel Gomes, Manuel de Lanções, João Pereira, a cross made by Tomé Lourenço, vouched by the notary]

Source: Arquivo Distrital de Viana do Castelo, Fundo Notarial (Monção), Francisco Pereira de Araújo (notary), no. 5.7.1.6. (1649–1651), f.24–25.

One of the witnesses, André Velho de Azevedo, *cavaleiro*, professed person ('professo de abito') of São Bento de Avis, was in fact a knight of the order of S. Bento de Avis, a military order. Some punctuation was added for clarity.

Appendix 3
Victim's pardon (*perdão de parte)* from Isabel Dias to Francisco Dias, 19 October 1579, Lisbon

[f.57] Be it known those who see this pardon factum that in the year of the birth of our lord Jesus Christ of one thousand and five hundred and seventy-nine on the nineteenth day of the month of October, in the city of Lisbon, by the old pillory, in the house where presently the notaries of this city reside, presently appeared Isabel Dias, woman who is not married, resident of the city by the Chafariz d'el Rey. Then it was said by her, in front of me, notary, and witnesses identified below, that in this present month of October, on a day that in truth she was at night in front of the Chafariz da Perguiça, Francisco Dias, shoemaker, resident of this city, on Rua da Padaria, attacked her and gave her slaps ['bofetadas'] and blows ['pancadas'], and he did the same in her house, and left her with marks and bruises, about all of which she complained and accused him in front of Doctor Duarte Lampais, *cidadão,* and criminal judge of this city, as is all better and more fully elaborated as contained in the *autos* of the said *querela* [writ of the criminal denunciation], of which the scribe is Francisco Vieira. And that now she, Isabel Dias, feeling responsible for the said incident, said that for the love of the Senhor Deus, and that he pardons her sins, and for other just and honest reasons, and that moved by her pleasure, good and free volition, and very proper motive, and without fear, pressure nor threat from anybody, [she] would pardon, as in effect she pardoned freely the said Francisco Dias, all the guilt for the said incident and convictions that he has or could have, and rectification, and [f.57v] penalty that there could be at any time imposed against him. And [she] wants nothing from him from [a] criminal or civil [procedure] as long as he frees himself from justice at his own cost, and at his expense, Francisco Dias, and if there are costs against her, he will not claim them against her, for as is stated she pardons him freely. And with this [she] asks the justices of these kingdoms and others whosoever to whom the case pertains that they not proceed against the said Francisco Dias for the above-mentioned reasons and in relation to it. Rather if it is necessary [she] asks that his discharge ['sentença de livramento'] be granted for she desists from the said *querela* and accusation that she has made and of any whatsoever [claim] that she could make later for the above-mentioned reasons, and all [of the *querela*] in fact is null and has no effect, force, or validity as if it [the *querela*] had not been made. Rather [she] wants that this pardon be upheld and kept, which she promises and obliges herself to adhere to it, and not to renege it, nor go against it in part or in whole, through the courts, or outside of it, effectively not in law nor in any other manner. And that in reneging or contradicting it, such reneging and contradiction is not worth anything except for adhering and maintaining it [the pardon] in its entirety according to the above-mentioned, to which end she obliged herself and her estate, and all costs, expenses, losses, and damages that result from and are applied to this [reneging] which she shall pay if thus she adheres not. And she promised and obliged herself to adhere to it in every way in its entirety, without breech whatsoever, [and] with truthful testimony thus she approved and requested that this document be done in this registry, and copies of it be made that the said Francisco Dias, who was present, asked for and accepted. And I, notary, [f.58] accept [this pardon] on behalf of those who are absent to whom this could affect, as a public person, stipulatory and receiver. [The] witnesses who were present are Afonso Fernandes, shoemaker, resident in this city at the entrance to the Misericórdia, in front of the tax house, and João Filgueira, also another shoemaker resident of this city, attached to the said Afonso Fernandes, [and] both said that they well recognized the said Isabel Dias to be the one contained in this document and is the one present. And as another witness, Belchior Fernandes, resident in this city on the Rua das Flores, who signed this *nota* [notarized deed] for the said Isabel Dias, on her behalf, because she stated that she did not know how to write, and I, Sebastião Mendes de Matos, notary, wrote it. And the said Isabel Dias stated that the said Francisco Dias shall not do her any harm nor offense whatsoever, nor revoke, because as stated she freely pardons him the past. The above-mentioned witnessed the above-said [that] I [notary] wrote [and] crossed out there that is Gls.

[following the above text] I sign on behalf of the said Isabel Dias who does not know how to write [signature of] Belchior Fernandes [the other two witnesses made a cross and the notary vouched for them]

Source: Instituto de Arquivos Nacionais/Torre do Tombo, Fundo Notarial (Lisbon), Caixa 2, no. 11 (1579), f.57–58.

The last comment regarding 'Gls' refers to an error that the notary had made in the text regarding Isabel Dias' last name, when he wrote Gls (for Gonçalves) instead of Dias, which error he crossed out, and vouched at the end that he had crossed out that word. Some punctuation was added for clarity.

Appendix 4

Criminal denunciation (*querela*) filed by Ana Gomes, prisoner, against Tomé Rodrigues, jail guard, 18 September 1629, Ponta Delgada

[f.66v] In the year of the birth of our lord Jesus Christ of one thousand six hundred twenty-nine years on the eighteenth day of the month of September in this city of Ponta Delgada, island of São Miguel, in the lodgings of Duarte Borges da Costa, most senior city councillor [and] judge, according to the ordinance in the absence of an outside judge, in this city of Ponta Delgada and its environs. And by him it was ordered that I, scribe, make this *auto* [writ] saying that Ana Gomes, prisoner in the jail of this city, sent him a petition stating in it that while she was a prisoner in the said jail, Tomé Rodrigues Leonardo, jail guard of it, took her and whipped her in front of all the [female] prisoners, and inflicted on her many black marks and bloody bruises, without she, supplicant, having had anything with him, with which he caused her much offense and injury. And since she [the] supplicant [f.67] complains of and denounces the said jail guard, she asked that she be given mercy [and the judge] send a scribe to see her, who will vouch for what he sees, and take her denunciation and complaint, for he [the jail guard] did everything as her enemy by offending and whipping her with a bull's pizzle, she being a woman of good repute, and will receive justice. By virtue of which petition, since the said supplicant is a prisoner in the said jail, he, the said judge, ordered me, scribe, and that I go to the said jail and see her marks and bruises that she had, and if truthfully she would make an oath on the holy gospels that she accused well and truthfully, since he [the judge] could not go do it personally for being busy. In complying with that order I, scribe, went to the said jail to see the said marks that the said supplicant had, who had on the right arm three black marks, and more on one leg a black one [and] five on one buttock, and that all were black and bloody, for which I [scribe] vouch, and gave the oath on the holy gospels to the said supplicant, Ana Gomes, with authority for which [the scribe received] from the said judge. And [the scribe] asked her if she wanted to complain and would complain of the defendant, well and truthfully, and since she accepted the oath that well and truth … [f.67v – top of folio is frayed, some words missing] … of the defendant for having done to her what is contained in her petition that she repeated in front of me, scribe, and all seen by the said judge, and the oath from me, scribe, [the judge] accepted the said *querela* [criminal denunciation] as by right he was to receive, from which he ordered that this *auto* be done so that she name her witnesses, that [presently] the said judge signed [and] Pedro Ferreira Serrão [scribe] wrote it. [signature of Duarte Borges, acting judge]

Source: Biblioteca Pública e Arquivo Regional de Ponta Delgada, Ponta Delgada, São Miguel (Azores), Fundo Judicial, *Livro de Autos de Querelas*, NOT.601 (1606–1654), f.66v–67v.

Sometimes the *querela* was referred to as an *auto* which can be translated as a writ. Some punctuation was added for clarity.

Appendix 5
Victim's pardon (*perdão de parte*) from Melchior Barbosa, painter, to Martinho da Cunha and others, 22 April 1577, Porto

[f.153] Be it known those who see this pardon factum that on the year of the birth of our Lord Jesus Christ of one thousand and five hundred and seventy-seven years on the twenty second day of the month of April, in the very noble [f.153v] and always loyal city of Porto, on the Rua Chã at the home of Francisco de Lemos, *cidadão*, of the said city, being present there Melchior Barbosa, painter, resident in the said city. And then by him, Melchior Barbosa, it was said that he denounced in front of the corregidor, of the said city, about certain persons regarding and for reasons of adultery with his wife, Isabel da Costa, among whom was Martinho da Cunha, scribe for the vicar of the said city, and that he [Melchior] after having filed the said *querela* [criminal denunciation] became informed of the truth and found [that] the said Martinho da Cunha did not have any guilt in this and is innocent of the said incident. And because of false information that they gave him he [Melchior] denounced him, Martinho da Cunha, so that to alleviate his conscience, knowing the truth, and [that] the said Martinho da Cunha has no guilt as previously stated, that he [Melchior] would freely pardon as he then in effect pardoned the said Martinho da Cunha all the guilt that he could have in this. And [Melchior] wanted nothing from him in [a] civil or criminal [procedure], rather he asked for mercy from the king our lord and all his justices that they pardon him [Martinho], and not to proceed against him, and not to apprehend him, and to let him go in peace, for he has no guilt as stated. And thus said further he, Melchior Barbosa, that after the said *querela*, on the fourth day of this present month of April and of this present year of MDLXXVII years, as he, Melchior Barbosa, went to apprehend the said Martinho da Cunha, and grabbing him, the said Martinho da Cunha, in his defence, also grabbed him [Melchior], from which he, Belchior [*sic*] Barbosa, came out injured with an injury on the left arm, and also with two [f.154] stones ['pedradas'] on the head that was inflicted on him [Melchior] by a lad named Manuel who was a servant of the said Martinho da Cunha. And of the above-mentioned injury as well as the blows to the head ['esmechadas'] and wound he [Melchior] made an *auto* [writ] with the corregidor, judge of the said city, and he complained of the said Martim da Cunha, and of the said Manuel, and of other people as stated in the said *autos*. And he, Melchior Barbosa, said that regarding how the incident happened from the said injury, and since he was the instigator, and wanted to apprehend the said Martim da Cunha, and since he [Melchior] is already healed of the said 'pedradas' and injury, and knowing that the said Martim da Cunha has no guilt in the said injury and 'pedradas', that he

[Melchior], to alleviate his conscience, would pardon as in fact he pardoned freely the said Martim da Cunha all of whatever guilt that he could have in the said injury and 'pedradas'. And thus in the same manner would pardon as in effect he pardoned the said Manuel, and more people included in the said *auto* and *querela*, all and whatever guilt that they could have in the said injury and 'pedradas'. And from him, Martim da Cunha, and of the said Manuel and more people about whom he [Melchior] complained in the said *auto* of the said injury, [he] did not want anything [from a] civil or criminal [procedure], rather he asked for mercy from the king our lord and his justices to pardon them and let them go in peace, and not apprehend them nor proceed against them. And as is contained in this pardon factum thus he promised to conform, uphold, and not go against it in part or in whole, in law or outside it, and in order not to go against it [he] renounced all laws, rights, and ordinances that could be applied, and the law that deals with general renunciations [f.154v] is void. And thus [Melchior] conceded this pardon factum, and all contained in it, and in this *nota* [notarized deed], he granted to the said Martim da Cunha and Manuel, and the additional people included in the said *auto* of injury, and to whomever else it pertains. And I, notary, as a public person, stipulatory and receiver, stipulated and received this pardon document from the said Melchior Barbosa for the said Martim da Cunha, and Manuel, and additional people to whom it pertains who are absent, as by right I can and should. [I] attest that the following are present: Dom Jerónimo de Meneses, and Garcia de Melo Pra [Pereira], *fidalgos* of His Majesty's household, our lord, and Sebastião Marinho, servant of the said Snr [Senhor] *Dom* Jerónimo, and Paulo Gonçalves, servant of mine, notary, residents of the said city, on Rua de Couros. I, notary, wrote this, and there be no doubt that between the lines is stated [reference to minor corrections in the text] Garcia Fernandes [notary].

[five signatures, that of the pardoner and the four witnesses]

Source: Arquivo Distrital do Porto, Fundo Notarial, Po.1, 3a Se, no. 58 (1577), f.153–154v.

The notary at one point wrote Belchior instead of Melchior, and also referred to the defendant variably as Martinho da Cunha or Martim da Cunha. In fact, the names, Belchior/Melchior and Martinho/Martim were used indistinctively in the early modern period. Some punctuation was added for clarity.

Appendix 6
Criminal denunciation (*querela*) filed by the *alcaide* António Pereira against Manuel Mendes, nicknamed *o rameligua*, and Maria Guerra, nicknamed *a bisquainha*, 12 August 1630, Ponta Delgada

[f.69v] In the year of the birth of our lord Jesus Christ of one thousand six hundred and thirty years on the twelfth day of the month of August of the said year, in this city of Ponta Delgada, island of São Miguel, in the residence and palace of the Count of Vila Franca, *Dom* Rodrigo de Câmara, general captain and governor in all of this island, with the seal of his majesty. Thus, before him and in the presence of me, scribe, appeared the *alcaide* António Pereira de Crasto, and he said that he was *alcaide* of this city, and as such it behoved him to accuse all crimes that were committed, according to the ordinance, for which he came before the count to accuse, as in effect he accused Manuel Mendes, nicknamed *o rameligua*, master of his boat, and Maria Guerra, [f.70] single woman, nicknamed *a bisquainha*, both residents in this city. And the reason for the accusation and denunciation was that being the said Manuel Mendes a married man, and being obliged to lead with her [the wife] a married life as God orders, and he [Manuel] did much to the contrary. And for many years he [Manuel] has been, and still nowadays is, in concubinage with the said Maria Guerra, [Maria] being by his hand kept and maintained without fear of God, nor of the justices of His Majesty, about which there is great scandal in the neighbourhood, as well as among the people in the city. And for the little care that he [Manuel] gives his wife, so that upon arriving on the tenth of the month of August of the present year, in the said his boat, from the island of Terceira, he [Manuel] did not go to his house nor to see the said his wife, and went to settle down in the house of the said his concubine, where he undresses and removes his clothes from the sea. And since, according to the ordinances of this realm, there are great penalties for any married man who engages in concubinage, and for the woman who was with him, he [*alcaide*] requested to him the said count that he [the count] receive his [*alcaide*'s] complaint and denunciation, and to proceed against the said defendants as the said ordinance mandates. And that he [*alcaide*] named as witnesses: Francisco Fernandes, Tomé and Pedro Lopes, night watch, and Maria Guerreira, washerwoman, and *o sarguete* whose name is unknown ['por nome não perca'], and António Dias, and his wife, Cosme Gonçalves, and António Fernandes, and Jerónimo Correia *o Leite*, and his wife, the wife of the *orta* [market gardener], whose name is unknown, the daughter of Manuel Rodrigues, Lucia Mendes … [f.70v … top part of the folio is frayed]. And he [*alcaide*] presented, as his guarantor and principal payer, Gonçalo Pires, agricultural worker, and resident in the Lugar da Relva in the jurisdiction of this city, who appeared then and said that he would oblige himself and in effect did oblige himself to be guarantor and principal payer for the said *alcaide*, to pay all the costs for which he [*alcaide*] is condemned due to this accusation and denunciation, or regarding the final sentence, [if] he [*alcaide*] comes out condemned, the said *alcaide*, for which reason, he [Gonçalo] obliges all his goods and properties, movable and immovable. And thus the said Conde de Vila Franca gave the oath of the holy gospels to the said *alcaide*, with which authority he [the count] directed him [*alcaide*] to declare himself if well and truthfully he made this accusation and denunciation, and he [*alcaide*] having accepted the said oath, he [*alcaide*] said that, according to the information that he had, he made this accusation and denunciation against the defendants for all has truly passed [as stated]. And the said count received it in as much as by right it was to be received, and of all this [the scribe] made this *auto de querela* [writ of criminal denunciation] per his [the count's] command, that he [the count] signed, with the said *alcaide* and guarantor who signed, Pedro Ferreira Serrão, [the] scribe, wrote it [three signatures].

Source: Biblioteca Pública e Arquivo Regional de Ponta Delgada, Ponta Delgada, São Miguel (Azores), Fundo Judicial, *Livro de Autos de Querelas*, NOT.601 (1606–1654), f.69v–70v.

Some punctuation was added for clarity.

Appendix 7
Royal pardon (*perdão régio*) granted to Pedro Gonçalves for taking the honour and virginity of Ana Gonçalves, 20 January 1610, Lisbon

I Dom Felipe etc. make it known that Pedro Gonçalves, from the Freguesia de Santa Cristina de Longas, now resident in Freguesia de São Lourenço, district of Villa de Guimarães, sent me word that when he was single he had had 'union' ['ajuntamento'] with Ana Gonçalves, and took her honour and virginity, which *querela* [criminal denunciation] [she] made to the outside judge, and with the witness depositions from the said *querela*, he [Pedro] was sentenced to jail. And afterward the said plaintiff pardoned him, and they got married, for which reason he asked me [the king] to pardon him for the guilt he had in the incident, and [the punishment he] received. And given his request, and things being as they are, it is well and pleases me that, if it is as stated, to pardon him for that which he mentions, according to his declaration, given what he alleges, and being married to the said Ana Gonçalves, and he will pay 3,000 *réis* for court costs ['despesas da mesa do despacho do dito desembargo'], and since he has already paid them to the receiver of the money for the said expenses, I grant this [pardon]. The king our lord granted it via the doctors Francisco Vaz Pinto and Luís Machado de Gouvea, and António Rodrigues did it in Lisbon, on the xx days of January of 1610.

Source: Instituto de Arquivos Nacionais/Torre do Tombo, Chancelaria de Dom Filipe II, *Perdões e Legitimações*, Livro 28, f.229v.

Some punctuation was added for clarity.

Bibliography

I. Manuscript Sources

Arquivo Distrital de Bragança
– Fundo Notarial

Arquivo Distrital de Evora
– Fundo Notarial

Arquivo Distrital de Faro
– Fundo Notarial

Arquivo Distrital de Porto
– Fundo Notarial
– Fundo Paroquiais

Arquivo Distrial de Viana do Castelo
– Fundo Notarial

Arquivo Histórico Municipal do Porto
– *Livros de Vereações*

Arquivo Municipal Alfredo Pimento de Guimarães
– *Livros de Vereações*

Arquivo da Santa Casa da Misericórdia de Ponta Delgada (São Miguel, Azores)
– *Livros de Receitas e Despesas*

Instituto de Arquivos Nacionais/Torre do Tombo (Lisbon)
– Chancelaria de Dom Manuel, *Perdões e Legitimações*
– Chancelaria de Dom João III, *Perdões e Legitimações*
– Chancelaria de Dom Sebastião, *Perdões e Legitimações*
– Chancelaria de Dom Felipe I, *Perdões e Legitimações*
– Chancelaria de Dom Felipe II, *Perdões e Legitimações*
– Chancelaria de Dom Felipe III, *Perdões e Legitimações*
– Chancelaria de Dom João IV, *Perdões e Legitimações*
– Chancelaria de Dom Afonso VI, *Perdões e Legitimações*
– Chancelaria de Dom Pedro II, *Perdões e Legitimações*
– Corpo Cronológico
– Fundo Notarial

Biblioteca Pública e Arquivo Regional de Angra do Heroísmo (Terceira, Azores)
– Fundo Judicial
– Fundo Notarial
– *Livros de Vereações*

Biblioteca Pública e Arquivo Regional da Madeira
– Fundo Judicial
– *Livros de Vereações*

Biblioteca Pública e Arquivo Regional de Ponta Delgada (São Miguel, Azores)
– Fundo Judicial. *Livro de Autos de Querellas dos Tabeliães Francisco Serrão, António Pereira, Jorge da Costa, Francisco Pavão, Pedro Ferreira Serrão, Gregório Sanches, Francisco de Carvalho[?], Lourenço Preto da Costa, Pedro Correia Chaves, Simão da Cunha, João de la Paz, Jerónimo Rebelo, Francisco Cardoso Machado* (1606–1654), NOT.601
– Fundo Judicial. *Livro para o Rol dos Culpados* (1644–1734), NOT. 554
– Fundo Notarial
– *Livros de Vereações*

II. Printed Sources

Almeida, Manuel Lopes de. *Acordos do Cabido de Coimbra, 1580–1640*. Coimbra: Coimbra Editora, 1973.

Andrade e Silva, José Justino de. *Collecção Chronologica da Legislação Portugueza (1603–1703)*. 10 vols. Lisbon: Imprensa de F.X. de Souza, 1854–1859.

Anjos, Luís dos. *Jardim de Portugal em que se da Noticia de alguas Sanctas & outras Molheres Illustres em Virtude*. Coimbra: N. Carvalho, 1626.

Anonymous. *The Anatomy of the English Nunnery at Lisbon in Portugal*. London: George Purslowe, 1622.

Arquivo Histórico da Madeira. *Documentos Históricos da Ilha do Porto Santo, Série Transcrições Documentais 2*. Maria Favila Vieira da Cunha Paredes, trans. Funchal: Secretaria Regional do Turismo e Cultura/Direcção Regional dos Assuntos Culturais, 2005.

Arrais, Frei Amador. *Diálogos*. Fidelino de Figueiredo, ed. Lisbon: Livraria Sá da Costa, 1944 [1589?].

Barreiros, Gaspar. *Chorographia de alguns lugares que stam em hum caminho que fez Gaspar Barreiros o anno de M.D.XXXXVI*. Coimbra: Universidade de Coimbra, 1968 [1561].

Barros, (Dr.) João de. *Espelho de Casados*. Porto: Imprensa Portugueza, 1874 [1540].

Barros, (Dr.) João de. *Geographia d'entre Douro e Minho e Tras-os-Montes*. Porto: Biblioteca Pública Municipal do Porto/Tipografia Progresso de Domingos Augusto da Silva, 1919 [1549?].

Basto, Artur de Magalhães, ed. *Livro Antigo de Cartas e Provisões dos Senhores Reis D. Afonso V, D. João II e D. Manuel I*. Porto: Câmara Municipal do Porto, 1940.

Basto, Artur de Magalhães, ed. *'Vereaçoens' Anos de 1390–1395*. Porto: Câmara Municipal do Porto, 1972.

Brandão (de Buarcos), João. *Grandeza e Abastança de Lisboa em 1552*. José da Felicidade Alves, org. Lisbon: Livros Horizonte, 1990 [1552].

Brandão, Mario, ed. *Documentos de D. João III*. 4 vols. Coimbra: Universidade de Coimbra, 1937.

Bronseval, Frère Claude de. *Peregrinatio Hispanica: Voyage de Dom Edme de Saulieu, Abbé de Clairvaux, en Espagne et au Portugal (1531–1533)*. Paris: Presses Universitaires de France/Fondation Calouste Gulbenkian, 1970.

Bueno, Silveira. *Auto das Regateiras de Lisboa Composto por um Frade Loyo Filho de hua dellas*. São Paulo: Edição Saraiva, 1969 [15??].

Câmara Municipal de Braga. 'Acordos e Vreaçõens [sic] da Câmara de Braga'. *Bracara Augusta: Revista Cultural de Regionalismo e História da Câmara Municipal de Braga*, vol. 24 (1970): 284–435; vol. 25/26 (1971/72): 418–70; vol. 27 (1973): 587–622; vol. 28 (1974): 533–42; vol. 29 (1975): 377–426; vol. 30 (1976): 681–792; vol. 31 (1977): 435–81; vol. 32 (1978): 415–75; vol. 33 (1979): 483–563; vol. 34 (1980): 937–92; vol. 35 (1981): 553–92; vol. 36 (1982): 545–601; vol. 37 (1983): 525–74; vol. 38 (1984): 393–448; vol. 40 (1986/87): 697–736; vol. 41 (1988/89): 553–70; vol. 42 (1991/92): 467–503.

Câmara Municipal de Lisboa. *Documentos do Arquivo Histórico da Câmara Municipal de Lisboa: Livros de Reis*. 8 vols. Lisbon: Câmara Municipal de Lisboa, 1957–1964.

Cartório Dominicano Português. *Livro da Visitação que se [a Inquisição] fez na Cydade de Braga e seu Arcebispado [1565]: Bartholomaeana Monumenta IV*. Porto: Arquivo Histórico Dominicano Português/Movimento Bartolomeano, 1974.

Canto, Ernesto, ed. *Archivo dos Açores*. 15 vols. Ponta Delgada: Typ. Do Archivo dos Açores, r.1980–1984.

Chiado, António Ribeiro. *Auto das Regateiras*. Rome: Edizioni dell'Ateneo, 1970 [15??].

Chojnacka, Monica, and Merry E. Wiesner-Hanks, eds. *Ages of Woman, Ages of Man: Sources of European Social History, 1400–1750*. London and New York: Longman/Pearson Education, 2002.

The Complete Works of William Shakespeare. New York: Avenel Books, 1975.

Cosman, Carol, Joan Keefe, and Kathleen Weaver, eds. *The Penguin Book of Women Poets*. London: Penguin Books, 1980.

Costa, Pe Agostinho Rebelo da. *Descrição Topográfica e Histórica da Cidade do Pôrto*. 2nd ed. Porto: Na Officina de António Alvarez Ribeiro, r.1945 [1789].

Couto, Diogo do. *Vida de D. Paulo de Lima Pereira Capitam Mor de Armadas do Estado da India*. Lisbon: Na Officina de Jozé Filipe, 1765.

Dias, Francisco. *Memorias Quinhentistas Dum Procurador Del-Rei No Pôrto*. Porto: Câmara Municipal do Porto, 1937 [158?].

Drummond, Francisco Ferreira. *Anais da Ilha Terceira*. Angra do Heroísmo: Governo Autónomo dos Açores, r.1981 [1850].

Drummond, Francisco Ferreira. *Apontamentos Topográficos. Políticos, Civis e Ecclesiásticos para a História das nove Ilhas dos Açores servindo de suplemento aos Anais da Ilha Terceira*. Angra do Heroísmo: Instituto Histórico da Ilha Terceira, r.1990.

Dumouriez, Charles François. *Etat Présent du Royaume de Portugal en l'Année MDCCLXVI*. Lausanne: Chez François Grasset & Comp., 1775.

Faria, Manoel Severim de. *Noticias de Portugal*. Lisbon: Na Offic. De Antonio Gomes, r.1791 [1655].

Faria y Sousa, Manuel de. *Epitome de las Historias Portuguesas*. Lisbon: Na Officina de Francisco Villela, 1673.

Freire, Braamcamp. 'Caderno da sisa da marçarya para 1502'. *Archivo Histórico Portuguez* 2 (Lisbon, 1904): 21–6.

Freire, Braamcamp. 'Povoação de Entre Douro e Minho no XVI século'. *Archivo Histórico Portuguez* 3 (Lisbon, 1905): 241–73.

Freire de Oliveira, Eduardo. *Elementos para a História do Município de Lisboa*. 17 vols. Lisbon: Tipografia Universal, 1882–1911.

Fructuoso, Gaspar (1522–1591). *Saudades da Terra*. 6 vols. Ponta Delgada: Tip. Do 'Diario dos Açores', 1926.

Gonçalves, Rui. *Dos privilegios & praerogativas q ho genero feminino tē por direito comū & ordenações do Reyno mais que ho genero masculino*. Lisbon: Biblioteca Nacional, 1992 [1557].

Gonçalves, Rui. *Memorial au rei D. João III sobre os perdões*. Lisbon: João Barreira, 15??.

Guedes, Lívio da Costa, ed. 'Aspectos do Reino de Portugal nos séculos XVI e XVII: A 'Descrição' de Alexandre Massaii (1621). II Tratado'. *Boletim do Arquivo Histórico Militar* 58 (Lisbon, 1989): 13–201.

Guerra Campos, Jose. 'Viaje de Lisboa a Santiago en 1594 por Juan Bautista Confalonieri'. *Cuadernos de Estudios Gallegos* 19 (1964): 185–250.

Guerreiro, Miguel do Couto. *Epigrammas Portuguezes*. Lisbon: Na Officina Patriarcal, 1793.

Jeay, Madeleine and Kathleen Garay, eds. *The Distaff Gospels*. Peterborough: Broadview Press, 2006.

Leão, Duarte Nunes de. *Descripção do Reino de Portugal*. Lisbon: Na Of. de Simão Thaddeo Ferreira, 1785 [1610].

Lima, Francisco Torrinha Augusto C. Pires de, ed. *Farsa de Inês Pereira de Gil Vicente*. Porto: Domingos Barreira – Editor, 1941 [1523?].

Lucena e Vale, Alexandre de. 'Livro dos Acordos da Câmara de Viseu, Actas de 1601 … 1605', *Beira Alta* 11 (Viseu, 1952): 225–54.

Maldonado, Pe Manuel Luis (1644–1711). *Fenix Angrence*. Helder Fernando Parreira de Sousa Lima, trans. 3 vols. Angra do Heroísmo: Instituto Histórico da Ilha Terceira, r.1990.

Manuel y Vasconcelos, D. Agustín. *Vida y Acciones del Rey Don Juan el Segundo, Decimotercio de Portugal*. Madrid: En la Imprensa de Maria de Quiñones, 1639.

Mello, D. Francisco Manuel de. *Carta de Guia de Casados*. 2nd ed. Porto: A 'Renascença Portuguesa', 1923 [1651].

Murray, Jacqueline, ed. *Love, Marriage, and Family in the Middle Ages: A Reader*. Peterborough: Broadview Press, 2001.

Oliveira, Cristovão Rodrigues de. *Sumário em que Brevemente se Contem Algumas Cousas (Assim Eclesiasticas como Seculares) que ha na Cidade de Lisboa*. Lisbon: Eds. Biblion, r.1938 [1551].

Pereira, António dos Santos. *Vereações de Velas (S. Jorge, 1559–1570–1571)*. Ponta Delgada: Universidade dos Açores/Departamento de História, 1984.

Pinto, Frei Heitor. *Imagem da Vida Cristã*, edited by Alves Correia. 4 vols. Lisbon: Livraria Sá da Costa, 1940 [1563; 1572].

Portugal. *Ordenações Filipinas*. 5 vols. Lisbon: Fundação Calouste Gulbenkian, 1985 [1870].

Portugal. *Ordenações Manuelinas*. 5 vols. Lisbon: Fundação Calouste Gulbenkian, 1984 [1797].

Rodrigues, Maria Teresa Campos, ed. *Livro das Posturas Antigas*. Lisbon: Câmara Municipal, 1974.

Sampaio, António de Villasboas de. *Auto da Lavradora de Ayró*. Coimbra: Na Impressa da Universidade, 1841 [1678].

Sampaio, Francisco Coelho de Sousa e. *Prelecções do direito pátrio, público e particular ... [1793]*. In *Poder e Instituições na Europa do Antigo Regime: Colectânia de Textos*, edited by António Manuel Hespanha. Lisbon: Fundação Calouste Gulbenkian, 1988.

Sanchez Rivero, Angel and Angela Mariutti de Sanchez Rivero, eds. *Viaje de Cosme de Médicis por España y Portugal (1668–1669)*. Madrid: Centro de Estudios Historicos, 1933.

Serrão, Joaquim Veríssimo, ed. *Viagens em Portugal de Manoel Severim de Faria, 1604–1609–1625*. Lisbon: Academia Portuguesa da História, 1974.

Telles, José Homem Correa. *Manual do Tabellião, ou Ensaio de Jurisprudencia Eurematica*. Lisbon: Na Impressão Regia, 1819.

Tours, P. François de. 'Voyage du P. François de Tours en Espagne et en Portugal (1698–1700)'. *Revue Hispanique* 53 (1921): 469–549.

Trancoso, Gonçalo Fernandez. *Primeira, Segvnda e Terceira Parte dos Contos e Historias de Proveito, e Exemplo, Dirigidos a Senhora Dona Joana D'Alburquerque, molher que foy do VisoRey da India, Ayres de Saldanha*. Lisbon: Antonio Alvarez, Impressor, 1608.

Vasconcelos, Basílio de. *'Itinerário' do Dr. Jerónimo Münzer (excertos)*. Coimbra: Imprensa da Universidade, 1931.

III. Secondary Sources

Abreu, Alberto Antunes de. 'O Arquivo e as Origens da Santa Casa da Misericórdia de Fão'. *Boletim Cultural de Esposende* no. 4 (December 1983): 105–12.

Afonso, Belarmino Augusto. 'Livros de devassa e etnotextos'. *Sociedade Portuguesa de Antropologia e Etnologia* 25 (Faculdade de Ciências do Porto, 1985): 347–58.

Ågren, Maria. *Domestic Secrets: Women & Property in Sweden, 1600–1857*. Chapel Hill: University of North Carolina Press, 2009.

Ågren, Maria. 'Individualism or Self-Sacrifice? Decision-Making and Retirement within the Early Modern Marital Economy in Sweden'. In *The Marital Economy in Scandinavia and Britain, 1400–1900*, edited by Maria Ågren and Amy Louise Erickson. Burlington: Ashgate, 2005, 221–36.

Albuquerque, Martim de. *Estudos de Cultura Portuguesa*. 3 vols. Lisbon: Imprensa Nacional, 1983.

Alloza Aparicio, Ángel. *La Vara Quebrada de la Justicia: un estúdio sobre la delincuencia madrileña entre los siglos XVI y XVIII*. Madrid: Catarata, 2000.

Almeida, A.A. Marques de. *Aritmética como Descrição do Real (1519–1679)*. 2 vols. Lisbon: Imprensa Nacional/Casa da Moeda, 1994.

Almeida, Angela Mendes de. 'Casamento, sexualidade e pecado – os manuais portugueses de casamento dos séculos XVI e XVII'. *Ler História*, no. 12 (1988): 3–21.

Almeida, Eduardo de. 'Regimento de salários e preços de 1522 (para Guimarães)'. *Revista de Guimarães* 40, no. 1/2 (January–June 1930): 41–63; 40 no. 3/4 (July–December 1930): 149–70.

Almeida, Fortunato de. 'Organização político-administrativa portuguesa dos sécs. XVII e XVIII'. In *Poder e Instituições na Europa do Antigo Regime: Colectânia de Textos*, edited by António Manuel Hespanha. Lisbon: Fundação Calouste Gulbenkian, 1988, 323–94.

Alves, Dina Catarina Duarte. 'Violência e perdão em Óbidos (1595–1680)'. Master's thesis, Faculdade de Letras, Universidade de Coimbra, 2003.

Amorim, Inês, Elisabete de Jesus, and Célia Rego. 'Mulher e religião na época moderna. A Ordem Terceira de S. Francisco, um modelo de sociabilidade religiosa'. *Portuguese Studies Review* 13, no. 1/2 (Fall–Winter 2005/2007): 369–99.

Amorim, Manuel. 'A Vila da Póvoa de Varzim no Século XVI'. In *Colóquio 'Santos Graça' de Etnografia Marítima, Actas III: Povoamento, Administração, Aspectos sociais*. Póvoa de Varzim: Câmara Municipal da Póvoa de Varzim, 1985, 97–201.

Amorim, Maria Norberta. 'Comportamentos demográficos de Antigo Regime na Península Ibérica'. *Ler História* 47 (2004): 147–70.

Andrade, Amélia, Teresa Teixeira, and Olga Magalhães. 'Subsídios para o Estudo do Adultério em Portugal no Século XV'. *Revista de História* 5 (1983–1984): 93–129.

Araújo, Ana Cristina. 'Cerimónias de execução pública no Antigo Regime – escatologia e justiça'. *Revista de História da Sociedade e da Cultura* 1 (2001): 169–211.

Araújo, Benedita. *Superstições populares portuguesas: contribuição para um estudo*. Lisbon: Edições Colibri, 1997.

Astarita, Tommaso. *Village Justice: Community, Family, and Popular Culture in Early Modern Italy*. Baltimore and London: Johns Hopkins University Press, 1999.

Barahona, Renato. *Sex Crimes, Honour, and the Law in Early Modern Spain: Vizcaya, 1528–1735*. Toronto, Buffalo and London: University of Toronto Press, 2003.

Barata, Filipe Themudo. 'Organizar a Procissão nos Finais do Século XV. O lugar de cada um e do grupo na cidade'. In *Categorias sociais e mobilidade urbana na Baixa Idade Média. Entre o Islão e a Cristandade*, edited by Hermínia Vasconcelos Vilar and Maria Filomena Lopes de Barros. Lisbon: Edições Colibri/CIDEHUS – Universidade de Evora, 2012, 187–94.

Barros, Amândio Jorge Morais. 'Mulheres e comércio. Linhas de intervenção de mulher portuense no negócio durante o século XVI'. *Portuguese Studies Review* 13, no. 1/2 (Fall–Winter 2005/2007): 229–68.

Beattie, Cordelia, and Matthew Frank Stevens, eds. *Married Women and the Law in Premodern Northwest Europe*. Rochester: Boydell Press, 2013.

Behrend-Martínez, Edward. '"She Wanted to Be Her Own Master": Women's Suits against Impotent and Abusive Husbands in a Spanish Church Court, 1650–1750', Ph.D. thesis, University of Chicago, 2002.

Behrend-Martínez, Edward. '"Taming Don Juan": Limiting Masculine Sexuality in Counter-Reformation Spain'. *Gender & History* 24, no. 2 (August 2012): 333–52.

Behrend-Martínez, Edward. *Unfit for Marriage: Impotent Spouses on Trial in the Basque Region of Spain, 1650–1750*. Reno and Las Vegas: University of Nevada Press, 2007.

Beirante, Maria Angela. 'Espaços de sociabilidade nas cidades medievais portuguesas'. In *Os Reinos Ibéricos na Idade Média: Livro de Homenagem ao Professor Doutor Humberto Carlos Baquero Moreno*, edited by Luís Adão da Fonseca, Luís Carlos Amaral, and Maria Fernanda Ferreira Santos. 2 vols. Porto: Faculdade de Letras da Universidade do Porto/Livraria Civilização Editora, 2003, II: 939–45.

Bellavitis, Anna. 'Dot et richesse des femmes à Venise au XVIe siècle'. *CLIO* 7 (1998): 91–100.

Bellavitis, Anna. 'Women, Family, and Property in Early Modern Venice'. In *Across the Religious Divide: Women, Property, and Law in the Wider Mediterranean (ca. 1300–1800)*, edited by Jutta Gisela Sperling and Shona Kelly Wray. London and New York: Routledge, 2010, 175–90.

Bennett, Judith M., and Amy M. Froide, eds. *Singlewomen in the European Past, 1250–1800*. Philadelphia: University of Pennsylvania Press, 1999.

Bettencourt, Olga. 'A Periferia das Pequenas Ilhas: o exemplo de São Jorge, a partir das Vereações de Velas (1559–1570–1571)'. In *O Faial e a Periferia Açoriana nos Sécs. XV a XIX. Actas do Colóquio realizado nas ilhas do Faial e Pico de 10 a 13 de Maio de 1993*. Horta: Núcleo Cultural da Horta, 1995 [183–8].

Birmingham, David. *A Concise History of Portugal*. 2nd ed. Cambridge: Cambridge University Press, 2003.

Bishop-Sánchez, Kathryn. 'Por detrás das alcoviteiras: prostituição e libertinagem na obra de Gil Vicente'. In *Gil Vicente 500 Anos Depois: Actas do Congresso Internacional realizado pelo Centro de Estudos de Teatro da Faculdade de Letras da Universidade de Lisboa*. 2 vols. Lisbon: Imprensa Nacional – Casa da Moeda, 2003, II: 9–24.

Blaikie, Andrew. 'Scottish Illegitimacy: Social Adjustment or Moral Economy?' *Journal of Interdisciplinary History* 29, no. 2 (Autumn 1998): 221–42.

Boes, Maria R. 'Women and the Penal System in Frankfurt am Main, 1562–1696'. *Criminal Justice History: An International Annual* 13 (1992): 61–73.

Boone III, James L. 'Parental Investment and Elite Family Structure in Preindustrial States: A Case Study of Late Medieval-Early Modern Portuguese Geneologies'. *American Anthropologist* 88, no. 4 (December 1986): 859–78.

Borges, Emília Salvado. *Homens, Fazenda e Poder no Alentejo de Setecentos: O Caso de Cuba*. Lisbon: Edições Colibri, 2000.

Brackett, John K. *Criminal Justice and Crime in Late Renaissance Florence, 1537–1609*. Cambridge: Cambridge University Press, 1992.

Braga, Isabel M.R. Mendes Drumond. 'A criminalidade em Portalegre no reinado de D. João III: delitos e perdões'. *A Cidade: Revista Cultural de Portalegre* no. 8, Nova Série (1993): 65–81.

Braga, Isabel M.R. Mendes Drumond. 'Para a história do medo no Portugal quinhentista: peste e religiosidade'. *Revista de Ciências Históricas* (Universidade Portucalense) 8 (1993): 83–96.

Braga, Isabel M.R. Mendes Drumond, and Paulo Drumond Braga. 'A criminalidade nos Açores no reinado de D. Sebastião: delitos e perdões'. In *O Faial e a Periferia Açoriana nos Sécs. XV a XIX. Actas do Colóquio realizado nas ilhas do Faial e Pico de 10 a 13 de Maio de 1993*. Horta: Núcleo Cultural da Horta, 1995, 523–43.

Braga, Paulo Drummond. *Do Crime ao Perdão Régio (Açores, Séculos XVI–XVIII)*. Ponta Delgada: Instituto Cultural de Ponta Delgada, 2003.

Braga, Paulo Drumond. 'Perdões concedidos a moradores em Évora no reinado de D. João IV'. In *Actas do Congresso de História no IV Centenário do Seminário de Évora*. Evora: s.n., 1994, 529–38.

Braun, Pierre. 'La Valeur Documentarie des Lettres de Rémission'. In *La Faute, la Répression et le Pardon: Actes du 107e Congrès National des Sociétés Savantes, Brest, 1982*. 2 vols. Paris: C.T.H.S./Comité des Travaux Historiques et Scientifiques, 1984, I: 207–21.

Brooks, Christopher W. *Lawyers, Litigants and English Society Since 1450*. London: Hambledon Press, 1998.

Butler, Sara M. 'Maintenance Agreements and Male Responsibility in Late Medieval England'. In *Boundaries of the Law: Geography, Gender and Jurisdiction in Medieval and Early Modern Europe*, edited by Anthony Musson. Burlington: Ashgate, 2005, 67–83.

Caeiro, Maria Margarida. 'Estereotipos femininos quinhentistas: O testemunho de António Ribeiro Chiado'. In *O Rosto Feminino da Expansão Portuguesa, Actas I, Congresso Internacional (Lisboa, 21–25 de Novembro de 1994)*. Lisbon: Comissão para a Igualdade e para os Direitos das Mulheres, 1995, 137–43.

Caeiro, Maria Margarida Castro Neves Mascarenhas. 'Concepções da vida e da morte na Madeira entre 1580 e 1640: alguns contributos para a história das mentalidades do arquipélago'. In *Actas III Colóquio Internacional de História da Madeira*. Funchal: Centro de Estudos do Atlântico, 1993, 575–83.

Caetano, Marcello. *História do Direito Português (sécs. xii–xvi)*. Lisbon: Editorial Verbo, 2000.

Cannon, Christopher. 'Chaucer and Rape: Uncertainty's Certainties'. In *Representing Rape in Medieval and Early Modern Literature*, edited by Elizabeth Robertson and Christine M. Rose. New York: Palgrave, 2001, 255–79.

Capel Martinez, Rosa María. 'Los protocolos notariales en la historia de la mujer en la España del antiguo régimen'. In *Ordenamiento jurídico y realidad social de las mujeres, siglos XVI a XX: Actas de las IV Jornadas de Investigación Interdisciplinaria*, edited by Valentina Fernandez Vargas and María Victoria Lopez-Cordon Cortezo. Madrid: Universidad Autónoma de Madrid, 1986, 169–79.

Cardoso, Maria Teresa Costa Ferreira. 'Os presos da Relação do Porto. Entre a cadeia e a Misericórdia (1735 a 1740)'. Master's thesis, Universidade do Minho, Braga, 2005.

Carita, Isabel. 'A mulher que fica – dois exemplos vicentinos'. In *O Rosto Feminino da Expansão Portuguesa, Actas I, Congresso Internacional (Lisboa, 21–25 de Novembro de 1994)*. Lisbon: Comissão para a Igualdade e para os Direitos das Mulheres, 1995, 131–5.

Carroll, Stuart. *Blood and Violence in Early Modern France*. Oxford: Oxford University Press, 2006.

Carvalho, Américo A. Taipa de. 'Condicionalidade sócio-cultural do Direito Penal'. *Boletim da Faculdade de Direito, Universidade de Coimbra* 58 (1982): 1039–45.

Carvalho, Joaquim Ramos de. 'Confessar e devassar: a igreija e a vida privada na epoca moderna' and 'As sexualidades'. In *História da Vida Privada em Portugal: A Idade Moderna*, edited by José Mattoso, 4 vols. Lisbon: Círculo de Leitores e Temas e Debates, 2011, II: 32–57, 96–129.

Carvalho, Joaquim Ramos de. 'A Jurisdição episcopal sobre leigos em matéria de pecados públicos: as visitas pastorais e o comportamento moral das populações portuguesas de antigo regime'. *Revista Portuguesa de História* 24 (1988): 121–63.

Casey, James. *Family and Community in Early Modern Spain: The Citizens of Granada, 1570–1739*. Cambridge: Cambridge University Press, 2007.

Cavallo, Sandra. *Artisans of the Body in Early Modern Italy: Identities, Families and Masculinities*. Manchester and New York: Manchester University Press, 2007.

Cavallo, Sandra. 'What Did Women Transmit? Ownership and Control of Household Goods and Personal Effects in Early Modern Italy'. In *Gender and Material Culture in Historical Perspective*, edited by Moira Donald and Linda Hurcombe. London: MacMillan Press, 2000, 38–53.

Cavallo, Sandra, and Lyndan Warner, eds. *Widowhood in Medieval and Early Modern Europe*. London and New York: Longman, 1999.

Cavallo, Sandra, and Simona Cerutti. 'Female Honor and the Social Control of Reproduction in Piedmont between 1600 and 1800'. In *Sex and Gender in Historical Perspective*, edited by Edward Muir and Guido Ruggiero. Baltimore: Johns Hopkins University Press, 1990, 73–109.

Chabot, Isabelle. 'Lineage Strategies and the Control of Widows in Renaissance Florence'. In *Widowhood in Medieval and Early Modern Europe*, edited by Sandra Cavallo and Lyndan Warner. London and New York: Longman, 1999, 127–44.

Chojnacki, Stanley. 'Daughters and Oligarchs: Gender and the Early Renaissance State'. In *Gender and Society in Renaissance Italy*, edited by Judith C. Brown and Robert C. Davis. London and New York: Longman, 1998, 63–86.

Coates, Timothy J. *Convicts and Orphans: Forced and State-Sponsored Colonizers in the Portuguese Empire, 1550–1755*. Stanford: Stanford University Press, 2001.

Coates, Timothy J. 'Crime and Punishment in the Fifteenth-Century Portuguese World: The Transition from Internal to Imperial Exile'. In *The Final Argument: The Imprint of Violence on Society in Medieval and Early Modern Europe*, edited by Donald J. Kagay and L.J. Andrew Villalon. Woodbridge: Boydell Press, 1998, 119–39.

Cohen, Elizabeth S. 'Honor and Gender in the Streets of Early Modern Rome'. *Journal of Interdisciplinary History* 22, no. 4 (Spring 1992): 597–625.

Cohen, Elizabeth S. 'The Trials of Artemisia Gentileschi: A Rape as History'. *Sixteenth Century Journal* 31, no. 1 (Spring 2000): 47–75.

Cohen, Elisabeth S. 'What's in a Name? Artemisia Gentileschi and the Politics of Reputation'. In *Artemisia Gentileschi: Taking Stock*, edited by Judith Mann. Turnhout: Brepols Publishers, 2005, 119–28.

Cohen, Elizabeth S., and Thomas V. Cohen. *Daily Life in Renaissance Italy*. Westport and London: Greenwood Press, 2001.

Cohen, Thomas V. 'Three Forms of Jeopardy: Honor, Pain, and Truth-Telling in a Sixteenth-Century Italian Courtroom'. *Sixteenth Century Journal* 29, no. 4 (Winter 1998): 975–98.

Cohn, Jr., Samuel K. *Women in the Streets: Essays on Sex and Power in Renaissance Italy*. Baltimore and London: Johns Hopkins University Press, 1996.

Coolidge, Grace E. '"Neither Dumb, Deaf, nor Destitute of Understanding": Women as Guardians in Early Modern Spain'. *Sixteenth Century Journal* 36, no. 3 (Fall 2005): 673–93.

Cordeiro, Ma Filipa de Meneses. 'Foral de Povos – 1195'. *Boletim Cultural* no. 1 (Câmara Municipal de Vila Franca de Xira, 1985): 149–75.

Córdoba de la Llave, Ricardo. *El instinto diabólico: Agresiones Sexuales en la Castilla Medieval*. Córdoba: Universidad de Córdoba, 1994.

Corrêa, Fernando Calapez. 'Aspectos da Criminalidade nos Açores: as Cartas de Perdão e de Legitimação Concedidas no Período das Guerras da Restauração'. In *O Faial e a Periferia Açoriana nos Sécs. XV a XIX. Actas do Colóquio realizado nas ilhas do Faial e Pico de 10 a 13 de Maio de 1993*. Horta: Núcleo Cultural da Horta, 1995 [545–57].

Correia, Eduardo. *Direito Criminal*. Coimbra: Livraria Almedina, 1963.

Correia, Eduardo. 'A evolução histórica das penas'. *Boletim da Faculdade de Direito* 53 (1977): 51–310.

Corteguera, Luis R. 'Encuentros imaginados entre súbdito y monarca: historias de perdón y petición en la España de la edad moderna'. In *Tradición y modernidad en la historia de la cultura política. España e Hispanoamérica, siglos XVI–XX*, edited by Riccardo Forte and Natalia Silva Prada. Mexico: Juan Pablos Editor/ Universidade Autónoma Metropolitana, 2009, 23–45.

Corteguera, Luis R. 'The Painter Who Lost His Hat: Artisans and Justice in Early Modern Barcelona'. *Sixteenth Century Journal* 29, no. 4 (Winter 1998): 1023–42.

Cosme, João dos Santos Ramalho. 'A população da comarca de Estremoz em 1538(?)'. *A Cidade: Revista Cultural de Portalegre* no. 8, Nova Série (1993): 83–107.

Cosme, João dos Santos Ramalho. 'Cartas de perdão e legitimação concedidas a açorianos (1642–1748)'. *Boletim do Instituto Histórico da Ilha Terceira* 48 (1990): 317–48.

Cosme, João dos Santos Ramalho, and Maria de Deus Beites Manso. 'Cartas de perdão e legitimação concedidas aos moradores do arquipélago da Madeira (1531–1557)'. In *Actas do II Colóquio Internacional de História da Madeira.* Funchal: Centro de Estudos de História do Atlântico, 1989, 155–70.

Costa, Elisa Maria Lopes da. 'História, Memória e Sabedoria: Tempos e "Ditos que se dizem" em algumas ilhas açorenses'. In *O Faial e a Periferia Açoriana nos Séculos XV a XX. Actas do IV Colóquio.* Horta: Núcleo Cultural da Horta, 2007 [431–59].

Costa, José Pereira da. 'O municipalismo no arquipélago da Madeira, 1470–1550'. In *O Município no Mundo Português: Seminário Internacional, Funchal, 26 a 30 Outubro de 1998*, edited by Alberto Vieira. Funchal: Região Autónoma da Madeira/Centro de Estudos de História do Atlântico, 1998, 183–210.

Costa, Maria Clara Pereira da. 'Testemunhos históricos acerca do papel de algumas mulheres no contexto social madeirense – séc. XV e XVI'. In *Actas III Colóquio Internacional de História da Madeira.* Funchal: Centro de Estudos do Atlântico, 1993, 291–324.

Cruz, António. *Os Mesteres do Pôrto: Subsídios para a História das Antigas Corporações dos Ofícios Mecânicos*. 2 vols. Porto: Edição do Sub-Secretariado de Estado das Corporações e Previdência Social/Empresa Industrial Gráfica do Pôrto, 1943.

Cunha, Mafalda Soares da, and Nuno Gonçalo Monteiro. 'Aristocracia, Poder e Família em Portugal, Séculos XV–XVIII'. In *Sociedade, Família e Poder na Peninsula Ibérica: Elementos para uma História Comparativa*, edited by Mafalda Soares da Cunha and Juan Hernández Franco. Lisbon and Murcia: Edições Colibri/CIDHUS/Universidade de Evora/Universidad de Murcia, 2010, 47–75.

Dabbs, Julia K. *Life Stories of Women Artists, 1550–1800: An Anthology.* Burlington: Ashgate, 2009.

Dantas, Júlio. *O amor em Portugal no século XVIII.* Porto: Livraria Chardron, 1916.

Davis, Natalie Zemon. *Fiction in the Archives: Pardon Tales and Their Tellers in Sixteenth-Century France.* Stanford: Stanford University Press, 1987.

DesBrisay, Gordon. 'Twisted by Definition: Women Under Godly Discipline in Seventeenth-Century Scottish Towns'. In *Twisted Sisters: Women, Crime and Deviance in Scotland Since 1400*, edited by Yvonne Galloway Brown and Rona Ferguson. East Lothian: Tuckwell Press, 2002, 137–55.

DesBrisay, Gordon, and Karen Sander Thomson. 'Crediting Wives: Married Women and Debt Litigation in the Seventeenth Century'. In *Finding the Family in Medieval and Early Modern Scotland*, edited by Elizabeth Ewan and Janay Nugent. Aldershot: Ashgate, 2008, 85–97.

Dewulf, Jeroen. 'As cartas do humanista Nicolau Clenardo sobre Portugal'. In *Os Reinos Ibéricos na Idade Média: Livro de Homenagem ao Professor Doutor Humberto Carlos Baquero Moreno*, 2 vols, edited by Luís Adão da Fonseca, Luís Carlos Amaral, and Maria Fernanda Ferreira Santos. Porto: Faculdade de Letras da Universidade do Porto/Livraria Civilização Editora, 2003, II: 581–89.

Di Simplicio, Oscar. 'Perpetuas: The Women Who Kept Priests, Siena 1600–1800'. In *History from Crime: Selections from Quaderni Storici*, edited by Edward Muir and Guido Ruggiero. Baltimore and London: Johns Hopkins University Press, 1994, 32–64.

Dias, Isabel de Barros. 'Uso pragmático do *topos* má na segunda redacção da *Crónica de 1344*'. In *Mulheres Más: Percepção da Mulher Transgressora no Mundo Luso-Hispânico*, 2 vols, edited by Ana María da Costa Toscano and Shelley Godsland. Porto: Universidade Fernando Pessoa, 2004, I: 123–40.

Dias, João José Alves. 'Os Fogos Femininos nos Municípios do Séc. XVI'. In *A Mulher na Sociedade Portuguesa: Visão Histórica e Perspectivas Actuais. Colóquio 1985, Actas*. 2 vols. Coimbra: Universidade de Coimbra, 1986, II: 223–7.

Dias, João José Alves. *Gentes e espaços: Edição crítica do 'Numeramento de 1527–1532' – Dicionário corográfico do Portugal Quinhentista – Comarca de Entre Douro e Minho*. Cascais: Patrimonia Histórica, 1999.

Dias, João José Alves. 'Prohibited Sex in Portugal in the Sixteenth Century: An Approach'. In *Pelo Vaso Traseiro: Sodomy and Sodomites in Luso-Brazilian History*, edited by Harold Johnson and Francis A. Dutra. Tucson: Fenestra Books, 2007, 49–61.

Dios, Salustiano de. *Gracia, Merced y Patronato Real: La Camara de Castilla Entre 1474–1530*. Madrid: Centro de Estudios Constitucionales, 1993.

Disney, A.R. *A History of Portugal and the Portuguese Empire*. 2 vols. Cambridge: Cambridge University Press, 2009.

Du Mont, Janice, and Deborah Parnis. 'Judging Women: The Pernicious Effects of Rape Mythology'. *Canadian Woman Studies/Les cahiers de la femme* 19, no. 1/2 (1999): 102–9.

Duarte, I. de Sousa. *Legislação do Notariado Portuguez até ao anno de 1882*. Lisbon: Livraria Ferreira, 1884.

Duarte, Luís Miguel. *Justiça e Criminalidade no Portugal Medievo (1459–1481)*. 2 vols. Lisbon: Fundação Calouste Gulbenkian, 1999.

Duarte, Luís Miguel, and Maria da Conceição Falcão Ferreira. 'Dependentes das Elites Vimarenses Face à Justiça no Reinado de D. Afonso V'. *Revista da Faculdade de Letras* 6 (Porto, 1989): 175–221.

Dupont-Bouchat, Marie-Sylvie. 'Le crime pardonné. La justice réparatrice sous l'Ancien Régime (XVIe–XVIIIe siècles)'. *Criminologie* 32, no. 1 (1999): 31–56.

Durães, Margarida. 'Os Camponeses do Noroeste de Portugal. Família, Património e Cultura Material (Séculos XVIII–XIX)'. In *Sociedade, Família e Poder na Peninsula Ibérica: Elementos para uma História Comparativa*, edited by Mafalda Soares da Cunha and Juan Hernández Franco. Lisbon and Murcia: Edições Colibri/CIDHUS/Universidade de Evora/Universidad de Murcia, 2010, 235–54.

Dutra, Francis A. 'Sodomy and the Portuguese Nobility: The Case of Dom Filipe de Moura and His Circle'. In *Pelo Vaso Traseiro: Sodomy and Sodomites in Luso-Brazilian History*, edited by Harold Johnson and Francis A. Dutra. Tucson: Fenestra Books, 2007, 165–94.

Dyer, Abigail. 'Seduction by Promise of Marriage: Law, Sex, and Culture in Seventeenth-Century Spain'. *Sixteenth Century Journal* 34, no. 2 (Summer 2003): 439–55.

Eisenach, Emlyn. *Husbands, Wives, and Concubines: Marriage, Family, and Social Order in Sixteenth-Century Verona*. Kirksville: Truman State University Press, 2004.

Elbl, Ivana. 'Status and Agency: Royal Grants to Portuguese Noblewomen, 1438–1481'. *Portuguese Studies Review* 13, no. 1/2 (Fall–Winter 2005/2007): 61–114.

Emigh, Rebecca Jean. 'Property Devolution in Tuscany'. *Journal of Interdisciplinary History* 33, no. 3 (Winter 2003): 385–420.

Erickson, Amy Louise. 'Property and Widowhood in England, 1660–1840'. In *Widowhood in Medieval and Early Modern Europe*, edited by Sandra Cavallo and Lyndan Warner. London and New York: Longman, 1999, 145–63.

Erickson, Amy Louise. *Women and Property in Early Modern England*. London and New York: Routledge, 1993.

Ewan, Elizabeth. 'Crime or Culture? Women and Daily Life in Late-Medieval Scotland'. In *Twisted Sisters: Women, Crime and Deviance in Scotland Since 1400*, edited by Yvonne Galloway Brown and Rona Ferguson. East Lothian: Tuckwell Press, 2002, 117–36.

Ewan, Elizabeth. '"To the Longer Liver": Provisions for the Dissolution of the Marital Economy in Scotland, 1470–1550'. In *The Marital Economy in Scandinavia and Britain, 1400–1900*, edited by Maria Ågren and Amy Louise Erickson. Burlington: Ashgate, 2005, 191–206.

Falconer, J.R.D. 'A Family Affair: Households, Misbehaving and the Community in Sixteenth-Century Aberdeen'. In *Finding the Family in Medieval and Early Modern Scotland*, edited by Elizabeth Ewan and Janay Nugent. Aldershot: Ashgate, 2008, 139–50.

Farr, James R. *A Tale of Two Murders: Passion and Power in Seventeenth-Century France*. Durham and London: Duke University Press, 2005.

Feeley, Malcolm M., and Deborah L. Little. 'The Vanishing Female: The Decline of Women in the Criminal Process, 1687–1912'. *Law & Society Review* 25, no. 4 (1991): 719–58.

Fernandes, Hirondino da Paixão. *Bibliografia do Distrito de Bragança: Documentos (textos) Publicados, 569–1870*. Bragança: Câmara Municipal de Bragança, 1996.

Fernandes, Maria de Lurdes Correia. '(Re)Constructions des Images du Couple dans la Péninsule Ibérique aux XVIe et XVIIe Siècles'. *Histoire Economie et Société* 21, no. 2 (2002): 133–44.

Fernandes, Maria de Lurdes C. 'As artes da Confissão: Em torno dos Manuais de Confessores do século XVI em Portugal'. *Humanística e Teologia* 11 (1990): 47–80.

Ferraro, Joanne M. *Marriage Wars in Late Renaissance Venice*. Oxford: Oxford University Press, 2001.

Ferraro, Joanne M. 'The Power to Decide: Battered Wives in Early Modern Venice'. *Renaissance Quarterly* 48, no. 3 (Autumn 1995): 492–512.

Ferreira, Ana Maria Pereira. 'Alguns sismos e vulcões nas ilhas do Faial, Pico e S. Jorge nos séculos XVI e XVII'. In *O Faial e a Periferia Açoriana nos Séculos XV a XX. Actas do Colóquio realizado nas ilhas do Faial e S. Jorge de 12 a 15 de Maio de 1997*. Horta: Núcleo Cultural da Horta, 1997, 103–11.

Ferreira, Fernando Bandeira, António Maria Pereira, and Augusto M. Veloso Ferreira. 'Le notariat portugais'. *Archivum: Revue Internationale des Archives* 12 (1962): 21–30.

Ferreira, Godofredo. 'Um Ricaço Lisboeta do Século XVII: Inventário de seus bens'. *Estremadura: Boletim da Junta de Província* no. 50/52 (January/December 1959): 1–32.

Ferreira, Maria Isabel Rodrigues. 'Tipos femininos em Gil Vicente: um olhar pela sociedade das descobertas'. In *O Rosto Feminino da Expansão Portuguesa, Actas I, Congresso Internacional (Lisboa, 21–25 de Novembro de 1994)*. Lisbon: Comissão para a Igualdade e para os Direitos das Mulheres, 1995, 127–9.

Ferreira, Susannah C. Humble. 'Agents of Political Change: Noblewomen in Portugal at the Turn of the Sixteenth Century'. *Portuguese Studies Review* 13, no. 1/2 (Fall–Winter 2005/2007): 115–34.

Fonseca, Jorge. *Montemor-O-Novo No Século XV*. Montemor-O-Novo: Câmara Municipal de Montemor-O-Novo, 1998.

Fontes, João Luís Inglês. 'A Pobre Vida no Feminino: O Caso das Galvoas de Évora'. In *O Corpo e o Gesto na Civilização Medieval*, edited by Ana Isabel Buescu, João Silva de Sousa, and Maria Adelaide Miranda. Lisbon: Edições Colibri/Universidade Nova de Lisboa, 2006, 157–78.

Fox, Gwyn. *Subtle Subversions: Reading Golden Age Sonnets by Iberian Women*. Washington: Catholic University of America Press, 2008.

Franco, Isabel Maria Madureira. 'As dinâmicas familiares e communitárias no couto de S. João da Foz (1449–1497)'. In *Os Reinos Ibéricos na Idade Média: Livro de Homenagem ao Professor Doutor Humberto Carlos Baquero Moreno*, 2 vols, edited by Luís Adão da Fonseca, Luís Carlos Amaral, and Maria Fernanda Ferreira Santos. Porto: Faculdade de Letras da Universidade do Porto/Livraria Civilização Editora, 2003, II: 529–38.

Franco, Luís F. Farinha. 'Um Livro de Visitações à Igreja de Sant'Ana de Lisboa (1570–1598)'. *Boletim Cultural* 79/80 (Lisbon, 1973/74): 61–90.

Freitas, Judite A. Gonçalves de. 'D. Leonor de Aragão: imagens de contestação e poder'. In *Mulheres Más: Percepção da Mulher Transgressora no Mundo Luso-Hispânico*, 2 vols, edited by Ana María da Costa Toscano and Shelley Godsland. Porto: Universidade Fernando Pessoa, 2004, I: 73–86.

Gamboa-Tusquets, Yolanda. 'María de Zayas, or Memory Chains and the Education of a Learned Woman'. In *Women's Literacy in Early Modern Spain and the New World*, edited by Anne J. Cruz and Rosilie Hernández. Burlington: Ashgate, 2011, 209–24.

García Fuentes, J. Ma. 'Inquisición y Sexualidad en el Reino de Granada en el Siglo XVI'. *Chronica Nova* 3 (Granada, 1986): 207–29.

García Herrero, María del Carmen. 'Imágenes matrimoniales en las obras juanmanuelinas'. In *Os Reinos Ibéricos na Idade Média: Livro de Homenagem ao Professor Doutor Humberto Carlos Baquero Moreno*, 3 vols, edited by Luís Adão da Fonseca, Luís Carlos Amaral, and Maria Fernanda Ferreira Santos, III: 1035–41. Porto: Faculdade de Letras da Universidade do Porto/Livraria Civilização Editora, 2003.

Garrido González, Elisa, ed. *Historia de las Mujeres en España*. Madrid: Editorial Síntesis, 1997.

Gaskill, Martin. 'Reporting Murder: Fiction in the Archives in Early Modern England'. *Social History* 23, no. 1 (January 1998): 1–30.

Gauvard, Claude. *'De Grace Especial': Crime, Etat et Société en France à la fin du Moyen Age*. 2 vols. Paris: Publications de la Sorbonne, 1991.

Gay, Jean-Pascal. 'Acheter la Grâce en France du XVe au XVIIe Siècle'. In *Justice et Argent: Les crimes et les peines pécuniaires du XIIIe au XXIe siècle*, edited by Benoît Garnot. Dijon: Editions Universitaires de Dijon, 2005, 237–57.

Gillespie, Raymond. 'Women and Crime in Seventeenth-Century Ireland'. In *Women in Early Modern Ireland*, edited by Margaret MacCurtain and Mary O'Dowd. Edinburgh: Edinburgh University Press, 1991, 43–52.

Gomes, Rita Costa. *The Making of a Court Society: Kings and Nobles in Late Medieval Portugal*. Alison Aiken, trans. Cambridge: Cambridge University Press, 2003.

Gonçalves, Flávio. 'Documentos Avulsos sobre a Póvoa de Varzim no século XVIII'. *Boletim Cultural Póvoa de Varzim* 27, no. 2 (1990): 585–607.

Gonçalves, Iria. *As Finanças do Porto na segunda metade do século XV*. Porto: Arquivo Histórico/Câmara Municipal do Porto, 1987.

Gonçalves, Iria. 'Um Problema a Resolver: A Vereação de Velas e os Consumos Essenciais'. In *O Faial e a Periferia Açoriana nos Sécs. XV a XIX: Actas do Colóquio realizado nas ilhas do Faial e Pico de 10 a 13 Maio de 1993*. Horta: Núcleo Cultural da Horta, 1995, 175–88.

Gottlieb, Beatrice. 'The Meaning of Clandestine Marriage'. In *Family and Sexuality in French History*, edited by Robert Wheaton and Tamara K. Hareven. Philadelphia: University of Pennsylvania Press, 1980, 49–83.

Gourlay, Kristi. 'A Pugnacious Pagan Princess: Aggressive Female Anger and Violence in *Fierabras*'. In *The Representation of Women's Emotions in Medieval and Early Modern Culture*, edited by Lisa Perfetti. Gainesville: University of Florida Press, 2005, 133–63.

Gouveia, António Camões. 'A linhagem ou o tempo da memória. D. Francisco Manuel de Melo e o nobre seiscentista'. *Ler História* 18 (1990): 3–24.

Gowing, Laura. *Domestic Dangers: Women, Words, and Sex in Early Modern London*. Oxford: Clarendon Press, 1998.

Gowing, Laura. 'Language, Power and the Law: Women's Slander Litigation in Early Modern London'. In *Women, Crime and the Courts in Early Modern England*, edited by Jennifer Kermode and Garthine Walker. Chapel Hill and London: University of North Carolina Press, 1994, 26–47.

Graham, Michael F. 'Women and the Church Courts in Reformation-Era Scotland'. In *Women in Scotland c.1100–c.1750*, edited by Elizabeth Ewan and Maureen M. Meikle, 187–98. Linton: Tuckwell Press, 1999.

Greenshields, Malcolm. *An Economy of Violence in Early Modern France: Crime and Justice in the Haute Auvergne, 1587–1664*. University Park: Pennsylvania State University Press, 1994.

Greenshields, Malcolm. 'Women, Violence, and Criminal Justice Records in Early Modern Haute Auvergne (1587–1664)'. *Canadian Journal of History/Annales Canadiennes d'Histoire* 22 (August 1987): 175–94.

Grubb, James S. 'Piero Amadi Acts Like His Betters'. In *A Renaissance of Conflicts: Visions and Revisions of Law and Society in Italy and Spain*, edited by John A. Marino and Thomas Kuehn. Toronto: Centre for Reformation and Renaissance Studies, 2004, 259–78.

Hanson, Carl A. *Economy and Society in Baroque Portugal, 1668–1703*. Minneapolis: University of Minnesota Press, 1981.

Hardwick, Julie. 'Women "Working" the Law: Gender, Authority, and Legal Process in Early Modern France'. *Journal of Women's History* 9, no. 3 (Autumn 1997): 28–49.

Heras Santos, José Luis de las. *La Justicia Penal de los Austrias en la Corona de Castilla*. Salamanca: Ediciones Universidad de Salamanca, 1991.

Hespanha, António Manuel. 'Les autres raisons de la politique: l'économie de la grâce'. In *Recherche sur l'histoire de l'état dans le monde ibérique (15e–20e siècle)*, edited by Jean-Frédéric Schaub. Paris: Presses de l'Ecole Normale Supérieure, 1993, 67–86.

Hespanha, António Manuel. 'Centro e periferia nas estruturas administrativas do Antigo Regime'. *Ler História* no. 8 (1986): 35–60.

Hespanha, António Manuel. 'O estatuto jurídico da mulher na época da expansão'. In *O Rosto Feminino da Expansão Portuguesa, Actas I, Congresso Internacional (Lisboa, 21–25 de Novembro de 1994)*. Lisbon: Comissão para a Igualdade e para os Direitos das Mulheres, 1995, 53–64.

Hespanha, António Manuel. 'Da "Iustitia" à "Disciplina": textos, poder e política penal no antigo regime'. In *Justiça e Litigiosidade: História e Prospectiva*. Lisbon: Fundação Calouste Gulbenkian, 1993, 287–379.

Hespanha, António Manuel. 'A monarquia: a legislação e os agentes'. In *História da Vida Privada em Portugal: A Idade Moderna*, 4 vols, edited by José Mattoso. Lisbon: Círculo de Leitores e Temas e Debates, 2011, II: 12–31.

Hespanha, António Manuel. 'Sábios e Rústicos: a violência doce da razão jurídica'. *Revista Critica de Ciências Sociais* no. 25/26 (December 1988): 31–60.

Hespanha, António Manuel. *As Vésperas do Leviathan: Instituições e Poder Poltítico, Portugal – Séc. XVII*. Coimbra: Livraria Almedina, 1994.

Higgs, David. 'A *Beata* and Biography: Leonarda Rosa and Her Detractors'. *Portuguese Studies Review* 13, no. 1/2 (Fall–Winter 2005/2007): 401–9.

Howell, Martha. *The Marriage Exchange: Property, Social Place and Gender in the Cities of the Low Countries 1300–1550*. Chicago: Chicago University Press, 1998.

Hunt, Margaret R. 'The Sailor's Wife, War Finance, and Coverture in Late Seventeenth-Century London'. In *Married Women and the Law: Coverture in England and the Common Law World*, edited by Tim Stretton and Krista J. Kesselring. Montreal and Kingston: McGill-Queen's University Press, 2013, 139–62.

Johansen, Hanne Marie. 'Marriage Trouble, Separation and Divorce in Early Modern Norway'. In *The Marital Economy in Scandinavia and Britain, 1400–1900*, edited by Maria Ågren and Amy Louise Erickson. Burlington: Ashgate, 2005, 175–89.

Johnson, Harold, and Francis A. Dutra, eds. *Pelo Vaso Traseiro: Sodomy and the Sodomites in Luso-Brazilian History*. Tucson: Fenestra Books, 2007.

Johnston, Wayne. *A World Elsewhere*. Toronto: Vintage Canada, 2011.

Jones, Karen. *Gender and Petty Crime in Late Medieval England: The Local Courts in Kent, 1460–1560*. Woodbridge: Boydell Press, 2006.

Kane, Bronach, and Fiona Williamson, eds. *Women, Agency and the Law, 1300–1700*. London: Pickering & Chatto, 2013.

Kasdagli, Aglaia E. *Land and Marriage Settlements in the Aegean: A Case Study of Seventeenth-Century Naxos*. Venice: Hellenic Institute of Byzantine and Post-Byzantine Studies, 1999.

Kaspersson, Maria. 'Prosecution and Public Participation – The Case of Early Modern Sweden'. In *Crime, Law and Popular Culture in Europe, 1500–1900*, edited by Richard Mc Mahon. Portland: Willan Publishing, 2008, 96–117.

Kesselring, K.J. *Mercy and Authority in the Tudor State*. Cambridge: Cambridge University Press, 2003.

Klapisch-Zuber, Christiane. 'The "Cruel Mother": Maternity, Widowhood, and the Dowry in Florence in the Fourteenth and Fifteenth Centuries'. In *Feminism & Renaissance Studies*, edited by Lorna Hutson. Oxford: Oxford University Press, 1999, 186–202.

Knox, Andrea. '"Barbarous and Pestiferous Women": Female Criminality, Violence and Aggression in Sixteenth- and Seventeenth-Century Scotland and Ireland'. In *Twisted Sisters: Women, Crime and Deviance in Scotland Since 1400*, edited by Yvonne Galloway Brown and Rona Ferguson. East Lothian: Tuckwell Press, 2002, 13–31.

Korpiola, Mia. 'Rethinking Incest and Heinous Sexual Crime: Changing Boundaries of Secular and Ecclesiastical Jurisdiction in Late Medieval Sweden'. In *Boundaries of the Law: Geography, Gender and Jurisdiction in Medieval and Early Modern Europe*, edited by Anthony Musson. Burlington: Ashgate, 2005, 102–17.

Kuehn, Thomas. 'Daughters, Mothers, Wives, and Widows: Women as Legal Persons'. In *Time, Space, and Women's Lives in Early Modern Europe*, edited by Anne Jacobson Schutte, Thomas Kuehn, and Silvana Seidel Menchi. Kirksville: Truman State University Press, 2001, 97–115.

Lafage, Valérie. '*Punir, récompenser*: l'enseignement des testaments montpelliérains (1554–1622)'. *Seizième Siècle* no. 3 (2007): 225–48.

Lalanda, Ma Margarida de Sá Nogueira. 'Os municípios micaelenses nos séculos XVI e XVII'. In *O Município no Mundo Português: Seminário Internacional, Funchal, 26 a 30 Outubro de 1998*, edited by Alberto Vieira. Funchal: Região Autónoma da Madeira/Centro de Estudos de História do Atlântico, 1998, 235–68.

Lello Universal: Novo Diccionário Encyclopédico Luso-Brasileiro. 2 vols. Porto: Lello & Irmão Editores/Propietários da Livraria Chardon, 1938.

Lencart e Silva, Maria Joana Corte-Real. 'A Mulher nas Ordenações Manuelinas'. *Revista de História* 12 (Porto, 1993): 59–79.

Levi, Giovanni. 'Reciprocidad Mediterránea'. *Hispania* 60/61, no. 204 (2000): 103–26.

Levy, Allison, ed. *Sex Acts in Early Modern Italy: Practice, Performance, Perversion, Punishments*. Burlington: Ashgate, 2010.

Lipscomb, Suzannah. 'Crossing Boundaries: Women's Gossip, Insults and Violence in Sixteenth-Century France'. *French History* 25 (2011): 408–26.

Llobet, Gabriel de. 'Attestation Notariée d'une Lettre de Rémission Roussillonnaise de 1604'. In *La Faute, la Répression et le Pardon: Actes du 107e Congrès National des Sociétés Savantes, Brest, 1982*. 2 vols. Paris: C.T.H.S./Comité des Travaux Historiques et Scientifiques, 1984, I: 383–86.

Lopes, Maria Antónia. 'Notas para o estudo do papel social da mãe: representações e normas no theatro de Manoel de Figueiredo'. *Revista Portuguesa de História* 24 (1988): 67–95.

López-Lázaro, Fabio T. *Crime in Early Bourbon Madrid (1700–1808): An Analysis of the Royal Judicial Court's Casebook*. Lewiston: Edwin Mellen Press, 2008.

Lorenzo Pinar, Francisco Javier. 'La mujer y el Tribunal Diocesano en Zamora durante el siglo XVI: divorcios y nulidades matrimoniales'. *Studia Zamorensia* 3 (1996): 77–88.

Lourenço, Maria Paula Marçal. *D. Pedro II, O Pacífico (1648–1706)*. Lisbon: Círculo de Leitores e Temas e Debates, 2010.

Magalhães, Joaquim Romero. 'O Pano de Fundo'. In *História de Portugal: No Alvorecer da Modernidade*, 4 vols, edited by José Mattoso. Lisbon: Editorial Estampa, 1997, III: 485–9.

Manso, Maria de Deus Beites, and Maria Margarida Caeiro. 'A Visitação de Francisco Cardoso de Torneo aos Açores (1618–1620) (Contribuição em torno de alguns processos)'. In *O Faial e a Periferia Açoriana nos Sécs. XV a XIX: Actas do Colóquio realizado nas ilhas do Faial e Pico de 10 a 13 Maio de 1993*. Horta: Núcleo Cultural da Horta, 1995, 515–21.

Mantecón Movellán, Tomás A. 'Mujeres forzadas y abusons deshonestos en la Castilla moderna'. *Manuscrits* 20 (2002): 157–85.

Marino, John A., ed. *Early Modern Italy*. Oxford and New York: Oxford University Press, 2002.

Mariz, José. *Tabeliães e Notários: Estudos e Documentos Técnicos*. Lisbon: Instituto Português de Arquivos, 1989.

Marques, A.H. de Oliveira. *História de Portugal*. 8th ed. Lisbon: Palas Editores, 1978.

Marques, A.H. de Oliveira. *Portugal Quinhentista (Ensaios)*. Lisbon: Quetzal Editores, 1987.

Marques, António Soares. 'A Mulher nos Sermões do Pe António de Vieira'. *MATHESIS* 2 (1993): 121–41.

Marques, Pedro Miguel Reboredo. '"Não são femeas, ou machos as almas com distinção": Estratégias de valorização da mulher em papéis volantes setecentistas'. *Portuguese Studies Review* 13, no. 1/2 (Fall–Winter 2005/2007): 305–29.

Martin, A. Lynn. *Alcohol, Violence, and Disorder in Traditional Europe*. Kirsksville: Truman State University Press, 2009.

Martín Casares, Aurelia. 'Las mujeres y la : "paz en la casa" en el discurso renacentista'. *Chronica Nova* 29 (2002): 217–44.

Martín Casares, Aurelia. 'La violencia contra las mujeres en al siglo XVI: un caso de violación en la provincia de Granada'. *Arenal: Revista de Historia de las Mujeres* 4, no. 1 (January–June 1997): 149–62.

McDonough, Susan. 'She Said, He Said, and They Said: Claims of Abuse and a Community's Response in Late Medieval Marseille'. *Journal of Women's History* 19, no. 4 (2007): 35–58.

McGough, Laura. 'Women, Private Property, and the Limitations of State Authority in Early Modern Venice'. *Journal of Women's History* 14, no. 3 (Autumn 2002): 32–52.

McIntosh, Marjorie K. 'The Benefits and Drawbacks of *Femme Sole* in England, 1300–1630'. *Journal of British Studies* 44, no. 3 (July 2005): 410–38.

Melo, Arnaldo Sousa. 'Women and Work in the Household Economy: The Social and Linguistic Evidence from Porto, c.1340–1450'. In *The Medieval Household in Christian Europe, c.850–c.1550: Managing Power, Wealth, and the Body*, edited by Cordelia Beattie, Anna Maslakovic, and Sarah Rees Jones. Turnhout: Brepols Publishers, 2003, 249–69.

Mendelson, Sara, and Patricia Crawford. *Women in Early Modern England*. Oxford: Oxford University Press, 2003.

Mendes, Isabel Maria Ribeiro. 'A Defesa do Termo de Lisboa em 1594–1595: Documento do Arquivo de Simancas'. *Revista da Faculdade de Letras* no. 12, 5a Série (December 1989): 97–116.

Meneses, Avelino de Freitas de. *Os Açores e o Domínio Filipino (1580–1590)*. 2 vols. Angra do Heroísmo: Instituto Histórico da Ilha Terceira, 1987.

Meneses, Avelino de Freitas de, and João Paulo Oliveira e Costa, eds. *O reino, as ilhas e o mar oceano: Estudos em homenagem a Artur Teodoro de Matos*. 2 vols. Lisbon and Ponta Delgada: Universidade dos Açores/Universidade de Lisboa, 2007.

Mentzer, Raymond A. 'Morals and Moral Regulation in Protestant France'. *Journal of Interdisciplinary History* 30, no. 1 (Summer 2000): 1–20.

Metcalf, Alida C. 'Fathers and Sons: The Politics of Inheritance in a Colonial Brazilian Township'. *Hispanic American Historical Review* 66, no. 3 (August 1986): 455–84.

Meyerson, Mark D., Daniel Thiery, and Oren Falk, eds. *'A Great Effusion of Blood'? Interpreting Medieval Violence*. Toronto: University of Toronto Press, 2004.

Monteiro, Isilda Braga da Costa. 'A litigiosidade e o "perdão" em Vila Nova de Gaia (séculos XVII e XVIII)'. *Revista de Ciências Históricas* (Universidade Portucalense) 11 (1996): 101–12.

Monteiro, Nuno Gonçalo. 'Casa, casamento e nome: fragmentos sobre relações familiares e indivíduos'. In *História da Vida Privada em Portugal: A Idade Moderna*, 4 vols, edited by José Mattoso. Lisbon: Círculo de Leitores e Temas e Debates, 2011, II: 130–58.

Monteiro, Nuno Gonçalo. 'Poderes municipais e elites locais (séculos XVII–XIX): estado de uma questão'. In *O Município no Mundo Português: Seminário Internacional, Funchal, 26 a 30 Outubro de 1998*, edited by Alberto Vieira. Funchal: Região Autónoma da Madeira/Centro de Estudos de História do Atlântico, 1998, 79–89.

Moreira, Manuel António Fernandes. *O Município e os Forais de Viana do Castelo*. Viana do Castelo: Edição da Câmara Municipal, 1986.

Moreira, Maria João Guardado, and Teresa Rodrigues Veiga. 'Modelos de mortalidade em Portugal'. *Ler História* 49 (2005): 145–69.

Moreno, Humberto Baquero. 'O município português nos séculos XIV a XVI'. In *O Município no Mundo Português: Seminário Internacional, Funchal, 26 a 30 Outubro de 1998*, edited by Alberto Vieira. Funchal: Região Autónoma da Madeira/Centro de Estudos de História do Atlântico, 1998, 37–47.

Morujão, Maria do Rosário Barbosa. 'Ecos do passado: marcas da oralidade em documentos medievais portugueses'. In *Os Reinos Ibéricos na Idade Média: Livro de Homenagem ao Professor Doutor Humberto Carlos Baquero Moreno*, 3 vols, edited by Luís Adão da Fonseca, Luís Carlos Amaral, and Maria Fernanda Ferreira Santos. Porto: Faculdade de Letras da Universidade do Porto/Livraria Civilização Editora, 2003, III: 1061–6.

Muchembled, Robert. *Le Temps des Supplices: De l'Obéissance sous les Rois Absolus, XVe–XVIIIe Siècle*. Paris: Armand Colin Editeur, 1992.

Muchembled, Robert. *La Violence au Village: Sociabilité et comportements populaires en Artois du XVe au XVIIe siècle*. Turnhout: Editions Brepols I.G.P., 1989.

Murray, Mary. *The Law of the Father? Patriarchy in the Transition from Feudalism to Capitalism*. London and New York: Routledge, 1995.

Nalle, Sarah T. 'Literacy and Culture in Early Modern Castile'. *Past and Present* no. 125 (November 1989): 65–96.

Narbona Vizcaíno, Rafael. *Pueblo, Poder y Sexo. Valencia Medieval (1306–1420)*. Valencia: Diputació de València, 1992.

Nazzari, Muriel. 'Parents and Daughters: Change in the Practice of Dowry in São Paulo (1600–1770)'. *Hispanic American Historical Review* 70, no. 4 (November 1990): 639–65.

Nazzari, Muriel. 'The Waxing and Waning of Matrilineality in São Paulo, Brazil: Historical Variations in an Ambilineal System, 1500–1900'. In *Gender, Kinship, Power: A Comparative and Interdisciplinary History*, edited by Mary Jo Maynes, Ann Waltern, Birgitte Soland, and Ulrike Strasser. New York and London: Routledge, 1996, 305–17.

Neto, Margarida Sobral. 'Uma Mulher nas Malhas da Justiça Senhorial na Gândara do Séc. XVII'. *Revista Portuguesa de História* 1, t.XXXI (1996): 529–53.

Netterstrom, Jeppe Büchert, and Bjorn Poulsen, eds. *Feud in Medieval and Early Modern Europe*. Aarhus: Aarhus University Press, 2007.

Nussdorfer, Laurie. *Brokers of Public Trust: Notaries in Early Modern Rome*. Baltimore: Johns Hopkins University Press, 2009.

Nussdorfer, Laurie. 'Writing and the Power of Speech: Notaries and Artisans in Baroque Rome'. In *Culture and Identity in Early Modern Europe (1500–1800): Essays in Honor of Natalie Zemon Davis*, edited by Barbara B. Diefendorf and Carla Hesse. Ann Arbor: University of Michigan Press, 1993, 103–18.

O'Dowd, Mary. 'Women and the Law in Early Modern Ireland'. In *Women in Renaissance and Early Modern Europe*, edited by Christine Meek. Dublin: Four Courts Press, 2000, 95–108.

Olival, Fernanda. 'Os lugares e espaços do privado nos grupos populares e intermédios'. In *História da Vida Privada em Portugal: A Idade Moderna*, 4 vols, edited by José Mattoso. Lisbon: Círculo de Leitores e Temas e Debates, 2011, II: 244–75.

Olival, Fernanda. 'A visita da inquisição à Madeira em 1591–92'. In *Actas III Colóquio Internacional de História da Madeira*. Funchal: Centro de Estudos do Atlântico, 1993, 493–519.

O'Neill, Brian Juan. *Social Inequality in a Portuguese Hamlet: Land, Late Marriage, and Bastardy, 1870–1978*. Cambridge: Cambridge University Press, 1987.

Paiva, José Pedro. *Bruxaria e superstição num país sem 'caça às bruxas', 1600–1774*. 2nd ed. Lisbon: Notícias Editorial, 2002.

Pereira, António dos Santos. *A Ilha de S. Jorge (Séculos XV–XVII): Contribuição para o seu estudo*. Ponta Delgada: Universidade dos Açores/Departamento de História, 1987.

Pereira, João Cordeiro. *Portugal na Era de Quinhentos*. Cascais: Patrimonia Histórica, 2003.

Pereira, Maria Teresa Lopes. *Alcácer do Sal na Idade Média*. Lisbon: Câmara Municipal de Alcácer do Sal/Edições Colibri, 2007.

Pereira, Pe Sérgio Augusto Gonçalves. 'Foral dado por D. Afonso III a Viana'. *Arquivo do Alto Minho* 8, no. 2 (1958): 7–19.

Pérez García, Pablo. *El Justicia Criminal de Valencia (1479–1707)*. Valencia: Generalitat Valenciana, 1991.

Pfeffer, Wendy. 'Constant Sorrow: Emotions and the Women Trouvères'. In *The Representation of Women's Emotions in Medieval and Early Modern Culture*, edited by Lisa Perfetti. Gainesville: University of Florida Press, 2005, 119–32.

Phillips, William D. Jr., and Carla Rahn Phillips. *A Concise History of Spain*. Cambridge: Cambridge University Press, 2010.

Pic, François. 'Pardon et "Grans Perdons"'. In *La Faute, la Répression et le Pardon: Actes du 107e Congrès National des Sociétés Savantes, Brest, 1982*. 2 vols. Paris: C.T.H.S./Comité des Travaux Historiques et Scientifiques, 1984, I: 447–62.

Pieroni, Geraldo. *Banidos: A Inquisição e a lista dos cristão-novos condenados a viver no Brasil*. Rio de Janeiro: Editora Bertrand Brasil, 2003.

Pieroni, Geraldo. 'Fui desterro para os culpados: A Inquisição portuguesa e os banidos no Brazil colonial'. *Portuguese Studies Review* 15, no. 1/2 (2007): 267–80.

Pina, Fernando Correia. 'O Regimento das Procissões da Vila de Fronteira em 1633'. *A Cidade: Revista Cultural de Portalegre* no. 8, Nova Série (1993): 167–72.

Pipkin, Amanda. *Rape in the Republic, 1609–1725: Formulating Dutch Identity*. Leiden and Boston: Brill, 2013.

Polónia, Amélia. 'Women's Contribution to Family, Economy and Social Range of Maritime Communities in Sixteenth-Century Portugal'. *Portuguese Studies Review* 13, no. 1/2 (Fall–Winter 2005/2007): 269–85.

Polónia, Amélia. *O Cardeal Infante D. Henrique, Arcebispo de Évora. Um prelado no limiar da viragem tridentina*. Porto: Fundação Eugénio de Almeida, 2005.

Polónia, Amélia. '"Mulheres que partem e mulheres que ficam": O protagonismo feminismo na expansão ultramarina'. *O Estudo da História* 4 (2001): 79–98.

Poska, Allyson M. *Women and Authority in Early Modern Spain: The Peasants of Galicia*. Oxford: Oxford University Press, 2005.

Pylkkänen, Anu. 'Forming the Marital Economy in the Early Modern Finnish Countryside'. In *The Marital Economy in Scandinavia and Britain, 1400–1900*, edited by Maria Ågren and Amy Louise Erickson. Burlington: Ashgate, 2005, 75–88.

Queirós, Isabel Maria de Moura Ribeiro. 'Theudas e Mantheudas: A criminalidade feminina no reinado de D. João II através das *cartas de perdão* (1481–1485)'. Master's thesis, Faculdade de Letras, Universidade do Porto, 1999.

Ramos, Anabela. *Violência e Justiça em Terras do Montemuro, 1708–1820*. Viseu: Palimage Editores, 1998.

Ribeiro, Ana Sofia Vieira. 'Convívios difíceis: viver, sentir e pensar a violência no Porto de setecentos (1750–1772)'. Master's thesis, Faculdade de Letras, Universidade do Porto, 2008.

Ribeiro, João Adriano. 'Reflexões sobre o estudo dos municípios rurais da Madeira'. In *O Município no Mundo Português: Seminário Internacional, Funchal, 26 a 30 Outubro de 1998*, edited by Alberto Vieira. Funchal: Região Autónoma da Madeira/Centro de Estudos de História do Atlântico, 1998, 473–82.

Ribeiro, Luciano. 'Uma Descrição de Entre Douro e Minho'. *Boletim Cultural da Câmara Municipal do Porto* (1959): 441–60.

Ribeiro, Margarida, and Fernando Portugal. 'Aspectos Linguísticos e Etnográficos das Cartas de Perdão: Lavrar de Correia'. *Separata da Revista de Portugal* 33 (Lisbon, 1968): 276–81.

Ribière, Pierre. 'Délits sexuels dans les lettres de rémission du comte Jean IV d'Armagnac'. In *La Faute, la Répression et le Pardon: Actes du 107e Congrès National des Sociétés Savantes, Brest, 1982*. 2 vols. Paris: C.T.H.S./Comité des Travaux Historiques et Scientifiques, 1984, I: 369–81.

Rodrigues, José Damião. 'Criminalidade e Violência em Ponta Delgada no Final do Antigo Regime (1706–1817): Para uma Outra Leitura das Relações Sociais'. In *Colóquio Comemorativo dos 450 Anos da Cidade de Ponta Delgada. Actas*. Ponta Delgada: Universidade dos Açores, 1999 [153–78].

Rodrigues, José Damião, and Rui Cunha Martins. 'A Construção de um Espaço: os Açores e o Olhar do Poder Cental'. In *O Faial e a Periferia Açoriana nos Sécs. XV a XIX. Actas do Colóquio realizado nas ilhas do Faial e Pico de 10 a 13 de Maio de 1993*. Horta: Núcleo Cultural da Horta, 1995 [75–83].

Rodrigues, Teresa. *Cinco Séculos de Quotidiano: A vida em Lisboa do século XV aos nossos dias*. Lisbon: Edições Cosmos, 1997.

Rodrigues, Teresa. *Crises de Mortalidade em Lisboa, Séculos XVI e XVII*. Lisbon: Livros Horizonte, 1990.

Rodrigues, Vítor Luís Pinto Gaspar da Conceição. 'A Guiné nas cartas de perdão (1463–1500)'. In *Sociedade, Cultura e Mentalidades na Época do 'Cancioneiro Geral' Volume IV das Actas do Congresso Internacional 'Bartolomeu Dias e sua Época'*. Lisbon: Instituto de Investigação Científica Tropical, 1989, 397–412.

Rodriguez Flores, Ma Immaculada. *El Perdon Real en Castilla (Siglos XIII–XVIII)*. Salamanca: Universidad de Salamanca, 1971.

Rollo-Koster, Joëlle. 'The Boundaries of Affection: Women and Property in Late Medieval Avignon'. In *Across the Religious Divide: Women, Property, and Law in the Wider Mediterranean (ca. 1300–1800)*, edited by Jutta Gisela Sperling and Shona Kelly Wray. New York and London: Routledge, 2010, 38–50.

Rosa, Maria de Lurdes de. *O Morgadio em Portugal, sécs. XIV–XV: modelos e práticas de comportamento linhagístico*. Lisbon: Editorial Estampa,1995.

Roth-Lochner, Barbara. 'L'Evolution de l'activité notariale à Genève aux XVIIe et XVIIIe siècles'. *Revue d'histoire moderne et contemporaine* 32 (January–March 1986): 97–113.

Rublack, Ulinka. *The Crimes of Women in Early Modern Germany*. Oxford: Oxford University Press, 1999.

Rudolph, Julia. 'Rape and Resistance: Women and Consent in Seventeenth-Century English Legal and Political Thought'. *Journal of British Studies* 39, no. 2 (April 2000): 157–84.

Ruff, Julius R. *Violence in Early Modern Europe*. Cambridge: Cambridge University Press, 2001.

Sá, Isabel dos Guimarães. 'As crianças e as idades da vida'. In *História da Vida Privada em Portugal: A Idade Moderna*, 4 vols, edited by José Mattoso. Lisbon: Círculo de Leitores e Temas e Debates, 2011, II: 72–95.

Sá, Isabel dos Guimarães. 'Os Espaços de reclusão e a vida nas margens'. In *História da Vida Privada em Portugal: A Idade Moderna*, 4 vols, edited by José Mattoso. Lisbon: Círculo de Leitores e Temas e Debates, 2011, II: 276–99.

Sá, Isabel dos Guimarães. *Quando o rico se faz pobre: Misericórdias, caridade e poder no império português,1500–1800*. Lisbon: Comissão Nacional para as Comemorações dos Descobrimentos Portugueses, 1997.

Sandvik, Hilde. 'Decision-Making on Marital Property in Norway, 1500–1800'. In *The Marital Economy in Scandinavia and Britain, 1400–1900*, edited by Maria Ågren and Amy Louise Erickson. Burlington: Ashgate, 2005, 111–26.

Santos, João Marinho dos. *Os Açores nos Sécs. XV e XVI*. 2 vols. Angra do Heroísmo: Dir. Regional dos Assuntos Culturais, 1989.

Santos, João Marinho dos. 'Ponta Delgada – Nascimento e Primeira Infância de uma Cidade'. *Revista de História Económica e Social* 1 (January–June 1978): 33–53.

Saraiva, José Hermano. *História de Portugal*. 5th ed. Mem Martins: Publicações Europa-América, 1998.

Schmugge, Ludwig. 'Barbara Zymermanin's Two Husbands'. In *Medieval Church Law and the Origins of the Western Legal Tradition: A Tribute to Kenneth Pennington*, edited by Wolfgang P. Müller and Mary E. Sommar. Washington: Catholic University of America Press, 2006, 289–98.

Schmugge, Ludwig. 'Female Petitioners in the Papal Penitentiary'. *Gender & History* 12, no. 3 (November 2000): 685–703.

Schneider, Zoë A. 'Women before the Bench: Female Litigants in Early Modern Normandy'. *French Historical Studies* 23, no. 1 (Winter 2000): 1–32.

Segura Graiño, Cristina. 'La Transición del Medievo a la Modernidad'. In *Historia de las Mujeres en España*, edited by Elisa Garrido. Madrid: Editorial Síntesis, 1997, 219–45.

Serrão, Joaquim Veríssimo. *O Tempo dos Filipes em Portugal e no Brasil (1580–1668): Estudos Históricos*. 2nd ed. Lisbon: Edições Colibri, 2004.

Shemek, Deanna. *Ladies Errant: Wayward Women and Social Order in Early Modern Italy*. Durham and London: Duke University Press, 1998.

Shepard, Alexandra and Judith Spicksley. 'Worth, Age, and Social Status in Early Modern England'. *The Economic History Review* 64, no. 2 (May 2011): 493–530.

Silva, Francisco Ribeiro da. 'Os concelhos e as cortes seiscentistas portuguesas: representação e intervenção (o caso do Porto)'. In *O Município no Mundo Português: Seminário Internacional, Funchal, 26 a 30 Outubro de 1998*, edited by Alberto Vieira. Funchal: Região Autónoma da Madeira/Centro de Estudos de História do Atlântico, 1998, 63–77.

Silva, Francisco Ribeiro da. *O Porto e o seu Termo (1580–1640): os Homens, as Instituições e o Poder*. 2 vols. Porto: Arquivo Histórico/Câmara Municipal do Porto, 1988.

Silva, Hugo Ribeiro da, and Susana Cardoso. 'Escrituras de perdão num notário do Porto (1650–1700)'. *Revista da Faculdade de Letras*, 5 (Porto, 2004): 167–92.

Silva, Júlia Maria Sousa Alves da. *A Mulher em Gil Vicente*. Braga: Edições APPACDM Distrital de Braga, 1995.

Silva, Mário Justino. *O rei e os nobres: Imagens do quotidiano nos 'Ditos Portugueses Dignos de Memória' (século XVI)*. Cascais: Patrimonia Histórica, 2004.

Silva, Nuno J. Espinosa Gomes da. *História do Direito Português: Fontes de Direito*. 4th ed. Lisbon: Fundação Calouste Gulbenkian, 2006.

Sperling, Jutta Gisela. 'Marriage, Kinship, and Property in Portuguese Testaments (1649–1650)'. In *Across the Religious Divide: Women, Property, and Law in the Wider Mediterranean (ca. 1300–1800)*, edited by Jutta Gisela Sperling and Shona Kelly Wray. New York and London: Routledge, 2010, 158–74.

Sperling, Jutta. 'Women's Property Rights in Portugal under D. João I (1385–1433): A Comparison with Renaissance Italy'. *Portuguese Studies Review* 13, no. 1/2 (Fall–Winter 2005/2007): 27–59.

Steenbergh, Kristine. 'Emotions and Gender: The Case of Anger in Early Modern English Revenge Tragedies'. In *A History of Emotions, 1200–1800*, edited by Jonas Liliequist. London: Pickering & Chatto, 2012, 119–33.

Stretton, Tim. *Women Waging Law in Elizabethan England.* Cambridge: Cambridge University Press, 1998.

Taylor, Scott. *Honor and Violence in Golden Age Spain*. New Haven and London: Yale University Press, 2008.

Teodoro, Leandro Alves. 'O comprometimento moralizante dos sínodos portugueses entre os séculos XIV e XV'. *Portuguese Studies Review* 21, no. 1 (Summer 2013): 7–18.

Todd, Barbara. 'Written in Her Heart: Married Women's Separate Allegiance in English Law'. In *Married Women and the Law: Coverture in England and the Common Law World*, edited by Tim Stretton and Krista J. Kesselring. Montreal and Kingston: McGill-Queen's University Press, 2013, 163–91.

Tomás y Valiente, Francisco. *El derecho penal de la monarquía absoluta*. Madrid: Tecnos, 1969.

Tomás y Valiente, Francisco. 'El perdon de la parte ofendida en el derecho penal castellano'. *Anuario de Historia del Derecho Español* 31, no. 1, Serie 1a (Madrid, 1961): 55–114.

Vann, Theresa M. 'Criminal Settlement in Medieval Castilian Towns'. In *The Final Argument: The Imprint of Violence on Society in Medieval and Early Modern Europe*, edited by Donald J. Kagay and L.J. Andrew Villalon. Woodbridge: Boydell Press, 1998, 83–94.

Veríssimo, Nelson. 'Poder municipal e vida quotidiana: Machico no século XVII'. In *O Município no Mundo Português: Seminário Internacional, Funchal, 26 a 30 Outubro de 1998*, edited by Alberto Vieira. Funchal: Região Autónoma da Madeira/Centro de Estudos de História do Atlântico, 1998, 291–302.

Vickers, Daniel. 'Credit and misunderstanding on Nantucket Island, Massachusetts (1683–1763)'. *Quaderni Storici* 2 (August 2011): 415–40.

Vieira, Aires dos Passos. 'Subsídios para a história da criminalidade da Madeira nas épocas de Filipe II e III'. In *Actas III Colóquio Internacional de História da Madeira*. Funchal: Centro de Estudos do Atlântico, 1993, 473–92.

Vieira, Alberto. 'História e municipalismo na Madeira: projectos e realizações, o município de S. Vicente'. In *O Município no Mundo Português: Seminário Internacional, Funchal, 26 a 30 Outubro de 1998*, edited by Alberto Vieira. Funchal: Região Autónoma da Madeira/Centro de Estudos de História do Atlântico, 1998, 327–48.

Vieira, Luís Filipe. 'Leitura social e cultural da morte em Santa Cruz das Flores (1676–1725)'. In *O Faial e a Periferia Açoriana nos Sécs. XV a XIX. Actas do III Colóquio. Nos 550 anos do Descobrimento das Flores e do Corvo*. Horta: Núcleo Cultural da Horta, 2002, 507–25.

Viejo Yharrassary, Julián. 'La Segunda Dote'. *Cuadernos de Sección. Historia-Geografia* 8 (1986): 33–46.

Vollendorf, Lisa. *The Lives of Women: A New History of Inquisitional Spain*. Nashville: Vanderbilt University Press, 2005.

Vollendorf, Lisa. 'Navigating the Atlantic Divide: Women, Education, and Literacy in Iberia and the Americas'. In *Women of the Iberian Atlantic*, edited by Sarah E. Owens and Jane E. Mangan. Baton Rouge: Louisiana University Press, 2012, 18–36.

Walker, Garthine. 'Rereading Rape and Sexual Violence in Early Modern England'. *Gender & History* 10, no. 1 (April 1998): 1–25.

Westphal, Sarah. 'Calefurnia's Rage: Emotions and Gender in Late Medieval Law and Literature'. In *The Representation of Women's Emotions in Medieval and Early Modern Culture*, edited by Lisa Perfetti. Gainesville: University of Florida Press, 2005, 164–90.

Wheeler, Douglas L. *Historical Dictionary of Portugal*. Metuchen and London: Scarecrow Press, 1993.

White, Landeg, trans. *The Collected Lyric Poems of Luís de Camões*. Princeton and Oxford: Princetown University Press, 2008.

Wiesner-Hanks, Merry E. *Women and Gender in Early Modern Europe*. 3rd ed. Cambridge: Cambridge University Press, 2008.

Wiesner-Hanks, Merry E. *Christianity and Sexuality in the Early Modern World: Regulating Desire, Reforming Practice*. London and New York: Routledge, 2000.

Wiesner-Hanks, Merry E. *The Marvelous Hairy Girls: The Gonzales Sisters and Their Worlds*. New Haven and London: Yale University Press, 2009.

Wright, Danya C. 'Coverture and Women's Agency: Informal Modes of Resistance to Legal Patriarchy'. In *Married Women and the Law: Coverture in England and the Common Law World*, edited by Tim Stretton and Krista J. Kesselring. Montreal and Kingston: McGill-Queen's University Press, 2013, 240–63.

Zorzi, Andrea. 'The Florentines and Their Public Offices in the Early Fifteenth Century: Competition, Abuses of Power, and Unlawful Acts'. In *History from Crime: Selections from Quaderni Storici*, edited by Edward Muir and Guido Ruggiero. Baltimore and London: Johns Hopkins University Press, 1994, 110–34.

Index

Page numbers followed by *t* indicate tables.

For Product Safety Concerns and Information please contact our EU representative GPSR@taylorandfrancis.com Taylor & Francis Verlag GmbH, Kaufingerstraße 24, 80331 München, Germany